Advances in Discrete Time Systems
http://dx.doi.org/10.5772/3432
Edited by Magdi S. Mahmoud

Contributors

Suchada Sitjongsataporn, Xiaojie Xu, Jun Yoneyama, Yuzu Uchida, Ryutaro Takada, Yuanqing Xia, Li Dai, Magdi Mahmoud, Meng-Yin Fu, Mario Alberto Jordan, Jorge Bustamante, Carlos Berger, Atsue Ishii, Takashi Nakamura, Yuko Ohno, Satoko Kasahara, Junmin Li, Jiangrong Li, Zhile Xia, Saïd Guermah, Gou Nakura

Published by InTech

Janeza Trdine 9, 51000 Rijeka, Croatia

Publishing Process Manager Iva Lipovic
Technical Editor InTech DTP team
Cover InTech Design team

Additional hard copies can be obtained from orders@intechopen.com

Advances in Discrete Time Systems, Edited by Magdi S. Mahmoud
p. cm.
ISBN 978-953-51-0875-7

For EU product safety concerns:
IN TECH d.o.o., Prolaz Marije Krucifikse Kozulić 3, 51000 Rijeka, Croatia, info@intechopen.com or visit our website at intechopen.com.

Meet the editor

Magdi Sadek Mahmoud is a Distinguished University Professor at KFUPM, Saudi Arabia. He worked at different universities world-wide including Egypt, Kuwait, UAE, UK, USA, Singapore and Australia. He lectured in Venezuela, Germany, UK, USA, Canada and China. He has been actively engaged in teaching and research in the development of modern methodologies to distributed control, switched time-delay systems, fault-tolerant systems and information technology. He is the principal author of thirty books, inclusive book-chapters and the author/co-author of more than 490 peer-reviewed papers. He is the recipient of two national, one regional and two university prizes for outstanding research in engineering. He is a fellow of the IEE, a senior member of the IEEE, the CEI (UK), and a registered consultant engineer of information engineering and systems (Egypt).

Contents

Preface

This volume brings about the contemporary results in the field of discrete-time systems. It covers technical reports written on the topics of robust control, nonlinear systems and recent applications. Although the research views are different, they all geared towards focusing on the up-to-date knowledge gain by the researchers and providing effective developments along the systems and control arena. Each topic has a detailed discussions and suggestions for future perusal by interested investigators.

The book is divided into three sections: Section I is devoted to 'robust control', Section II deals with 'nonlinear control' and Section III provides 'applications'

Section I 'robust control' comprises of three chapters. In what follows we provide brief account of each. In the first chapter titled "Stochastic mixed LQR/H⊚ control for linear discrete-time systems" Xiaojie Xu considered the static state feedback stochastic mixed LQR/ Hoo control problem for linear discrete-time systems. In this chapter, the author established sufficient conditions for the existence of all admissible static state feedback controllers solving this problem. Then, sufficient conditions for the existence of all static output feedback controllers solving the discrete-time stochastic mixed LQR/ Hoo control problem are presented.

In the second chapter titled "Robust control design of uncertain discrete-time descriptor systems with delays" by Yoneyama, Uchida, and Takada, the authors looked at the robust H_∞ non-fragile control design problem for uncertain discrete-time descriptor systems with time-delay. The controller gain uncertainties under consideration are supposed to be time-varying but norm-bounded. The problem addressed was the robust stability and stabilization problem under state feedback subject to norm-bounded uncertainty. The authors derived sufficient conditions for the solvability of the robust non-fragile stabilization control design problem for discrete-time descriptor systems with time-delay obtained with additive controller uncertainties.

In the third chapter, the authors Jun-min, Jiang-rong and Zhi-le of "Delay-dependent generalized H2 control for discrete-time fuzzy systems with infinite-distributed delays" examined the generalized H2 control problem for a class of discrete time T-S fuzzy systems with infinite-distributed delays. They constructed a new delay-dependent piecewise Lyapunov-Krasovskii functional (DDPLKF) and based on which the stabilization condition and controller design method are derived. They have shown that the control laws can be obtained by solving a set of LMIs. A simulation example has been presented to illustrate the effectiveness of the proposed design procedures.

Section II 'nonlinear control' is subsumed of three chapters. In the first chapter of this section, Dai, Xia, Fu and Mahmoud, in an overview setting, wrote the chapter "Discrete model-predictive control" and introduced the principles, mathematical formulation and properties of MPC for constrained dynamic systems, both linear and nonlinear. In particular, they addressed the issues of feasibility, closed loop stability and open-loop performance objective versus closed loop performance. Several technical issues pertaining to robust design, stochastic control and MPC over networks are stressed.

The authors Jordan, Bustamante and Berger presented "Stability Analysis of Nonlinear Discrete-Time Adaptive Control Systems with Large Dead-Times" as the second chapter in this section. They looked at the guidance, navigation and control systems of unmanned underwater vehicles (UUVs) which are digitally linked by means of a control communication with complex protocols and converters. Of particular interest is to carefully examine the effects of time delays in UUVs that are controlled adaptively in six degrees of freedom. They performed a stability analysis to obtain guidelines for selecting appropriate sampling periods according to the tenor of perturbations and delay.

In the third chapter "Adaptive step-size orthogonal gradient-based per-tone equalization in discrete multitone systems" by Suchada Sitjongsataporn, the author focused on discrete multitone theory and presented orthogonal gradient-based algorithms with reduced complexity for per-tone equalizer (PTEQ) based on the adaptive step-size approaches related to the mixed-tone criterion. The convergence behavior and stability analysis of the proposed algorithms are investigated based on the mixed-tone weight-estimated errors.

Section III provides 'applications' in terms of three chapters. In one chapter "An approach to hybrid smoothing for linear discrete-time systems with non-Gaussian noises" by Gou Nakura, the author critically examined hybrid estimation for linear discrete-time systems with non- Gaussian noises and assumed that modes of the systems are not directly accessible. In this regard, he proceeded to determine both estimated states of the systems and a candidate of the distributions of the modes over the finite time interval based on the most probable trajectory (MPT) approach.

In the following chapter "Discrete-time fractional-order systems: modeling and stability issues" by Guermah, Djennoune and Bettayeb, the authors reviewed some basic tools for modeling and analysis of fractional-order systems (FOS) in discrete time and introduced state-space representation for both commensurate and non commensurate fractional orders. They revealed new properties and focused on the analysis of the controllability and the observability of linear discrete-time FOS. Further, the authors established testable sufficient conditions for guaranteeing the controllability and the observability.

In the third chapter "Investigation of a methodology for the quantitative estimation of nursing tasks on the basis of time study data" by Atsue Ishii, Takashi Nakamura, Yuko Ohno and Satoko Kasahara, the authors concentrated on establishing a methodology for the purpose of linking the data to the calculation of quantities of nursing care required or to nursing care management. They focused on the critical issues including estimates of ward task times based on time study data, creation of a computer-based virtual ward environment using the estimated values and test experiment on a plan for work management using the virtual ward environment

To sum up, the collection of such variety of chapters presents a unique opportunity to research investigators who are interested to catch up with accelerated progress in the world of discrete-time systems.

Magdi S. Mahmoud
KFUPM, Saudi Arabia

Section 1

Robust Control

Chapter 1

Stochastic Mixed LQR/H$_\infty$ Control for Linear Discrete-Time Systems

Xiaojie Xu

Additional information is available at the end of the chapter

http://dx.doi.org/10.5772/51019

1. Introduction

Mixed H_2/H_∞ control has received much attention in the past two decades, see Bernstein & Haddad (1989), Doyle et al. (1989b), Haddad et al. (1991), Khargonekar & Rotea (1991), Doyle et al. (1994), Limebeer et al. (1994), Chen & Zhou (2001) and references therein. The mixed H_2/H_∞ control problem involves the following linear continuous-time systems

$$\begin{aligned}\dot{x}(t)&=Ax(t)+B_0w_0(t)+B_1w(t)+B_2u(t),\ x(0)=x_0\\ z(t)&=C_1x(t)+D_{12}u(t)\\ y(t)&=C_2x(t)+D_{20}w_0(t)+D_{21}w(t)\end{aligned} \tag{1}$$

where, $x(t)\in R^n$ is the state, $u(t)\in R^m$ is the control input, $w_0(t)\in R^{q_1}$ is one disturbance input, $w(t)\in R^{q_2}$ is another disturbance input that belongs to $L_2[0,\infty)$, $y(t)\in R^r$ is the measured output.

Bernstein & Haddad (1989) presented a combined LQG/H_∞ control problem. This problem is defined as follows: Given the stabilizable and detectable plant (1) with $w_0(t)=0$ and the expected cost function

$$J(A_c, B_c, C_c) = \lim_{t\to\infty} E\left\{x^T(t)Qx(t) + u^T(t)Ru(t)\right\} \tag{2}$$

determine an nth order dynamic compensator

$$\begin{aligned} \dot{x}_c(t) &= A_c x(t) + B_c y(t) \\ u(t) &= C_c x_c(t) \end{aligned} \tag{3}$$

which satisfies the following design criteria: (i) the closed-loop system (1) (3) is stable; (ii) the closed-loop transfer matrix T_{zw} from the disturbance input $w$to the controlled output z satisfies$\| T_{zw}\|_\infty < \gamma$; (iii) the expected cost function $J(A_c, B_c, C_c)$is minimized; where, the disturbance input w is assumed to be a Gaussian white noise. Bernstein & Haddad (1989) considered merely the combined LQG/H_∞ control problem in the special case of $Q = C_1^T C_1$ and $R = D_{12}^T D_{12}$ and$C_1^T D_{12} = 0$. Since the expected cost function $J(A_c, B_c, C_c)$ equals the square of the H_2-norm of the closed-loop transfer matrix T_{zw} in this case, the combined LQG/H_∞ problem by Bernstein & Haddad (1989) has been recognized to be a mixed H_2/H_∞ problem. In Bernstein & Haddad (1989), they considered the minimization of an "upper bound" of $\| T_{zw}\|_2^2$ subject to$\| T_{zw}\|_\infty < \gamma$, and solved this problem by using Lagrange multiplier techniques. Doyle et al. (1989b) considered a related output feedback mixed H_2/H_∞ problem (also see Doyle et al. 1994). The two approaches have been shown in Yeh et al. (1992) to be duals of one another in some sense. Haddad et al. (1991) gave sufficient conditions for the exstence of discrete-time static output feedback mixed H_2/H_∞controllers in terms of coupled Riccati equations. In Khargonekar & Rotea (1991), they presented a convex optimisation approach to solve output feedback mixed H_2/H_∞ problem. In Limebeer et al. (1994), they proposed a Nash game approach to the state feedback mixed H_2/H_∞ problem, and gave necessary and sufficient conditions for the existence of a solution of this problem. Chen & Zhou (2001) generalized the method of Limebeer et al. (1994) to output feedback multiobjective H_2/H_∞ problem. However, up till now, no approach has involved the combined LQG/H_∞ control problem (so called stochastic mixed LQR/H_∞ control problem) for linear continuous-time systems (1) with the expected cost function (2), where, $Q \geq 0$and $R > 0$are the weighting matrices, $w_0(t)$is a Gaussian white noise, and $w(t)$is a disturbance input that belongs to$L_2[0,\infty)$.

In this chapter, we consider state feedback stochastic mixed LQR/H_∞ control problem for linear discrete-time systems. The deterministic problem corresponding to this problem (so called mixed LQR/H_∞ control problem) was first considered by Xu (2006). In Xu (2006), an algebraic Riccati equation approach to state feedback mixed quadratic guaranteed cost and H_∞ control problem (so called state feedback mixed QGC/H_∞ control problem) for linear discrete-time systems with uncertainty was presented. When the parameter uncertainty equals zero, the discrete-time state feedback mixed QGC/H_∞ control problem reduces to the discrete-time state feedback mixed LQR/H_∞ control problem. Xu (2011) presented respectively a state space approach and an algebraic Riccati equation approach to discrete-time state feedback mixed LQR/H_∞ control problem, and gave a sufficient condition for the existence of an admissible state feedback controller solving this problem.

On the other hand, Geromel & Peres (1985) showed a new stabilizability property of the Riccati equation solution, and proposed, based on this new property, a numerical procedure to design static output feedback suboptimal LQR controllers for linear continuous-time systems. Geromel et al. (1989) extended the results of Geromel & Peres (1985) to linear discrete-time systems. In the fact, comparing this new stabilizability property of the Riccati equation solution with the existing results (de Souza & Xie 1992, Kucera & de Souza 1995, Gadewadikar et al. 2007, Xu 2008), we can show easily that the former involves sufficient conditions for the existence of all state feedback suboptimal LQR controllers. Untill now, the technique of finding all state feedback controllers by Geromel & Peres (1985) has been extended to various control problems, such as, static output feedback stabilizability (Kucera & de Souza 1995), H_∞control problem for linear discrete-time systems (de Souza & Xie 1992), H_∞control problem for linear continuous-time systems (Gadewadikar et al. 2007), mixed LQR/H_∞ control problem for linear continuous-time systems (Xu 2008).

The objective of this chapter is to solve discrete-time state feedback stochastic mixed LQR/H_∞ control problem by combining the techniques of Xu (2008 and 2011) with the well known LQG theory. There are three motivations for developing this problem. First, Xu (2011) parametrized a central controller solving the discrete-time state feedback mixed LQR/H_∞ control problem in terms of an algebraic Riccati equation. However, no stochastic interpretation was provided. This paper thus presents a central solution to the discrete-time state feedback stochastic mixed LQR/H_∞ control problem. This result may be recognied to be a stochastic interpretation of the discrete-time state feedback mixed LQR/H_∞ control problem considered by Xu (2011). The second motivation for our paper is to present a characterization of all admissible state feedback controllers for solving discrete-time stochastic mixed LQR/H_∞ control problem for linear continuous-time systems in terms of a single algebraic Riccati equation with a free parameter matrix, plus two constrained conditions: One is a free parameter matrix constrained condition on the form of the gain matrix, another is an assumption that the free parameter matrix is a free admissible controller error. The third motivation for our paper is to use the above results to solve the discrete-time static output feedback stochastic mixed LQR/H_∞ control problem.

This chapter is organized as follows: Section 2 introduces several preliminary results. In Section 3, first,we define the state feedback stochastic mixed LQR/H_∞ control problem for linear discrete-time systems. Secondly, we give sufficient conditions for the existence of all admissible state feedback controllers solving the discrete-time stochastic mixed LQR/H_∞ control problem. In the rest of this section, first, we parametrize a central discrete-time state feedback stochastic mixed LQR/H_∞ controller, and show that this result may be recognied to be a stochastic interpretation of discrete-time state feedback mixed LQR/H_∞ control problem considered by Xu (2011). Secondly, we propose a numerical algorithm for calclulating a kind of discrete-time state feedback stochastic mixed LQR/H_∞ controllers. Also, we compare our main result with the related well known results. As a special case, Section 5 gives sufficient conditions for the existence of all admissible static output feedback controllers solving the discrete-time stochastic mixed LQR/H_∞ control problem, and proposes a numerical algorithm for calculating a discrete-time static output feedback stochastic mixed LQR/H_∞ controller. In Section 6, we give two examples to illustrate the design procedures and their effectiveness. Section 7 is conclusion.

2. Preliminaries

In this section, we will review several preliminary results. First, we introduce the new stabilizability property of Riccati equation solutions for linear discrete-time systems which was presented by Geromel et al. (1989). This new stabilizability property involves the following linear discrete-time systems

$$\begin{aligned} x(k+1)&=Ax(k)+Bu(k); x(0)=x_0 \\ y(k)&=Cx(k) \end{aligned} \tag{4}$$

with quadratic performance index

$$J_2:=\sum_{k=0}^{\infty}\{x^T(k)Qx(k)+u^T(k)Ru(k)\}$$

under the influence of state feedback of the form

$$u(k)=Kx(k) \tag{5}$$

where,$x(k)\in R^n$ is the state, $u(k)\in R^m$is the control input, $y(k)\in R^r$is the measured output, $Q=Q^T\geq 0$and$R=R^T>0$. We make the following assumptions

Assumption 2.1(A, B) is controllable.

Assumption 2.2$(A, Q^{1/2})$ is observable.

Define a discrete-time Riccati equation as follows:

$$A^TSA-A-A^TSB(R+B^TSB)^{-1}B^TSA+Q=0 \tag{6}$$

For simplicity the discrete-time Riccati equation (6) can be rewritten as

$$\Pi_d(S)=Q \tag{7}$$

http://dx.doi.org/10.5772/51019

Geromel & Peres (1985) showed a new stabilizability property of the Riccati equation solution, and proposed, based on this new property, a numerical procedure to design static output feedback suboptimal LQR controllers for linear continuous-time systems. Geromel et al. (1989) extended this new stabilizability property displayed in Geromel & Peres (1985) to linear discrete-time systems. This resut is given by the following theorem.

Theorem 2.1 (Geromel et al. 1989) For the matrix $L \in R^{m\times n}$ such that

$$K = -(R + B^T SB)^{-1} B^T SA + L \tag{8}$$

holds, $S \in R^{n\times n}$is a positive definite solution of the modified discrete-time Riccati equation

$$\Pi_d(S) = Q + L^T (R + B^T SB)L \tag{9}$$

Then the matrix $(A + BK)$is stable.

When these conditions are met, the quadratic cost function J_2 is given by

$J_2 = x^T(0)Sx(0)$

Second, we introduce the well known discrete-time bounded real lemma (see Zhou et al., 1996; Iglesias & Glover, 1991; de Souza & Xie, 1992).

Lemma 2.1 (Discrete Time Bounded Real Lemma)

Suppose that$\gamma > 0$, $M(z) = \begin{bmatrix} A & B \\ C & D \end{bmatrix} \in RH_\infty$, then the following two statements are equivalent:

i.$\| M(z) \|_\infty < \gamma$.

ii. There exists a stabilizing solution $X \geq 0$ ($X > 0$if $(C, A)$is observable) to the discrete-time Riccati equation

$A^T XA - X + \gamma^{-2}(A^T XB + C^T D)U_1^{-1}(B^T XA + D^T C) + C^T C = 0$

such that$U_1 = I - \gamma^{-2}(D^T D + B^T XB) > 0$.

Next, we will consider the following linear discrete-time systems

$$\begin{aligned} x(k+1) &= Ax(k) + B_1 w(k) + B_2 u(k) \\ z(k) &= C_1 x(k) + D_{12} u(k) \end{aligned} \tag{10}$$

under the influence of state feedback of the form

$$u(k)=Kx(k) \tag{11}$$

where, $x(k)\in R^n$ is the state, $u(k)\in R^m$ is the control input, $w(k)\in R^q$ is the disturbance input that belongs to $L_2[0,\infty)$, $z(k)\in R^p$ is the controlled output. Let $x(0)=x_0$.

The associated with this systems is the quadratic performance index

$$J_2:=\sum_{k=0}^{\infty}\{x^T(k)Qx(k)+u^T(k)Ru(k)\} \tag{12}$$

where, $Q=Q^T\geq 0$ and $R=R^T>0$.

The closed-loop transfer matrix from the disturbance input w to the controlled output z is

$$T_{zw}(z)=\begin{bmatrix} A_K & B_K \\ C_K & 0 \end{bmatrix}:=C_K(zI-A_K)^{-1}B_K$$

where, $A_K:=A+B_2K, B_K:=B_1, C_K:=C_1+D_{12}K$.

The following lemma is an extension of the discrete-time bounded real lemma (see Xu 2011).

Lemma 2.2 Given the system (10) under the influence of the state feedback (11), and suppose that $\gamma>0, T_{zw}(z)\in RH_\infty$; then there exists an admissible controller K such that $\|T_{zw}(z)\|_\infty<\gamma$ if there exists a stabilizing solution $X_\infty\geq 0$ to the discrete time Riccati equation

$$A_K^TX_\infty A_K-X_\infty+\gamma^{-2}A_K^TX_\infty B_KU_1^{-1}B_K^TX_\infty A_K+C_K^TC_K+Q+K^TRK=0 \tag{13}$$

such that $U_1=I-\gamma^{-2}B_K^TX_\infty B_K>0$.

Proof: See the proof of Lemma 2.2 of Xu (2011). Q.E.D.

Finally, we review the result of discrete-time state feedback mixed LQR/H_∞ control problem. Xu (2011) has defined this problem as follows: Given the linear discrete-time systems (10)(11) with $w\in L_2[0,\infty)$ and $x(0)=x_0$, for a given number $\gamma>0$, determine an admissible controller that achieves

$$\sup_{w\in L_{2+}}\inf_{K}\{J_2\} \text{ subject to } \|T_{zw}(z)\|_\infty<\gamma.$$

If this controller K exists, it is said to be a discrete-time state feedback mixed LQR/H_∞ controller.

The following assumptions are imposed on the system

Assumption 2.3 (C_1, A) is detectable.

Assumption 2.4$(A,\ B_2)$ is stabilizable.

*Assumption 2.5*$D_{12}^T[C_1\ \ D_{12}]=[0\ \ I]$.

The solution to the problem defined in the above involves the discrete-time Riccati equation

$$A^T X_\infty A - X_\infty - A^T X_\infty \hat{B}(\hat{B}^T X_\infty \hat{B} + \hat{R})^{-1}\hat{B}^T X_\infty A + C_1^T C_1 + Q = 0 \tag{14}$$

where, $\hat{B}=[\gamma^{-1}B_1\ \ B_2]$, $\hat{R}=\begin{bmatrix} -I & 0 \\ 0 & R+I \end{bmatrix}$.

Xu (2011) has provided a solution to discrete-time state feedback mixed LQR/H_∞control problem, this result is given by the following theorem.

Theorem 2.2 There exists a discrete-time state feedback mixed LQR/H_∞ controller if the discrete-time Riccati equation (14) has a stabilizing solution X_∞ and $U_1= I-\gamma^{-2}B_1^T X_\infty B_1>0$.

Moreover, this discrete-time state feedback mixed LQR/H_∞controller is given by

$K=-U_2^{-1}B_2^T U_3 A$

where,$U_2=R+I+B_2^T U_3 B_2$, and$U_3=X_\infty+\gamma^{-2}X_\infty B_1 U_1^{-1}B_1^T X_\infty$.

In this case, the discrete-time state feedback mixed LQR/H_∞controller will achieve

$$\sup_{w\in L_{2+}}\inf_K\{J_2\}=x_0^T(X_\infty+\gamma^{-2}X_w-X_z)x_0 \text{ subject to} \| T_{zw}\|_\infty<\gamma.$$

where, $\hat{A}_K=A_K+\gamma^{-2}B_K U_1^{-1}B_K^T X_\infty A_K$, $X_w=\sum_{k=0}^{\infty}\{(\hat{A}_K^k)^T A_K^T X_\infty B_K U_1^{-2}B_K^T X_\infty A_K \hat{A}_K^k\}$, and $X_z=\sum_{k=0}^{\infty}\{(\hat{A}_K^k)^T C_K^T C_K \hat{A}_K^k\}$.

3. State Feedback

In this section, we consider the following linear discrete-time systems

$$\begin{aligned} x(k+1)&=Ax(k)+B_0w_0(k)+B_1w(k)+B_2u(k)\\ z(k)&=C_1x(k)+D_{12}u(k)\\ y(k)&=C_2x(k)\end{aligned} \tag{15}$$

with state feedback of the form

$$u(k)=Kx(k) \tag{16}$$

where, $x(k)\in R^{n}$ is the state, $u(k)\in R^{m}$ is the control input, $w_0(k)\in R^{q_1}$ is one disturbance input, $w(k)\in R^{q_2}$ is another disturbance that belongs to $L_2[0,\infty)$, $z(k)\in R^{p}$ is the controlled output, $y(k)\in R^{r}$ is the measured output.

It is assumed that $x(0)$ is Gaussian with mean and covariance given by

$E\{x(0)\}=\bar{x}_0$

$\text{cov}\{x(0),\ x(0)\}:=E\{(x(0)-\bar{x}_0)(x(0)-\bar{x}_0)^T\}=R_0$

The noise process $w_0(k)$ is a Gaussain white noise signal with properties

$E\{w_0(k)\}=0, E\{w_0(k)w_0^T(\tau)\}=R_1(k)\delta(k-\tau)$

Furthermore, $x(0)$ and $w_0(k)$ are assumed to be independent, $w_0(k)$ and $w(k)$ are also assumed to be independent, where, $E[\bullet]$ denotes expected value.

Also, we make the following assumptions:

Assumption 3.1 $(C_1,\ A)$ is detectable.

Assumption 3.2 $(A,\ B_2)$ is stabilizable.

Assumption 3.3 $D_{12}^T[C_1\quad D_{12}]=[0\quad I]$.

The expected cost function corresponding to this problem is defined as follows:

$$J_E:=\lim_{T\to\infty}\frac{1}{T}E\left\{\sum_{k=0}^{T}(x^T(k)Qx(k)+u^T(k)Ru(k)-\gamma^2\|w\|^2)\right\} \tag{17}$$

where, $Q=Q^T\geq 0$, $R=R^T>0$, and $\gamma>0$ is a given number.

As is well known, a given controller K is called admissible (for the plant G) if K is real-rational proper, and the minimal realization of K internally stabilizes the state space realization (15) of G.

Recall that the discrete-time state feedback optimal LQG problem is to find an admissible controller that minimizes the expected quadratic cost function (17) subject to the systems (15) (16) with $w(k)=0$, while the discrete-time state feedback H_∞ control problem is to find an admissible controller such that $\|T_{zw}\|_\infty<\gamma$ subject to the systems (15) (16) for a given number $\gamma>0$. While we combine the two problems for the systems (15) (16) with $w\in L_2[0,\infty)$, the expected cost function (17) is a function of the control input $u(k)$ and disturbance input $w(k)$ in the case of γ being fixed and $x(0)$ being Gaussian with known statistics and $w_0(k)$ being a Gaussain white noise with known statistics. Thus it is not possible to pose a discrete-time state feedback stochastic mixed LQR/H_∞ control problem that achieves the minimization of the expected cost function (17) subject to $\| T_{zw}\|_\infty < \gamma$ for the systems (15) (16) with $w \in L_2[0,\infty)$ because the expected cost function (17) is an uncertain function depending on disturbance input $w(k)$. In order to eliminate this difficulty, the design criteria of discrete-time state feedback stochastic mixed LQR/H_∞ control problem should be replaced by the following design criteria:

$$\sup_{w\in L_{2+}} \inf_K \left\{J_E\right\} \text{ subject to } \| T_{zw}\|_\infty < \gamma$$

because for all $w \in L_2[0,\infty)$, the following inequality always exists.

$$\inf_K \left\{J_E\right\} \le \sup_{w\in L_{2+}} \inf_K \left\{J_E\right\}$$

Based on this, we define the discrete-time state feedback stochastic mixed LQR/H_∞ control problem as follows:

Discrete-time state feedback stochastic mixed LQR/H_∞ control problem: Given the linear discrete-time systems (15) (16) satisfying Assumption 3.1-3.3 with $w(k) \in L_2[0,\infty)$ and the expected cost functions (17), for a given number $\gamma > 0$, find all admissible state feedback controllers K such that

$$\sup_{w\in L_{2+}} \left\{J_E\right\} \text{ subject to } \| T_{zw}\|_\infty < \gamma$$

where, $T_{zw}(z)$ is the closed loop transfer matrix from the disturbance input w to the controlled output z.

If all these admissible controllers exist, then one of them $K = K^*$ will achieve the design criteria

$$\sup_{w\in L_{2+}} \inf_K \left\{J_E\right\} \text{ subject to } \| T_{zw}\|_\infty < \gamma$$

and it is said to be a central discrete-time state feedback stochastic mixed LQR/H_∞ controller.

Remark 3.1 The discrete-time state feedback stochastic mixed LQR/H_∞ control problem defined in the above is also said to be a discrete-time state feedback combined LQG/H_∞ control problem in general case. When the disturbance input $w(k)=0$, this problem reduces to a discrete-time state feedback combined LQG/H_∞ control problem arisen from Bernstein & Haddad (1989) and Haddad et al. (1991).

Remark 3.2 In the case of $w(k)=0$, it is easy to show (see Bernstein & Haddad 1989, Haddad et al. 1991) that J_E in (17) is equivalent to the expected cost function

$$J_E = \lim_{k\to\infty} E\left\{x^T(k)Qx(k) + u^T(k)Ru(k)\right\}$$

Define $Q = C_1^T C_1$ and $R = D_{12}^T D_{12}$ and suppose that$C_1^T D_{12} = 0$, then J_E may be rewritten as

$$\begin{aligned} J_E &= \lim_{k\to\infty} E\left\{ x^T(k)Qx(k) + u^T(k)Ru(k) \right\} \\ &= \lim_{k\to\infty} E\left\{ x^T(k)C_1^T C_1 x(k) + u^T(k)D_{12}^T D_{12} u(k) \right\} \\ &= \lim_{k\to\infty} E\left\{ z^T(k)z(k) \right\} \end{aligned}$$

Also, the controlled output z may be expressed as

$$z = T_{zw_0}(z) w_0 \tag{18}$$

where,$T_{zw_0}(z) = \begin{bmatrix} A_K & B_0 \\ C_K & 0 \end{bmatrix}$. If w_0 is white noise with indensity matrix I and the closed-loop systems is stable then

$$J_E = \lim_{k\to\infty} E\left\{ z^T(k)z(k) \right\} = \| T_{zw_0} \|_2^2$$

This implies that the discrete-time state feedback combined LQG/H_∞ control problem in the special case of $Q = C_1^T C_1$ and $R = D_{12}^T D_{12}$ and $C_1^T D_{12} = 0$ arisen from Bernstein & Haddad (1989) and Haddad et al. (1991) is a mixed H_2/H_∞ control problem.

Based on the above definition, we give sufficient conditions for the existence of all admissible state feedback controllers solving the discrete-time stochastic mixed LQR/H_∞ control problem by combining the techniques of Xu (2008 and 2011) with the well known LQG theory. This result is given by the following theorem.

Theorem 3.1 There exists a discrete-time state feedback stochastic mixed LQR/ H_∞ controller if the following two conditions hold:

i. There exists a matrix ΔK such that

$$\Delta K = K + U_2^{-1} B_2^T U_3 A \tag{19}$$

and X_∞ is a symmetric non-negative definite solution of the following discrete-time Riccati equation

$$\begin{aligned} &A^T X_\infty A - X_\infty - A^T X_\infty \hat{B}(\hat{B}^T X_\infty \hat{B} + \hat{R})^{-1} \hat{B}^T X_\infty A \\ &+ C_1^T C_1 + Q + \Delta K^T U_2 \Delta K = 0 \end{aligned} \tag{20}$$

and $\hat{A}_c = A - \hat{B}(\hat{B}^T X_\infty \hat{B} + \hat{R})^{-1} \hat{B}^T X_\infty A$ is stable and$U_1 = I - \gamma^{-2} B_1^T X_\infty B_1 > 0$;

where, $\hat{B}=[\gamma^{-1}B_1 \quad B_2]$, $\hat{R}=\begin{bmatrix} -I & 0 \\ 0 & R+I \end{bmatrix}$, $U_3=X_\infty+\gamma^{-2}X_\infty B_1 U_1^{-1} B_1^T X_\infty$, $U_2=R+I+B_2^T U_3 B_2$.

ii. ΔK is an admissible controller error.

In this case, the discrete-time state feedback stochastic mixed LQR/H_∞ controller will achieve

$$\sup_{w\in L_{2+}}\left\{J_E\right\}=\lim_{T\to\infty}\frac{1}{T}\sum_{k=0}^{T} tr(B_0^T X_\infty B_0 R_1(k)) \text{ subject to } \| T_{zw}\|_\infty<\gamma$$

Remark 3.3 In Theorem 3.1, the controller error is defined to be the state feedback controller K minus the suboptimal controller $K^*=-U_2^{-1}B_2^T U_3 A$, where, $X_\infty\geq 0$ satisfies the discrete-time Riccati equation (20), that is,

$$\Delta K=K-K^*$$

where, ΔK is the controller error, K is the state feedback controller and K^* is the suboptimal controller. Suppose that there exists a suboptimal controller K^* such that $A_{K^*}=A+B_2K^*$ is stable, then K and ΔK is respectively said to be an admissible controller and an admissible controller error if it belongs to the set

$$\Omega:=\left\{\Delta K: A_{K^*}+B_2\Delta K \text{ is stable}\right\}$$

Remark 3.4 The discrete-time state feedback stochastic mixed LQR/H_∞ controller satisfying the conditions i-ii displayed in Theorem 3.1 is not unique. All admissible state feedback controllers satisfying these two conditions lead to all discrete-time state feedback stochastic mixed LQR/H_∞ controllers.

Astrom (1971) has given the mean value of a quadratic form of normal stochastic variables. This result is given by the following lemma.

Lemma 3.1 Let x be normal with mean m and covariance R. Then

$$E\{x^T Sx\}=m^T Sm+trSR$$

For convenience, let $A_K=A+B_2K$, $B_K=B_1$, $C_K=C_1+D_{12}K$, $A_{K^*}=A+B_2K^*$, $B_{K^*}=B_1$, $C_{K^*}=C_1+D_{12}K^*$, and $K^*=-U_2^{-1}B_2^T U_3 A$, where, $X_\infty\geq 0$ satisfies the discrete-time Riccati equation (20); then we have the following lemma.

Lemma 3.2 Suppose that the conditions i-ii of Theorem 3.1 hold, then the both A_{K^*} and A_K are stable.

Proof: Suppose that the conditions i-ii of Theorem 3.1 hold, then it can be easily shown by using the similar standard matrix manipulations as in the proof of Theorem 3.1 in de Souza & Xie (1992) that

$$(\hat{B}^T X_\infty \hat{B} + \hat{R})^{-1} = \begin{bmatrix} -U_1^{-1} + U_1^{-1}\hat{B}_1 U_2^{-1}\hat{B}_1^T U_1^{-1} & U_1^{-1}\hat{B}_1 U_2^{-1} \\ U_2^{-1}\hat{B}_1^T U_1^{-1} & U_2^{-1} \end{bmatrix}$$

where, $\hat{B}_1 = \gamma^{-1} B_1^T X_\infty B_2$. Thus we have

$$A^T X_\infty \hat{B}(\hat{B}^T X_\infty \hat{B} + \hat{R})^{-1}\hat{B}^T X_\infty A = -\gamma^2 A^T X_\infty B_1 U_1^{-1} B_1^T X_\infty A + A^T U_3 B_2 U_2^{-1} B_2^T U_3 A$$

Rearranging the discrete-time Riccati equation (20), we get

$$\begin{aligned} X_\infty &= A^T X_\infty A + \gamma^{-2} A^T X_\infty B_1 U_1^{-1} B_1^T X_\infty A - A^T U_3 B_2 U_2^{-1} B_2^T U_3 A \\ &+ C_1^T C_1 + Q + \Delta K^T U_2 \Delta K \\ &= A_{K^*}^T X_\infty A_{K^*} + \gamma^{-2} A_{K^*}^T X_\infty B_{K^*} U_1^{-1} B_{K^*}^T X_\infty A_{K^*} + C_{K^*}^T C_{K^*} + Q \\ &+ K^{*T} R K^* + \Delta K^T U_2 \Delta K \end{aligned}$$

that is,

$$\begin{aligned} &A_{K^*}^T X_\infty A_{K^*} - X_\infty + \gamma^{-2} A_{K^*}^T X_\infty B_{K^*} U_1^{-1} B_{K^*}^T X_\infty A_{K^*} + C_{K^*}^T C_{K^*} + Q \\ &+ K^{*T} R K^* + \Delta K^T U_2 \Delta K = 0 \end{aligned} \tag{21}$$

Since the discrete-time Riccati equation (20) has a symmetric non-negative definite solution X_∞ and $\hat{A}_c = A - \hat{B}(\hat{B}^T X_\infty \hat{B} + \hat{R})^{-1}\hat{B}^T X_\infty A$ is stable, and we can show that $\hat{A}_c = A_{K^*} + \gamma^{-2} B_{K^*} U_1^{-1} B_{K^*}^T X_\infty A_{K^*}$, the discrete-time Riccati equation (21) also has a symmetric non-negative definite solution X_∞ and $A_{K^*} + \gamma^{-2} B_{K^*} U_1^{-1} B_{K^*}^T X_\infty A_{K^*}$ also is stable. Hence, $(U_1^{-1} B_{K^*}^T X_\infty A_{K^*}, A_{K^*})$is detectable. Based on this, it follows from standard results on Lyapunov equations (see Lemma 2.7 a), Iglesias & Glover 1991) that A_{K^*} is stable. Also, note that ΔK is an admissible controller error, so $A_K = A_{K^*} + B_2 \Delta K$ is stable. Q. E. D.

Proof of Theorem 3.1: Suppose that the conditions i-ii hold, then it follows from Lemma 3.2 that the both A_{K^*} and A_K are stable. This implies that $T_{zw}(z) \in RH_\infty$.

Define $V(x(k)) = x^T(k) X_\infty x(k)$, where, X_∞ is the solution to the discrete-time Riccati equation (20), then taking the difference $\Delta V(x(k))$, we get

$$\begin{aligned} \Delta V(x(k)) &= x^T(k+1) X_\infty x(k+1) - x^T(k) X_\infty x(k) \\ &= x^T(k)(A_K^T X_\infty A_K - X_\infty)x(k) + 2w^T(k) B_K^T X_\infty A_K x(k) \\ &+ w^T(k) B_K^T X_\infty B_K w(k) + 2w_0^T(k) B_0^T X_\infty A_K x(k) \\ &+ 2w_0^T(k) B_0^T X_\infty B_1 w(k) + w_0^T(k) B_0^T X_\infty B_0 w_0(k) \end{aligned} \tag{22}$$

On the other hand, we can rewrite the discrete-time Riccati equation (20) by using the same standard matrix manipulations as in the proof of Lemma 3.2 as follows:

$$A^T X_\infty A - X_\infty + \gamma^{-2} A^T X_\infty B_1 U_1^{-1} B_1^T X_\infty A - A^T U_3 B_2 U_2^{-1} B_2^T U_3 A$$
$$+C_1^T C_1 + Q + \Delta K^T U_2 \Delta K = 0$$

or equivalently

$$A_K^T X_\infty A_K - X_\infty + \gamma^{-2} A_K^T X_\infty B_K U_1^{-1} B_K^T X_\infty A_K + C_K^T C_K + Q + K^T R K = 0 \tag{23}$$

It follows from Lemma 2.2 that$\| T_{zw} \|_\infty < \gamma$.Completing the squares for (22) and substituting (23) in (22), we get

$$\Delta V(x(k)) = -\| z \|^2 + \gamma^2 \| w \|^2 - \gamma^2 \| U_1^{1/2}(w - \gamma^{-2} U_1^{-1} B_K^T X_\infty A_K x) \|^2$$
$$+ x^T(k)(A_K^T X_\infty A_K - X_\infty + \gamma^{-2} A_K^T X_\infty B_K U_1^{-1} B_K^T X_\infty A_K + C_K^T C_K) x(k)$$
$$+ 2 w_0^T(k) B_0^T X_\infty A_K x(k) + 2 w_0^T(k) B_0^T X_\infty B_1 w(k) + w_0^T(k) B_0^T X_\infty B_0 w_0(k)$$
$$= -\| z \|^2 + \gamma^2 \| w \|^2 - \gamma^2 \| U_1^{1/2}(w - \gamma^{-2} U_1^{-1} B_K^T X_\infty A_K x) \|^2 - x^T(k)(Q + K^T R K) x(k)$$
$$+ 2 w_0^T(k) B_0^T X_\infty A_K x(k) + 2 w_0^T(k) B_0^T X_\infty B_1 w(k) + w_0^T(k) B_0^T X_\infty B_0 w_0(k)$$

Thus, we have

$$J_E = \lim_{T\to\infty} \frac{1}{T} E\left\{ \sum_{k=0}^{T} (x^T(k) Q x(k) + u^T(k) R u(k) - \gamma^2 \| w \|^2) \right\}$$
$$= \lim_{T\to\infty} \frac{1}{T} E\left\{ \sum_{k=0}^{T} (-\Delta V(x(k)) - \| z \|^2 - \gamma^2 \| U_1^{1/2}(w - \gamma^{-2} U_1^{-1} B_K^T X_\infty A_K x) \|^2 \right.$$
$$\left. + 2 w_0^T(k) B_0^T X_\infty A_K x(k) + 2 w_0^T(k) B_0^T X_\infty B_1 w(k) + w_0^T(k) B_0^T X_\infty B_0 w_0(k)) \right\}$$
$$\le \lim_{T\to\infty} \frac{1}{T} E\left\{ \sum_{k=0}^{T} (-\Delta V(x(k)) + 2 w_0^T(k) B_0^T X_\infty A_K x(k) + 2 w_0^T(k) B_0^T X_\infty B_1 w(k) \right.$$
$$\left. + w_0^T(k) B_0^T X_\infty B_0 w_0(k)) \right\}$$

Note that $x(\infty) = \lim_{T\to\infty} x(T) = 0$and

$$x(k) = A_K^k x_0 + \sum_{i=0}^{k-1} A_K^{k-i-1} B_0 w_0(i) + \sum_{i=0}^{k-1} A_K^{k-i-1} B_1 w(i)$$
$$w_0^T(k) B_0^T X_\infty A_K x(k) = w_0^T(k) B_0^T X_\infty A_K A_K^k x_0$$
$$+ w_0^T(k) B_0^T X_\infty A_K \sum_{i=0}^{k-1} A_K^{k-i-1} B_0 w_0(i) + w_0^T(k) B_0^T X_\infty A_K \sum_{i=0}^{k-1} A_K^{k-i-1} B_0 w(i)$$

we have

$$E\left\{\sum_{k=0}^{T} w_0^T(k)B_0^T X_\infty A_K x(k)\right\}=E\left\{\sum_{k=0}^{T}(w_0^T(k)B_0^T X_\infty A_K\sum_{i=0}^{k-1}A_K^{k-i-1}B_0w_0(i))\right\}$$
$$=\sum_{k=0}^{T}\sum_{i=0}^{k-1}tr\left\{B_0^T X_\infty A_K^{k-i}B_0E(w_0(i)w_0^T(k))\right\}=0$$

Based on the above, it follows from Lemma 3.1 that

$$\sup_{w\in L_{2+}}\left\{J_E\right\}=\lim_{T\to\infty}\frac{1}{T}E\left\{x^T(0)X_\infty x(0)+\sum_{k=0}^{T}w_0^T(k)B_0^T X_\infty B_0w_0(k)\right\}$$
$$=\lim_{T\to\infty}\frac{1}{T}\left\{\bar{x}_0^T X_\infty \bar{x}_0+tr(X_\infty R_0)+\sum_{k=0}^{T}tr(B_0^T X_\infty B_0R_1(k))\right\}$$
$$=\lim_{T\to\infty}\frac{1}{T}\sum_{k=0}^{T}tr(B_0^T X_\infty B_0R_1(k))$$

Thus, we conclude that

$$\sup_{w\in L_{2+}}\left\{J_E\right\}=\lim_{T\to\infty}\frac{1}{T}\sum_{k=0}^{T}tr(B_0^T X_\infty B_0R_1(k)) \text{ subject to } \| T_{zw}\|_\infty<\gamma \text{ Q.E.D.}$$

In the rest of this section, we give several discussions.

A. A Central Discrete-Time State Feedback Stochastic Mixed LQR/ H_∞ Controller

We are to find a central solution to the discrete-time state feedback stochastic mixed LQR/ H_∞ control problem.This central solution involves the discrete-time Riccati equation

$$A^T X_\infty A-X_\infty-A^T X_\infty \hat{B}(\hat{B}^T X_\infty \hat{B}+\hat{R})^{-1}\hat{B}^T X_\infty A+C_1^T C_1+Q=0 \quad (24)$$

where, $\hat{B}=[\gamma^{-1}B_1 \quad B_2],\hat{R}=\begin{bmatrix}-I & 0\\ 0 & R+I\end{bmatrix}$. Using the similar argument as in the proof of Theorem 3.1 in Xu (2011), the expected cost function J_E can be rewritten as:

$$J_E=\lim_{T\to\infty}\frac{1}{T}E\left\{\sum_{k=0}^{T}(x^T(k)Qx(k)+u^T(k)Ru(k)-\gamma^2\| w\|^2)\right\}$$
$$=\lim_{T\to\infty}\frac{1}{T}E\left\{\sum_{k=0}^{T}[-\Delta V(x(k))-\| z\|^2-\gamma^2\| U_1^{1/2}(w-\gamma^{-2}U_1^{-1}B_K^T X_\infty A_K x)\|^2\right.$$
$$+x^T(A_K^T X_\infty A_K-X_\infty+\gamma^{-2}A_K^T X_\infty B_K U_1^{-1}B_K^T X_\infty A_K+C_K^T C_K+Q+K^T RK)x$$
$$\left.+2w_0^T(k)B_0^T X_\infty A_K x(k)+2w_0^T(k)B_0^T X_\infty B_1w(k)+w_0^T(k)B_0^T X_\infty B_0w_0(k)]\right\} \quad (25)$$

Note that

$$\begin{aligned}&A_K^T X_\infty A_K - X_\infty + \gamma^{-2} A_K^T X_\infty B_K U_1^{-1} B_K^T X_\infty A_K + C_K^T C_K + Q + K^T R K\\&= A^T X_\infty A - X_\infty - A^T X_\infty \hat{B}(\hat{B}^T X_\infty \hat{B} + \hat{R})^{-1} \hat{B}^T X_\infty A + C_1^T C_1 + Q\\&+(K + U_2^{-1} B_2^T U_3 A)^T U_2 (K + U_2^{-1} B_2^T U_3 A)\end{aligned} \tag{26}$$

It follows from (25) and (26) that

$$\begin{aligned}J_E &= \lim_{T\to\infty} \frac{1}{T} E\left\{\sum_{k=0}^{T} (x^T(k)Qx(k) + u^T(k)Ru(k))\right\}\\&= \lim_{T\to\infty} \frac{1}{T} E\left\{\sum_{k=0}^{T} [-\Delta V(x(k)) - \| z\|^2 + \gamma^2 \| w\|^2 - \gamma^2 \| U_1^{1/2}(w - \gamma^{-2} U_1^{-1} B_K^T X_\infty A_K x)\|^2\right.\\&\left.+\| U_2^{1/2}(K + U_2^{-1} B_2^T U_3 A)x\|^2 + 2w_0^T(k) B_0^T X_\infty A_K x(k) + w_0^T(k) B_0^T X_\infty B_0 w_0(k)]\right\}\end{aligned} \tag{27}$$

If $K = -U_2^{-1} B_2^T U_3 A$, then we get that

$$\begin{aligned}&\sup_{w\in L_{2+}} \inf_K \left\{J_E\right\} = \lim_{T\to\infty} \frac{1}{T}\left\{\bar{x}_0^T X_\infty \bar{x}_0 + tr(X_\infty R_0) + \sum_{k=0}^{T} tr(B_0^T X_\infty B_0 R_1(k))\right\}\\&= \lim_{T\to\infty} \frac{1}{T} \sum_{k=0}^{T} tr(B_0^T X_\infty B_0 R_1(k))\end{aligned}$$

by using Lemma 3.1 and the similar argument as in the proof of Theorem 3.1. Thus, we have the following theorem:

Theorem 3.2 There exists a central discrete-time state feedback stochastic mixed LQR/H_∞ controller if the discrete-time Riccati equation (24) has a stabilizing solution $X_\infty \ge 0$ and $U_1 = I - \gamma^{-2} B_1^T X_\infty B_1 > 0$.

Moreover, if this condition is met, the central discrete-time state feedback stochastic mixed LQR/ H_∞ controller is given by

$$K = -U_2^{-1} B_2^T U_3 A$$

where, $U_3 = X_\infty + \gamma^{-2} X_\infty B_1 U_1^{-1} B_1^T X_\infty$, $U_2 = R + I + B_2^T U_3 B_2$.

In this case, the central discrete-time state feedback stochastic mixed LQR/H_∞ controller will achieve

$$\sup_{w\in L_{2+}} \inf_K \left\{J_E\right\} = \lim_{T\to\infty} \frac{1}{T} \sum_{k=0}^{T} tr(B_0^T X_\infty B_0 R_1(k)) \text{ subject to } \| T_{zw}\|_\infty < \gamma$$

Remark 3.5 When $\Delta K = 0$, Theorem 3.1 reduces to Theorem 3.2.

Remark 3.6 Notice that the condition displayed in Theorem 3.2 is the same as one displayed in Theroem 2.2. This implies that the result given by Theorem 3.2 may be recognied to be a stochastic interpretation of the discrete-time state feedback mixed LQR/H_∞ control problem considered by Xu (2011).

B. Numerical Algorithm

In order to calculate a kind of discrete-time state feedback stochastic mixed LQR/ H_∞ controllers, we propose the following numerical algorithm.

Algorithm 3.1

Step 1: Fix the two weighting matrices Q and$R$, set$i=0$, $\Delta K_i=0$, $U_{2(i)}=0$and a small scalarδ, and a matrix M which is not zero matrix of appropriate dimensions.

Step 2: Solve the discrete-time Riccati equation

$$A^T X_i A - X_i - A^T X_i \hat{B}(\hat{B}^T X_i \hat{B} + \hat{R})^{-1} \hat{B}^T X_i A + C_1^T C_1 + Q + \Delta K_i^T U_{2(i)} \Delta K_i = 0$$

for X_i symmetric non-negative definite such that

$$\hat{A}_{ci} = A - \hat{B}(\hat{B}^T X_i \hat{B} + \hat{R})^{-1} \hat{B}^T X_i A \text{ is stable and} U_{1(i)} = I - \gamma^{-2} B_1^T X_i B_1 > 0.$$

Step 3: Calculate$U_{3(i)}$, $U_{2(i)}$and K_i by using the following formulas

$$\begin{aligned} U_{3(i)} &= X_i + \gamma^{-2} X_i B_1 U_{1(i)}^{-1} B_1^T X_i \\ U_{2(i)} &= R + I + B_2^T U_{3(i)} B_2 \\ K_i &= -U_{2(i)}^{-1} B_2^T U_{3(i)} A + \Delta K_i \end{aligned} \tag{28}$$

Step 4: Let $\Delta K_{i+1} = \Delta K_i + \delta M$ (or$\Delta K_{i+1} = \Delta K_i - \delta M$) and$U_{2(i+1)} = U_{2(i)}$.

Step 5: If $A_i = A + B_2 K_i$ is stable, that is, $\Delta K_i$is an admissible controller error, then increase i by1, goto Step 2; otherwise stop.

Using the above algorithm, we obtain a kind of discrete-time state feedback stochastic mixed LQR/H_∞ controllers as follows:

$$K_i = -U_{2(i)}^{-1} B_2^T U_{3(i)} A \pm i\delta M$$
$$(i = 0, 1, 2, \cdots, n, \cdots)$$

C. Comparison with Related Well Known Results

Comparing the result displayed in Theorem 3.1 with the earlier results, such as, Geromel & Peres (1985), Geromel et al. (1989), de Souza & Xie (1992), Kucera & de Souza (1995) and Gadewadikar et al. (2007); we know easily that all these earlier results are given in terms of a single algebraic Riccati equation with a free parameter matrix, plus a free parameter constrained condition on the form of the gain matrix. Although the result displayed in Theorem 3.1 is also given in terms of a single algebraic Riccati equation with a free parameter matrix, plus a free parameter constrained condition on the form of the gain matrix; but the free parameter matrix is also constrained to be an admissible controller error. In order to give some interpretation for this fact, we provided the following result of discrete-time state feedback stochastic mixed LQR/H_∞ control problem by combining directly the proof of Theorem 3.1, and the technique of finding all admissible state feedback controllers by Geromel & Peres (1985) (also see Geromel et al. 1989, de Souza & Xie 1992, Kucera & de Souza 1995).

Theorem 3.3 There exists a state feedback stochastic mixed LQR/H_∞controller if there exists a matrix L such that

$$L = K + U_2^{-1} B_2^T U_3 A \tag{29}$$

and X_∞ is a symmetric non-negative definite solution of the following discrete-time Riccati equation

$$\begin{aligned} &A^T X_\infty A - X_\infty - A^T X_\infty \hat{B}(\hat{B}^T X_\infty \hat{B} + \hat{R})^{-1} \hat{B}^T X_\infty A \\ &+ C_1^T C_1 + Q + L^T U_2 L = 0 \end{aligned} \tag{30}$$

and $A_K + \gamma^{-2} B_K U_1^{-1} B_K^T X_\infty A_K$ is stable and$U_1 = I - \gamma^{-2} B_1^T X_\infty B_1 > 0$.

Where, $\hat{B} = [\gamma^{-1} B_1 \quad B_2]$, $\hat{R} = \begin{bmatrix} -I & 0 \\ 0 & R+I \end{bmatrix}$, $U_3 = X_\infty + \gamma^{-2} X_\infty B_1 U_1^{-1} B_1^T X_\infty$,$U_2 = R + I + B_2^T U_3 B_2$.

Note that$A_K = A_{K^*} + B_2 \Delta K, K = K^* + \Delta K$ and

$\hat{A}_c = A - \hat{B}(\hat{B}^T X_\infty \hat{B} + \hat{R})^{-1} \hat{B}^T X_\infty A = A_{K^*} + \gamma^{-2} B_{K^*} U_1^{-1} B_{K^*}^T X_\infty A_{K^*}$

This implies that $A_K + \gamma^{-2} B_K U_1^{-1} B_K^T X_\infty A_K$ is stable if $\hat{A}_c$ is stable and $\Delta K$is an admissible controller error. Thus we show easily that in the case of$\Delta K = L$, there exists a matrix L such that (29) holds, where, $X_\infty$is a symmetric non-negative definite solution of discrete-time Riccati equation (30) and $A_K + \gamma^{-2} B_K U_1^{-1} B_K^T X_\infty A_K$ is stable if the conditions i-ii of Theorem 3.1 hold.

At the same time, we can show also that if $\Delta K = L$ is an admissble controller error, then the calculation of the algotithm 3.1 will become easilier. For an example, for a given admissible controller errorΔK_i, the step 2 of algorithm 3.1 is to solve the discrete-time Riccati equation

$$A^T X_i A - X_i - A^T X_i \hat{B}(\hat{B}^T X_i \hat{B} + \hat{R})^{-1} \hat{B}^T X_i A + \hat{Q} = 0$$

for X_i being a stabilizing solution, where,$\hat{Q} = C_1^T C_1 + Q + \Delta K_i^T U_{2(i)} \Delta K_i$. Since $\hat{A}_{ci} = A - \hat{B}(\hat{B}^T X_i \hat{B} + \hat{R})^{-1} \hat{B}^T X_i A$ is stable and ΔK_i is an admissible controller error, so $A_K + \gamma^{-2} B_K U_{1(i)}^{-1} B_K^T X_i A_K$ is stable. This implies the condition ii displayed in Theorem 3.1 makes the calculation of the algorithm 3.1 become easier.

4. Static Output Feedback

This section consider discrete-time static output feedback stochastic mixed LQR/H_∞ control problem. This problem is defined as follows:

Discrete-time static ouput feedback stochastic mixed LQR/H_∞ control problem: Consider the system (15) under the influence of static output feedback of the form

$u(k)=F_\infty y(k)$

with$w \in L_2[0,\infty)$, for a given number$\gamma>0$, determine an admissible static output feedback controller F_∞ such that

$\sup_{w\in L_{2+}}\{J_E\}$ subject to $\| T_{zw}\|_\infty<\gamma$

If this admissible controller exists, it is said to be a discrete-time static output feedback stochastic mixed LQR/H_∞ controller. As is well known, the discrete-time static output feedback stochastic mixed LQR/H_∞ control problem is equivalent to the discrete-time state feedback stochastic mixed LQR/H_∞ control problem for the systems (15) (16), where, $K$is constrained to have the form of$K=F_\infty C_2$. This problem is also said to be a structural constrained state feedback stochastic mixed LQR/H_∞ control problem.Based the above, we can obtain all solution to discrete-time static output feedback stochastic mixed LQR/H_∞ control problem by using the result of Theorem 3.1 as follows:

Theorem 4.1 There exists a discrete-time static output feedback stochastic mixed LQR/ H_∞ controller if the following two conditions hold:

i.There exists a matrix ΔK such that

$$\Delta K=FC_2+U_2^{-1}B_2^T U_3 A \tag{31}$$

and X_∞ is a symmetric non-negative definite solution of the following discrete-time Riccati equation

$$\begin{aligned}&A^T X_\infty A-X_\infty-A^T X_\infty \hat{B}(\hat{B}^T X_\infty \hat{B}+\hat{R})^{-1}\hat{B}^T X_\infty A\\&+C_1^T C_1+Q+\Delta K^T U_2 \Delta K=0\end{aligned} \tag{32}$$

and $\hat{A}_c=A-\hat{B}(\hat{B}^T X_\infty \hat{B}+\hat{R})^{-1}\hat{B}^T X_\infty A$ is stable and$U_1=I-\gamma^{-2}B_1^T X_\infty B_1>0$.

Where, $\hat{B}=[\gamma^{-1}B_1 \quad B_2]$, $\hat{R}=\begin{bmatrix}-I & 0\\ 0 & R+I\end{bmatrix}$, $U_3=X_\infty+\gamma^{-2}X_\infty B_1 U_1^{-1}B_1^T X_\infty$,$U_2=R+I+B_2^T U_3 B_2$.

ii. $\Delta K$is an admissible controller error.

In this case, the discrete-time static output feedback stochastic mixed LQR/H_∞ controller will achieve

$$\sup_{w \in L_{2+}} \left\{ J_E \right\} = \lim_{T \to \infty} \frac{1}{T} \sum_{k=0}^{T} tr(B_0^T X_\infty B_0 R_1(k)) \text{ subject to } \| T_{zw} \|_\infty < \gamma$$

Remark 4.1 In Theorem 4.1, define a suboptimal controller as $K^* = -U_2^{-1} B_2^T U_3 A$, then $\Delta K = F_\infty C_2 - K^*$. As is discussed in Remark 3.1, suppose that there exists a suboptimal controller K^* such that $A_{K^*} = A + B_2 K^*$ is stable, then ΔK is an admissible controller error if it belongs to the set:

$\Omega := \{\Delta K : A + B_2 F_\infty C_2 \text{ is stable}\}$

It should be noted that Theorem 4.1 does not tell us how to calculate a discrete-time static output feedback stochastic mixed LQR/H_∞ controller F_∞. In order to do this, we present, based on the algorithms proposed by Geromel & Peres (1985) and Kucera & de Souza (1995), a numerical algorithm for computing a discrete-time static output feedback stochastic mixed LQR/H_∞ controller F_∞ and a solution X_∞ to discrete-time Riccati equation (32). This numerical algorithm is given as follows:

Algorithm 4.1

Step 1: Fix the two weighting matrices Q and R, set $i=0$, $\Delta K_i = 0$, and $U_{2(i)} = 0$.

Step 2: Solve the discrete-time Riccati equation

$$A^T X_i A - X_i - A^T X_i \hat{B}(\hat{B}^T X_i \hat{B} + \hat{R})^{-1} \hat{B}^T X_i A$$
$$+ C_1^T C_1 + Q + \Delta K_i^T U_{2(i)} \Delta K_i = 0$$

for X_i symmetric non-negative definite such that

$\hat{A}_{ci} = A - \hat{B}(\hat{B}^T X_i \hat{B} + \hat{R})^{-1} \hat{B}^T X_i A$ is stable and $U_{1(i)} = I - \gamma^{-2} B_1^T X_i B_1 > 0$.

Step 3: Calculate $U_{3(i+1)}$, $U_{2(i+1)}$ and ΔK_{i+1} by using the following formulas

$$U_{3(i+1)} = X_i + \gamma^{-2} X_i B_1 U_{1(i)}^{-1} B_1^T X_i$$
$$U_{2(i+1)} = R + I + B_2^T U_{3(i+1)} B_2$$
$$\Delta K_{i+1} = -U_{2(i+1)}^{-1} B_2^T U_{3(i+1)} A \left(C_2^T (C_2 C_2^T)^{-1} C_2 - I \right)$$

Step 4: If ΔK_{i+1} is an admissible controller error, then increase i by 1, and goto Step 2; otherwise stop.

If the four sequences $X_0, X_1, \cdots, X_i, \cdots, U_{1(1)}, U_{1(2)}, \cdots, U_{1(i)}, \cdots, U_{2(1)}, U_{2(2)}, \cdots, U_{2(i)}, \cdots$, and $U_{3(1)}, U_{3(2)}, \cdots, U_{3(i)}, \cdots$ converges, say to X_∞, U_1, U_2 and U_3, respectively; then the both two conditions displayed in Theorem 4.1 are met. In this case, a discrete-time static output feedback stochastic mixed LQR/H_∞ controllers is parameterized as follows:

$$F_{\infty} = -U_2^{-1} B_2^T U_3 A C_2^T (C_2 C_2^T)^{-1}$$

In this chapter, we will not prove the convergence of the above algorithm. This will is another subject.

5. Numerical Examples

In this section, we present two examples to illustrate the design methods displayed in Section 3 and 4 respectively.

Example 5.1 Consider the following linear discrete-time system (15) under the influence of state feedback of the form$u(k) = Kx(k)$, its parameter matrices are

$$A = \begin{bmatrix} 0 & 2 \\ 4 & 0.2 \end{bmatrix},\ B_0 = \begin{bmatrix} 0.1 \\ 0.2 \end{bmatrix},\ B_1 = \begin{bmatrix} 0.5 \\ 0.3 \end{bmatrix},\ B_2 = \begin{bmatrix} 1 \\ 0 \end{bmatrix}$$
$$C_1 = \begin{bmatrix} 1 & 0 \\ 0 & 0 \end{bmatrix},\ C_2 = \begin{bmatrix} 1 & 0 \\ 0 & 1 \end{bmatrix},\ D_{12} = \begin{bmatrix} 0 \\ 1 \end{bmatrix}$$

The above system satisfies Assumption 3.1-3.3, and the open-loop poles of this system are $p_1 = -2.7302, p_2 = 2.9302$; thus it is open-loop unstable.

Let$R = 1, Q = \begin{bmatrix} 1 & 0 \\ 0 & 1 \end{bmatrix}$, $\gamma = 9.5,\ \delta = 0.01, M = [-0.04 \quad -1.2]$; by using algorithm 3.1, we solve the discrete-time Riccati equation (20) to get$X_i, U_{1(i)}$, $K_i (i = 0,1,2,\cdots,10)$and the corresponding closed-loop poles. The calculating results of algorithm 3.1 are listed in Table 1.

It is shown in Table 1 that when the iteration index$i = 10, X_{10} 0$ and $U_{1(10)} = -0.2927$ 0, thus the discrete-time state feedback stochastic mixed LQR/H_{∞} controller does not exist in this case. Of course, Table 1 does not list all discrete-time state feedback stochastic mixed LQR/H_{∞} controllers because we do not calculating all these controllers by using Algorithm in this example. In order to illustrate further the results, we give the trajectories of state of the system (15) with the state feedback of the form $u(k) = Kx(k)$ for the resulting discrete-time state feedback stochastic mixed LQR/H_{∞} controller $K = [-0.3071 \quad -2.0901]$. The resulting closed-loop system is

$$x(k+1) = (A + B_2 K) x(k) + B_0 w_0(k) + B_1 w(k)$$
$$z(k) = (C_1 + D_{12} K) x(k)$$

where, $A + B_2 K = \begin{bmatrix} -0.3071 & -0.0901 \\ 4.0000 & 0.2000 \end{bmatrix}, C_1 + D_{12} K = \begin{bmatrix} 1.0000 & 0 \\ -0.3071 & -2.0901 \end{bmatrix}$.

http://dx.doi.org/10.5772/51019

Iteration Index i	Solution of DARE X_i	Additional Condition $U_{1(i)}$	State Feedback Controller K_i	The Closed-Loop Poles
0	$X_0>0$	0.5571	$[-0.2886 \quad -1.9992]$	$p_1=-0.2951$, $p_2=0.2065$
1	$X_1>0$	0.5553	$[-0.2892 \quad -2.0113]$	$p_1=-0.1653$, $p_2=0.0761$
2	$X_2>0$	0.5496	$[-0.2903 \quad -2.0237]$	$p_{1,2}=-0.0451 \pm j0.1862$
3	$X_3>0$	0.5398	$[-0.2918 \quad -2.0363]$	$p_{1,2}=-0.0459 \pm j0.2912$
4	$X_4>0$	0.5250	$[-0.2940 \quad -2.0492]$	$p_{1,2}=-0.0470 \pm j0.3686$
5	$X_5>0$	0.5040	$[-0.2969 \quad -2.0624]$	$p_{1,2}=-0.0485 \pm j0.4335$
6	$X_6>0$	0.4739	$[-0.3010 \quad -2.0760]$	$p_{1,2}=-0.0505 \pm j0.4911$
7	$X_7>0$	0.4295	$[-0.3071 \quad -2.0901]$	$p_{1,2}=-0.0535 \pm j0.5440$
8	$X_8>0$	0.3578	$[-0.3167 \quad -2.1049]$	$p_{1,2}=-0.0584 \pm j0.5939$
9	$X_9>0$	0.2166	$[-0.3360 \quad -2.1212]$	$p_{1,2}=-0.0680 \pm j0.6427$
10	$X_{10}>0$	-0.2927		

Table 1. The calculating results of algorithm 3.1.

To determine the mean value function, we take mathematical expectation of the both hand of the above two equations to get

$$\bar{x}(k+1)=(A+B_2K)\bar{x}(k)+B_1w(k)$$
$$\bar{z}(k)=(C_1+D_{12}K)\bar{x}(k)$$

where, $E\{x(k)\}=\bar{x}(k)$, $E\{z(k)\}=\bar{z}(k)$,$E\{x(0)\}=\bar{x}_0$.

Let$w(k)=\gamma^{-2}U_1^{-1}B_1^T X_\infty(A+B_2K)\bar{x}(k)$, then the trajectories of mean values of states of resulting closed-loop system with $\bar{x}_0=[3 \quad 2]^T$ are given in Fig. 1.

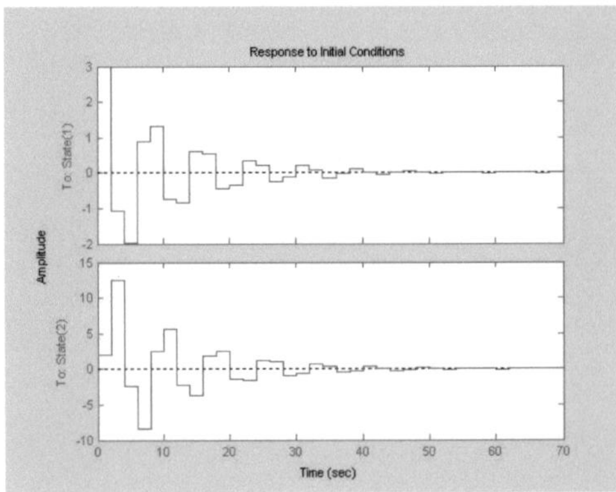

Figure 1. The trajectories of mean values of states of resulting system in Example 5.1.

Example 5.2 Consider the following linear discrete-time system (15) with static output feedback of the form$u(k)=F_\infty y(k)$, its parameter matrices are as same as Example 5.1.

When C_2 is quare and invertible, that is, all state variable are measurable, we may assume without loss of generality that $C_2=I$; let$\gamma=6.5$, $R=1$and$Q=\begin{bmatrix}1 & 0\\ 0 & 1\end{bmatrix}$, by solving the discrete-time Riccati equation (24), we get that the central discrete-time state feedback stochastic mixed LQR/H_∞ controller displayed in Theorem 3.2 is

$$K^*=[-0.3719 \quad -2.0176]$$

and the poles of resulting closed-loop system are$p_1=-0.1923, p_2=0.0205$.

When$C_2=[1 \quad 5.4125]$, let$\gamma=6.5, R=1$, $Q=\begin{bmatrix}1 & 0\\ 0 & 1\end{bmatrix}$, by using Algorithm 4.1, we solve the discrete-time Riccati equation (32) to get

$$X_\infty=\begin{bmatrix}148.9006 & 8.8316\\ 8.8316 & 9.5122\end{bmatrix}>0, U_1=0.0360$$

Thus the discrete-time static output feedback stochastic mixed LQR/H_∞ controller displayed in Theorem 4.1 is$F_\infty=-0.3727$. The resulting closed-loop system is

$$x(k+1)=(A+B_2F_\infty C_2)x(k)+B_0w_0(k)+B_1w(k)$$
$$z(k)=(C_1+D_{12}F_\infty C_2)x(k)$$

where, $A + B_2F_\infty C_2 = \begin{bmatrix} -0.3727 & -0.0174 \\ 4.0000 & 0.2000 \end{bmatrix}$, $C_1 + D_{12}F_\infty C_2 = \begin{bmatrix} 1.0000 & 0 \\ -0.3727 & -2.0174 \end{bmatrix}$.

Taking mathematical expectation of the both hand of the above two equations to get

$$\bar{x}(k+1) = (A + B_2F_\infty C_2)\bar{x}(k) + B_1 w(k)$$
$$z(k) = (C_1 + D_{12}F_\infty C_2)\bar{x}(k)$$

where, $E\{x(k)\} = \bar{x}(k)$, $E\{z(k)\} = \bar{z}(k)$, $E\{x(0)\} = \bar{x}_0$.

Let$w(k) = \gamma^{-2}U_1^{-1}B_1^T X_\infty(A + B_2F_\infty C_2)\bar{x}(k)$, then the trajectories of mean values of states of resulting closed-loop system with $\bar{x}_0 = [1 \quad 2]^T$ are given in Fig. 2.

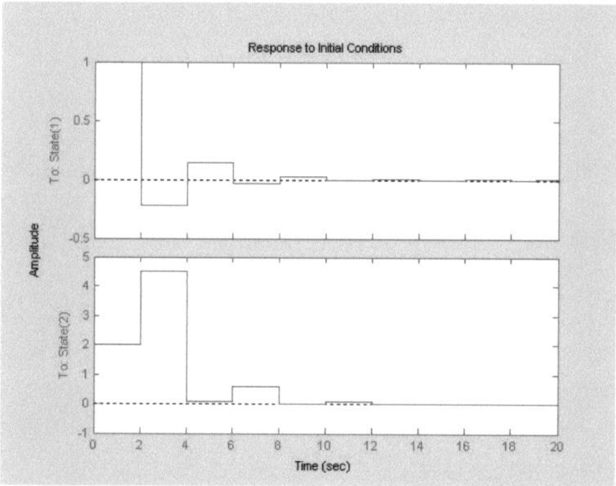

Figure 2. The trajectories of mean values of states of resulting system in Example 5.2.

6. Conclusion

In this chapter, we provide a characterization of all state feedback controllers for solving the discrete-time stochastic mixed LQR/H_∞ control problem for linear discrete-time systems by the technique of Xu (2008 and 2011) with the well known LQG theory. Sufficient conditions for the existence of all state feedback controllers solving the discrete-time stochastic mixed LQR/H_∞ control problem are given in terms of a single algebraic Riccati equation with a free parameter matrix, plus two constrained conditions: One is a free parameter matrix constrained condition on the form of the gain matrix, another is an assumption that the free parameter matrix is a free admissible controller error. Also, a numerical algorithm for calculating a kind of discrete-time state feedback stochastic mixed LQR/H_∞ controllers are proposed. As one special case, the central discrete-time state feedback stochastic mixed LQR./H_∞ controller is given in terms of an algebraic Riccati equation. This provides an interpretation of discrete-time state feedback mixed LQR/H_∞ control problem. As another special case, sufficient conditions for the existence of all static output feedback controllers solving the discrete-time stochastic mixed LQR/H_∞ control problem are given. A numerical algorithm for calculating a static output feedback stochastic mixed LQR/H_∞ controller is also presented.

Author details

Xiaojie Xu*

Address all correspondence to: xiaojiex@public.wh.hb.cn

School of Electrical Engineering, Wuhan University, P. R. China

References

[1] Astrom, K. J. (1970). Introduction to stochastic control theory. *Academic Press*, INC.

[2] Athans, M. (1971). The role and use of thr stochastic linear-quadratic-Gaussian problem in control system design. *IEEE Trans. Aut. Control*, 16(6), 529-552.

[3] Basar, T., & Bernhard, P. (1991). H_∞-optimal control and related minmax design problems: a dynamic approach, Boston, MA: Birkhauser.

[4] Bernstein, D. S., & Haddad, W. M. (1989). LQG control with an H_∞ performance bound: A Riccati equation approach. *IEEE Trans. Aut. Control*, 34(3), 293-305.

[5] Chen, X., & Zhou, K. (2001). Multiobjective H_2/H_∞ control design. *SIAM J. Control Optim.*, 40(2), 628-660.

[6] de Souza, C. E., & Xie, L. (1992). On the discrete-time bounded real lemma with application in the characterization of static state feedback H_∞ controllers. *Systems & Control Letters*, 18, 61-71.

[7] Doyle, J. C., Glover, K., Khargonekar, P. P., & Francis, B. A. (1989a). State-space solutions to standard H_2 and H_∞ control problems. *IEEE Trans. Aut. Control*, 34(8), 831-847.

[8] Doyle, J. C., Zhou, K., & Bodenheimer, B. (1989b). Optimal control with mixed H_2 and H_∞ performance objectives. *Proceedings of 1989 American Control Conference*, Pittsb-urh, PA, 2065-2070.

[9] Doyle, J. C., Zhou, K., Glover, K., & Bodenheimer, B. (1994). Mixed H_2 and H_∞ perfor-mance objectives II: optimal control. *IEEE Trans. Aut. Control*, 39(8), 1575-1587.

http://dx.doi.org/10.5772/51019

[10] Furata, K., & Phoojaruenchanachai, S. (1990). An algebraic approach to discrete-time H_∞ control problems. *Proceedings of 1990 American Control Conference,* San Diego, 2067-3072.

[11] Gadewadikar, J., Lewis, F. L., Xie, L., Kucera, V., & Abu-Khalaf, M. (2007). Parameterization of all stabilizing H_∞ static state-feedback gains: application to output-feedback design. *Automatica,* 43, 1597-1604.

[12] Geromel, J. C., & Peres, P. L. D. (1985). Decentrailised load-frequency control. *IEE Proceedings,* 132(5), 225-230.

[13] Geromel, J. C., Yamakami, A., & Armentano, V. A. (1989). Structrual constrained controllers for discrete-time linear systems. *Journal of Optimization and Applications,* 61(1), 73-94.

[14] Haddad, W. M., Bernstein, D. S., & Mustafa, D. (1991). Mixed-norm H_2/H_∞ regulation and estimation: the discrete-time case. *Systems & Control Letters,* 16, 235-247.

[15] Iglesias, P. A., & Glover, K. (1991). State-space approach to discrete-time H_∞ control. *INT. J. Control,* 54(5), 1031-1073.

[16] Khargonekar, P. P., & Rotea, M. A. (1991). Mixed H_2/H_∞ control: A convex optimization approach. *IEEE Trans. Aut. Control,* 36(7), 824-837.

[17] Kucera, V., & de Souza, C. E. (1995). A necessary and sufficient condition for output feedback stabilizability. *Automatica,* 31(9), 1357-1359.

[18] Kwakernaak, H. (2002). H_2-optimization-theory and application to robust control design. *Annual Reviews in Control,* 26, 45-56.

[19] Limebeer, D. J. N., Anderson, B. D. O., Khargonekar, P. P., & Green, M. (1992). A game theoretic approach to H_∞ control for time-varying systems. *SIAM J. Control and Optimization,* 30(2), 262-283.

[20] Limebeer, D. J. N., Anderson, B. D. O., & Hendel, B. (1994). A Nash game approach to mixed H_2/H_∞ control. *IEEE Trans. Aut. Control,* 39(1), 69-82.

[21] Tse, E. (1971). On the optimal control of stochastic linear systems. *IEEE Trans. Aut. Control,* 16(6), 776-785.

[22] Xu, X. (1996). A study on robust control for discrete-time systems with uncertainty. *A Master Thesis of 1995,* Kobe university, Kobe, Japan, January, 1996.

[23] Xu, X. (2008). Characterization of all static state feedback mixed LQR/H_∞ controllers for linear continuous-time systems. *Proceedings of the 27th Chinese Control Conference,* Kunming, Yunnan, China, 678-682, July 16-18, 2008.

[24] Xu, X. (2011). Discrete time mixed LQR/H_∞ control problems. *Discrete Time Systems*, Mario Alberto Jordan (Ed.), 978-9-53307-200-5, InTech, Available from, http://www.intechopen.com/.

[25] Yeh, H., Banda, S. S., & Chang, B. C. (1992). Necessary and sufficient conditions for mixed H_2 and H_∞ optimal control. *IEEE Trans. Aut. Control*, 37(3), 355-358.

[26] Zhou, K., Doyle, J. C., & Glover, K. (1996). Robust and optimal control. *Prentice-Hall, INC.*

Chapter 2

Robust Control Design of Uncertain Discrete-Time Descriptor Systems with Delays

Jun Yoneyama, Yuzu Uchida and Ryutaro Takada

Additional information is available at the end of the chapter

http://dx.doi.org/10.5772/ 51538

1. Introduction

A descriptor system describes a natural representation for physical systems. In general, the continuous-time descriptor representation consists of differential and algebraic equations, and the discrete-time descriptor system has difference and algebraic equations. Hence, the descriptor system is a generalized representation of the state-space system. This system appears in various physical systems. In fact, descriptor systems can be found in electrical circuits, moving robots and many other practical systems which are modeled with additional algebraic constraints. The descriptor system is also referred to as singular system, implicit system, generalized state-space system, differential-algebraic system, or semistate system. System analysis and control design of descriptor systems have been extensively investigated in the past years due to their potential representation ([4], [6], [7], [17], [23]). An important characteristic of continuous-time descriptor systems is the possible impulse modes, which are harmful to physical systems and are undesirable in system control. The discrete-time descriptor system may not have causality, which leads to no solution of the system states. In [4], [32], such descriptor system behaviors are described and notion of regularity, non-impulse, causality, and admissibility are given. In [1] and [22], quadratic stability for continuous-time descriptor systems was considered. Its discrete-time system counterpart was investigated in [31] and [32].

When we make a mathematical model for a physical system, time-delay is another phenomenon. We often see time-delay in the process of control algorithms and the transmission of information. Time-delay often appear in many practical systems and mathematical formulations such as electrical system, mechanical system, biological system, and transportation system. Hence, a system with time-delay is also a natural representation, and its analysis and synthesis are of theoretical and practical importance. In the past decades, research on continuous-time delay systems has been active. Difficulty that arises in continuous time-delay systems is that the system is infinite dimensional and a corresponding controller can be a memory feedback. This class of a controller may minimize a certain performance index, but it is difficult to implement it to practical systems because it feeds back past information of the system. To overcome such a difficulty, a memoryless controller is used for time-delay systems. In the last decade, sufficient stability conditions for time-delay systems have been given via linear matrix inequalities (LMIs), and stabilization methods by memoryless controllers have been investigated by many researchers. Since Li and de Souza considered robust stability and stabilization problems in [18], less conservative stability conditions for continuous time-delay systems have been obtained in [14] and [26]. Recently, H_∞ disturbance attenuation conditions have also been given ([25], [34], [35]). The results in [10], [27], [33], [36] considered discrete-time systems with time-invariant delays. Gao and Chen [11], Hara and Yoneyama [12], [13] gave robust stability conditions. Fridman and Shaked [8] solved a guaranteed cost control problem. Fridman and Shaked [9], Zhang and Han [37] considered the H_∞ disturbance attenuation. The results have been extended to a class of discrete-time descriptor delay systems in [2], [3], [24].

In general, control systems are designed not only for the stability, but also for robustness with respect to system parameters. In addition, they are designed for the optimization of multiple control performance measures. Most designed control systems require accurate controllers. Thus, when a desired controller is implemented, all of the controller coefficients are required to be the exact values as those to be designed. However, it is not always possible in practical applications since actuators may be of malfunction, and round-off errors in numerical computations by calculations are possibly encountered. Therefore, it is necessary that the designed controller should be able to tolerate some uncertainty in its control gains. Since controller fragility problem has to be considered when implementing a designed controller in practical applications, the non-fragile control design problem has been investigated in [5], [15], [16], [19], [20], [21]. For state-space systems, several recent research works have been devoted to the design problem of non-fragile robust control ([5], [19], [20], [21]). Most of these are derived via either Riccati matrix equation approach or linear matrix inequality (LMI) approach. The design problem of non-fragile robust controllers of continuous-time descriptor systems was investigated in [15] and [16]. The discrete-time counterpart was given in [28].

In this chapter, the robust non-fragile control design problem and the robust H_∞ non-fragile control design problem for uncertain discrete-time descriptor systems are considered. The controller gain uncertainties and uncertain system parameters under consideration are supposed to be time-varying but norm-bounded. The problem to be addressed is the control design problem of state feedback controller, which is subject to norm-bounded uncertainty, such that the resulting closed-loop system is regular, causal and robustly admissible with H_∞ disturbance attenuation for all admissible uncertainties. Sufficient conditions for the solvability of the robust H_∞ non-fragile control design problem for descriptor systems are obtained, for the cases with multiplicative controller uncertainties. The results are developed for a class of uncertain discrete-time descriptor systems with time-delay. Finally, some numerical examples are shown to illustrate our proposed controller design methods.

2. Descriptor systems

Consider the discrete-time descriptor system

$$Ex(k+1) = Ax(k) + Bu(k) \tag{1}$$

where $x(k) \in \Re^n$ is the state and $u(k) \in \Re^m$ is the control. E, A and B are system matrices with appropriate dimensions. E satisfies $rankE = r \leq n$. Unforced descriptor system (1) with $u(k) = 0$ is denoted by the pair $(E,\ A)$.

Definition 2.1. *(Dai [4]) (i) The pair $(E,\ A)$ is said to be regular if $det(zE - A)$ is not identically zero.*
(ii) The pair $(E,\ A)$ is said to be causal if it is regular and $deg(det(zE - A)) = rank(E)$.
(iii) Define the generalized spectral radius as $\rho(E,\ A) = \max_{\lambda \in \{det(zE-A)=0\}} |\lambda|$. The pair $(E,\ A)$ is said to be stable if $\rho(E,\ A) < 1$.
(iv) The pair $(E,\ A)$ is said to be admissible if it is regular, causal and stable.

Lemma 2.2. *(Dai [4]) (i) The descriptor system*

$$Ex(k+1) = Ax(k)$$

where

$$(E,\ A) = \left(\begin{bmatrix} I_r & 0 \\ 0 & 0 \end{bmatrix},\ \begin{bmatrix} A_1 & A_2 \\ A_3 & A_4 \end{bmatrix} \right)$$

is regular and causal if and only if A_4 is invertible.
(ii) The pair $(E,\ A)$ is admissible if and only if A_4 is nonsingular and $\rho(A_1 - A_2 A_4^{-1} A_3) < 1$.

Unlike the standard state-space system, a descriptor system may not be regular and causal. These unique characteristics lead to no solution of the system (1), and thus should be taken care of.

Next, we consider the uncertain descriptor system

$$Ex(k+1) = (A + \Delta A)x(k) + Bu(k) \tag{2}$$

where an uncertain matrix is of the form

$$\Delta A = HF(k)G \tag{3}$$

where $F(k) \in \Re^{l \times j}$ is an unknown time-varying matrix satisfying $F^T(k)F(k) \leq I$ and H and G are constant matrices of appropriate dimensions.

3. Non-fragile control

This section provides system analysis and control design for uncertain descriptor systems. First, the non-fragile controller is discussed in Section 3.1, and then the system analysis of the closed-loop system with a non-fragile controller is investigated in Section 3.2. Finally, Section 3.3 proposes non-fragile control design methods.

3.1. Form of controller and preliminary results

The ideal form of a feedback controller is given by

$$u(k) = Kx(k)$$

where K is a feedback gain to be determined. In practical situations where malfunction in the actuator and uncertain calculation of control gain may occur, the actual controller is assumed to be of the form

$$u(k) = [I + \alpha\Phi(k)]\, Kx(k) \tag{4}$$

where $\alpha\Phi(k)K$ shows uncertainty in the control gain. $\Phi(k)$ is an unknown time-varying matrix satisfying

$$\Phi^T(k)\Phi(k) \leq I, \tag{5}$$

and α is a known positive constant which indicates the measure of non-fragility against controller gain variation. Applying the controller (4) to the system (2), we have the closed-loop system

$$Ex(k+1) = (A + BK + H_c F_c(k) G_c)x(k) \tag{6}$$

where

$$H_c = [H \;\; \alpha B],\; F_c(k) = \mathrm{diag}[F(k) \;\; \Phi(k)],\; G_c = \begin{bmatrix} G \\ K \end{bmatrix}.$$

Definition 3.1. *The system (6) is said to be robustly admissible if it is admissible for all admissible uncertainties (3) and (5).*

The problem is to find a controller (4) which makes the system (2) robustly admissible. In the following, we consider the robust admissibility of the closed-loop system (6). The following lemmas are useful to prove our results.

Lemma 3.2. *(Xie [29]) Given matrices $Q = Q^T$, H, G and $R = R^T > 0$ with appropriate dimensions.*

$$Q + HF(k)G + G^T F^T(k) H^T < 0$$

for all $F(k)$ satisfying $F^T(k)F(k) \leq R$ if and only if there exists a scalar $\varepsilon > 0$ such that

$$Q + \frac{1}{\varepsilon} HH^T + \varepsilon G^T R G < 0.$$

Lemma 3.3. *(Xu & Lam [32]) (i) The descriptor system (1) is admissible if and only if there exist matrices $P > 0$ and Q such that*

$$A^T PA - E^T PE + A^T SQ^T + QS^T A < 0 \tag{7}$$

where $S \in \Re^{n\times(n-r)}$ is any matrix with full column rank and satisfies $E^T S = 0$.
(ii) The descriptor system (1) is admissible if and only if there exists a matrix P such that

$$\begin{aligned} E^T PE &\geq 0, \\ A^T PA - E^T PE &< 0. \end{aligned}$$

Lemma 3.4. *(Xie and de Souza [30]) Given matrices X, $Y > 0$ and Z with appropriate dimensions, we have*

$$X^T Z + Z^T X + X^T YX \geq -Z^T Y^{-1} Z.$$

3.2. Robust admissibility analysis

The following two theorems give a necessary and sufficient condition for the closed-loop system (6) to be robustly admissible.

Theorem 3.5. *Given K, the descriptor system (6) is robustly admissible if and only if there exist matrices $P > 0$, Q and scalar $\varepsilon > 0$ such that*

$$\begin{bmatrix} \begin{pmatrix} QS^T(A+BK) + (A+BK)^T SQ^T \\ -E^T PE + \varepsilon(G^T G + K^T K) \end{pmatrix} & (A+BK)^T P & QS^T H & \alpha QS^T B \\ P(A+BK) & -P & PH & \alpha PB \\ H^T SQ^T & H^T P & -\varepsilon I & 0 \\ \alpha B^T SQ^T & \alpha B^T P & 0 & -\varepsilon I \end{bmatrix} < 0 \tag{8}$$

where $S \in \Re^{n\times(n-r)}$ is any matrix with full column rank and satisfies $E^T S = 0$.

Proof: (Sufficiency) Suppose that there exist matrices $P > 0$, Q and scalar $\varepsilon > 0$ such that the condition (8) holds. Then, by Schur complement formula, we have

$$\begin{aligned} &\begin{bmatrix} QS^T(A+BK) + (A+BK)^T SQ^T - E^T PE & (A+BK)^T P \\ P(A+BK) & -P \end{bmatrix} \\ &+\varepsilon^{-1} \begin{bmatrix} QS^T H_c \\ PH_c \end{bmatrix} \begin{bmatrix} H_c^T SQ^T & H_c^T P \end{bmatrix} + \varepsilon \begin{bmatrix} G_c^T \\ 0 \end{bmatrix} \begin{bmatrix} G_c & 0 \end{bmatrix} < 0. \end{aligned} \tag{9}$$

Now, using Lemma 3.2, we have

$$\begin{aligned}
&\begin{bmatrix} \begin{pmatrix} QS^T(A+BK+H_cF_c(k)G_c) \\ +(A+BK+H_cF_c(k)G_c)^T SQ^T - E^T PE \end{pmatrix} & (A+BK+H_cF_c(k)G_c)^T P \\ P(A+BK+H_cF_c(k)G_c) & -P \end{bmatrix} \\
&= \begin{bmatrix} QS^T(A+BK)+(A+BK)^T SQ^T - E^T PE & (A+BK)^T P \\ P(A+BK) & -P \end{bmatrix} \\
&\quad + \begin{bmatrix} QS^T H_c \\ PH_c \end{bmatrix} \Phi(k) \begin{bmatrix} G_c & 0 \end{bmatrix} + \begin{bmatrix} G_c^T \\ 0 \end{bmatrix} \Phi(k) \begin{bmatrix} H_c^T SQ^T & H_c^T P \end{bmatrix} \\
&\leq \begin{bmatrix} QS^T(A+BK)+(A+BK)^T SQ^T - E^T PE & (A+BK)^T P \\ P(A+BK) & -P \end{bmatrix} \\
&\quad \varepsilon^{-1} \begin{bmatrix} QS^T H_c \\ PH_c \end{bmatrix} \begin{bmatrix} H_c^T SQ^T & H_c^T P \end{bmatrix} + \varepsilon \begin{bmatrix} G_c^T \\ 0 \end{bmatrix} \begin{bmatrix} G_c & 0 \end{bmatrix}.
\end{aligned}$$

It follows from (9) that

$$\begin{bmatrix} \begin{pmatrix} QS^T(A+BK+H_c\Phi(k)G_c) \\ +(A+BK+H_c\Phi(k)G_c)^T SQ^T - E^T PE \end{pmatrix} & (A+BK+H_c\Phi(k)G_c)^T P \\ P(A+BK+H_c\Phi(k)G_c) & -P \end{bmatrix} < 0.$$

This implies by Schur complement formula and Lemma 3.3(i) that the descriptor system (6) is robustly admissible.
(Necessity) Assume that the descriptor system (6) is robustly admissible. Then, it follows from Definition 3.1 and Lemma 3.3 that there exist matrices $P > 0$, Q and scalar $\varepsilon > 0$ such that (7) with A replaced by $A + BK + H_c\Phi(k)G_c$ holds. Thus, for all admissible $F(k)$ and $\Phi(k)$, the following inequality holds:

$$\begin{bmatrix} \begin{pmatrix} QS^T(A+BK+H_cF_c(k)G_c) \\ +(A+BK+H_c\Phi(k)_cG_c)^T SQ^T - E^T PE \end{pmatrix} & (A+BK+H_cF_c(k)G_c)^T P \\ P(A+BK+H_cF_c(k)G_c) & -P \end{bmatrix} < 0.$$

That is,

$$\begin{aligned}
&\begin{bmatrix} QS^T(A+BK)+(A+BK)^T SQ^T - E^T PE & (A+BK)^T P \\ P(A+BK) & -P \end{bmatrix} \\
&+ \begin{bmatrix} QS^T H_c \\ PH_c \end{bmatrix} \Phi(k) \begin{bmatrix} G_c & 0 \end{bmatrix} + \begin{bmatrix} G_c^T \\ 0 \end{bmatrix} \Phi(k) \begin{bmatrix} H_c^T SQ^T & H_c^T P \end{bmatrix} < 0
\end{aligned}$$

is satisfied for all admissible $F(k)$ and $\Phi(k)$. It follows from Lemma 3.2 that

$$\begin{aligned}
&\begin{bmatrix} QS^T(A+BK)+(A+BK)^T SQ^T - E^T PE & (A+BK)^T P \\ P(A+BK) & -P \end{bmatrix} \\
&+\varepsilon^{-1} \begin{bmatrix} QS^T H_c \\ PH_c \end{bmatrix} \begin{bmatrix} H_c^T SQ^T & H_c^T P \end{bmatrix} + \varepsilon \begin{bmatrix} G_c^T \\ 0 \end{bmatrix} \begin{bmatrix} G_c & 0 \end{bmatrix} < 0,
\end{aligned}$$

which leads to the condition (8) by Schur complement formula. This completes the proof.

Similarly, using Lemma 3.3(ii), we obtain the following result.

Theorem 3.6. *Given K, the descriptor system (6) is robustly admissible if and only if there exist matrix P and scalar ε > 0 such that*

$$E^T PE \geq 0, \tag{10}$$

$$\begin{bmatrix} -E^T PE + \varepsilon(G^T G + K^T K) & (A+BK)^T P & 0 & 0 \\ P(A+BK) & -P & PH & \alpha PB \\ 0 & H^T P & -\varepsilon I & 0 \\ 0 & \alpha B^T P & 0 & -\varepsilon I \end{bmatrix} < 0. \tag{11}$$

3.3. Robust control design

In the previous section, we have obtained robust admissibility conditions of the closed-loop system (6). Based on those conditions, we now seek how to calculate a feedback gain K in the controller (4).

Theorem 3.7. *There exists a controller (4) that makes the descriptor system (2) robustly admissible if there exist matrices $P > 0$, Q and scalar $\varepsilon > 0$ such that*

$$\Gamma = P^{-1} - \varepsilon^{-1} H_c H_c^T > 0, \tag{12}$$

$$QS^T A + A^T SQ^T - E^T PE + \varepsilon G^T G + \varepsilon^{-1} QS^T H_c H_c^T SQ^T + \Theta^T \Gamma^{-1} \Theta - \Psi \Lambda^{-1} \Psi^T < 0 \tag{13}$$

where $S \in \Re^{n\times(n-r)}$ is any matrix with full column rank and satisfies $E^T S = 0$, and

$$\begin{aligned} \Psi &= QS^T B + \Theta^T \Gamma^{-1} B, \\ \Lambda &= B^T \Gamma^{-1} B + \varepsilon I, \\ \Theta &= A + \varepsilon^{-1} H_c H_c^T SQ^T. \end{aligned}$$

In this case, a feedback gain in the controller (4) is given

$$K = -\Lambda^{-1} \Psi^T. \tag{14}$$

Proof: (Sufficiency) The closed-loop system (6) with the feedback gain (14) is given by

$$Ex(k+1) = (A - B\Lambda^{-1}\Gamma^T + H_c F_c(k) G_c) x(k).$$

where $G_c = \left[G^T \ -\Psi\Lambda^{-1}\right]^T$. Then, by some mathematical manipulation and (13), it can be verified that

$$
\begin{aligned}
& QS^T(A - B\Lambda^{-1}\Psi^T) + (A - B\Lambda^{-1}\Psi^T)^T SQ^T - E^T PE + \varepsilon G_c^T G_c + \varepsilon^{-1} QS^T H_c H_c^T SQ^T \\
& +(A - B\Lambda^{-1}\Psi^T + \varepsilon^{-1} H_c H_c^T SQ^T)^T \Gamma^{-1} (A - B\Lambda^{-1}\Psi^T + \varepsilon^{-1} H_c H_c^T SQ^T) \\
= \; & QS^T A + A^T SQ^T - E^T PE + (A + \varepsilon^{-1} H_c H_c^T SQ^T)^T \Gamma^{-1} (A + \varepsilon^{-1} H_c H_c^T SQ^T) \\
& +\varepsilon G^T G - QS^T B\Lambda^{-1}\Psi^T - (A + \varepsilon^{-1} H_c H_c^T SQ^T)^T \Gamma^{-1} B\Lambda^{-1}\Psi^T - \Psi\Lambda^{-1} B^T SQ^T \\
& -\Psi\Lambda^{-1} B^T \Gamma^{-1} (A + \varepsilon^{-1} H_c H_c^T SQ^T) + \Psi\Lambda^{-1} B^T \Gamma^{-1} B\Lambda^{-1} \Gamma^T + \varepsilon \Psi\Lambda^{-1}\Lambda^{-1}\Psi^T \\
& +\varepsilon^{-1} QS^T H_c H_c^T SQ^T \\
= \; & QS^T A + A^T SQ^T - E^T PE + (A + \varepsilon^{-1} H_c H_c^T SQ^T)^T \Gamma^{-1} (A + \varepsilon^{-1} H_c H_c^T SQ^T) \\
& +\varepsilon G^T G - [QS^T + (A + \varepsilon^{-1} H_c H_c^T SQ^T)^T \Gamma^{-1}] B\Lambda^{-1}\Psi^T \\
& -\Psi\Lambda^{-1} B^T [SQ^T + \Gamma^{-1}(A + \varepsilon^{-1} H_c H_c^T SQ^T)] + \Psi\Lambda^{-1}\Psi^T + \varepsilon^{-1} QS^T H_c H_c^T SQ^T \\
= \; & QS^T A + A^T SQ^T - E^T PE + \varepsilon G^T G + \varepsilon^{-1} QS^T H_c H_c^T SQ^T + \Theta^T \Gamma^{-1} \Theta - \Psi\Lambda^{-1}\Psi^T < 0.
\end{aligned}
$$

By Schur complement formula, we obtain

$$
\begin{bmatrix}
\begin{pmatrix} QS^T(A - B\Lambda^{-1}\Psi^T) + (A - B\Lambda^{-1}\Psi^T)^T SQ^T \\ -E^T PE + \varepsilon G^T G + \varepsilon \Psi\Lambda^{-1}\Lambda^{-1}\Psi^T \end{pmatrix} & (A - B\Lambda^{-1}\Psi^T)^T P & QS^T H_c \\
P(A - B\Lambda^{-1}\Psi^T) & -P & PH_c \\
H_c^T SQ^T & H_c^T P & -\varepsilon I
\end{bmatrix} < 0.
$$

Hence, by Theorem 3.5 we can show that the closed-loop system (6) is robustly admissible. (Necessity) Assume there exists a feedback control of the form (4) which makes the descriptor system (1) robustly admissible. Then, it follows from Theorem 3.5 that there exists a scalar $\varepsilon > 0$ such that

$$
\begin{bmatrix}
QS^T(A + BK) + (A + BK)^T SQ^T - E^T PE + \varepsilon G_c^T G_c & (A + BK)^T P & QS^T H_c \\
P(A + BK) & -P & PH_c \\
H_c^T SQ^T & H_c^T P & -\varepsilon I
\end{bmatrix} < 0.
$$

It follows from Schur complement formula that

$$
QS^T A + A^T SQ^T - E^T PE + \varepsilon^{-1} QS^T H_c H_c^T SQ^T + \Theta^T \Gamma^{-1} \Theta + K^T \Psi^T + \Psi K + K^T \Lambda K < 0.
$$

By Lemma 3.4, we have

$$
K^T \Psi^T + \Psi K + K^T \Lambda K \geq -\Psi\Lambda^{-1}\Psi^T.
$$

Therefore, we obtain the conditions (12) and (13), and the feedback gain K is calculated as in (14).

Similarly, we can prove the following theorem by using Theorem 3.6.

Theorem 3.8. *There exists a controller (4) that makes the descriptor system (1) robustly admissible if there exist matrix P and scalar $\varepsilon > 0$ such that (10), (12), and*

$$
-E^T PE + \varepsilon G^T G + A^T \Gamma^{-1} A - A^T \Gamma^{-1} B\Lambda^{-1} B^T \Gamma^{-1} A < 0 \tag{15}
$$

where Γ, Λ are given in Theorem 3.7. In this case, the feedback gain in the controller (4) is given as in (14).

4. H_∞ non-fragile control

In this section, we consider the robust admissibility with H_∞ disturbance attenuation. H_∞ disturbance attenuation problem plays an important role in control systems. Section 4.1 discusses the analysis of H_∞ disturbance attenuation, and Section 4.2 gives design methods of the H_∞ non-fragile controllers.

4.1. Robust H_∞ disturbance attenuation for uncertain systems

First, we consider the robust H_∞ disturbance attenuation γ for the following uncertain descriptor system

$$\begin{aligned} Ex(k+1) &= (A+\Delta A)x(k) + B_1 w(k) + B_2 u(k), \\ z(k) &= Cx(k) + Du(k) \end{aligned} \tag{16}$$

where $w(k) \in \Re^{m_1}$ is the disturbances and $z(k) \in \Re^p$ is the controlled output. A, B_1, B_2, C and D are system matrices with appropriate dimensions. Uncertain matrix ΔA is assumed to be of the form (3).

The controller is assumed to be of the form (4). Applying the controller (4) to the system (16), we have the closed-loop system

$$\begin{aligned} Ex(k+1) &= (A+B_2K+H_cF_c(k)G_c)x(k) + B_1 w(k), \\ z(k) &= (C+DK+\alpha D\Phi(k)K)x(k) \end{aligned} \tag{17}$$

where

$$H_c = [H \;\; \alpha B_2], \; F_c(k) = \mathrm{diag}[F(k) \;\; \Phi(k)], \; G_c = \begin{bmatrix} G \\ K \end{bmatrix}.$$

Define the cost function

$$J = \sum_{k=0}^{\infty} (z^T(k)z(k) - \gamma^2 w^T(k)w(k)). \tag{18}$$

The problem is to find a controller (4) which makes the system (16) with $w(k) = 0$ robustly admissible, and makes it satisfy $J < 0$ in (18). If there exists such a controller, it is said to be an H_∞ non-fragile controller and the closed-loop system is said to be robustly admissible with H_∞ disturbance attenuation γ.

The following is a well-known result for the admissibility with H_∞ disturbance attenuation γ of linear descriptor systems.

Lemma 4.1. *(Xu & Lam [32]) Consider the system*

$$\begin{aligned} Ex(k+1) &= Ax(k) + Bw(k), \\ z(k) &= Cx(k) + Dw(k) \end{aligned} \tag{19}$$

where A, B, C and D are matrices of appropriate dimensions.
(i) Given a scalar $\gamma > 0$. The descriptor system (19) is robustly admissible with H_∞ disturbance attenuation γ if and only if there exist matrices $P > 0$, Q such that

$$\begin{bmatrix} A^TPA - E^TPE + C^TC & A^TPB + C^TD \\ B^TPA + D^TC & B^TPB + D^TD - \gamma^2 I \end{bmatrix} + \begin{bmatrix} A^T \\ B^T \end{bmatrix} SQ^T + QS^T \begin{bmatrix} A & B \end{bmatrix} < 0 \tag{20}$$

where $S \in \Re^{n\times(n-r)}$ is any matrix with full column rank and satisfies $E^TS = 0$.
(ii) Given a scalar $\gamma > 0$. The descriptor system (19) is robustly admissible with H_∞ disturbance attenuation γ if and only if there exist matrix P such that

$$E^TPE \geq 0, \tag{21}$$

$$\begin{bmatrix} A^TPA - E^TPE + C^TC & A^TPB + C^TD \\ B^TPA + D^TC & B^TPB + D^TD - \gamma^2 I \end{bmatrix} < 0. \tag{22}$$

The following theorem provides a necessary and sufficient condition for the robust admissibility with H_∞ disturbance attenuation of (17).

Theorem 4.2. *Given γ and K, the descriptor system (17) is robustly admissible with H_∞ disturbance attenuation γ if and only if there exist matrices $P > 0$, $Q = [Q_1^T \ Q_2^T]^T$ and scalars $\varepsilon_1 > 0, \varepsilon_2 > 0$ such that*

$$\begin{bmatrix} \Pi_{11} & A_K^TSQ_2^T + Q_1S^TB_1 & A_K^TP & (C+DK)^T & Q_1S^TH_c & 0 \\ Q_2S^TA_K + B_1^TSQ^T & \Pi_{22} & B_1^TP & 0 & Q_2S^TH_c & 0 \\ PA_K & PB_1 & -P & 0 & PH_c & 0 \\ C+DK & 0 & 0 & -I & 0 & \alpha D \\ H_c^TSQ_1^T & H_c^TSQ_2^T & H_c^TP & 0 & -\varepsilon_1 I & 0 \\ 0 & 0 & 0 & \alpha D^T & 0 & -\varepsilon_2 I \end{bmatrix} < 0 \tag{23}$$

where $A_K = A + B_2K$, $S \in \Re^{n\times(n-r)}$ is any matrix with full column rank and satisfies $E^TS = 0$, and

$$\begin{aligned} \Pi_{11} &= Q_1S^TA_K - E^TPE + A_K^TSQ_1^T + \varepsilon_1 G_c^TG_c + \varepsilon_2 K^TK, \\ \Pi_{22} &= -\gamma^2 I + Q_2S^TB_1 + B_1^TSQ_2^T. \end{aligned}$$

Proof: (Sufficiency) Suppose that there exist matrices $P > 0$, $Q = [Q_1^T \ Q_2^T]^T$ and scalars $\varepsilon_1 > 0$, $\varepsilon_2 > 0$ such that the condition (23) holds. Then, by Schur complement formula, we have

$$\bar{Q} + \varepsilon_1^{-1}\bar{H}_1\bar{H}_1^T + \varepsilon_1\bar{G}_2^T\bar{G}_1 + \varepsilon_2^{-1}\bar{H}_2\bar{H}_2^T + \varepsilon_2\bar{G}_2^T\bar{G}_2 < 0. \tag{24}$$

where

$$\bar{Q} = \begin{bmatrix} Q_1 S^T A_K - E^T PE + A_K^T S Q_1^T & A_K^T S Q_2^T + Q_1 S^T B_1 & A_K^T P & (C+DK)^T \\ Q_2 S^T A_K + B_1^T S Q^T & -\gamma^2 I + Q_2 S^T B_1 + B_1^T S Q_2^T & B_1^T P & 0 \\ PA_K & PB_1 & -P & 0 \\ C+DK & 0 & 0 & -I \end{bmatrix},$$
$$\bar{H}_1 = \left[H_c^T S Q_1^T \; H_c^T S Q_2^T \; H_c^T P \; 0\right]^T,$$
$$\bar{H}_2 = \left[0 \; 0 \; 0 \; \alpha D^T\right]^T,$$
$$\bar{G}_1 = \left[G_c \; 0 \; 0 \; 0\right],$$
$$\bar{G}_2 = \left[K \; 0 \; 0 \; 0\right].$$

Now, using Lemma 3.2, we have

$$\begin{bmatrix} \Delta_{11} & \Delta_{12} & \Delta_{13} & (C+DK+D\Phi(k)K)^T \\ \Delta_{12}^T & \Delta_{22} & B_1^T P & 0 \\ \Delta_{13}^T & PB_1 & -P & 0 \\ C+DK+D\Phi(k)K & 0 & 0 & -I \end{bmatrix}$$
$$= \bar{Q} + \bar{H}_1 F_c(k) \bar{G}_1 + \bar{G}_1^T F^T(k) \bar{H}_1^T + \bar{H}_2 \Phi(k) \bar{G}_2 + \bar{G}_2^T \Phi^T(k) \bar{H}_2^T$$
$$\leq \bar{Q} + \varepsilon_1^{-1} \bar{H}_1 H_1^T + \varepsilon_1 \bar{G}_1^T \bar{G}_1 + \varepsilon_2^{-1} \bar{H}_2 H_2^T + \varepsilon_2 \bar{G}_2^T \bar{G}_2$$

where

$$\Delta_{11} = Q_1 S^T (A + B_2 K + H_c F_c(k) G_c) + (A + B_2 K + H_c F_c(k) G_c)^T S Q_1^T - E^T PE,$$
$$\Delta_{12} = (A + B_2 K + H_c F_c(k) G_c)^T S Q_2^T + Q_1 S^T B_1,$$
$$\Delta_{13} = (A + B_2 K + H_c F_c(k) G_c)^T P,$$
$$\Delta_{22} = -\gamma^2 I + Q_2 S^T B_1 + B_1^T S Q_2^T.$$

It follows from (24) that

$$\begin{bmatrix} \Delta_{11} & \Delta_{12} & \Delta_{13} & (C+DK+D\Phi(k)K)^T \\ \Delta_{12}^T & \Delta_{22} & B_1^T P & 0 \\ \Delta_{13}^T & PB_1 & -P & 0 \\ C+DK+D\Phi(k)K & 0 & 0 & -I \end{bmatrix} < 0.$$

This implies by Schur complement formula and Lemma 4.1(i) that the descriptor system (17) is robustly admissible with H_∞ disturbance attenuation γ.

(Necessity) Assume that the descriptor system (17) is robustly admissible with H_∞ disturbance attenuation γ. Then, it follows from Lemma 4.1 that there exist matrices $P > 0$, Q and scalars $\varepsilon_1 > 0$, $\varepsilon_2 > 0$ such that (20) with A replaced by $A + BK + H_c F_c(k) G_c$ and C by $C + DK + \alpha\Phi(k)K$ holds. Thus, for all admissible $F(k)$ and $\Phi(k)$, the following inequality holds:

$$\begin{bmatrix} \Delta_{11} & \Delta_{12} & \Delta_{13} & (C+DK+D\Phi(k)K)^T \\ \Delta_{12}^T & \Delta_{22} & B_1^T P & 0 \\ \Delta_{13}^T & PB_1 & -P & 0 \\ C+DK+D\Phi(k)K & 0 & 0 & -I \end{bmatrix} < 0.$$

That is,

$$\bar{Q} + \bar{H}_1 F_c(k)\bar{G}_1 + \bar{G}_1^T F_c^T(k)\bar{H}_1^T + \bar{H}_2\Phi(k)\bar{G}_2 + \bar{G}_2^T\Phi^T(k)\bar{H}_2^T < 0$$

is satisfied for all admissible $F(k)$ and $\Phi(k)$. It follows from Lemma 3.2 that

$$\bar{Q} + \varepsilon_1^{-1}\bar{H}_1\bar{H}_1^T + \varepsilon_1\bar{G}_1^T\bar{G}_1 + \varepsilon_2^{-1}\bar{H}_2\bar{H}_2^T + \varepsilon_2\bar{G}_2^T\bar{G}_2 < 0,$$

which leads to the condition (23). This completes the proof.

Based on Lemma 4.1(ii), we have the following theorem. The proof is similar to that of Theorem 4.2, and is thus omitted.

Theorem 4.3. *Given γ and K, the descriptor system (17) is robustly admissible with H_∞ disturbance attenuation γ if and only if there exist matrix P and scalars $\varepsilon_1 > 0, \varepsilon_2 > 0$ such that (21), and*

$$\begin{bmatrix} -E^TPE + \varepsilon_1 G_c^T G_c + \varepsilon_2 K^T K & 0 & (A+B_2K)^T P & (C+DK)^T & 0 & 0 \\ 0 & -\gamma^2 I & B_1^T P & 0 & 0 & 0 \\ P(A+B_2K) & PB_1 & -P & 0 & PH_c & 0 \\ C+DK & 0 & 0 & -I & 0 & \alpha D \\ 0 & 0 & H_c^T P & 0 & -\varepsilon_1 I & 0 \\ 0 & 0 & 0 & \alpha D^T & 0 & -\varepsilon_2 I \end{bmatrix} < 0. \qquad (25)$$

4.2. H∞ non-fragile control design for uncertain systems

Now, we are at the position to propose design methods of H_∞ non-fragile controller for uncertain descriptor systems.

Theorem 4.4. *There exists a controller (4) that makes the descriptor system (16) robustly admissible with H_∞ disturbance attenuation γ if there exist matrices $P > 0$, $Q = [Q_1^T\ Q_2^T]^T$ and scalars $\varepsilon_1 > 0$, $\varepsilon_2 > 0$ such that*

$$\Gamma = P^{-1} - \varepsilon_1^{-1} H_c H_c^T > 0, \qquad (26)$$

$$Z = I - \varepsilon_2^{-1}\alpha^2 DD^T > 0, \qquad (27)$$

$$W = \gamma^2 I - Q_2 S^T B_1 - B_1^T S Q_2^T - \varepsilon_1^{-1} Q_2 S^T H_c H_c^T S Q_2^T - \Theta_B^T \Gamma^{-1}\Theta_B > 0, \qquad (28)$$

$$\begin{aligned} &Q_1 S^T A + A^T S Q_1^T - E^T P E + \varepsilon_1 G^T G + \varepsilon_1^{-1} Q_1 S^T H_c H_c^T S Q_1^T \\ &+ C^T Z^{-1} C + Y W^{-1} Y^T + \Theta_A^T \Gamma^{-1}\Theta_A - \Psi\Lambda^{-1}\Psi^T < 0 \end{aligned} \qquad (29)$$

where $S \in \Re^{n\times(n-r)}$ is any matrix with full column rank and satisfies $E^T S = 0$, and

$$\begin{aligned} \Psi &= (Q_1 S^T + \Theta_A^T \Gamma^{-1})B_2 + C^T Z^{-1} D + Y W^{-1}(Q_2 S^T + \Theta_B^T \Gamma^{-1})B_2, \\ \Lambda &= B_2^T \Gamma^{-1} B_2 + D^T Z^{-1} D + (\varepsilon_1 + \varepsilon_2) I + B_2^T (S Q_2^T + \Gamma^{-1}\Theta_B) W^{-1} (Q_2 S^T + \Theta_B^T \Gamma^{-1}) B_2, \\ \Theta_A &= A + \varepsilon_1^{-1} H_c H_c^T S Q_1^T, \\ \Theta_B &= B_1 + \varepsilon_1^{-1} H_c H_c^T S Q_2^T, \\ Y &= A^T S Q_2^T + (Q_1 S^T + \Theta_A^T \Gamma^{-1})\Theta_B. \end{aligned}$$

In this case, a feedback gain in the controller (4) is given by

$$K = -\Lambda^{-1}\Psi^T. \tag{30}$$

Proof: (Sufficiency) The closed-loop system (17) with the feedback gain (30) is given by

$$\begin{aligned} Ex(k+1) &= (A - B_2\Lambda^{-1}\Psi^T + H_c F_c(k) G_c)x(k) + B_1 w(k), \\ z(k) &= (C - D\Lambda^{-1}\Psi^T - \alpha D\Phi(k)\Lambda^{-1}\Psi^T)x(k) \end{aligned} \tag{31}$$

where $G_c = \begin{bmatrix} G^T & -\Psi\Lambda^{-1} \end{bmatrix}^T$. Then, by some mathematical manipulation, we have

$$\begin{aligned} &Q_1 S^T(A - B_2\Lambda^{-1}\Psi^T) + (A - B_2\Lambda^{-1}\Psi^T)^T S Q_1^T + \varepsilon_1 G_c^T G_c + \varepsilon_2 \Psi\Lambda^{-1}\Lambda^{-1}\Psi^T \\ &= Q_1 S^T A - Q_1 S^T B_2 \Lambda^{-1}\Psi^T + A^T S Q_1^T - \Psi\Lambda^{-1}B_2^T S Q_1^T + \varepsilon_1 G^T G \\ &\quad + (\varepsilon_1 + \varepsilon_2)\Psi\Lambda^{-1}\Lambda^{-1}\Psi^T, \end{aligned}$$

$$\begin{aligned} &(C - D\Lambda^{-1}\Psi^T)^T Z^{-1}(C - D\Lambda^{-1}\Psi^T) \\ &= C^T Z^{-1} C - \Psi\Lambda^{-1} D Z^{-1} C - C^T Z^{-1} D \Lambda^{-1}\Psi^T + \Psi\Lambda^{-1} D Z^{-1} D \Lambda^{-1}\Psi^T, \end{aligned}$$

$$\begin{aligned} &(A - B_2\Lambda^{-1}\Psi^T + \varepsilon_1^{-1} H_c H_c^T S Q_1^T)^T \Gamma^{-1}(A - B_2\Lambda^{-1}\Psi^T + \varepsilon_1^{-1} H_c H_c^T S Q_1^T) \\ &= \Theta_A^T \Gamma^{-1}\Theta_A - \Psi\Lambda^{-1}B_2^T\Gamma^{-1}\Theta_A - \Theta_A^T\Gamma^{-1}B_2\Lambda^{-1}\Psi^T + \Psi\Lambda^{-1}B_2^T\Gamma^{-1}B_2\Lambda^{-1}\Psi^T, \end{aligned}$$

$$\begin{aligned} &[(A - B_2\Lambda^{-1}\Psi^T)^T S Q_2^T + (Q_1 S^T + (A - B_2\Lambda^{-1}\Psi^T + \varepsilon_1^{-1} H_c H_c^T S Q_1^T)^T \Gamma^{-1})\Theta_B] W^{-1} \\ &\qquad \times [(A - B_2\Lambda^{-1}\Psi^T)^T S Q_2^T + (Q_1 S^T + (A - B_2\Lambda^{-1}\Psi^T + \varepsilon_1^{-1} H_c H_c^T S Q_1^T)^T \Gamma^{-1})\Theta_B)]^T \\ &= Y W^{-1} Y^T - \Psi\Lambda^{-1} B_2^T (S Q_2^T + \Gamma^{-1}\Theta_B)^T W^{-1} Y^T - Y W^{-1}(S Q_2^T + \Gamma^{-1}\Theta_B)^T B_2 \Lambda^{-1}\Psi^T \\ &\quad + \Psi\Lambda^{-1} B_2^T (S Q_2^T + \Gamma^{-1}\Theta_B) W^{-1} (S Q_2^T + \Gamma^{-1}\Theta_B)^T B_2 \Lambda^{-1}\Psi^T. \end{aligned}$$

Thus, it can be verified with (29) that

$$\begin{aligned} &Q_1 S^T(A - B_2\Lambda^{-1}\Psi^T) + (A - B_2\Lambda^{-1}\Psi^T)^T S Q_1^T + \varepsilon_1 G_c^T G_c + \varepsilon_2 \Psi\Lambda^{-1}\Lambda^{-1}\Psi^T \\ &\quad + (C - D\Lambda^{-1}\Psi^T)^T Z^{-1}(C - D\Lambda^{-1}\Psi^T) - E^T P E + \varepsilon_1^{-1} Q_1 S^T H_c H_c^T S Q_1^T \\ &\quad + (A - B_2\Lambda^{-1}\Psi^T + \varepsilon_1^{-1} H_c H_c^T S Q_1^T)^T \Gamma^{-1}(A - B_2\Lambda^{-1}\Psi^T + \varepsilon_1^{-1} H_c H_c^T S Q_1^T) \\ &\quad + [(A - B_2\Lambda^{-1}\Psi^T)^T S Q_2^T + (Q_1 S^T + (A - B_2\Lambda^{-1}\Psi^T + \varepsilon_1^{-1} H_c H_c^T S Q_1^T)^T \Gamma^{-1})\Theta_B] W^{-1} \\ &\qquad \times [(A - B_2\Lambda^{-1}\Psi^T)^T S Q_2^T + (Q_1 S^T + (A - B_2\Lambda^{-1}\Psi^T + \varepsilon_1^{-1} H_c H_c^T S Q_1^T)^T \Gamma^{-1})\Theta_B)]^T \\ &= Q_1 S^T A + A^T S Q_1^T + \varepsilon_1 G^T G - E^T P E + \varepsilon_1^{-1} Q_1 S^T H_c H_c^T S Q_1^T + C^T Z^{-1} C + \Theta_A^T \Gamma^{-1}\Theta_A \\ &\quad + Y W^{-1} Y^T - \Psi\Lambda^{-1}\Psi^T < 0. \end{aligned}$$

By Schur complement formula, we obtain

$$\begin{bmatrix} \begin{pmatrix} Q_1 S^T A_K + A_K^T S Q_1^T \\ -E^T P E + \varepsilon_1 G_c^T G_c \\ +\varepsilon_2 \Psi \Lambda^{-1} \Lambda^{-1} \Psi^T \end{pmatrix} & A_K^T S Q_2^T + Q_1 S^T B_1 & A_K^T P & C_K^T & Q_1 S^T H_c & 0 \\ Q_2 S^T A_K + B_1^T S Q_1^T & \begin{pmatrix} -\gamma^2 I + Q_2 S^T B_1 \\ +B_1^T S Q_2^T \end{pmatrix} & B_1^T P & 0 & Q_2 S^T H_c & 0 \\ P A_K & P B_1 & -P & 0 & P H_c & 0 \\ A_K & 0 & 0 & -I & 0 & \alpha D \\ H_c^T S Q_1^T & H_c^T S Q_2^T & H_c^T P & 0 & -\varepsilon_1 I & 0 \\ 0 & 0 & 0 & \alpha D^T & 0 & -\varepsilon_2 I \end{bmatrix} < 0.$$

where $A_K = A - B_2 \Lambda^{-1} \Psi^T$ and $C_K = C - D \Lambda^{-1} \Psi^T$. Hence, by Theorem 4.2 we can show that the closed-loop system (17) is robustly admissible with H_∞ disturbance attenuation γ. (Necessity) Assume there exists a feedback control of the form (4) which makes the descriptor system (16) robustly admissible with H_∞ disturbance attenuation γ. Then, it follows from Theorem 4.2 that there exist scalars $\varepsilon_1 > 0$ and $\varepsilon_2 > 0$ such that

$$\begin{bmatrix} \Pi_{11} & A_K^T S Q_2^T + Q_1 S^T B_1 & A_K^T P & (C + DK)^T & Q_1 S^T H_c & 0 \\ Q_2 S^T A_K + B_1^T S Q^T & \Pi_{22} & B_1^T P & 0 & Q_2 S^T H_c & 0 \\ P A_K & P B_1 & -P & 0 & P H_c & 0 \\ C + DK & 0 & 0 & -I & 0 & \alpha D \\ H_c^T S Q_1^T & H_c^T S Q_2^T & H_c^T P & 0 & -\varepsilon_1 I & 0 \\ 0 & 0 & 0 & \alpha D^T & 0 & -\varepsilon_2 I \end{bmatrix} < 0$$

where

$$\begin{aligned} \Pi_{11} &= Q_1 S^T A_K + A_K^T S Q_1^T - E^T P E + \varepsilon_1 G_c^T G_c + \varepsilon_2 K^T K, \\ \Pi_{22} &= -\gamma^2 I + Q_2 S^T B_1 + B_1^T S Q_2^T. \end{aligned}$$

It follows from Schur complement formula that we obtain the conditions (26), (27), (28), and

$$\begin{aligned} &Q_1 S^T A + A^T S Q_1^T - E^T P E + \varepsilon_1 G^T G + \varepsilon_1^{-1} Q S^T H_c H_c^T S Q^T + C^T Z^{-1} C + Y W^{-1} Y^T \\ &+\Theta_A^T \Gamma^{-1} \Theta_A + K^T \Psi^T + \Psi K + K^T \Lambda K < 0. \end{aligned}$$

By Lemma 3.4, we have

$$K^T \Psi^T + \Psi K + K^T \Lambda K \geq -\Psi \Lambda^{-1} \Psi^T.$$

Therefore, we finally obtain the condition (29), and the feedback gain K as in (30).

Based on Theorem 4.3, we can deduce the following theorem.

Theorem 4.5. *There exists a controller (4) that makes the descriptor system (16) robustly admissible with* H_∞ *disturbance attenuation* γ *if there exist matrix* P *and scalars* $\varepsilon_1 > 0,\ \varepsilon_2 > 0$ *such that (21), (26), (27) and*

$$W = \gamma^2 I - B_1^T \Gamma^{-1} B_1 > 0, \quad (32)$$

$$-E^T PE + \varepsilon_1 G^T G + C^T Z^{-1} C + A^T \Gamma^{-1} B_1 W^{-1} B_1^T \Gamma^{-1} A + A^T \Gamma^{-1} A - \Psi \Lambda^{-1} \Psi^T < 0 \quad (33)$$

where

$$\Psi = A^T \Gamma^{-1} B_2 + C^T Z^{-1} D + A^T \Gamma^{-1} B_1 W^{-1} B_1^T \Gamma^{-1} B_2,$$
$$\Lambda = B_2^T \Gamma^{-1} B_2 + D^T Z^{-1} D + (\varepsilon_1 + \varepsilon_2) I + B_2^T \Gamma^{-1} B_1 W^{-1} B_1^T \Gamma^{-1} B_2.$$

In this case, a feedback gain in the controller (4) is given as in (30).

5. Time-delay systems

This section investigates the robust admissibility of uncertain descriptor delay systems and provides a non-fragile control design method for such systems. Section 5.1 gives a robust admissibility condition for uncertain descriptor delay systems, and Section 5.2 proposes non-fragile control design methods.

5.1. Robust admissibility for uncertain systems

Consider the following descriptor system with time-delay and uncertainties:

$$Ex(k+1) = (A + \Delta A)x(k) + (A_d + \Delta A_d)x(k-d) + Bu(k) \quad (34)$$

where $x(k) \in \Re^n$ is the state and $u(k) \in \Re^m$ is the control. A, A_d and B are system matrices with appropriate dimensions. d is a constant delay and may be unknown. Uncertain matrices are given by

$$\left[\Delta A\ \Delta A_d\right] = HF(k)\left[G\ G_d\right]$$

where $F(k) \in \Re^{l \times j}$ is an unknown time-varying matrix satisfying $F^T(k)F(k) \leq I$ and H, G and G_d are constant matrices of appropriate dimensions. Unforced nominal descriptor system (34) with $u(k) = 0$ and $\Delta A = \Delta A_d = 0$ is denoted by the triplet $(E,\ A,\ A_d)$.

Definition 5.1. *(i) The triplet* $(E,\ A,\ A_d)$ *is said to be regular if* $det(z^{d+1}E - z^d A - A_d)$ *is not identically zero.*
(ii) The triplet $(E,\ A,\ A_d)$ *is said to be causal if it is regular and* $deg(z^{nd} det(zE - A - z^d A_d)) = nd + rank(E)$.
(iii) Define the generalized spectral radius as $\rho(E,\ A,\ A_d) = \max_{z|\lambda \in \{det(z^{d+1}E - z^d A - A_d) = 0\}} |\lambda|$. *The triplet* $(E,\ A,\ A_d)$ *is said to be stable if* $\rho(E,\ A,\ A_d) < 1$.
(iv) The triplet $(E,\ A,\ A_d)$ *is said to be admissible if it is regular, causal and stable.*

Applying the controller (4) to the system (34), we have the closed-loop system

$$Ex(k+1) = (A + BK + H_c F_c(k) G_c)x(k) + (A_d + HF(k)G_d)x(k-d) \tag{35}$$

where

$$H_c = [H \;\; \alpha B],\; F_c(k) = \mathrm{diag}[F(k) \;\; \Phi(k)],\; G_c = \begin{bmatrix} G \\ K \end{bmatrix}.$$

First, we consider the robust admissibility of the closed-loop system (35). In order to show a robust admissibility condition, we need the following theorem.

Theorem 5.2. *(Xu & Lam [32]) (i) The descriptor delay system (34) with $u(k) = 0$ and $\Delta A = \Delta A_d = 0$ is admissible if and only if there exist matrices $P > 0,\; Q > 0,\; X$ such that*

$$\begin{bmatrix} A^T PA - E^T PE + Q & A^T PA_d \\ A_d^T PA & A_d^T PA_d - Q \end{bmatrix} + \begin{bmatrix} A^T \\ A_d^T \end{bmatrix} SX^T + XS^T \begin{bmatrix} A^T \\ A_d^T \end{bmatrix}^T < 0 \tag{36}$$

where $S \in \Re^{n\times(n-r)}$ is any matrix with full column rank and satisfies $E^T S = 0$.
(ii) The descriptor delay system (34) with $u(k) = 0$ and $\Delta A = \Delta A_d = 0$ is admissible if and only if there exist matrices $P,\; Q > 0$ such that

$$E^T PE \geq 0, \tag{37}$$

$$\begin{bmatrix} A^T PA - E^T PE + Q & A^T PA_d \\ A_d^T PA & A_d^T PA_d - Q \end{bmatrix} < 0. \tag{38}$$

Robust admissibility conditions for uncertain descriptor delay system (35) are given in the following theorems.

Theorem 5.3. *Given γ and K, the descriptor system (35) is robustly admissible if there exist matrices $P > 0,\; Q > 0,\; X = [X_1^T \; X_2^T]^T$ and scalars $\varepsilon_1 > 0, \varepsilon_2 > 0$ such that*

$$\begin{bmatrix} \begin{pmatrix} X_1 S^T A_K - E^T PE + Q \\ +A_K^T SX_1^T + \varepsilon_1 G_c^T G_c \end{pmatrix} & A_K^T SX_2^T + X_1 S^T A_d & A_K^T P & X_1 S^T H_c & X_1 S^T H \\ X_2 S^T A_K + A_d^T SX^T & \begin{pmatrix} -Q + X_2 S^T A_d \\ +A_d^T SX_2^T + \varepsilon_2 G_d^T G_d \end{pmatrix} & A_d^T P & X_2 S^T H_c & X_2 S^T H \\ PA_K & PA_d & -P & PH_c & PH \\ H_c^T SX_1^T & H_c^T SX_2^T & H_c^T P & -\varepsilon_1 I & 0 \\ H^T SX_1^T & H^T SX_2^T & H^T P & 0 & -\varepsilon_2 I \end{bmatrix} < 0 \tag{39}$$

where $A_K = A + BK$ and $S \in \Re^{n\times(n-r)}$ is any matrix with full column rank and satisfies $E^T S = 0$.

Proof: Suppose that there exist matrices $P > 0$, $Q > 0$, $X = [X_1^T \; X_2^T]^T$ and scalars $\varepsilon_1 > 0$, $\varepsilon_2 > 0$ such that the condition (39) holds. Then, by Schur complement formula, we have

$$\begin{bmatrix} X_1 S^T A_K - E^T P E + A_K^T S X_1^T + Q & A_K^T S X_2^T + X_1 S^T A_d & A_K^T P \\ X_2 S^T A_K + A_d^T S X^T & -Q + X_2 S^T A_d + A_d^T S X_2^T & A_d^T P \\ P A_K & P A_d & -P \end{bmatrix}$$
$$+\varepsilon_1^{-1} \begin{bmatrix} X_1 S^T H_c \\ X_2 S^T H_c \\ P H_c \end{bmatrix} \begin{bmatrix} H_c^T S X_1^T & H_c^T S X_2^T & H_c^T P \end{bmatrix} + \varepsilon_1 \begin{bmatrix} G_c^T \\ 0 \\ 0 \end{bmatrix} \begin{bmatrix} G_c & 0 & 0 \end{bmatrix} \tag{40}$$
$$+\varepsilon_2^{-1} \begin{bmatrix} X_1 S^T H \\ X_2 S^T H \\ P H \end{bmatrix} \begin{bmatrix} H^T S X_1^T & H^T S X_2^T & H^T P \end{bmatrix} + \varepsilon_2 \begin{bmatrix} 0 \\ G_d^T \\ 0 \end{bmatrix} \begin{bmatrix} 0 & G_d & 0 \end{bmatrix} < 0.$$

Now, using Lemma 3.2, we have

$$\begin{bmatrix} \Delta_{11} & \Delta_{12} & (A_K + H_c F_c(k) G_c)^T P \\ \Delta_{12}^T & \Delta_{22} & (A_d + H F(k) G_d)^T P \\ P(A_K + H_c F_c(k) G_c) & P(A_d + H F(k) G_d) & -P \end{bmatrix}$$
$$= \begin{bmatrix} X_1 S^T A_K - E^T P E + A_K^T S X_1^T + Q & A_K^T S X_2^T + X_1 S^T A_d & A_K^T P \\ X_2 S^T A_K + A_d^T S X^T & -Q + X_2 S^T A_d + A_d^T S X_2^T & A_d^T P \\ P A_K & P A_d & -P \end{bmatrix}$$
$$+ \begin{bmatrix} X_1 S^T H_c \\ X_2 S^T H_c \\ P H_c \end{bmatrix} F_c(k) \begin{bmatrix} G_c & 0 & 0 \end{bmatrix} + \begin{bmatrix} G_c^T \\ 0 \\ 0 \end{bmatrix} F_c^T(k) \begin{bmatrix} H_c^T S X_1^T & H_c^T S X_2^T & H_c^T P \end{bmatrix}$$
$$+ \begin{bmatrix} X_1 S^T H_c \\ X_2 S^T H_c \\ P H_c \end{bmatrix} F(k) \begin{bmatrix} 0 & G_d & 0 \end{bmatrix} + \begin{bmatrix} 0 \\ G_d^T \\ 0 \end{bmatrix} F^T(k) \begin{bmatrix} H_c^T S X_1^T & H_c^T S X_2^T & H_c^T P \end{bmatrix}$$
$$\leq \begin{bmatrix} X_1 S^T A_K - E^T P E + A_K^T S X_1^T + Q & A_K^T S X_2^T + X_1 S^T A_d & A_K^T P \\ X_2 S^T A_K + A_d^T S X^T & -Q + X_2 S^T A_d + A_d^T S X_2^T & A_d^T P \\ P A_K & P A_d & -P \end{bmatrix}$$
$$+\varepsilon_1^{-1} \begin{bmatrix} X_1 S^T H_c \\ X_2 S^T H_c \\ P H_c \\ 0 \end{bmatrix} \begin{bmatrix} H_c^T S X_1^T & H_c^T S X_2^T & H_c^T P \end{bmatrix} + \varepsilon_1 \begin{bmatrix} G_c^T \\ 0 \\ 0 \end{bmatrix} \begin{bmatrix} G_c & 0 & 0 \end{bmatrix}$$
$$+\varepsilon_2^{-1} \begin{bmatrix} X_1 S^T H_c \\ X_2 S^T H_c \\ P H_c \\ 0 \end{bmatrix} \begin{bmatrix} H_c^T S X_1^T & H_c^T S X_2^T & H_c^T P \end{bmatrix} + \varepsilon_2 \begin{bmatrix} 0 \\ G_d^T \\ 0 \end{bmatrix} \begin{bmatrix} 0 & G_d & 0 \end{bmatrix}$$

where

$$\Delta_{11} = X_1 S^T (A + BK + H_c F_c(k) G_c) + (A + BK + H_c F_c(k) G_c)^T S X_1^T - E^T P E + Q,$$
$$\Delta_{12} = (A_K + H_c F_c(k) G_c)^T S X_2^T + X_1 S^T (A_d + H F(k) G_d),$$
$$\Delta_{22} = -Q + X_2 S^T (A_d + H F(k) G_d) + (A_d + H F(k) G_d)^T S X_2^T.$$

It follows from (40) that

$$\begin{bmatrix} \Delta_{11} & \Delta_{12} & (A_K + H_cF_c(k)G_c)^T P \\ \Delta_{12}^T & \Delta_{22} & (A_d + HF(k)G_d)^T P \\ P(A_K + H_cF_c(k)G_c) & P(A_d + HF(k)G_d) & -P \end{bmatrix} < 0.$$

This implies by Schur complement formula and Theorem 5.2(i) that the descriptor system (35) is robustly admissible.

Similarly, we can prove the following theorem by using Theorem 5.2(ii).

Theorem 5.4. *Given γ and K, the descriptor system (35) is robustly admissible if there exist matrices $P > 0,\ Q > 0$ and scalars $\varepsilon_1 > 0, \varepsilon_2 > 0$ such that (37), and*

$$\begin{bmatrix} -E^T PE + Q + \varepsilon_1 G_c^T G_c & 0 & A_K^T P & 0 & 0 \\ 0 & -Q + \varepsilon_2 G_d^T G_d & A_d^T P & 0 & 0 \\ PA_K & PA_d & -P & PH_c & PH \\ 0 & 0 & H_c^T P & -\varepsilon_1 I & 0 \\ 0 & 0 & H^T P & 0 & -\varepsilon_2 I \end{bmatrix} < 0 \tag{41}$$

where $A_K = A + BK$.

5.2. Control design for time-delay systems

Now, we are ready to propose control design methods for uncertain descriptor delay systems. The following theorems propose design methods of a non-fragile controller that makes the system (34) robustly admissible.

Theorem 5.5. *There exists a controller (4) that makes the descriptor system (34) robustly admissible if there exist matrices $P > 0,\ Q > 0,\ X = [X_1^T\ X_2^T]^T$ and scalars $\varepsilon_1 > 0,\ \varepsilon_2 > 0$ such that*

$$\Gamma = P^{-1} - \varepsilon_1^{-1} H_c H_c^T - \varepsilon_2^{-1} HH^T > 0, \tag{42}$$

$$\begin{aligned} W = Q - X_2 S^T A_d - A_d^T S X_2^T - \varepsilon_2 G_d^T G_d - \Theta_D^T \Gamma^{-1} \Theta_D \\ -X_2 S^T(\varepsilon_1^{-1} H_c H_c^T + \varepsilon_2^{-1} HH^T) S X_2^T > 0, \end{aligned} \tag{43}$$

$$\begin{aligned} X_1 S^T A + A^T S X_1^T - E^T PE + Q + \varepsilon_1 G^T G + X_1 S^T(\varepsilon_1^{-1} H_c H_c^T + \varepsilon_2^{-1} HH^T) S X_1^T \\ + \Theta_A^T \Gamma^{-1} \Theta_A + YW^{-1} Y^T - \Psi \Lambda^{-1} \Psi^T < 0 \end{aligned} \tag{44}$$

where $S \in \Re^{n \times (n-r)}$ is any matrix with full column rank and satisfies $E^T S = 0$, and

$$\begin{aligned} &\Psi = (X_1 S^T + \Theta_A^T \Gamma^{-1}) B + YW^{-1}(S X_2^T + \Theta_D^T \Gamma^{-1}) B, \\ &\Lambda = B^T \Gamma^{-1} B + \varepsilon_1 I + B^T (S X_2^T + \Gamma^{-1} \Theta_D) W^{-1} (X_2 S^T + \Theta_D^T \Gamma^{-1}) B, \\ &Y = A^T S X_2^T + (X_1 S^T + \Theta_A^T \Gamma^{-1}) \Theta_D, \\ &\Theta_A = A + (\varepsilon_1^{-1} H_c H_c^T + \varepsilon_2^{-1} HH^T) S X_1^T, \\ &\Theta_D = A_d + (\varepsilon_1^{-1} H_c H_c^T + \varepsilon_2^{-1} HH^T) S X_2^T. \end{aligned}$$

In this case, a feedback gain in the controller (4) is given by

$$K = -\Lambda^{-1}\Psi^T. \tag{45}$$

Proof: The closed-loop system (35) with the feedback gain (45) is given by

$$Ex(k+1) = (A - B\Lambda^{-1}\Psi^T + H_c F_c(k) G_c)x(k) + (A_d + HF(k)G_d)x(k-d) \tag{46}$$

where $G_c = \begin{bmatrix} G^T & -\Psi\Lambda^{-1} \end{bmatrix}^T$. Then, by some mathematical manipulation, we have

$$\begin{aligned}
&X_1 S^T (A - B\Lambda^{-1}\Psi^T) + (A - B\Lambda^{-1}\Psi^T)^T S X_1^T + \varepsilon_1 G_c^T G_c \\
&= X_1 S^T A - X_1 S^T B \Lambda^{-1}\Psi^T + A^T S X_1^T - \Psi\Lambda^{-1} B^T S X_1^T + \varepsilon_1 G^T G + \varepsilon_1 \Psi \Lambda^{-1}\Lambda^{-1}\Psi^T,
\end{aligned}$$

$$\begin{aligned}
&[A - B\Lambda^{-1}\Psi^T + (\varepsilon_1^{-1} H_c H_c^T + \varepsilon_2^{-1} H H^T) S X_1^T]^T \Gamma^{-1} \\
&\qquad \times [A - B\Lambda^{-1}\Psi^T + (\varepsilon_1^{-1} H_c H_c^T + \varepsilon_2^{-1} H H^T) S X_1^T] \\
&= \Theta_A^T \Gamma^{-1} \Theta_A - \Psi\Lambda^{-1} B^T \Gamma^{-1} \Theta_A - \Theta_A^T \Gamma^{-1} B \Lambda^{-1} \Psi^T + \Psi \Lambda^{-1} B^T \Gamma^{-1} B \Lambda^{-1} \Psi^T,
\end{aligned}$$

$$\begin{aligned}
&[(A - B\Lambda^{-1}\Psi^T)^T S X_2^T + (X_1 S^T + (A - B\Lambda^{-1}\Psi^T + \varepsilon_1^{-1} H_c H_c^T S X_1^T)^T \Gamma^{-1})\Theta_D] W^{-1} \\
&\qquad \times [(A - B\Lambda^{-1}\Psi^T)^T S X_2^T + (X_1 S^T + (A - B\Lambda^{-1}\Psi^T + \varepsilon_1^{-1} H_c H_c^T S X_1^T)^T \Gamma^{-1})\Theta_D)]^T \\
&= Y W^{-1} Y^T - \Psi\Lambda^{-1} B^T (S X_2^T + \Gamma^{-1}\Theta_D)^T W^{-1} Y^T - Y W^{-1} (S X_2^T + \Gamma^{-1}\Theta_D)^T B \Lambda^{-1} \Psi^T \\
&\quad + \Psi \Lambda^{-1} B^T (S X_2^T + \Gamma^{-1}\Theta_D) W^{-1} (S X_2^T + \Gamma^{-1}\Theta_D)^T B \Lambda^{-1} \Psi^T.
\end{aligned}$$

Thus, it can be verified with (44) that

$$\begin{aligned}
&X_1 S^T (A - B\Lambda^{-1}\Psi^T) + (A - B\Lambda^{-1}\Psi^T)^T S X_1^T + \varepsilon_1 G_c^T G_c - E^T P E + Q \\
&+ X_1 S^T (\varepsilon_1^{-1} H_c H_c^T + \varepsilon_2^{-1} H H^T) S X_1^T + [A - B\Lambda^{-1}\Psi^T + (\varepsilon_1^{-1} H_c H_c^T + \varepsilon_2^{-1} H H^T) S X_1^T]^T \\
&\qquad \times \Gamma^{-1} [A - B\Lambda^{-1}\Psi^T + (\varepsilon_1^{-1} H_c H_c^T + \varepsilon_2^{-1} H H^T) S X_1^T] \\
&+ [(A - B\Lambda^{-1}\Psi^T)^T S X_2^T + (X_1 S^T + (A - B\Lambda^{-1}\Psi^T + \varepsilon_1^{-1} H_c H_c^T S X_1^T)^T \Gamma^{-1})\Theta_D] W^{-1} \\
&\qquad \times [(A - B\Lambda^{-1}\Psi^T)^T S X_2^T + (X_1 S^T + (A - B\Lambda^{-1}\Psi^T + \varepsilon_1^{-1} H_c H_c^T S X_1^T)^T \Gamma^{-1})\Theta_D)]^T \\
&= X_1 S^T A + A^T S X_1^T + \varepsilon_1 G^T G - E^T P E + Q + X_1 S^T (\varepsilon_1^{-1} H_c H_c^T + \varepsilon_2^{-1} H H^T) S X_1^T \\
&\quad + \Theta_A^T \Gamma^{-1} \Theta_A + Y W^{-1} Y^T - \Psi \Lambda^{-1} \Psi^T < 0.
\end{aligned}$$

By Schur complement formula, we obtain

$$\begin{bmatrix}
\begin{pmatrix} X_1 S^T A_K - E^T P E + Q \\ + A_K^T S X_1^T + \varepsilon_1 G_c^T G_c \end{pmatrix} & A_K^T S X_2^T + X_1 S^T A_d & A_K^T P & X_1 S^T H_c & X_1 S^T H \\
X_2 S^T A_K + A_d^T S X^T & \begin{pmatrix} -Q + X_2 S^T A_d \\ + A_d^T S X_2^T + \varepsilon_2 G_d^T G_d \end{pmatrix} & A_d^T P & X_2 S^T H_c & X_2 S^T H \\
P A_K & P A_d & -P & P H_c & P H \\
H_c^T S X_1^T & H_c^T S X_2^T & H_c^T P & -\varepsilon_1 I & 0 \\
H^T S X_1^T & H^T S X_2^T & H^T P & 0 & -\varepsilon_2 I
\end{bmatrix} < 0$$

where $A_K = A - B\Lambda^{-1}\Psi^T$. Hence, by Theorem 5.3 we can show that the closed-loop system (35) is robustly admissible.

The following theorem can similarly be obtained from Theorem 5.4.

Theorem 5.6. *There exists a controller (4) that makes the descriptor system (34) robustly admissible if there exist matrices $P > 0$, $Q > 0$ and scalars $\varepsilon_1 > 0$, $\varepsilon_2 > 0$ such that (37), (42),*

$$W = Q - \varepsilon_2 G_d^T G_d - A_d^T \Gamma^{-1} A_d > 0, \tag{47}$$

$$-E^T PE + Q + \varepsilon_1 G^T G + A^T \Gamma^{-1} A + A^T \Gamma^{-1} A_d W^{-1} A_d^T \Gamma^{-1} A - \Psi \Lambda^{-1} \Psi^T < 0 \tag{48}$$

where Γ is given in (42), and

$$\begin{aligned} \Psi &= A^T \Gamma^{-1} B + A^T \Gamma^{-1} A_d W^{-1} A_d^T \Gamma^{-1} B, \\ \Lambda &= B^T \Gamma^{-1} B + \varepsilon_1 I + B^T \Gamma^{-1} A_d W^{-1} A_d^T \Gamma^{-1} B. \end{aligned}$$

In this case, a feedback gain in the controller (4) is given as in (45).

6. Numerical examples

In order to illustrate our control design methods, we consider the following two examples. The first one shows a non-fragile controller design method for an uncertain system, and the second gives the same class of a controller design method for a time-delay counterpart.

Consider an uncertain system:

$$\begin{bmatrix} 1 & 0 \\ 0 & 0 \end{bmatrix} x(k+1) = \left(\begin{bmatrix} 0 & 1 \\ 1 & 0.2 \end{bmatrix} + \begin{bmatrix} 0.06 \\ 0.08 \end{bmatrix} F(k) \begin{bmatrix} 0.2 & 0 \end{bmatrix} \right) x(k) + \begin{bmatrix} 0.2 \\ 0.3 \end{bmatrix} u(k).$$

Assuming the measure of non-fragility $\alpha = 0.3$, we apply Theorem 3.7 or 3.8, which gives a non-fragile control gain K in (4):

$$K = \begin{bmatrix} -4.0650 & -0.8131 \end{bmatrix}.$$

Next, we consider a uncertain time-delay system

$$\begin{aligned} \begin{bmatrix} 1 & 0 \\ 0 & 0 \end{bmatrix} x(k+1) &= \left(\begin{bmatrix} 1 & 0.2 \\ 0.1 & 0.3 \end{bmatrix} + \begin{bmatrix} 0.06 \\ 0.08 \end{bmatrix} F(k) \begin{bmatrix} 0.1 & 0 \end{bmatrix} \right) x(k) \\ &\quad + \begin{bmatrix} 1 & 0.2 \\ 0.1 & 0.3 \end{bmatrix} x(k-3) + \begin{bmatrix} 0.1 \\ 0.2 \end{bmatrix} u(k). \end{aligned}$$

Assuming the measure of non-fragility $\alpha = 0.35$, we apply Theorem 5.5 or 5.6, which gives a non-fragile control gain K in (4):

$$K = \begin{bmatrix} -0.6349 & -1.9048 \end{bmatrix}.$$

http://dx.doi.org/10.5772/51538

7. Conclusions

In this chapter, we investigated non-fragile control system analysis and design for uncertain discrete-time descriptor systems when the controller has some uncertainty in gain matrix. The controller is assumed to have multiplicative uncertainty in gain matrix. First, the robust admissibility of uncertain descriptor systems was discussed and the non-fragile control design methods were proposed. Then, theory was developed to the robust admissibility with H_∞ disturbance attenuation. Necessary and Sufficient conditions for the robust admissibility with H_∞ disturbance attenuation were obtained. Based on such conditions, the H_∞ non-fragile controller design methods were proposed. Next, uncertain descriptor systems with delay were considered. Based on system analysis of such systems, the non-fragile control design methods were proposed. Numerical examples were finally given to illustrate our controller design methods.

Author details

Jun Yoneyama, Yuzu Uchida and Ryutaro Takada

Department of Electronics and Electrical Engineering, College of Science and Engineering, Aoyama Gakuin University, Japan

References

[1] Boukas, E.K. & Liu, Z.K. Delay-dependent stability analysis of singular linear continuous-time system, IEE Proceedings on Control Theory and Applications, 2003;150 325-330.

[2] Chen, S.-H. & Chou, J.-H. Stability robustness of linear discrete singular time-delay systems with structured parameter uncertainties, IEE Proceedings on Control Theory and Applications, 2003;150 295-302.

[3] Chen, S.-J. & Lin, J.-L. Robust stability of discrete time-delay uncertain singular systems, IEE Proceedings on Control Theory and Applications, 2004;151 45-52.

[4] Dai, L. Singular Control Systems, Springer, Berlin, Germany; 1981.

[5] Du, H.: Lam, J. and Sze, K. Y. Non-fragile output feedback H_∞ vehicle suspension control using genetic algorithm, Engineering Applications of Artificial Intelligence, 2003;16 667-680.

[6] Fridman, E. Stability of linear descriptor system with delay: a Lyapunov-based approach, Journal of Mathematical Analysis and Applications, 2002;273 24-44.

[7] Fridman, E. & Shaked, U. H_∞-control of linear state-delay descriptor systems: an LMI approach, Linear Algebra and its Applications, 2002;351 271-302.

[8] Fridman, E. & Shaked, U. Stability and guaranteed cost control of uncertain discrete delay systems, International Journal of Control, 2005;78 235-246.

[9] Fridman, E. & Shaked, U. Delay-dependent H_∞ control of uncertain discrete delay systems, European Journal of Control, 2005;11 29-37.

[10] Gao, H., Lam, J., Wang, C. & Wang, Y. delay-dependent output feedback stabilization of discrete-time systems with time-varying state delay, IEE Proc. Control Theory Appl., 2004;151 691-698.

[11] Gao, H. & Chen, T. New results on stability of discrete-time systems with time-varying state delay, IEEE Transactions on Automatic Control, 2007;52 328-334.

[12] Hara, M. & Yoneyama, J. New robust stability condition for uncertain discrete-time systems with time-varying delay, in SICE Annual Conference 2008, 2008;743-747, Tokyo, August 2008.

[13] Hara, M. & Yoneyama, J. An improved robust stability condition for uncertain discrete time-varying delay systems, Journal of Cybernetics and Systems, 2009;2 23-27.

[14] He, Y., Wang, Q., Xie, L. & Lin, C. Further improvement of free-weighting matrices technique for systems with time-varying delay, IEEE Transactions on Automatic Control, 2007;52 293-299.

[15] Hou, Y., Liao, T., Yan, J. & Lien, C. Non-fragile H_∞ control for singular systems with state and input time-varying delays, International Journal of Nonlinear Sciences and Numerical Simulation, 2007;8 31-40.

[16] Kim, J. & Oh, D.-C. Robust and non-fragile H_∞ control for descriptor systems with parameter uncertainties and time delay, International Journal of Control, Automation, and Systems, 2007;5 8-14.

[17] Lin, C., Lam, J., Wang, J.L. & Yang, G.H. Analysis of robust stability for interval descriptor system, Systems and Control Letters, 2001;42 267-278.

[18] Li, X. & de Souza, C. E. Delay dependent robust stability and stabilization of uncertain linear delay systems: a linear matrix inequality approach, IEEE Transactions on Automatic Control, 1997;42 1144-1148.

[19] Lien, C. Non-fragile guaranteed cost control for uncertain neutral dynamic systems with time-varying delays in state and control input, Chaos, Solitons and Fractals, 2007;31 889-899.

[20] Lien, C. H_∞ non-fragile observer-based controls of dynamical systems via LMI optimization approach, Chaos, Solitons and Fractals, 2007;34 428-436.

[21] Lien, C. Cheng, W. Tsai, C. & Yu, K. Non-fragile observer-based controls of linear system via LMI approach, Chaos, Solitons and Fractals, 2007;32 1530-1537.

[22] Lu, G. & Ho, D.W.C. Generalized quadratic stability for continuous-time singular systems with nonlinear perturbation, IEEE Transactions on Automatic Control, 2006;51 818-823.

[23] Lv, L. & Lin, Z. Analysis and design of singular linear systems under actuator saturation and disturbances, Systems and Control Letters, 2008;57 904-912.

[24] Ma, S., Cheng, Z. & Zhang, C. Delay-dependent robust stability and stabilisation for uncertain discrete singular systems with time-varying delays, IEE Proceedings on Control Theory and Applications, 2007;1 1086-1095.

[25] Ma, S., Zhang, C. & Cheng, Z. Delay-dependent Robust H_∞ Control for Uncertain Discrete-Time Singular Systems with Time-Delays, Journal of Computational and Applied Mathematics, 2008;217 194-211.

[26] Mahmoud, M.S. Robust Control and Filtering for Time-Delay Systems, New York: Marcel Dekker, Inc; 2000.

[27] Palhares, R.M., Campos, C.D., Ekel, P. Ya., Leles, M.C.R. & D'Angelo, M.F.S.V. Delay-dependent robust H_∞ control of uncertain linear systems with lumped delays, IEE Proc. Control Theory Appl., 2005;152 27-33

[28] Wo, S., Zou, Y., Chen, Q., & Xu, S. Non-fragile controller design for discrete descriptor systems, Journal of the Franklin Institute, 2009;346 914-922.

[29] Xie, L. Output Feedback H_∞ Control of systems with parameter uncertainty, International Journal of Control, 1996;63, 741-750.

[30] Xie, L. & de Souza, C.E. Robust H_∞ control for linear systems with norm-bounded time-varying uncertainty, IEEE Transactions on Automatic Control, 1992;37 1188-1191.

[31] Xu, S., Van Dooren, P., Stefan, R. and Lam, J. Robust stability and stabilization for singular systems with state delay and parameter uncertainty, IEEE Transactions on Automatic Control, 2002;47 1122-1128.

[32] Xu, S. & Lam, J. Robust Control and Filtering of Singular Systems, Springer-Verlag Berlin Heidelberg; 2006.

[33] Xu, S., Lam, J. & Zou, Y. Improved conditions for delay-dependent robust stability and stabilization of uncertain discrete-time systems, Asian Journal of Control, 2005;7 344-348.

[34] Xu, S., Lam, J. & Zou, Y. New results on delay-dependent robust H_∞ control for systems with time-varying delays, Automatica, 2006;42 343-348.

[35] Ye, D. & Yang, G. H. Adaptive robust H_∞ state feedback control for linear uncertain systems with time-varying delay, International Journal of Adaptive Control and Signal Processing, 2008;22 845-858.

[36] Yoneyama, J. & Tsuchiya, T. New delay-dependent conditions on robust stability and stabilisation for discrete-time systems with time-delay, International Journal of Systems Science, 2008;39 1033-1040.

[37] Zhang, X.-M. & Han, Q.-L. A new finite sum inequality approach to delay-dependent H_∞ control of discrete-time systems with time-varying delay, International Journal of Robust and Nonlinear Control, 2008;18 630-647.

Chapter 3

Delay-Dependent Generalized H_2 Control for Discrete-Time Fuzzy Systems with Infinite-Distributed Delays

Jun-min Li, Jiang-rong Li and Zhi-le Xia

Additional information is available at the end of the chapter

http://dx.doi.org/10.5772/51778

1. Introduction

In recent years, there has been significant interest in the study of stability analysis and controller synthesis for Takagi-Sugeno(T-S) fuzzy systems, which has been used to approximate certain complex nonlinear systems [1]. Hence it is important to study their stability analysis and controller synthesis. A rich body of literature has appeared on the stability analysis and synthesis problems for T-S fuzzy systems [2-6]. However, these results rely on the existence of a common quadratic Lyapunov function (CQLF) for all the local models. In fact, such a CQLF might not exist for many fuzzy systems, especially for highly nonlinear complex systems. Therefore, stability analysis and controller synthesis based on CQLF tend to be more conservative. At the same time, a number of methods based on piecewise quadratic Lyapunov function (PQLF) for T-S fuzzy systems have been proposed in [7-14]. The basic idea of these methods is to design a controller for each local model and to construct a global piecewise controller from closed-loop fuzzy control system is established with a PQLF. The authors in [7,13] considered the information of membership function, a novel piecewise continuous quadratic Lyapunov function method has been proposed for stability analysis of T-S fuzzy systems. It is shown that the PQLF is a much richer class of Lyapunov function candidates than CQLF, it is able to deal with a large class of fuzzy systems and obtained results are less conservative.

On the other hand, it is well known that time delay is a main source of instability and bad performance of the dynamic systems. Recently, a number of important analysis and synthesis results have been derived for T-S fuzzy delay systems [4-7, 11, 13]. However, it should be pointed out that most of the time-delay results for T-S fuzzy systems are constant delay or time-varying delay [4-5, 7, 11, and 13]. In fact, Distributed delay occurs very often in reality and it has been drawing increasing attention. However, almost all existing works on distributed delays have focused on continuous-time systems that are described in the form of either finite or infinite integral and delay-independent. It is well known that the discrete-time system is in a better position to model digitally transmitted signals in a dynamic way than its continuous-time analogue. Generalized H_2 control is an important branch of modern control theories, it is useful for handling stochastic aspects such as measurement noise and random disturbances [10]. Therefore, it becomes desirable to study the generalized H_2 control problem for the discrete-time systems with distributed delays. The authors in [6] have derived the delay-independent robust H_∞ stability criteria for discrete-time T-S fuzzy systems with infinite-distributed delays. Recently, many robust fuzzy control strategies have been proposed a class of nonlinear discrete-time systems with time-varying delay and disturbance [15-33]. These results rely on the existence CLKF for all local models, which lead to be conservative. It is observed, based on the PLKF, the delay-dependent generalized H_2 control problem for discrete-time T-S fuzzy systems with infinite-distributed delays has not been addressed yet and remains to be challenging.

Motivated by the above concerns, this paper deals with the generalized H_2 control problem for a class of discrete time T-S fuzzy systems with infinite-distributed delays. Based on the proposed Delay-dependent PLKF(DDPLKF), the stabilization condition and controller design method are derived for discrete time T-S fuzzy systems with infinite-distributed delays. It is shown that the control laws can be obtained by solving a set of LMIs. A simulation example is presented to illustrate the effectiveness of the proposed design procedures.

Notation: The superscript "T" stands for matrix transposition, R^n denotes the n-dimensional Euclidean space, $R^{n\times m}$ is the set of all $n\times m$ real matrices, I is an identity matrix, the notation $P>0(P\geq 0)$ means that P is symmetric and positive(nonnegative) definite, $diag\{\ldots\}$ stands for a block diagonal matrix. Z^- denotes the set of negative integers. For symmetric block matrices, the notation * is used as an ellipsis for the terms that are induced by symmetry. In addition, matrices, if not explicitly stated, are assumed to have compatible dimensions.

2. Problem Formulation

The following discrete-time T-S fuzzy dynamic systems with infinite-distributed delays [6] can be used to represent a class of complex nonlinear time-delay systems with both local analytic linear models and fuzzy inference rules:

$$R^j: if\ s_1(t)\ is\ F_{j1} and\ s_2(t) is\ F_{j2}\ and \cdots and\ s_g(t) is F_{jg}, then$$

$$\begin{aligned} &x(t+1) = A_j x(t) + A_{dj} \sum_{d=1}^{\infty} \mu_d x(t-d) + B_{1j} u(t) + D_j v(t) \\ &z(t) = C_j x(t) + B_{2j} u(t) \\ &x(t) = \varphi(t) \qquad \forall t \in Z^- \qquad j = 1, 2 \cdots r \end{aligned} \tag{1}$$

where R^j, $j \in N := \{1,2,\ldots,r\}$ denotes the j-th fuzzy inference rule, r the number of the inference rules. F_{ji} (i=1, 2,…, g) are the fuzzy sets, $s(t)=[s_1(t), s_2(t),\ldots, s_g(t)] \in R^s$ the premise variable vector, $x(t)\in R^n$ the state vector, $z(t)\in R^q$ the controlled output vector, $u(t)\in R^m$ the control input vector, $v(t)\in l_2[0\ \infty)$ the disturbance input, $\varphi(t)$ the initial state, and $(A_j, A_{dj}, B_{1j}, D_j, C_j, B_{2j})$ represent the j-th local model of the fuzzy system (1).

The constants $\mu_d \geq 0$ (d =1,2, …) satisfy the following convergence conditions:

$$\bar{\mu} := \sum_{d=1}^{+\infty} \mu_d \leq \sum_{d=1}^{+\infty} d\mu_d < +\infty \tag{2}$$

***Remark* 1.** The delay term $\sum_{d=1}^{+\infty} \mu_d x(t-d)$ in the fuzzy system (1), is the so-called infinitely distributed delay in the discrete-time setting. The description of the discrete-time-distributed delays has been firstly proposed in the [6], and we aim to study the generalized H_2 control problem for discrete-time fuzzy systems with such kind of distributed delays in this paper, which is different from one in [6].

***Remark* 2.** In this paper, similar to the convergence restriction on the delay kernels of infinite-distributed delays for continuous-time systems, the constants μ_d (d =1,2, …)are assumed to satisfy the convergence condition (2), which can guarantee the convergence of the terms of infinite delays as well as the DDPLKF defined later.

By using a standard fuzzy inference method, that is using a center-average defuzzifiers product fuzzy inference, and singleton fuzzifier, the dynamic fuzzy model (1) can be expressed by the following global model:

$$\begin{aligned} &x(t+1) = \sum_{j=1}^{r} h_j(s(t))[A_j x(t) + A_{dj} \sum_{d=1}^{\infty} \mu_d x(t-d) + B_{1j} u(t) + D_j v(t)] \\ &z(t) = \sum_{j=1}^{r} h_j(s(t))[C_j x(t) + B_{2j} u(t)] \end{aligned} \tag{3}$$

where $h_j(s(t)) = \dfrac{\omega_j(s(t))}{\sum_{j=1}^{r} \omega_j(s(t))}$, $\omega_j(s(t)) = \prod_{i=1}^{g} F_{ji}(s(t))$, with $F_{ji}(s(t))$ being the grade of membership of $s_i(t)$inF_{ij},$\omega_j(s(t)) \geq 0$ has the following basic property:

$$\omega_j(s(t)) \geq 0, \sum_{j=1}^{r} \omega_j(s(t)) > 0, j \in N \quad \forall t \tag{4}$$

and therefore

$$h_j(s(t)) \geq 0, \sum_{j=1}^{r} h_j(s(t)) = 1, j \in N \quad \forall t \tag{5}$$

In order to facilitate the design of less conservative H_2 controller, we partition the premise variable space $\Omega \subseteq R^s$ into m polyhedral regions Ω_i by the boundaries [7]

$$\partial\Omega_i^v = \{s(t) \mid h_i(s(t)) = 1, 0 \leq \underset{0<|\delta|<1}{h_i(s(t+\delta))} < 1, i \in N\} \tag{6}$$

where v is the set of the face indexes of the polyhedral hull with satisfying $\partial\Omega_i = \cup_v (\partial\Omega_i^v)$

Based on the boundaries (6), m independent polyhedral regions Ω_l, $l \in L = \{1, 2 \cdots m\}$ can be obtained satisfying

$$\Omega_l \cap \Omega_j = \partial\Omega_i^v, l \neq j, l, j \in L \tag{7}$$

where L denotes the set of polyhedral region indexes.

In each region Ω_l, we define the set

$$M(l) := \{i \mid h_i(s(t)) > 0, s(t) \in \Omega_l, i \in N\}, l \in L \tag{8}$$

Considering (5) and (8), in each region Ω_l, we have

$$\sum_{i \in M(l)} h_i(s(t)) = 1 \tag{9}$$

and then, the fuzzy infinite-distributed delays system (1) can be expressed as follows:

$$\begin{aligned} x(t+1) &= \sum_{i \in M(l)} h_i(s(t))[A_i x(t) + A_{di} \sum_{d=1}^{\infty} \mu_d x(t-d) + B_{1i} u(t) + D_i v(t)] \\ z(t) &= \sum_{i \in M(l)} h_i(s(t))[C_i x(t) + B_{2i} u(t)] \qquad s(t) \in \Omega_l \end{aligned} \tag{10}$$

***Remark* 3.** According to the definition of (8), the polyhedral regions can be divided into two folds: operating and interpolation regions. For an operating region, the set *M(l)* contains only one element, and then, the system dynamic is governed by the *s*-th local model of the fuzzy system. For an interpolation region, the system dynamic is governed by a convex combination of several local models.

In this paper, we consider the generalized H_2 controller design problem for the fuzzy system (1) or equivalently (10), give the following assumptions.

***Assumption* 1.** When the state of the system transits from the region Ω_l to Ω_j at the time *t*, the dynamics of the system is governed by the dynamics of the region model of Ω_l at that time *t*.

For future use, we define a setΘthat represents all possible transitions from one region to itself or another regions, that is

$$\Theta = \{(l,j) \mid s(t) \in \Omega_l, s(t+1) \in \Omega_j \forall l, j \in L\} \tag{11}$$

Here $l = j$, when the system stays in the same region Ω_l, and $l \neq j$, when the system transits from the region Ω_l to another one Ω_j.

Considering the fuzzy system (10), choose the following non-fragile piecewise state feedback controller

$$u(t) = -(K_l + \Delta K_l)x(t) \qquad s(t) \in \Omega_l \quad l \in L \tag{12}$$

here ΔK_l are unknown real matrix functions representing time varying parametric uncertainties, which are assumed to be of the form

$$\Delta K_l = E_l U_l(t) H_l, U_l^T(t) U_l(t) \le I, U_l(t) \in R^{l_1 \times l_2} \tag{13}$$

where E_l, H_l are known constant matrices, and $U_l(t) \in R^{l_1 \times l_2}$ are unknown real time varying matrix satisfying$\Delta U_l^T(t) \Delta U_l \le I$.

Then, the closed-loop T-S system is governed by

$$\begin{aligned} x(t+1) &= \bar{A}_{cl} x(t) + A_{dl} \sum_{d=1}^{\infty} \mu_d x(t-d) + D_l v(t) \\ z(t) &= \bar{C}_{cl} x(t) \end{aligned} \tag{14}$$

for $s(t) \in \Omega_l$, $l \in L$ where

$$\bar{A}_{cl}=\sum_{i\in M(l)} h_i A_{il},\ A_{dl}=\sum_{i\in M(l)} h_i A_{di},\ D_l=\sum_{i\in M(l)} h_i D_i,\ \bar{C}_{cl}=\sum_{i\in M(l)} h_i C_{il}$$

$$A_{il}=A_i-B_{1i}\bar{K}_l,\ C_{il}=C_i-B_{2i}\bar{K}_l$$

Before formulation the problem to be investigated, we first introduce the following concept for the system (14).

***Definition* 1.** [10] Let a constant $\gamma>0$ be given. The closed-loop fuzzy system (14) is said to be stable with generalized H_2 performance if both of the following conditions are satisfied:

- The disturbance-free fuzzy system is globally asymptotically stable.
- Subject to assumption of zero initial conditions, the controlled output satisfies

$$\| z \|_\infty < \gamma \| v \|_2 \tag{15}$$

for all non-zero v $\in I_2$.

Now, we introduce the following lemmas that will be used in the development of our main result.

***Lemma* 1.**[6] Let $M\in R^{n\times n}$ be a positive semi-definite matrix, $x_i(t)\in R^n$and constant

$a_i>0(i=1,\ 2,\ \cdots)$, if the series concerned is convergent, then we have

$$(\sum_{i=1}^{\infty} a_i x_i)^T M(\sum_{i=1}^{\infty} a_i x_i)\le(\sum_{i=1}^{\infty} a_i)\sum_{i=1}^{\infty} a_i x_i M x_i \tag{16}$$

***Lemma* 2.** [14] For the real matrices $P_1,\ P_2,\ P_3,\ P_4,\ A,\ A_d,\ B,\ X_j(j=1,\cdots,5)$ and $D_i(i=1,\cdots,10)$ with compatible dimensions, the inequalities show in (17) and (18) at the following are equivalent, where U is an extra slack nonsingular matrix.

$$(a)\quad \begin{bmatrix} He\{P_1^T A\}+D_1 & P_1^T A_d + A^T P_2 + D_2 & A^T P_3 + D_3 & A^T P_4 + P_1^T B + D_4 & X_1 \\ * & He\{P_2^T A_d\}+D_5 & A_d^T P_3 + D_6 & A_d^T P_4 + P_2^T B + D_7 & X_2 \\ * & * & D_8 & P_3^T B + D_9 & X_3 \\ * & * & * & He\{B^T P_4\}+D_{10} & X_4 \\ * & * & * & * & X_5 \end{bmatrix}<0 \tag{17}$$

http://dx.doi.org/10.5772/51778

$$(b)\quad \begin{bmatrix} -He\{U\} & P_1+U^TA_2 & P_2+U^TA_d & P_3 & P_4+U^TB & 0 \\ * & D_1 & D_2 & D_3 & D_4 & X_1 \\ * & * & D_5 & D_6 & D_7 & X_2 \\ * & * & * & D_8 & D_9 & X_3 \\ * & * & * & * & D_{10} & X_4 \\ * & * & * & * & * & X_5 \end{bmatrix} < 0 \tag{18}$$

where $He\{*\}$ stands for $* + *^T$.

3. Main Results

Based on the proposed partition method, the following DDPLKF is proposed to develop the stability condition for the closed-loop system of (14).

$$\begin{aligned} &V(t) = V_1(t) + V_2(t) + V_3(t) \\ &V_1(t) = 2x(t)^T \overline{P}_l x(t),\ V_2(t) = \sum_{d=1}^{\infty} \mu_d \sum_{k=t-d}^{t-1} x(k)^T \overline{Q} x(k) \\ &V_3(t) = \sum_{d=1}^{\infty} \mu_d \sum_{i=-d}^{-1} \sum_{l=t+i}^{t-1} \eta(l)^T \overline{Z} \eta(l) \qquad\qquad l \in L \end{aligned} \tag{19}$$

where $\overline{P}_l = F^{-T} P_l F$, $\overline{Q} = F^{-T} QF$, $\overline{Z} = F^{-T} ZF$, and $P_l,\ Q,\ Z > 0$, F is nonsingular matrix, and $\eta(t) = x(t+1) - x(t)$.

Then, we are ready to present the generalized H$_2$ stability condition of (14) in terms of LMIs as follows

***Theorem* 1.** Given a constant $\gamma > 0$, the closed-loop fuzzy system (14) with infinite distributed delays is stable with generalized H$_2$ performance γ, if there exists a set of positive definite matrices $P_l,\ Q,\ Z > 0$, the nonsingular matrix F and matrices $X_{li},\ Y_{li},\ l \in L$, $i = 1, \cdots, 4$ satisfying the following LMIs:

$$C_{il}^T C_{il} - \gamma^2 P_l < 0 \quad i \in M(l), l \in L \tag{20}$$

$$\Pi_{ill} < 0 \quad i \in M(l), l \in L \tag{21}$$

$$\Pi_{ilj} < 0 \quad i \in M(l), (l, j) \in \Theta \tag{22}$$

where

$$\Pi_{ilj}=\begin{bmatrix} -He\{F\} & \Lambda_{ilj} & Y_{l_2}+A_{di}F & P_j+Y_{l_3} & Y_{l_4}+D_i & 0 \\ * & \Sigma_{l1} & \Sigma_{l2} & \Sigma_{l3} & \Sigma_{l4} & X_{l1} \\ * & * & \Sigma_{l5} & \Sigma_{l6} & \Sigma_{l7} & X_{l2} \\ * & * & * & \Sigma_{l8} & \Sigma_{l9} & X_{l3} \\ * & * & * & * & \Sigma_{l10} & X_{l4} \\ * & * & * & * & * & (-\sum_{d=1}^{\infty} d\mu_d)^{-1}Z \end{bmatrix}$$

with

$$\Lambda_{ilj}=P_j+Y_{l1}+A_iF-B_{1i}\bar{K}_lF,$$
$$\Sigma_{l1}=\bar{\mu}Q-2P_l+\mathrm{He}\{\bar{\mu}X_{l1}-Y_{l1}\},\ \Sigma_{l2}=-X_{l1}+X_{l2}^T-Y_{l2},\ \Sigma_{l3}=X_{l3}-Y_{l1}^T-Y_{l3},$$
$$\Sigma_{l4}=X_{l4}^T+Y_{l4},\ \Sigma_{l5}=\frac{1}{\bar{\mu}}Q-\mathrm{He}\{X_{l2}\},\ \Sigma_{l6}=-X_{l3}^T-Y_{l2},\ \Sigma_{l7}=X_{l4},$$
$$\Sigma_{l8}=\sum_{d=1}^{\infty}\mu_d dZ-\mathrm{He}\{Y_{l3}\},\ \Sigma_{l9}=Y_{l4}{}^T,\ \Sigma_{l10}=-I.$$

Proof. Taking the forward difference of (19) along the solution of the system (14), we have $\Delta V(t)=V(t+1)-V(t)=\Delta V_1+\Delta V_2+\Delta V_3$

Assuming that $s(t)\in\Omega_l$, $s(t+1)\in\Omega_j$. The difference of $V_i(t)$, $i=1,2,3$ can be calculated, respectively, showing at the following

$$\Delta V_1(t)=2[\bar{A}_{cl}x(t)+A_{dl}\sum_{d=1}^{\infty}\mu_d x(t-d)+D_l v(t)]^T\bar{P}_j[\eta(t)+x(t)]-2x^T(t)\bar{P}_l x(t) \quad (23)$$

$$\begin{aligned}\Delta V_2(t)&=\sum_{d=1}^{\infty}\mu_d\sum_{\tau=t+1-d}^{t}x^T(\tau)\bar{Q}x(\tau)-\sum_{d=1}^{\infty}\mu_d\sum_{\tau=t-d}^{t-1}x^T(\tau)\bar{Q}x(\tau)\\&=\bar{\mu}x^T(t)\bar{Q}x(t)-\sum_{d=1}^{\infty}\mu_d x^T(t-d)\bar{Q}x(t-d)\end{aligned} \quad (24)$$

From Lemma1, we have

$$-\sum_{d=1}^{\infty}\mu_d x^T(t-d)\bar{Q}x(t-d)\le-\frac{1}{\bar{\mu}}(\sum_{d=1}^{\infty}\mu_d x(t-d))^T\bar{Q}(\sum_{d=1}^{\infty}\mu_d x(t-d)) \quad (25)$$

Substituting (25) into (24), we have

$$\Delta V_2(t)\le\bar{\mu}x^T(t)\bar{Q}x(t)-\frac{1}{\bar{\mu}}(\sum_{d=1}^{\infty}\mu_d x(t-d))^T\bar{Q}(\sum_{d=1}^{\infty}\mu_d x(t-d)) \quad (26)$$

$$\Delta V_3(t)=\sum_{d=1}^{\infty}\mu_d d\eta(t)^T\overline{Z}\eta(t)-\sum_{d=1}^{\infty}\mu_d\sum_{l=t-d}^{t-1}\eta(l)^T\overline{Z}\eta(l) \tag{27}$$

Observing of the definition of $\eta(t)$and system (14), we can get the following equations:

$$\begin{aligned}\Xi_1&=2[x^T(t)\overline{X}_{l1}+\sum_{d=1}^{\infty}\mu_d x^T(t-d)\overline{X}_{l2}+\eta^T(t)\overline{X}_{l3}+v^T(t)X_{l4}U]\\&\times[\overline{\mu}x(t)-\sum_{d=1}^{\infty}\mu_d x^T(t-d)-\sum_{d=1}^{\infty}\mu_d\sum_{l=t-d}^{t-1}\eta(l)]=0\end{aligned} \tag{28}$$

$$\begin{aligned}\Xi_2&=2[x^T(t)\overline{Y}_{l1}+\sum_{d=1}^{\infty}\mu_d x^T(t-d)\overline{Y}_{l2}+\eta^T(t)\overline{Y}_{l3}+v^T(t)Y_{l4}U]\\&\times[(\overline{A}_{li}-I)x(t)+A_{di}+D_i v(t)-\eta(t)]=0\end{aligned} \tag{29}$$

where $\overline{X}_{li}=F^{-T}X_{li}F^{-1}(i=1,2,3)$

Since $\pm 2a^Tb\le a^TMa+b^TM^{-1}b$holds for compatible vectors$a$and$b$, and any compatible matrix $M>0$, we have

$$\begin{aligned}&-2[x^T(t)\overline{X}_{l1}+\sum_{d=1}^{\infty}\mu_d x^T(t-d)\overline{X}_{l2}+\eta^T(t)\overline{X}_{l3}+v^T(t)X_{l4}U]\times\sum_{d=1}^{\infty}\mu_d\sum_{l=t-d}^{t-1}\eta(l)\\&\le\sum_{d=1}^{\infty}d\mu_d\xi^T(t)\begin{bmatrix}\overline{X}_{l1}\\\overline{X}_{l2}\\\overline{X}_{l3}\\X_{l4}U\end{bmatrix}\overline{Z}^{-1}\begin{bmatrix}\overline{X}_{l1}\\\overline{X}_{l2}\\\overline{X}_{l3}\\X_{l4}U\end{bmatrix}^T\xi(t)+\sum_{d=1}^{\infty}\mu_d\sum_{l=t-d}^{t-1}\eta(l)\overline{Z}\eta(l)\end{aligned} \tag{30}$$

with$\xi(t)=[x^T(t),\ \sum_{d=1}^{\infty}\mu_d x^T(t-d),\ \eta^T(t),\ v^T(t)]^T$

Then, from (23-30) and considering (14), we have

$$\Delta V(t)-v^T(t)v(t)+v^T(t)v(t)+\Xi_1+\Xi_2\le\sum_{i\in M(l)}h_i\xi^T(t)\Psi_{ilj}\xi(t)+v^T(t)v(t) \tag{31}$$

where

$$\Psi_{ilj} = \begin{bmatrix} \Phi^1_{ilj} & \Phi^2_{ilj} & \Phi^3_{ilj} & \Phi^4_{ilj} \\ * & \Phi^5_{ilj} & \Phi^6_{ilj} & \Phi^7_{ilj} \\ * & * & \Phi^8_{ilj} & \Phi^9_{ilj} \\ * & * & * & \Phi^{10}_{ilj} \end{bmatrix} + \sum_{d=1}^{\infty} d\mu_d \begin{bmatrix} \overline{X}_{l1} \\ \overline{X}_{l2} \\ \overline{X}_{l3} \\ X_{l4}U \end{bmatrix} \overline{Z}^{-1} \begin{bmatrix} \overline{X}_{l1} \\ \overline{X}_{l2} \\ \overline{X}_{l3} \\ X_{l4}U \end{bmatrix}^T \tag{32}$$

with

$$\begin{aligned}
&\Phi_{l1} = \mathrm{He}\{(\overline{P}_j + \overline{Y}_{l1})^T \overline{A}_{li}\} + \overline{\mu} Q - 2\overline{P}_l + \mathrm{He}\{\overline{\mu}\overline{X}_{l1} - \overline{Y}_{l1}\} \\
&\Phi_{l2} = (\overline{P}_j + \overline{Y}_{l1})^T A_{di} + \overline{A}_{li}^T \overline{Y}_{l2} - \overline{X}_{l1} + \overline{X}_{l2}^T - \overline{Y}_{l2}, \Phi_{l3} = \overline{A}_{li}^T (\overline{P}_j + \overline{Y}_{l1}) + \overline{X}_{l3} + \overline{Y}_{l1}^T - \overline{Y}_{l3} \\
&\Phi_{l4} = (\overline{P}_j + \overline{Y}_{l1})^T D_i + \overline{A}_{li}^T U^T Y_{l4} + U^T X_{l4}^T + U^T Y_{l4} \\
&\Phi_{l5} = \mathrm{He}\{\overline{Y}_{l2}^T A_{di}\} - \frac{1}{\overline{\mu}} Q - \mathrm{He}\{\overline{X}_{l2}\}, \Phi_{l6} = A_{di}^T (\overline{P}_j + \overline{Y}_{l3}) - \overline{X}_{l3}^T - \overline{Y}_{l2}^T \\
&\Phi_{l7} = A_{di}^T U Y_{l4} + \overline{Y}_{l2}^T D_i - U X_{l4}^T, \Phi_{l8} = \sum_{d=1}^{\infty} \mu_d d \overline{Z} - \mathrm{He}\{\overline{Y}_{l3}\} \\
&\Phi_{l9} = (\overline{P}_j + \overline{Y}_{l3})^T D_i - U^T Y_{l4}, \Phi_{l10} = \mathrm{He}\{D_i^T U^T Y_{l4}\} - I
\end{aligned}$$

Then

$$\Delta V(t) - v^T(t) v(t) < 0 \tag{33}$$

if

$$\Psi_{ilj} < 0 \tag{34}$$

Using lemma 2, (32) is equivalent to (33)

$$\Xi_{ilj} = \begin{bmatrix} -He\{U\} & \overline{P}_i + \overline{Y}_{l1} + U^T \overline{A}_{li} & \overline{Y}_{l2} + U^T A_{di} & \overline{P}_j + \overline{Y}_{l3} & U^T (Y_{l4} + D_i) & 0 \\ * & \overline{\Sigma}_{l1} & \overline{\Sigma}_{l2} & \overline{\Sigma}_{l3} & U\Sigma_{l4} & \overline{X}_{l1} \\ * & * & \overline{\Sigma}_{l5} & \overline{\Sigma}_{l6} & U\Sigma_{l7} & \overline{X}_{l1} \\ * & * & * & \overline{\Sigma}_{l8} & U\Sigma_{l9} & \overline{X}_{l1} \\ * & * & * & * & \Sigma_{l10} & X_{l4}U \\ * & * & * & * & * & (-\sum_{d=1}^{\infty} \mu_d d)^{-1} \overline{Z} \end{bmatrix} \tag{35}$$

where $\overline{\Sigma}_{li} = F^{-T}\Sigma_{li}F^{-1}(i = 1, 2, 3, 5, 6, 8, 10)$

Let $U = F^{-1}$, $G = diag(F, F, F, F, I, F)$, pre- and post multiplying (35) by G^T, G respectively, then Ξ_{ilj} is equivalent to Π_{ilj}.

Thus, if (21) and (22) holds, (32) is satisfied, which implies that

$$\Delta V(t) < v^T(t)v(t) \tag{36}$$

It is noted that if the disturbance term $v(t) = 0$, it follows from (31) that

$$\Delta V(t) < \sum_{i \in M(l)} h_i \zeta^T(t)\Omega_{ilj}\zeta(t) \tag{37}$$

with $\zeta(t) = [x^T(t), \sum_{d=1}^{\infty} \mu_d x^T(t-d), \eta^T(t)]^T$

$$\Omega_{ilj} = \begin{bmatrix} \Phi_{ilj}^1 & \Phi_{ilj}^2 & \Phi_{ilj}^3 \\ * & \Phi_{ilj}^5 & \Phi_{ilj}^6 \\ * & * & \Phi_{ilj}^8 \end{bmatrix} + \sum_{d=1}^{\infty} d\mu_d \begin{bmatrix} \overline{X}_{l1} \\ \overline{X}_{l2} \\ \overline{X}_{l3} \end{bmatrix} \overline{Z}^{-1} \begin{bmatrix} \overline{X}_{l1} \\ \overline{X}_{l2} \\ \overline{X}_{l3} \end{bmatrix}^{\mathrm{T}} \tag{38}$$

By Schur's complement, LMI (32) implies $\Omega_{ilj} < 0$, then $\Delta V(t) < 0$. Therefore, the closed-loop system (14) with v(t) = 0 is globally asymptotically stable.

Now, to establish the generalized H_2 performance for the closed-loop system (14), under zero-initial condition, and v(t)≠0, taking summation for the both sides of (36) leads to

$$V(x(\mathrm{T}+1)) < \sum_{t=0}^{\mathrm{T}} v^T(t)v(t) \tag{39}$$

It follows from (20) that

$$\begin{aligned} z^T(t)z(t) = x^T(t)\overline{C}_{cl}^T\overline{C}_{cl}x(t) = \sum_{i \in M(l)} h_i \lambda^T(t) \begin{bmatrix} C_{il}^T C_{il} & 0 & 0 \\ 0 & 0 & 0 \\ 0 & 0 & 0 \end{bmatrix} \lambda(t) \\ < \gamma^2 \lambda^T(t) \begin{bmatrix} P & 0 & 0 \\ 0 & Q & 0 \\ 0 & 0 & Z \end{bmatrix} \lambda(t) = \gamma^2 V(t) \end{aligned} \tag{40}$$

with

$$\Lambda(t)=\left[x(t),\ \sum_{d=1}^{\infty}\mu_d\sum_{\tau=t-d}^{t-1}x(\tau),\ \sum_{d=1}^{\infty}\mu_d\sum_{i=-d}^{-1}\sum_{l=t-d}^{t-1}\eta(l)\right]$$

From (39) and (40), we have

$$\|z(t)\|_{\infty}^{2}<\gamma^{2}\|v(t)\|_{2}^{2} \tag{41}$$

The proof is completed.

The following theorem shows that the desired controller parameters and considered controller uncertain can be determined based on the results of Theorem 1.This can be easily proved along the lines of Theorem 1, and we, therefore, only keep necessary details in order to avoid unnecessary duplication.

***Theorem* 2.** Consider the uncertain terms (12). Given a constant$\gamma>0$, the closed-loop fuzzy system (14) with infinite-distributed delays is stable with generalized H_2 performanceγ, if there exists a set of positive definite matricesP_l, Q, $Z>0$, the nonsingular matrix F and matrices X_{li}, Y_{li}, M_l, $l\in L$, i=1,2,3,4satisfying the following LMIs:

$$\begin{bmatrix} -P_l & C_iF-B_{2i}M_l & -B_{2i}H_lF \\ * & -\gamma^2 I+\varepsilon_l E_l^T E_l & 0 \\ * & * & -\varepsilon_l I \end{bmatrix}<0 \quad i\in M(l),l\in L \tag{42}$$

$$\Upsilon_{ill}<0 \quad i\in M(l),l\in L \tag{43}$$

$$\Upsilon_{ilj}<0 \quad i\in M(l),(l,j)\in\Theta \tag{44}$$

where

$$ilj=\begin{bmatrix} -He\{F\} & T_{ilj} & Y_{l_2}+A_{di}F & P_j+Y_{l_3} & Y_{l_4}+D_i & 0 & 0 \\ * & \Sigma_{l1} & \Sigma_{l2} & \Sigma_{l3} & \Sigma_{l4} & X_{l1} & -B_{1i}H_lF \\ * & * & \Sigma_{l5} & \Sigma_{l6} & \Sigma_{l7} & X_{l2} & 0 \\ * & * & * & \Sigma_{l8} & \Sigma_{l9} & X_{l3} & 0 \\ * & * & * & * & \Sigma_{l10} & X_{l4} & 0 \\ * & * & * & * & * & \Gamma_l & 0 \\ * & * & * & * & * & * & -\varepsilon_l I \end{bmatrix}$$

with

$$T_{ilj}=P_j+Y_{l1}+A_iF-B_{1i}M_l, \quad \Gamma_l=(-\sum_{d=1}^{\infty}d\mu_d)^{-1}Z+\varepsilon_l E_l^T E_l.$$

Furthermore, the control law is given by

$$K_l=M_lF^{-1} \tag{45}$$

Proof. In (20) and (21), replace $\overline{K_l}$ with $K_l+\Delta K_l$, and then by S-procedure, we can easily obtain the results of this theorem, and the details are thus omitted.

***Remark* 4.** If the global state space replace the transitions Θ and all P_ls in Theorem 2 become a common P, Theorem 2 is regressed to Corollary 1, shown in the following.

***Corollary* 1.** Consider the uncertain terms (12). Given a constant $\gamma>0$, the closed-loop fuzzy system (14) with infinite-distributed delays is stable with generalized H_2 performance γ, if there exists a set of positive definite matrices P_l, Q, $Z>0$, the nonsingular matrix F and matrices X_{li}, Y_{li}, M_l, $l\in L$, $i=1,2,3,4$ satisfying the following LMIs:

$$\begin{bmatrix} -P & C_iF-B_{2i}M_l & -B_{2i}H_lF \\ * & -\gamma^2 I+\varepsilon_l E_l^T E_l & 0 \\ * & * & -\varepsilon_l I \end{bmatrix}<0 \quad i\in M(l), l\in L \tag{46}$$

$$\Upsilon_{il}<0 \quad i\in M(l), l\in L \tag{47}$$

where

$$_{il}=\begin{bmatrix} -He\{F\} & T_{il} & Y_{l_2}+A_{di}F & P_j+Y_{l_3} & Y_{l_4}+D_i & 0 & 0 \\ * & \Sigma_{l1} & \Sigma_{l2} & \Sigma_{l3} & \Sigma_{l4} & X_{l1} & -B_{1i}H_lF \\ * & * & \Sigma_{l5} & \Sigma_{l6} & \Sigma_{l7} & X_{l2} & 0 \\ * & * & * & \Sigma_{l8} & \Sigma_{l9} & X_{l3} & 0 \\ * & * & * & * & \Sigma_{l10} & X_{l4} & 0 \\ * & * & * & * & * & \Gamma_l & 0 \\ * & * & * & * & * & * & -\varepsilon_l I \end{bmatrix}$$

with

$$\mathrm{T}_{il} = P + Y_{l1} + A_i F - B_{1i} M_l,\ \Gamma_l = (-\sum_{d=1}^{\infty} d\mu_d)^{-1} Z + \varepsilon_l E_l^T E_l,$$
$$\Sigma_{l1} = \bar{\mu} Q - 2P + \mathrm{He}\{\bar{\mu} X_{l1} - Y_{l1}\},\ \Sigma_{l2} = -X_{l1} + X_{l2}^T - Y_{l2},\ \Sigma_{l3} = X_{l3} - Y_{l1}^T - Y_{l3},$$
$$\Sigma_{l4} = X_{l4}^T + Y_{l4},\ \Sigma_{l5} = -\frac{1}{\mu} Q - \mathrm{He}\{X_{l2}\},\ \Sigma_{l6} = -X_{l3}^T - Y_{l2},\ \Sigma_{l7} = X_{l4},$$
$$\Sigma_{l8} = \sum_{d=1}^{\infty} \mu_d dZ - \mathrm{He}\{Y_{l3}\},\ \Sigma_{l9} = Y_{l4}^{\ T},\ \Sigma_{l10} = -I.$$

4. Numerical Examples

In this section, we will present two simulation examples to illustrate the controller design method developed in this paper.

***Example* 1.** Consider the following modified Henon system with infinite distributed delays and external disturbance

$$\begin{aligned} x_1(t+1) &= -\{cx_1(t) + (1-c)\sum_{d=1}^{+\infty} \mu_d x_1(t-d)\}^2 + 0.1x_2(t) - 0.5\sum_{d=1}^{+\infty} \mu_d x_2(t-d) + u(t) + 0.1v(t) \\ x_2(t+1) &= x_2(t) - 0.5x_1(t) \\ z_1(t) &= (1-c)x_1(t) + u(t) \\ z_2(t) &= 0.2x_2(t) \end{aligned} \tag{48}$$

where the constant $c \in [0,1]$ is the retarded coefficient.

Let $s(t) = cx_1(t) + (1-c)\sum_{d=1}^{+\infty} \mu_d x_1(t-d)$. Assume that $s(t) \in [-1,1]$. The nonlinear term $s^2(t)$ can be exactly represented as
$s^2(t) = h_1(s(t))(-1)s(t) + h_2(s(t))(1)s(t)$

where the $h_1(s(t))$, $h_2(s(t)) \in [0,1]$, and $h_1(s(t)) + h_2(s(t)) = 1$. By solving the equations, the membership functions $h_1(s(t))$ and $h_2(s(t))$ are obtained as

$$h_1(s(t)) = \frac{1}{2}(1 - s(t)), \quad h_2(s(t)) = \frac{1}{2}(1 + s(t))$$

It can be seen from the aforementioned expressions that $h_1(s(t)) = 1$ and $h_2(s(t)) = 0$ when $s(t) = -1$, and that $h_1(s(t)) = 0$ and $h_2(s(t)) = 1$ when $s(t) = 1$. Then the nonlinear system in (48) can be approximately represented by the following T-S fuzzy model:

$$R^1: if\ s(t)\ is\ -1,\ then$$

$$x(t+1)=A_1x(t)+A_{d1}\sum_{d=1}^{\infty}\mu_d x(t-d)+B_{11}u(t)+D_1V(t)$$

$$z(t)=C_1x(t)+B_{21}u(t)$$

$$R^2: if\ s(t)\ is\ 1,\ then$$

$$x(t+1)=A_2x(t)+A_{d2}\sum_{d=1}^{\infty}\mu_d x(t-d)+B_{12}u(t)+D_2v(t)$$

$$z(t)=C_2x(t)+B_{22}u(t)$$

where

$$A_1=\begin{bmatrix}0.9 & 0.1\\ -0.5 & 1\end{bmatrix},\ A_{1d}=\begin{bmatrix}0.1 & -0.5\\ 0 & 0\end{bmatrix},\ B_{11}=B_{12}=\begin{bmatrix}1\\ 0\end{bmatrix},$$

$$A_2=\begin{bmatrix}-0.9 & 0.1\\ -0.5 & 1\end{bmatrix},\ A_{2d}=\begin{bmatrix}-0.1 & -0.5\\ 0 & 0\end{bmatrix},\ D_1=D_2=\begin{bmatrix}0.1\\ 0\end{bmatrix},$$

$$C_1=C_2=\begin{bmatrix}-0.1 & 0\\ 0 & -0.2\end{bmatrix},\ B_{21}=B_{22}=\begin{bmatrix}1\\ 0\end{bmatrix},\ E_1=E_2=[0.05\ \ 0],$$

$$H_1=H_2=[0.1\ \ 0],$$

$$e_1=10, e_2=11,$$

$$V(t)=0.1\cos(t)\times\exp(-0.05t).$$

The subspaces can be described by

$$\Omega_1=\{s(t)\mid -1\le s(t)\le 0\},\ \Omega_2=\{s(t)\mid 0\le s(t)\le 1\}$$

Choosing the constants $c=0.9$, $\mu_d=2^{-3-d}$, $d=10$ we easily find that $\bar{\mu}=\sum_{d=1}^{\infty}\mu_d=2^{-3}<\sum_{d=1}^{\infty}d\mu_d=2<+\infty$, which satisfies the convergence condition (2).

with the H_2 performance index $\gamma_{\min}=0.11$, we solve (42)-(44) and obtain

$$P_1=\begin{bmatrix}0.1944 & 0.0248\\ 0.0248 & 0.3342\end{bmatrix},\ P_2=\begin{bmatrix}0.1951 & 0.0252\\ 0.0252 & 0.3358\end{bmatrix},\ Q=\begin{bmatrix}0.2876 & 0.0746\\ 0.0746 & 0.1636\end{bmatrix},$$

$$Z=\begin{bmatrix}0.0048 & 0.0019\\ 0.0019 & 0.1275\end{bmatrix},\ F=\begin{bmatrix}0.3939 & 0.1516\\ 0.0476 & 0.6285\end{bmatrix},\ K_1=[-0.0223\ \ 0.1702],$$

$$K_2=[\ -0.0171\ \ 0.1685]\ .$$

Simulation results with the above solutions for the H_2 controller designs are shown Fig.1 and Fig.2

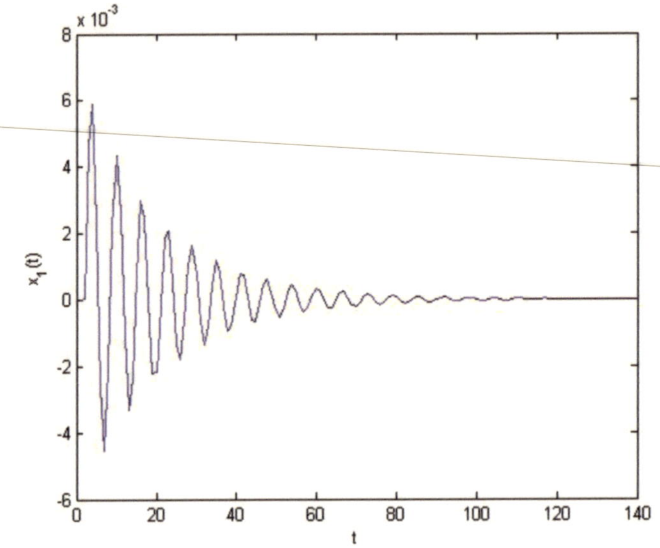

Figure 1. The state evolution $x_1(t)$ of controlled system.

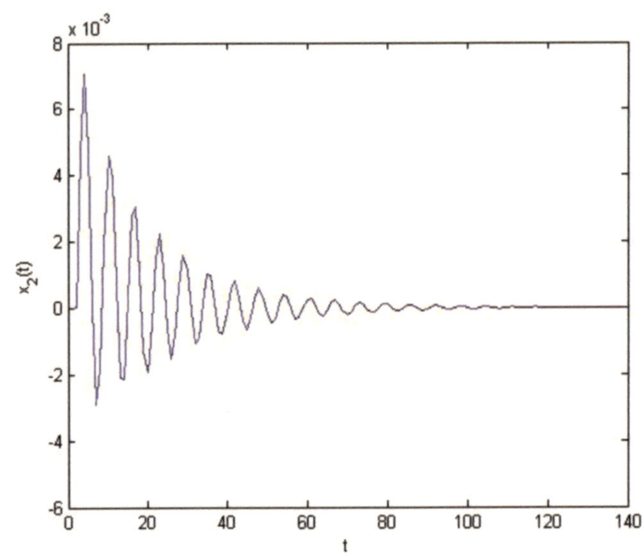

Figure 2. The state evolution $x_2(t)$ of controlled systems.

***Example* 2.** Consider a fuzzy discrete time system with the same form as in Example, but with different system matrices given by

http://dx.doi.org/10.5772/51778

$$A_1=\begin{bmatrix}-0.986 & 0.1\\ -0.5 & 1\end{bmatrix},\ A_{1d}=\begin{bmatrix}-0.1 & -0.5\\ 0 & 0\end{bmatrix},\ B_{11}=\begin{bmatrix}0\\ 0.5\end{bmatrix},\ B_{12}=\begin{bmatrix}1\\ 0\end{bmatrix},$$

$$A_2=\begin{bmatrix}0.5 & -0.6\\ 0.6 & 0.5\end{bmatrix},\ A_{2d}=\begin{bmatrix}-0.05 & -0.6\\ 0 & 0\end{bmatrix},\ D_1=D_2=\begin{bmatrix}0.1\\ 0\end{bmatrix},$$

$$C_1=\begin{bmatrix}-0.02 & 0\\ 0 & -0.1\end{bmatrix},\ C_2=\begin{bmatrix}-0.1 & 0\\ 0 & -0.3\end{bmatrix},\ B_{21}=B_{22}=\begin{bmatrix}1\\ 0\end{bmatrix},$$

$$E_1=E_2=[0.05\ \ 0],\ H_1=H_2=[0.1\ \ 0],e_1=10,e_2=11,\ e_3=12,$$

$$v(t)=0.1\cos(t)\times\exp(-0.05t).$$

We expanded the state space from [-1,1] to [- 3,3], the membership functions are given as

$$h_1(s(t))=\begin{cases}1 & s(t)\in[-3,\ -1],\\ -0.5s(t)+0.5 & s(t)\in[-1,\ 1].\end{cases}$$

$$h_2(s(t))=\begin{cases}0.5s(t)+0.5 & s(t)\in[-1,\ 1],\\ 1 & s(t)\in[1,\ 3].\end{cases}$$

The subspaces are given as shown in Fig.3

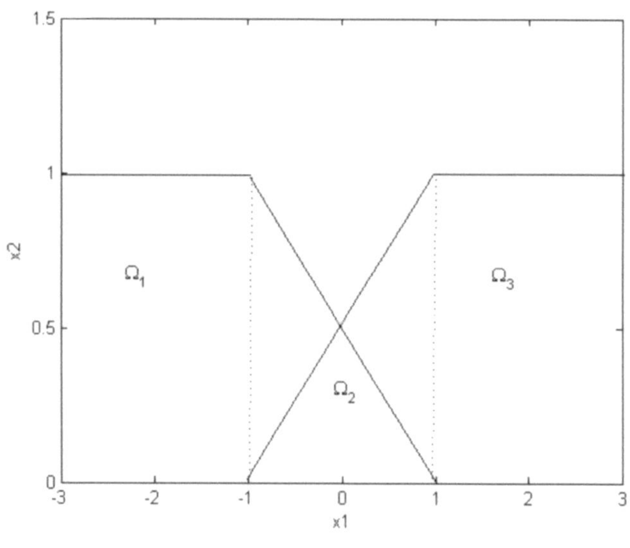

Figure 3. Membership functions and partition of subspaces.

Using the Theorem 2 and Corollary 1, respectively, the achievable minimum performance index for the H_2 controller can be obtained and is summarized in Table 1.

Approach	**Performance**

Common Lyapunov function based generalized H_2 performance (Theorem 2)	γ_{min}=0,4586
Piecewise Lyapunov function based generalized H_2 performance (Corollary1)	γ_{min}=0,3975

Table 1. Comparison for generalized H_2 performance.

By using the LMI toolbox, we have

$$P_1=\begin{bmatrix}1.5359 & 0.5771\\ 0.5771 & 1.4293\end{bmatrix},\ P_2=\begin{bmatrix}1.5254 & 0.6540\\ 0.6540 & 1.5478\end{bmatrix},\ P_3=\begin{bmatrix}1.2754 & 0.5634\\ 0.5634 & 1.4983\end{bmatrix},$$
$$Q=\begin{bmatrix}1.8101 & 0.1568\\ 0.1568 & 0.5915\end{bmatrix},\ Z=\begin{bmatrix}0.0399 & 0.0285\\ 0.0285 & 0.4640\end{bmatrix},\ F=\begin{bmatrix}3.1076 & 0.7119\\ 0.8671 & 2.5352\end{bmatrix},$$
$$K_1=[0.0003\ \ -0.2297],\ K_2=[0.1311\ \ -0.0371],\ K_3=[-0.1125\ \ -0.0005].$$

The simulation results with the initial conditions are shown Fig.4 and Fig.5

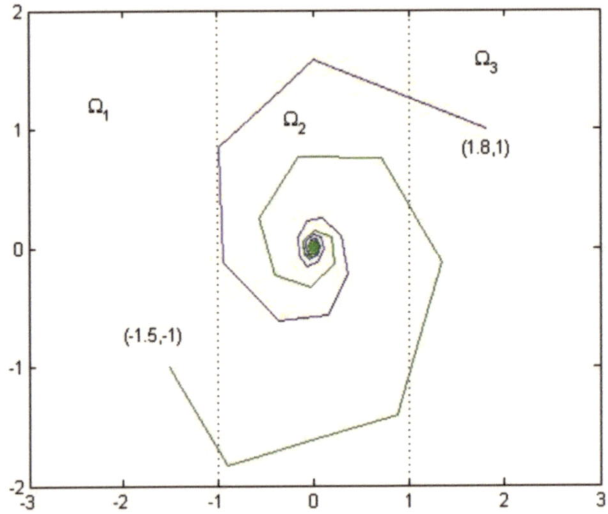

Figure 4. Trajectories from two initial conditions

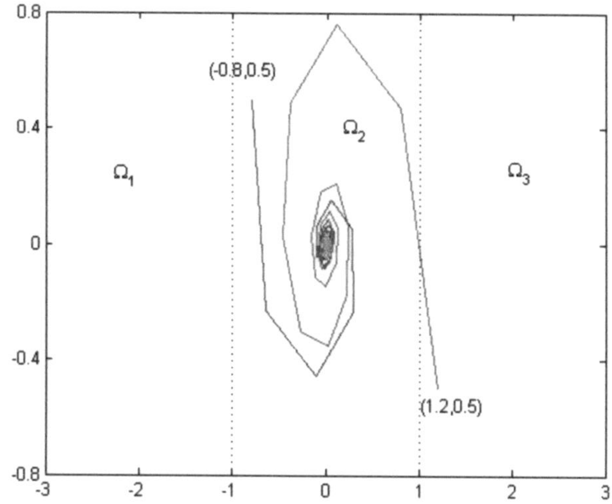

Figure 5. Trajectories from two initial conditions

5. Conclusions

This paper presents delay-dependent analysis and synthesis method for discrete-time T-S fuzzy systems with infinite-distributed delays. Based on a novel DDPLKF, the proposed stability and stabilization results are less conservative than the existing results based on the CLKF and delay independent method. The non-fragile stated feedback controller law has been developed so that the closed-loop fuzzy system is generalized H_2 stable. It is also shown that the controller gains can be determined by solving a set of LMIs. A simulation example was presented to demonstrate the advantages of the proposed approach.

Author details

Jun-min Li[1*], Jiang-rong Li[1,2] and Zhi-le Xia[1,3]

*Address all correspondence to: jmli@mail.xidian.edu.cn

1 Department of Applied Mathematics, Xidian University, China

2 College of mathematics & Computer Science, Yanan University, China

3 School of Mathematics and Information Engineering, Taizhou University, China

References

[1] Takagi, T., & Sugeno, M. (1985). Fuzzy identification of systems and its applications to modeling and control. *IEEE Transactions on Systems, Man, Cybernetics*, 15(1), 116-132.

[2] Zhang, J. H., & Xia, Y. Q. (2009). New results on H_∞ filtering for fuzzy time-delay systems. *IEEE Transactions on Fuzzy Systems*, 17(1), 128-137.

[3] Zhang, B. Y., Zhou, S. S., & Li, T. (2007). A new approach to robust and non-fragile H_∞ control for uncertain fuzzy systems. *Information Sciences*, 17-5118.

[4] Zhou, S. S., & Li, T. (2005). Robust stabilization for delayed discrete-time fuzzy systems via basis dependent Lyapunov-Krasovskii function. *Fuzzy Sets and Systems*, 151-139.

[5] Xu, S. H. Y., & Lam, J. (2005). Robust H_∞ control for uncertain discrete-time delay fuzzy systems via output feedback controllers. *IEEE Transactions on Fuzzy Systems*, 13(1), 82-93.

[6] Wei, G. L., Feng, G., & Wang, Z. D. (2009). Robust H_∞ control for discrete-time fuzzy systems with infinite distributed delays. *IEEE Transactions on Fuzzy Systems*, 17(1), 224-232.

[7] Chen, M., Feng, G. H. B., & Chen, G. (2009). Delay-Dependent H_∞ filter design for discrete-time fuzzy systems with time-varying delays. *IEEE Transactions on Fuzzy Systems*, 17(3), 604-616.

[8] Johansson, M., Rantzer, A., & Arzen, K. E. (1999). Piecewise quadratic stability of fuzzy systems. *IEEE Transactions on Fuzzy Systems*, 7(6), 713-722.

[9] Zhang, H. B., & Dang, C. H. Y. (2008). Piecewise H_∞ controller design of uncertain discrete-time fuzzy systems with time delays. *IEEE Transactions on Fuzzy Systems*, 16(6), 1649-1655.

[10] Wang, L., Feng, G., & Hesketh, T. (2004). Piecewise generalized H_2 controller synthesis of discrete-time fuzzy systems. *IEE Proceeding on Control Theory and Application*, 9-554.

[11] Huang, H., & Feng, G. (2009). Delay-dependent H_∞ and generalized H_2 filtering for delayed neural network. *IEEE Transactions on Circuits, Systems-I: Regular papers,*, 56(4), 846-857.

[12] Zhang, H. B., & Feng, G. (2008). Stability analysis and H_∞ controller design of discrete-time fuzzy Large scale systems based on piecewise Lyapunov functions. *IEEE Transactions on Systems, Man, Cybernetics*, 38(5), 1390-1401.

[13] Chen, C. L., Feng, G., Sun, D., & Guan, X. P. (2005). H_∞ output feedback control of discrete-time fuzzy systems with application to chaos controller. *IEEE Transactions on Fuzzy Systems*, 13(4), 531-543.

[14] Xia, Z. L., & Li, J. M. (2009). Delay-dependent H∞ Control for T-S Fuzzy Systems Based on a Switching Fuzzy Model and Piecewise Lyapunov Function. *Acta Automatica Sinica*, 35(9), 1347-1350.

[15] Li, J. R., Li, J. M., & Xia, Z. L. (2011). Delay-dependent generalized H_2 control for discrete T-S fuzzy large-scale stochastic systems with mixed delays. *International Journal of Applied Mathematics and Computer Science*, 21(4), 585-604.

[16] Li, J. M., & Zhang, G. (2012). Non-fragile guaranteed cost control of T-S fuzzy time-varying state and control delays systems with local bilinear models. *Iranian Journal of Fuzzy Systems*, 9(2), 45-64.

[17] Bing, C., et al. (2007). Guaranteed cost control of T-S fuzzy systems with state and input delays. *Fuzzy Sets and Systems,*, 158-2251.

[18] Chang, W. J., et al. (2011). Robust Fuzzy Control for Discrete Perturbed Time-Delay Affine Takagi-Sugeno Fuzzy Models. *International Journal of Control Automation and Systems*, 9-86.

[19] Chiang, T. S., & Liu, P. (2012). Robust output tracking control for discrete-time nonlinear systems with time-varying delay: Virtual fuzzy model LMI-based approach. *Expert Systems with Applications*, 39-8239.

[20] Choi, H. H. (2010). Robust Stabilization of Uncertain Fuzzy-Time-Delay Systems Using Sliding-Mode-Control Approach. IEEE Transactions on Fuzzy Systems; , 18-979.

[21] Gassara, H., et al. (2010). Observer-Based Robust H-infinity Reliable Control for Uncertain T-S Fuzzy Systems With State Time Delay. IEEE Transactions on Fuzzy Systems; , 18-1027.

[22] Gassara, H., et al. (2010). Robust control of T-S fuzzy systems with time-varying delay using new approach. International Journal of Robust and Nonlinear Control; , 20-1566.

[23] Hu, S., et al. (2012). Robust H-infinity control for T-S fuzzy systems with probabilistic interval time varying delay. *Nonlinear Analysis-Hybrid Systems*, 6-871.

[24] Huang, J., et al. (2010). Robust control of delay-dependent T-S fuzzy system based on method of descriptor model transformation. *Artificial Intelligence Review*, 34-205.

[25] Kchaou, M., et al. (2011). Robust reliable guaranteed cost piecewise fuzzy control for discrete-time nonlinear systems with time-varying delay and actuator failures. *International Journal of General Systems*, 40-531.

[26] Kchaou, M., et al. (2011). Delay-dependent H-infinity resilient output fuzzy control for nonlinear discrete-time systems with time-delay. *International Journal of Uncertainty Fuzziness and Knowledge-Based Systems*, 19-229.

[27] Lien, C. H., et al. (2010). Robust H-infinity control for uncertain T-S fuzzy time-delay systems with sampled-data input and nonlinear perturbations. *Nonlinear Analysis-Hybrid Systems*, 4-550.

[28] Liu, X., et al. (2010). Delay-dependent robust and reliable H-infinity fuzzy hyperbolic decentralized control for uncertain nonlinear interconnected systems. *Fuzzy Sets and Systems*, 161-872.

[29] Mozelli, L. A., et al. (2011). A new discretized Lyapunov-Krasovskii functional for stability analysis and control design of time-delayed T-S fuzzy systems. *International Journal of Robust and Nonlinear Control*, 21-93.

[30] Peng, C., & Han, Q. L. (2011). Delay-range-dependent robust stabilization for uncertain T-S fuzzy control systems with interval time-varying delays. *Information Sciences*, 181-4287.

[31] Wu, Z. G., et al. (2012). Reliable H-infinity Control for Discrete-Time Fuzzy Systems With Infinite-Distributed Delay. *IEEE Transactions on Fuzzy Systems*, 20-22.

[32] Mourad, K., Mansour, S., & Ahmed, T. (2011). Robust H_2 Guaranteed cost fuzzy control for uncertain discrete-time fuzzy systems via poly-quadratic Lyapunov functions. *Asian Journal of Control*, 13(2), 309-316.

[33] Zhang, G., & Li, J. M. (2010). Non-Fragile Guaranteed Cost Control of discrete-time Fuzzy Bilinear System. *Journal of Systems Engineering and Electronics*, 21(4), 629-634.

Section 2

Nonlinear Systems

Chapter 4

Discrete-Time Model Predictive Control

Li Dai, Yuanqing Xia, Mengyin Fu and
Magdi S. Mahmoud

Additional information is available at the end of the chapter

http://dx.doi.org/10.5772/51122

1. Introduction

More than 25 years after model predictive control (MPC) or receding horizon control (RHC) appeared in industry as an effective tool to deal with multivariable constrained control problems, a theoretical basis for this technique has started to emerge, see [1-3] for reviews of results in this area.

The focus of this chapter is on MPC of constrained dynamic systems, both linear and nonlinear, to illuminate the ability of MPC to handle constraints that makes it so attractive to industry. We first give an overview of the origin of MPC and introduce the definitions, characteristics, mathematical formulation and properties underlying the MPC. Furthermore, MPC methods for linear or nonlinear systems are developed by assuming that the plant under control is described by a discrete-time one. Although continuous-time representation would be more natural, since the plant model is usually derived by resorting to first principles equations, it results in a more difficult development of the MPC control law, since it in principle calls for the solution of a functional optimization problem. As a matter of fact, the performance index to be minimized is defined in a continuous-time setting and the overall optimization procedure is assumed to be continuously repeated after any vanishingly small sampling time, which often turns out to be a computationally intractable task. On the contrary, MPC algorithms based on discrete-time system representation are computationally simpler. The system to be controlled which usually described, or approximated by an ordinary differential equation is usually modeled by a difference equation in the MPC literature since the control is normally piecewise constant. Hence, we concentrate our attention from now onwards on results related to discrete-time systems.

By and large, the main disadvantage of the MPC is that it cannot be able of explicitly dealing with plant model uncertainties. For confronting such problems, several robust model predictive control (RMPC) techniques have been developed in recent decades. We review different RMPC methods which are employed widely and mention the advantages and disadvantages of these methods. The basic idea of each method and some method applications are stated as well.

Most MPC strategies consider hard constraints, and a number of RMPC techniques exist to handle uncertainty. However model and measurement uncertainties are often stochastic, and therefore RMPC can be conservative since it ignores information on the probabilistic distribution of the uncertainty. It is possible to adopt a stochastic uncertainty description (instead of a set-based description) and develop a stochastic MPC (SMPC) algorithm. Some of the recent advances in this area are reviewed.

In recent years, there has been much interest in networked control systems (NCSs), that is, control systems close via possibly shared communication links with delay/bandwidth constraints. The main advantages of NCSs are low cost, simple installation and maintenance, and potentially high reliability. However, the use of the network will lead to intermittent losses or delays of the communicated information. These losses will tend to deteriorate the performance and may even cause the system to become unstable. MPC framework is particularly appropriate for controlling systems subject to data losses because the actuator can profit from the predicted evolution of the system. In section 7, results from our recent research are summarized. We propose a new networked control scheme, which can overcome the effects caused by the network delay.

At the beginning of research on NCSs, more attention was paid on single plant through network. Recently, fruitful research results on multi-plant, especially, on multi-agent networked control systems have been obtained. MPC lends itself as a natural control framework to deal with the design of coordinated, distributed control systems because it can account for the action of other actuators while computing the control action of a given set of actuators in real-time. In section 8, a number of distributed control architectures for interconnected systems are reviewed. Attention is focused on the design approaches based on model predictive control.

2. Model Predictive Control

Model predictive control is a form of control scheme in which the current control action is obtained by solving, at each sampling instant, a finite horizon open-loop optimal control problem, using the current state of the plant as the initial state. Then the optimization yields an optimal control sequence and the first control in this sequence is applied to the plant. This is the main difference from conventional control which uses a pre-computed control law.

2.1. Characteristics of MPC

MPC is by now a mature technology. It is fair to mention that it is the standard approach for implementing constrained, multivariable control in the process industries today. Furthermore, MPC can handle control problems where off-line computation of a control law is difficult or impossible.

Specifically, an important characteristic of this type of control is its ability to cope with hard constraints on controls and states. Nearly every application imposes constraints. For instance, actuators are naturally limited in the force (or equivalent) they can apply, safety limits states such as temperature, pressure and velocity, and efficiency, which often dictates steady-state operation close to the boundary of the set of permissible states. In this regard, MPC is one of few methods having applied utility, and this fact makes it an important tool for the control engineer, particularly in the process industries where plants being controlled are sufficiently slow to permit its implementation.

In addition, another important characteristic of MPC is its ability to handle control problems where off-line computation of a control law is difficult or impossible. Examples where MPC may be advantageously employed include unconstrained nonlinear plants, for which online computation of a control law usually requires the plant dynamics to possess a special structure, and time-varying plants.

A fairly complete discussion of several design techniques based on MPC and their relative merits and demerits can be found in the review article by [4].

2.2. Essence of MPC

As mentioned in the excellent review article [2], MPC is not a new method of control design. Rather, it essentially solves standard optimal control problems which is required to have a finite horizon in contrast to the infinite horizon usually employed in $H_2$and H_∞linear optimal control. Where it differs from other controllers is that it solves the optimal control problem on-line for the current state of the plant, rather than providing the optimal control for all states, that is determining a feedback policy on-line.

The on-line solution is to solve an open-loop optimal control problem where the initial state is the current state of the system being controlled which is just a mathematical programming problem. However, determining the feedback solution, requires solution of Hamilton-Jacobi-Bellman (Dynamic Programming) differential or difference equation, a vastly more difficult task (except in those cases, such as $H_2$and H_∞linear optimal control, where the value function can be finitely parameterized). From this point of view, MPC differs from other control methods merely in its implementation. The requirement that the open-loop optimal control problem be solvable in a reasonable time (compared with plant dynamics) necessitates, however, the use of a finite horizon and this raises interesting problems.

3. Linear Model Predictive Control

MPC has become an attractive feedback strategy, especially for linear processes. By now, linear MPC theory is quite mature. The issues of feasibility of the on-line optimization, stability and performance are largely understood for systems described by linear models.

3.1. Mathematical formulation

The idea of MPC is not limited to a particular system description, but the computation and implementation depend on the model representation. Depending on the context, we will readily switch between state space, transfer matrix and convolution type models [4]. In addition, nowadays in the research literature, MPC is formulated almost always in the state space. We will assume the system to be described in state space by a linear discrete-time model.

$$x(k+1)=Ax(k)+Bu(k),\ \ x(0)=x_0 \tag{1}$$

where $x(k)\in\mathbb{R}^n$is the state vector at time$k$, and $u(k)\in\mathbb{R}^r$ is the vector of manipulated variables to be determined by the controller. The control and state sequences must satisfy $u(k)\in\mathsf{U}$, $x(k)\in\mathsf{X}$. Usually, $\mathsf{U}$is a convex, compact subset of $\mathbb{R}^r$ and X convex, closed subset of$\mathbb{R}$^{n}, each set containing the origin in its interior.

The control objective is usually to steer the state to the origin or to an equilibrium state x_r for which the output $y_r=h(x_r)=r$ where $r$is the constant reference. A suitable change of coordinates reduces the second problem to the first which, therefore, we consider in the sequel. Assuming that a full measurement of the state $x(k)$ is available at the current time$k$. Then for event $(x,\ k)$(i.e. for state x at time$k$), a receding horizon implementation is typically formulated by introducing the following open-loop optimization problem.

$$J_{(p,m)}(x(k)) \tag{2}$$

subject to

$$\begin{aligned} &u(k)\in\mathsf{U},\\ &x(k)\in\mathsf{X}, \end{aligned} \tag{3}$$

$(p\geq m)$where$p$ denotes the length of the prediction horizon or output horizon, and m denotes the length of the control horizon or input horizon. (When, $p=\infty$we refer to this as the infinite horizon problem, and similarly, when$p$ is finite, we refer to it as a finite horizon problem). For the problem to be meaningful we assume that the origin $(x=0,\ u=0)$ is in the interior of the feasible region.

Several choices of the objective function $J_{(p,m)}(x(k))$ in the optimization eq.(2) have been reported in [4-7] and have been compared in [8]. In this Chapter, we consider the following quadratic objective

$$
\begin{aligned}
J_{(p,m)}(x(k)) &= \min_{u(\cdot)}[x^T(k+p|k)P_0x(k+p|k)+\sum_{i=0}^{p-1}x^T(k+i|k)Qx(k+i|k) \\
&+ \sum_{i=0}^{m-1}u^T(k+i|k)Ru(k+i|k)]
\end{aligned}
\tag{4}
$$

where $u(\cdot):=[u(k)^T, \ldots, u(k+m-1 \mid k)^T]^T$ is the sequence of manipulated variables to be optimized; $x(k+i \mid k)$, $i=1, 2, \ldots, p$denote the state prediction generated by the nominal model (1) on the basis of the state informations at time $k$under the action of the control sequence $u(k)$, $u(k+1 \mid k)$, ..., $u(k+i-1 \mid k)$; P_0, Q and$R$ are strictly positive definite symmetric weighting matrices. Let $u^*_{(p,m)}(i \mid k)$, $i=k, \ldots, k+m-1$ be the minimizing control sequence for $J_{(p,m)}(x(k))$ subject to the system dynamics (1) and the constraint (3), and $J^*_{(p,m)}$ be the optimizing value function.

A receding horizon policy proceeds by implementing only the first control $u^*_{(p,m)}(k \mid k)$ to obtain$x(k+1)=Ax(k)+Bu^*_{(p,m)}(k \mid k)$. The rest of the control sequence $u^*_{(p,m)}(i \mid k)$, $i=k+1, \ldots, k+m-1$ is discarded and $x(k+1)$ is used to update the optimization problem (2) as a new initial condition. This process is repeated, each time using only the first control action to obtain a new initial condition, then shifting the cost ahead one time step and repeating. This is the reason why MPC is also sometimes referred to as receding horizon control (RHC) or moving horizon control (MHC). The purpose of taking new measurements at each time step is to compensate for unmeasured disturbances and model inaccuracy, both of which cause the system output to be different from the one predicted by the model. Fig.1 presents a conceptual picture of MPC.

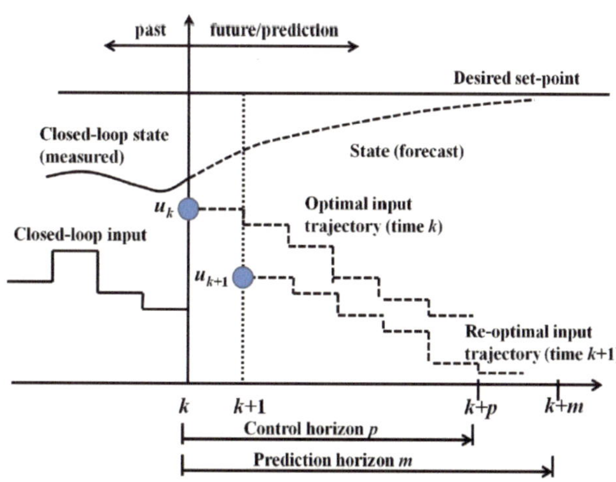

Figure 1. Principle of model predictive control.

Three practical questions are immediate [1]:

1. When is the problem formulated above feasible, so that the algorithm yields a control action which can be implemented?

2. When does the sequence of computed control actions lead to a system which is closed-loop stable?

3. What closed-loop performance results from repeated solution of the specified open-loop optimal control problem?

These questions will be explained in the following sections.

3.2. Feasibility

The constraints stipulated in (3) may render the optimization problem infeasible. It may happen, for example, because of a disturbance, that the optimization problem posed above becomes infeasible at a particular time step. It may also happen, that the algorithm which minimizes an open-loop objective, inadvertently drives the closed-loop system outside the feasible region.

3.3. Closed loop stability

In either the infinite or the finite horizon constrained case it is not clear under what conditions the closed loop system is stable. Much research on linear MPC has focused on this problem. Two approaches have been proposed to guarantee stability: one based on the original problem (1), (2), and (3) and the other where a contraction constraint is added [9, 10]. With the contraction constraint the norm of the state is forced to decrease with time and stability follows trivially independent of the various parameters in the objective function. Without the contraction constraint the stability problem is more complicated.

General proofs of stability for constrained MPC based on the monotonicity property of the value function have been proposed by [11] and [12]. The most comprehensive and also most compact analysis has been presented by [13] and [14] whose arguments we will sketch here.

To simplify the exposition we assume $p=m=N$, then $J_{(p,m)}=J_N$ as defined in eq.(2). The key idea is to use the optimal finite horizon cost J_N^*, the value function, as a Lyapunov function. One wishes to show that

$$J_N^*(x(k))-J_N^*(x(k+1))>0, \quad for\ x\neq 0 \tag{5}$$

Rewriting $J_N^*(x(k))-J_N^*(x(k+1))$ gives,

$$\begin{aligned} J_N^*(x(k))-J_N^*(x(k+1)) &= [x^T(k)Qx(k)+u^{*T}(x(k))Ru^*(x(k))] \\ &\quad +[J_{N-1}^*(x(k+1))-J_N^*(x(k+1))] \end{aligned} \tag{6}$$

If it can be shown that the right hand side of (6) is positive, then stability is proven. Due to $Q>0$ and $R>0$, the first term $[x^T(k)Qx(k)+u^{*T}(x(k))Ru^*(x(k))]$ is positive. In general, it cannot be asserted that the second term $[J_{N-1}^*(x(k+1))-J_N^*(x(k+1))]$ is nonnegative.

Several approaches have been presented to assure that the right hand side of (6) is positive, please refer to [1]. The various constraints introduced to guarantee stability (end constraint for all states, end constraint for unstable modes, terminal region, etc.) may lead to feasibility problems. For instance, the terminal equality constraint may become infeasible unless a sufficiently large horizon is used.

3.4. Open-loop performance objective versus closed loop performance

In receding horizon control only the first of the computed control moves is implemented, and the remaining ones are discarded. Therefore the sequence of actually implemented control moves may differ significantly from the sequence of control moves calculated at a particular time step. Consequently the finite horizon objective which is minimized may have only a tentative connection with the value of the objective function as it is obtained when the control moves are implemented.

4. Nonlinear model predictive control

Linear MPC has been developed, in our opinion, to a stage where it has achieved sufficient maturity to warrant the active interest of researchers in nonlinear control. While linear model predictive control has been popular since the 70s of the past century, the 90s have witnessed a steadily increasing attention from control theorists as well as control practitioners in the area of nonlinear model predictive control (NMPC).

The practical interest is driven by the fact that many systems are in general inherently nonlinear and today's processes need to be operated under tighter performance specifications. At the same time more and more constraints for example from environmental and safety considerations, need to be satisfied. In these cases, linear models are often inadequate to describe the process dynamics and nonlinear models have to be used. This motivates the use of nonlinear model predictive control.

The system to be controlled is described, or approximated by a discrete-time model

$$\begin{aligned} x(k+1) &= f(x(k), u(k)), \\ y(k) &= h(x(k)), \end{aligned} \tag{7}$$

where $f(\cdot)$ is implicitly defined by the originating differential equation that has an equilibrium point at the origin (i.e. $f(0, 0)=0$). The control and state sequences must satisfy (3).

4.1. Difficulties of NMPC

The same receding horizon idea which we discussed in section 3 is also the principle underlying nonlinear MPC, with the exception that the model describing the process dynamics is nonlinear. Contrary to the linear case, however, feasibility and the possible mismatch between the open-loop performance objective and the actual closed loop performance are largely unresolved research issues in nonlinear MPC. An additional difficulty is that the optimization problems to be solved on line are generally nonlinear programs without any redeeming features, which implies that convergence to a global optimum cannot be assured. For the quadratic programs arising in the linear case this is guaranteed. As most proofs of stability for constrained MPC are based on the monotonicity property of the value function, global optimality is usually not required, as long as the cost attained at the minimizer decreases (which is usually the case, especially when the optimization algorithm is initialized from the previous shifted optimal sequence). However, although stability is not altered by local minimum, performance clearly deteriorates.

The next section focuses on system theoretical aspects of NMPC. Especially the question on closed-loop stability is considered.

4.2. Closed-loop stability

One of the key questions in NMPC is certainly, whether a finite horizon NMPC strategy does lead to stability of the closed-loop or not. Here only the key ideas are reviewed and no detailed proofs are given. Furthermore, notice that we will not cover all existing NMPC approaches, instead we refer the reader to the overview papers [2, 15, 16]. For all the following sections it is assumed that the prediction horizon is set equal to the control horizon, that is, $p=m$.

4.2.1. Infinite horizon NMPC

As pointed out, the key problem with a finite prediction and control horizon stems from the fact that the predicted open and the resulting closed-loop behavior is in general different. The most intuitive way to achieve stability is the use of an infinite horizon cost [17, 18], that is, p in (4) is set to ∞. As mentioned in [19], in the nominal case, feasibility at one sampling instance also implies feasibility and optimality at the next sampling instance. This follows from Bellman's Principle of Optimality [20], that is the input and state trajectories computed as the solution of the NMPC optimization problem (2), (3) and (7) at a specific instance in time, are in fact equal to the closed-loop trajectories of the nonlinear system, i.e. the remaining parts of the trajectories after one sampling instance are the optimal solution at the next sampling instance. This fact also implies closed-loop stability. When the system is both infinite-horizon and constrained, [21] considered this case for T-S fuzzy systems with PDC law and non-PDC law. New sufficient conditions were proposed in terms of LMIs. Both the corresponding PDC and non-PDC state-feedback controllers were designed, which could guarantee that the resulting closed-loop fuzzy system be asymptotically stable. In addition, the feedback controllers would meet the specifications for the fuzzy systems with input or output constraints.

4.2.2. Finite horizon NMPC

In this section, different possibilities to achieve closed-loop stability for NMPC using a finite horizon length have been proposed. Just as outlined for the linear case, in the proof the value function is employed as a Lyapunov function. A global optimum must be found at each time step to guarantee stability. As mentioned above, when the horizon is infinity, feasibility at a particular time step implies feasibility at all future time steps. Unfortunately, contrary to the linear case, the infinite horizon problem cannot be solved numerically.

Most of approaches modify the NMPC setup such that stability of the closed-loop can be guaranteed independently of the plant and performance specifications. This is usually achieved by adding suitable equality or inequality constraints and suitable additional penalty terms to the objective functional. These additional constraints are usually not motivated by physical restrictions or desired performance requirements but have the sole purpose to enforce stability of the closed-loop. Therefore, they are usually termed stability constraints.

Terminal equality constraint. The simplest possibility to enforce stability with a finite prediction horizon is to add a so called zero terminal equality constraint at the end of the prediction horizon [17, 23, 28], i.e. to add the equality constraint $x(k+p \mid k)=0$to the optimization problem (2), (3) and (7). This leads to stability of the closed-loop, if the optimal control problem possesses a solution at$k$, since the feasibility at one time instance does also lead to feasibility at the following time instances and a decrease in the value function.

The first proposal for this form of model predictive control for time-varying, constrained, nonlinear, discrete-time systems was made by [17]. This paper is particularly important, because it provides a definitive stability analysis of this version of discrete-time receding horizon control (under mild conditions of controllability and observability) and shows the value function J_N^* associated with the finite horizon optimal control problem approaches that of the infinite horizon problem as the horizon approaches infinity. This paper remains a key reference on the stabilizing properties of model predictive control and subsumes much of the later literature on discrete-time MPC that uses a terminal equality constraint.

In fact, the main advantages of this version are the straightforward application and the conceptual simplicity. On the other hand, one disadvantage of a zero terminal constraint is that the system must be brought to the origin in finite time. This leads in general to feasibility problems for short prediction/control horizon lengths, i.e. a small region of attraction. From a computational point of view, the optimization problem with terminal constraint can be solved in principle, but equality constraints are computationally very expensive and can only be met asymptotically [24]. In addition, one cannot guarantee convergence to a feasible solution even when a feasible solution exists, a discomforting fact. Furthermore, specifying a terminal constraint which is not met in actual operation is always somewhat artificial and may lead to aggressive behavior. Finally, to reduce the complexity of the optimization problem it is desirable to keep the control horizon small, or, more generally, characterize the control input sequence with a small number of parameters. However, a small number of degrees of freedom may lead to quite a gap between the open-loop performance objective and the actual closed loop performance.

Terminal constraint set and terminal cost function. Many schemes have been proposed [24, 26-28, 30, 31, 36, 37], to try to overcome the use of a zero terminal constraint. Most of them either use the so called terminal region constraint

$$x(k+p \mid k) \in X_f \subseteq \mathsf{X} \tag{8}$$

and/or a terminal penalty term $E(x(k+p \mid k))$ which is added to the cost functional. Note that the terminal penalty term is not a performance specification that can be chosen freely. Rather E and the terminal region X_f in (8) are determined off-line such that stability is enforced.

- *Terminal constraint set.* In this version of model predictive control, X_f is a subset of X containing a neighborhood of the origin. The purpose of the model predictive controller is to steer the state to X_f in finite time. Inside X_f, a local stabilizing controller $k_f(\cdot)$ is employed. This form of model predictive control is therefore sometimes referred to as dual mode, and was proposed. Fixed horizon versions for constrained, nonlinear, discrete-time systems are proposed in [32] and [33].
- *Terminal cost function.* One of the earliest proposals for modifying (2), (3) and (7) to ensure closed-loop stability was the addition of a terminal cost. In this version of model predictive control, the terminal cost $E(\cdot)$ is nontrivial and there is no terminal constraint so that $X_f = \mathbb{R}^n$. The proposal [34] was made in the context of predictive control of unconstrained linear system. Can this technique for achieving stability (by adding only a terminal cost) be successfully employed for constrained and/or nonlinear systems? From the literature the answer may appear affirmative. However, in this literature there is an implicit requirement that $x(k+p \mid k) \in X_f$ is satisfied for every initial state in a given compact set, and this is automatically satisfied if N is chosen sufficiently large. The constraint $x(k+p \mid k) \in X_f$ then need not be included explicitly in the optimal control problem actually solved on-line. Whether this type of model predictive control is regarded as having only a terminal cost or having both a terminal cost and a terminal constraint is a matter of definition. We prefer to consider it as belonging to the latter category as the constraint is necessary even though it is automatically satisfied if N is chosen sufficiently large.

Terminal cost and constraint set. Most recent model predictive controllers belong to this category. There are a variety of good reasons for incorporating both a terminal cost and a terminal constraint set in the optimal control problem. Ideally, the terminal cost $E(\cdot)$ should be the infinite horizon value function $J_\infty^*(\cdot)$ if this were the case, then $J_N^*(\cdot) = J_\infty^*(\cdot)$, on-line optimization would be unnecessary, and the known advantages of an infinite horizon, such as stability and robustness, would automatically accrue. Nonlinearity and/or constraints render this impossible, but it is possible to choose $E(\cdot)$ so that it is exactly or approximately equal to $J_{\infty}^{*}(\cdot)$ in a suitable neighborhood of the origin. Choosing X_f to be an appropriate subset of this neighborhood yields many advantages and motivates the choice of $E(\cdot)$ and X_f in most of the examples of this form of model predictive control.

For the case when the system is nonlinear but there are no state or control constraints, [35] use a stabilizing local control law$k_f(\cdot)$, a terminal cost function $E(\cdot)$ that is a (local) Lyapunov function for the stabilized system, and a terminal constraint set X_f that is a level set of $E(\cdot)$ and is positively invariant for the system$x(k+1)=f(x(k), k_f(x(k)))$. The terminal constraint is omitted from the optimization problem solved on-line, but it is nevertheless shown that this constraint is automatically satisfied for all initial states in a level set of$J_N^{*}(\cdot)$. The resultant closed-loop system is asymptotically (or exponentially) stabilizing with a region of attraction that is this level set of$J_N^{*}(\cdot)$.

When the system is both nonlinear and constrained, $E(\cdot)$and $X_f$include features from the example immediately above. In [36], $k_f(\cdot)$ is chosen to stabilize the linearized system $x(k+1)=Ax(k)+Bu(k)$, where $A:=f_x(0, 0)$ and$B:=f_u(0, 0)$. Then the author of [36] employs a non-quadratic terminal cost $E(\cdot)$ and a terminal constraint set X_f that is positively invariant for the nonlinear system $x(k+1)=f(x(k), k_f(x(k)))$ and that satisfies $X_f \subset \mathsf{X}$ and $k_f(X_f) \subset \mathsf{U}$.

Variable horizon/Hybrid model predictive control. These techniques were proposed by [37] and developed by [38] to deal with both the global optimality and the feasibility problems, which plague nonlinear MPC with a terminal constraint. Variable horizon MPC also employs a terminal constraint, but the time horizon at the end of which this constraint must be satisfied is itself an optimization variable. It is assumed that inside this region another controller is employed for which it is somehow known that it asymptotically stabilizes the system. Variable horizon has also been employed in contractive model predictive control (see the next section). With these modifications a global optimum is no longer needed and feasibility at a particular time step implies feasibility at all future time steps. The terminal constraint is somewhat less artificial here because it may be met in actual operation. However, a variable horizon is inconvenient to handle on-line, an exact end constraint is difficult to satisfy, and the exact determination of the terminal region is all but impossible except maybe for low order systems. In order to show that this region is invariant and that the system is asymptotically stable in this region, usually a global optimization problem needs to be solved.

Contractive model predictive control. The idea of contractive MPC was mentioned by [39], the complete algorithm and stability proof were developed by [40]. In this approach a constraint is added to the usual formulation which forces the actual and not only the predicted state to contract at discrete intervals in the future. From this requirement a Lyapunov function can be constructed easily and stability can be established. The stability is independent of the objective function and the convergence of the optimization algorithm as long as a solution is found which satisfies the contraction constraint. The feasibility at future time steps is not necessarily guaranteed unless further assumptions are made. Because the contraction parameter implies a specific speed of convergence, its choice comes natural to the operating personnel.

Model predictive control with linearization. All the methods discussed so far require a nonlinear program to be solved on-line at each time step. The effort varies somewhat because some methods require only that a feasible (and not necessarily optimal) solution be found or that only an improvement be achieved from time step to time step. Nevertheless the effort is usually formidable when compared to the linear case and stopping with a feasible rather than optimal solution can have unpredictable consequences for the performance. The computational effort can be greatly reduced when the system is linearized first in some manner and then the techniques developed for linear systems are employed on-line. Some approaches have been proposed.

Linearization theory may, in some applications, be employed to transform the original nonlinear system, using state and feedback control transformations, into a linear system. Model predictive control may be applied to the transformed system [41, 42]. [42] applies first feedback linearization and then uses MPC in a cascade arrangement for the resulting linear system. The optimal control problem is not, however, transformed into a convex problem, because the transformed control and state constraint sets and the transformed cost are no longer necessarily convex. [43, 44] employ linear transformation ($x(k+1)=Ax+Bu$ is replaced by $x(k+1)=(A+BK)x+Bv$, where $v:=u-Kx$ is the re-parameterized control) to improve conditioning of the optimal control problem solved on-line.

Conclusions. MPC for linear constrained systems has been shown to provide an excellent control solution both theoretically and practically. The incorporation of nonlinear models poses a much more challenging problem mainly because of computational and control theoretical difficulties, but also holds much promise for practical applications. In this section an overview over the stability analysis of NMPC is given. As outlined some of the challenges occurring in NMPC are already solvable. Nevertheless in the nonlinear area a variety of issues remain which are technically complex but have potentially significant practical implications for stability and performance.

5. Robust model predictive control

MPC is a class of model-based control theories that use linear or nonlinear process models to forecast system behavior. The success of the MPC control performance depends on the accuracy of the open loop predictions, which in turn depends on the accuracy of the process models. It is possible for the predicted trajectory to differ from the actual plant behavior [45]. Needless to say, such control systems that provide optimal performance for a particular model may perform very poorly when implemented on a physical system that is not exactly described by the model (see e.g. [46]).

When we say that a control system is robust we mean that stability is maintained and that the performance specifications are met for a specified range of model variations (uncertainty range). To be meaningful, any statement about robustness of a particular control algorithm must make reference to a specific uncertainty range as well as specific stability and performance criteria.

Predictive controllers that explicitly consider the process and model uncertainties, when determining the optimal control policies, are called robust predictive controllers. The main concept of such controllers is similar to the idea of H_{∞}controllers and consists on the minimization of worst disturbance effect to the process behavior [47]. Several applications for the formulation of robust predictive control laws began to appear in the literature in the 1990s, focusing on both model uncertainties and disturbances.

Although a rich theory has been developed for the robust control of linear systems, very little is known about the robust control of linear systems with constraints. Most studies on robustness consider unconstrained systems. According to the Lyapunov theory, we know that if a Lyapunov function for the nominal closed-loop system maintains its descent property if the disturbance (uncertainty) is sufficiently small, then stability is maintained in the presence of uncertainty. However, when constraints on states and controls are present, it is necessary to ensure, in addition, that disturbances do not cause transgression of the constraints. This adds an extra level of complexity.

In this section, we review two robust model predictive control (RMPC) methods and mention the advantages and disadvantages of methods below. The basic idea of each method and some method applications are stated.

5.1. Min-Max RMPC methods

In the main stream robust control literature, "robust performance" is measured by determining the worst performance over the specified uncertainty range. In direct extension of this definition it is natural to set up a new RMPC objective where the control action is selected to minimize the worst value the objective function can attain as a function of the uncertain model parameters. This describes the first attempt toward a RMPC algorithm which was proposed by [48]. They showed that for FIR models the optimization problem which must be solved on-line at each time step is a linear program of moderate size with uncertain coefficients and an ∞-norm objective function. Unfortunately, it is well known now that robust stability is not guaranteed with this algorithm [46].

In literature [48], the Campo algorithm fails to address the fact that only the first element of the optimal input trajectory is implemented and the whole min-max optimization is repeated at the next time step with a feedback update. In the subsequent optimization, the worst-case parameter values may change because of the feedback's update. In the case of a system with uncertainties, the open-loop optimal solution differs from the feedback optimal solution, thereby violating the basic premise behind MPC. This is why robust stability cannot be assured with the Campo algorithm.

The literature [49] proposed the RMPC formulations which explicitly take into account uncertainties in the prediction model

$$f(x_k, u_k, w_k, v_k) = A(w_k)x_k + B(w_k)u_k + Ev_k \tag{9}$$

where $A(w) = A_0 + \sum_{i=1}^{q} A_i w_i,\ B(w) = B_0 + \sum_{i=1}^{q} B_i w_i$

$w_k \in \mathsf{W} \in \mathbb{R}^{n_w},\ v_k \in \mathsf{V} \in \mathbb{R}^{n_v}$

Letv_k, $w_k$be modeled as unknown but bounded exogenous disturbances and parametric uncertainties and$\mathsf{W}$, Vbe polytopes respectively. A RMPC strategy often used is to solve a min-max problem that minimize the worst-case performance while enforcing input and state constraints for all possible disturbances. The following min-max control problem is referred as *open-loop constrained robust optimal control problem* (OL-CROC).

$$\begin{aligned} &\min_{u_0,\dots,u_{N-1}} \left\{ \max_{\substack{v_0,\dots,v_{N-1} \in \mathsf{V} \\ w_0,\dots,w_{N-1} \in \mathsf{W}}} \sum_{k=0}^{N-1} l(x_k, u_k) + F(x_N) \right\} \\ &s.t. \quad \text{dynamics (9), constraints (3) satisfied} \quad \forall v_k \in \mathsf{V},\ \forall w_k \in \mathsf{W} \end{aligned} \tag{10}$$

Other papers in the literature aim at explicitly or implicitly approximating the problem above by simplifying the objective and uncertainty description, and making the on-line effort more manageable, but still guaranteeing at least robust stability. For example, the authors of [50] use an ∞-norm open-loop objective function and both assume FIR models with uncertain coefficients. A similar but more general technique has also been proposed for state-space systems with a bounded input matrix [51].

The authors of [52] have defined a dynamic programming problem (thus accounting for feedback) to determine the control sequence minimizing the worst case cost. They show that with the horizon set to infinity this procedure guarantees robust stability. However, the approach suffers from the curse of dimensionality and the optimization problem at each stage of the dynamic program is non-convex. Thus, in its generality the method is unsuitable for on-line (or even off-line) use except for low order systems with simple uncertainty descriptions.

These formulations may be conservative for certain problems leading to sluggish behavior because of three reasons. First of all, arbitrarily time-varying uncertain parameters are usually not a good description of the model uncertainty encountered in practice, where the parameters may be either constant or slowly varying but unknown. Second, the computationally simple open-loop formulations neglect the effect of feedback. Third, the worst-case error minimization itself may be a conservative formulation for most problems.

The authors of [50, 53, 54] propose to optimize nominal rather than robust performance and to achieve robust stability by enforcing a robust contraction constraint, i.e.requiring the worst-case prediction of the state to contract. With this formulation robust global asymptotic stability can be guaranteed for a set of linear time-invariant stable systems. The optimization problem can be cast as a quadratic program of moderate size for a broad class of uncertainty descriptions.

To account for the effect of feedback, the authors of [55] propose to calculate at each time step not a sequence of control moves but a state feedback gain matrix which is determined to minimize an upper bound on robust performance. For fairly general uncertainty descriptions, the optimization problem can be expressed as a set of linear matrix inequalities for which efficient solution techniques exist.

5.2. LMI-based RMPC methods

In the above method, a cost function is minimized considering the worst case into all the plants described by the uncertainties. Barriers of RMPC algorithms include: the computational cost, the applicability depending on the speed and size of the plant on which the control will act. In this section, we present one such MPC-based technique for the control of plants with uncertainties. This technique is motivated by developments in the theory and application (to control) of optimization involving linear matrix inequalities (LMIs) [56].

In this regard, the authors in [55] used the formulation in LMIs to solve the optimization problem. The basic idea of LMIs is to interpret a control problem as a semi-definite programming (SDP), that is, an optimization problem with linear objective and positive-definite constraints involving symmetric matrices that are related to the decision variables.

There are two reasons why LMI optimization is relevant to MPC. Firstly, LMI-based optimization problems can be solved in polynomial time, which means that they have low computational complexity. From a practical standpoint, there are effective and powerful algorithms for the solution of these problems, that is, algorithms that rapidly compute the global optimum, with non-heuristic stopping criteria. It is comparable to that required for the elevation of an analytical solution for a similar problem. Thus LMI optimization is well suited for online implementation, which is essential for MPC. Secondly, it is possible to recast much of existing robust control theory in the framework of LMIs [55].

The implication is that we can devise an MPC scheme where, at each time instant, an LMI optimization problem (as opposed to conventional linear or quadratic programs) is solved that incorporates input/output constraints and a description of the plant uncertainty. What's more, it can guarantee certain robustness properties.

5.3. Our works

In recent decades, many research results in the design of RMPC have appeared, see for examples, [55-62] and the references therein. The main drawback associated with the abovementioned methods proposed in MPC is that a single Lyapunov matrix is used to guarantee the desired closed-loop multi-objective specifications. This must work for all matrices in the uncertain domain to ensure that the hard constraints on inputs and outputs are satisfied. This condition is generally conservative if used in time-invariant systems. Furthermore, the hard constraints on outputs of closed-loop systems cannot be transformed into a linear matrix inequality (LMI) form using the method proposed in [57, 58, 60].

We present a multi-model paradigm for robust control. Underlying this paradigm is a linear time-varying (LTV) system.

$$\begin{aligned} x(k+1) &= A(k)x(k) + B(k)u(k) \\ y(k) &= C(k)x(k) \\ \begin{bmatrix} A(k) & B(k) \\ C(k) & 0 \end{bmatrix} &\in \Omega \end{aligned} \tag{11}$$

where $u(k) \in \mathbb{R}^{n_u}$ is the control input, $x(k) \in \mathbb{R}^{n_x}$ is the state of the plant and $y(k) \in \mathbb{R}^{n_y}$ is the plant output, and Ω is some pre-specified set.

For polytopic systems, the set Ω is the polytope

$$\Omega = Co\left\{ \begin{bmatrix} A_1 & B_1 \\ C_1 & 0 \end{bmatrix}, \begin{bmatrix} A_2 & B_2 \\ C_2 & 0 \end{bmatrix}, \ldots, \begin{bmatrix} A_L & B_L \\ C_L & 0 \end{bmatrix} \right\}, \tag{12}$$

where Co devotes to the convex hull. In other words, if $\begin{bmatrix} A(k) & B(k) \\ C(k) & 0 \end{bmatrix} \in \Omega$, then, for some non-negative $\xi_1(k)$, $\xi_2(k)$,...,ξ_L (k) summing to one, we have

$$\begin{bmatrix} A(k) & B(k) \\ C(k) & 0 \end{bmatrix} = \sum_{i=1}^{L} \xi_i(k) \begin{bmatrix} A_i & B_i \\ C_i & 0 \end{bmatrix}, \tag{13}$$

where $L = 1$ corresponds to the nominal LTI system. The system described in equation (11) subject to input and output constraints

$$\begin{aligned} |u_h(k+i \mid k)| &\le u_{h,max}, \; i \ge 0, \; h = 1, 2, \ldots, \mathbb{R}^{n_u}, \\ |y_h(k+i \mid k)| &\le y_{h,max}, \; i \ge 1, \; h = 1, 2, \ldots, \mathbb{R}^{n_y}. \end{aligned}$$

In 2001, the authors of [63] firstly put forward the idea of using the parameter-dependent Lyapunov function to solve the problem of robust constrained MPC for linear continuous-time uncertain systems, and hereafter, this idea was applied to linear discrete-time uncertain systems in [64, 65].

Inspired by above-mentioned work, we addressed the problem of robust constrained MPC based on parameter-dependent Lyapunov functions with polytopic-type uncertainties in [66]. The results are based on a new extended LMI characterization of the quadratic objective, with hard constraints on inputs and outputs. Sufficient conditions in LMI do not involve the product of the Lyapunov matrices and the system dynamic matrices. The state feedback control guarantees that the closed-loop system is robustly stable and the hard constraints on inputs and outputs are satisfied. The approach provides a way to reduce the conservativeness of the existing conditions by decoupling the control parameterization from the Lyapunov matrix. An example will be provided to illustrate the effectiveness of the techniques developed in [66]. As the method proposed in [55] is a special case of our results, the optimization problem should be feasible using the method proposed in our paper since it is solvable using the approach in [55]. However, the optimization may not have a solution by the result in [55], while it has a solution by our result.

Example (Input and Output Constraints) Consider the linear discrete-time parameter uncertain system (11) with

$$\begin{aligned} &A_1=\begin{bmatrix}-0.90 & 0.80\\ 0.35 & 0.45\end{bmatrix},\ A_2=\begin{bmatrix}0.90 & 0.85\\ 0.40 & -0.85\end{bmatrix},\ A_3=\begin{bmatrix}0.96 & 0.13\\ 0.28 & -0.90\end{bmatrix},\\ &B_1=\begin{bmatrix}1\\ -1\end{bmatrix},\ B_2=\begin{bmatrix}1\\ -0.8\end{bmatrix},\ B_3=\begin{bmatrix}1\\ -0.86\end{bmatrix},\\ &C_1=[1\ \ 0.3],\ C_2=[0.8\ \ 0.2],\ C_3=[1.2\ \ 0.4]. \end{aligned} \tag{14}$$

It is shown that the optimization is infeasible with the method proposed in [55] without the constraints. However, taking output constraints with $y_{1,max}=2$ and input constraints with $u_{1,max}=0.8$, and with uncertain parameters assumed to be$\xi_1(k)=0.5cos(k)^2$, $\xi_2(k)=0.6sin(k)^2$, $\xi_3(k)=0.5cos(k)^2+0.4sin(k)^2$, it is feasible using the method proposed in this paper. The simulation results are given in Figure 2 and Figure 3.

5.4. Conclusion

An overview of some methods on RMPC is presented. The methods are studied based on LMI and Min-Max. The basic idea and applications of methods are stated in each part. Advantages and disadvantages of methods are stated in this section too.

6. Recent developments in stochastic MPC

Despite the extensive literature that exists on predictive control and robustness to uncertainty, both multiplicative (e.g. parametric) and additive (e.g. exogenous), very little attention

has been paid to the case of stochastic uncertainty. Although robust predictive control can handle constrained systems that are subject to stochastic uncertainty, it will propagate the effects of uncertainty over a prediction horizon which can be computationally expensive and conservative. Yet this situation arises naturally in many control applications. The aim of this section is to review some of the recent advances in stochastic model predictive control (SMPC).

The basic SMPC problem is defined in Subsection 6.1. and a review of earlier work is given in Subsection 6.2.

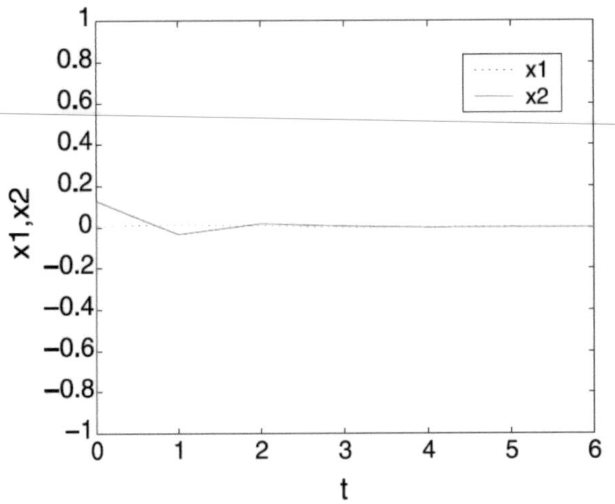

Figure 2. States (x_1, x_2) (method in [66]).

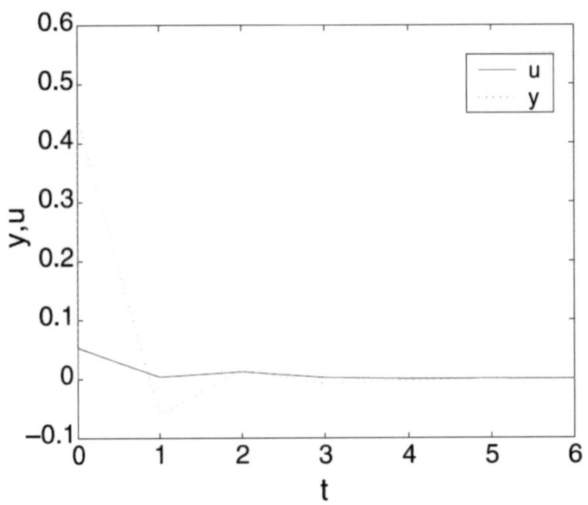

Figure 3. Output $y$and input u(method in [66]).

6.1. Basic SMPC problem

Consider the system described by the model

$$x(k+1) = Ax(k) + Bu(k) + w(k) \quad (15)$$

where $x \in \mathbb{R}^n$ is the state, $u \in \mathbb{R}^m$is the input and the disturbance w_k are assumed to be independent and identically distributed (i.i.d.), with zero mean, known distribution, and

$$-\alpha \leq w_k \leq \alpha \tag{16}$$

where $\alpha > 0$and inequalities apply element wise. (15) is subject to probabilistic constraints

$$P(e_j^T \phi_k \leq h_j) \geq p_j, \ j = 1, \ldots, \rho \qquad \phi_k = G x_{k+1} + F u_k \tag{17}$$

where$G \in \mathbb{R}^{\rho \times n}$, $F \in \mathbb{R}^{\rho \times m}$and e_j^T denotes the jth row of the identity matrix. This formulation covers the case of state only, input only and state/input constraints which can be probabilistic (soft) or deterministic (hard) since $p_j = 1$can be chosen for some or all$j$. For each j (17) can be invoked separately so that in this section is taken to be scalar

$$\phi_k = g^T x_{k+1} + f^T u_k \tag{18}$$

The problem is to devise a receding horizon MPC strategy that minimizes the cost

$$J = \sum_{k=0}^{\infty} \mathsf{E}(x^T(k) Q x(k) + u^T(k) R u(k)) \tag{19}$$

(where Edenotes expectation) and guarantees that the closed loop system is stable, while its state converges to a neighborhood of the origin subject to the constraint (17).

As is common in the literature on probabilistic robustness (e.g. [67]), all stochastic uncertainties are assumed to have bounded support. Not only is this necessary for asserting feasibility and stability, but it matches the real world more closely than the mathematically convenient Gaussian assumption which permits $w$to become arbitrarily large (albeit with small probability), since noise and disturbances derived from physical processes are finite.

6.2. Earlier work

Stochastic predictive control (SMPC) is emerging as a research area of both practical and theoretical interest.

MPC has proved successful because it attains approximate optimality in the presence of constraints. In addition, RMPC can maintain a satisfactory level of performance and guarantee constraint satisfaction when the system is subject to bounded uncertainty [2]. However, such an approach does not cater for the case in which model and measurement uncertainties are stochastic in nature, subject to some statistical regularity, and neither can it handle the case of random uncertainty whose distribution does not have finite support (e.g. normal distributions). Therefore RMPC can be conservative since it ignores information on the probabilistic distribution of the uncertainty.

It is possible to adopt a stochastic uncertainty description (instead of a set-based description) and develop an MPC algorithm that minimizes the expected value of a cost function. In general, the same difficulties that plagued the set-based approach are encountered here. One notable exception is that, when the stochastic parameters are independent sequences, the true closed-loop optimal control problem can be solved analytically using dynamic programming [68]. In many cases, the expected error may be a more meaningful performance measure than the worst-case error.

SMPC also derives from the fact that most real life applications are subject to stochastic uncertainty and have to obey constraints. However, not all constraints are hard (i.e. inviolable), and it may be possible to improve performance by tolerating violations of constraints providing that the frequency of violations remains within allowable limits, namely soft constraints (see e.g. [69, 70] or [71, 73]).

These concerns are addressed by stochastic MPC. Early work [74] considered additive disturbances and ignored the presence of constraints. Later contributions [68, 75-78] took constraints into account, but suffered from either excessive computation or a high degree of conservativeness, or did not consider issues of closed loop stability/feasibility.

An approach that arose in the context of sustainable development [70, 79] overcame some of these difficulties by using stochastic moving average models and equality stability constraints. This was extended to state space models with stochastic output maps and to inequality maps involving terminal invariant sets [81]. The restriction of model uncertainty to the output map was removed in [81], but the need to propagate the effects of uncertainty over the prediction horizon prevented the statement of results in respect of feasibility. [82] overcomes these issues through an augmented autonomous prediction formulation, and provides a method of handling probabilistic constraints and ensuring closed loop stability through the use of an extension of the concept of invariance, namely invariance with probability p.

Recent work [83, 84] proposed SMPC algorithms that use probabilistic information on additive disturbances in order to minimize the expected value of a predicted cost subject to hard and soft (probabilistic) constraints. Stochastic tubes were used to provide a recursive guarantee of feasibility and thus ensure closed loop stability and constraint satisfaction. Moreover, the authors of [84] proposed conditions that, for the parameterization of predictions employed, are necessary and sufficient for recursive feasibility, thereby incurring no additional conservatism. The approach was based on state feedback, which assumed that the states are measurable. In practice this is often not the case, and it is then necessary to estimate the state via an observer. The introduction of state estimation into RMPC is well understood and uses lifting to describe the combined system and observer dynamics. In [85], these ideas are extended to include probabilistic information on measurement noise and the unknown initial plant state, and extends the approach of [84].

http://dx.doi.org/10.5772/51122

Applications

In the next two sections, we will show that many important practical and theoretical problems can be formulated in the MPC framework. Pursuing them will assure MPC of its stature as a vibrant research area, where theory is seen to support practice more directly than in most other areas of control research.

7. Networked control systems

Traditionally, the different components (i.e., sensor, controller, and actuator) in a control system are connected via wired, point-to-point links, and the control laws are designed and operate based on local continuously-sampled process output measurements.

In recent years, there has been a growing interest in the design of controllers based on the network systems in several areas such as traffic, communication, aviation and spaceflight [86]. The networked control systems (NCSs) is defined as a feedback control system where control loops are closed through a real-time network [96, 97], which is different from traditional control systems. For an overview, the readers can refer to [97], which systematically addresses several key issues (band-limited channels, sampling and delay, packet loss, system architecture) that make NCSs distinct from other control systems.

7.1. Characteristics of NCSs

Advantages. Communication networks make the transmission of data much easier and provide a higher degree of freedom in the configuration of control systems. Network-based communication allows for easy modification of the control strategy by rerouting signals, having redundant systems that can be activated automatically when component failure occurs. Particularly, NCSs allow remote monitoring and adjustment of plants over the Internet. This enables the control system to benefit from the way it retrieves data and reacts to plant fluctuations from anywhere around the world at any time, see for example, [98-101] and references therein.

Disadvantages. Although the network makes it convenient to control large distributed systems, new issues arise in the design of a NCSs. Augmenting existing control networks with real-time wired or wireless sensor and actuator networks challenges many of the assumptions made in the development of traditional process control methods dealing with dynamical systems linked through ideal channels with flawless, continuous communication. In the context of networked control systems, key issues that need to be carefully handled at the control system design level include data losses due to field interference and time-delays due to network traffic as well as due to the potentially heterogeneous nature of the additional measurements (for example, continuous, asynchronous and delayed) [102]. These issues will deteriorate the performance and may even cause the system to be unstable.

Hence, the main question is how to design the NCSs include the handling of data losses, time-varying delays, and the utilization of heterogeneous measurements to maintain the closed-loop stability while improving the closed-loop performance.

7.2. Results on NCSs

To solve these problems, various methods have been developed, e.g., augmented deterministic discrete-time model, queuing, optimal stochastic control, perturbation, sampling time scheduling, robust control, fuzzy logic modulation, event-based control, end-user control adaptation, data packet dropout analysis, and hybrid systems stability analysis. However, these methods have put some strict assumptions on NCSs, e.g., the network time delay is less than the sampling period [109, 110]. The work of [111] presents an approach for stability analysis of NCSs that decouples the scheduling protocol from properties of the network-free nominal closed-loop system. The problem of the design of robust H_∞controllers for uncertain NCSs with the effects of both the network-induced delay and data dropout has been considered in [112] the network-induced time delay is larger than one sampling period, but there is no compensation for the time delay and data dropout.

A common approach is to insert network behavior between the nodes of a conventional control loop, designed without taking the network behavior into account. More specifically, in [114], it was proposed to first design the controller using established techniques considering the network transparent, and then to analyze the effect of the network on closed-loop system stability and performance. This approach was further developed in [115] using a small gain analysis approach.

In the last few years, however, several research papers have studied control using the *IEEE*802.11 and Bluetooth wireless networks, see, for example, [116-119] and the references therein. In the design and analysis of networked control systems, the most frequently studied problem considers control over a network having constant or time-varying delays. This network behavior is typical of communications over the Internet but does not necessarily represent the behavior of dedicated wireless networks in which the sensor, controller, and actuator nodes communicate directly with one another but might experience data losses. An appropriate framework to model lost data, is the use of asynchronous systems [120-122] and the process is considered to operate in an open-loop fashion when data is lost.

The most destabilizing cause of packet loss is due to bursts of poor network performance in which case large groups of packets are lost nearly consecutively. A more detailed description of bursty network performance using a two-state Markov chain was considered in [123]. Modeling networks, using Markov chains results in describing the overall closed-loop system as a stochastic hybrid system [120]. Stability results have been presented for particular cases of stochastic hybrid systems (e.g., [124, 125]). However, these results do not directly address the problem of augmentation of dedicated, wired control systems with networked actuator and sensor devices to improve closed-loop performance.

With respect to other results on networked control, in [126], stability and disturbance attenuation issues for a class of linear networked control systems subject to data losses modeled as a discrete-time switched linear system with arbitrary switching was studied. In [127], (see also [128-130]), optimal control of linear time-invariant systems over unreliable communication links under different communication protocols (with and without acknowledgment of successful communication) was investigated and sufficient conditions for the existence of stabilizing control laws were derived.

Although, within control theory, the study of control over networks has attracted considerable attention in the literature, most of the available results deal with linear systems (e.g., [100, 131]).

7.3. Our works

MPC framework is particularly appropriate for controlling systems subject to data losses because the actuator can profit from the predicted evolution of the system. In this section, results from our works are summarized.

Several methodologies have been reported in the open literature to handle with the problems mentioned above in networked systems. Among these papers, two basic control strategies are applied when the packet dropping happens, they are zero-input schemes, by which the actuator input is set to zero when the control packet is lost, and hold-input scheme which implies the previous control input is used again when the control packet drops. The further research is proposed in [132] by directly comparing the two control methods.

The work of [133] presents a novel control technique combining modified MPC and modified Smith predictor to guarantee the stability of NCSs. Especially, the key point in this paper is that the future control sequence is used to compensate for the forward communication time delay and predictor is responsible for compensating the time delay in the backward channel.

Although much research work have been done in NCSs, many of those results simply treat the NCSs as a system with time delay, which ignores NCSs features, e.g., random network delay and data transmission in packets [134]. In order to solve the problem, Markovian jump system can be used to model the random time-delay. Moreover, most work have also ignored another important feature of NCSs. This feature is that the communication networks can transmit a packet of data at the same time, which is not done in traditional control systems. We have proposed a new networked control scheme – networked predictive control which mainly consists of a control prediction generator and a network dropout/delay compensator. It is first assumed that control predictions based on received data are packed and sent to the plant side through a network. Then the network dropout/delay compensator chooses the latest control value from the control prediction sequences available on the plant side, which can compensate for the time delay and data dropouts. The structure of the networked predictive control system (NPCS) is shown as Figure 4. The random network delay in the forward channel in NCS has been studied in [135]. Some other results has been obtained in [136] and [137], where the network-induced delay is not in the form of a Markov chain.

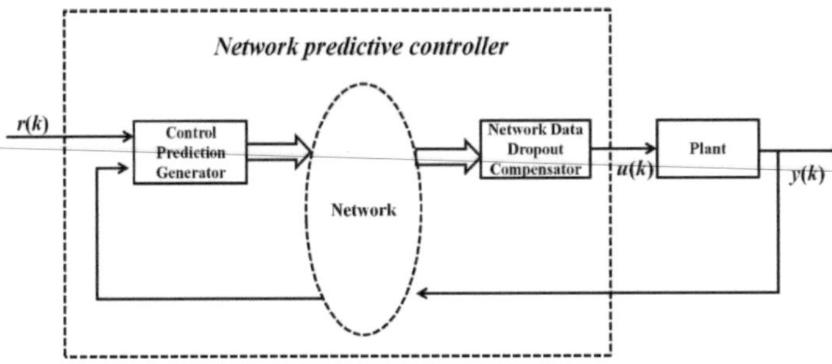

Figure 4. The networked predictive control system.

But, the random network delay in the forward and feedback channels makes the control design and stability analysis much more difficult. In [100] proposes a predictive control scheme for NCS with random network delay in both the feedback and forward channels and also provides an analytical stability criteria for closed-loop networked predictive control (NPC) systems. Furthermore, [138] can overcome the effects caused by both the unknown network delay and data dropout. Recently, [139] mainly focus on the random transmission data dropout existing in both feedback and forward channels in NCSs. So, the network-induced time delay is not discussed here.

In fact, using the networked predictive control scheme presented in this section, the control performance of the closed-loop system with data dropout is very similar to the one without data dropout.

8. Distributed MPC

At the beginning of research on NCSs, more attention was paid on single plant through network. Recently, fruitful research results on multi-plant, especially, on multi-agent networked control systems have been obtained. The aim of this section is to review a classification of a number of distributed control architectures for large scale systems. Attention is focused on the design approaches based on model predictive control. The controllers apply MPC policies to their local subsystems. They exchange their predictions by communication and incorporate the information from other controllers into their local MPC problem so as to coordinate with each other. For the considered architecture, the underlying rationale, the fields of application, the merits and limitations are discussed and the main references to the literature are reported.

8.1. Background

Technological and economical reasons motivate the development of process plants, manufacturing systems, traffic networks, water or power networks [140] with an ever increasing complexity. In addition, there is an increasing interest in networked control systems, where dedicated local control networks can be augmented with additional networked (wired and/or wireless) actuator/sensor devices have become cheap and easy-to-install [141, 142]. These large scale systems are composed by many physically or geographically divided subsystems. Each subsystem interacts with some so called neighbouring subsystems by their states and their inputs. The technical target is to achieve some global performance of entire system (or a common goal of all subsystems). Actually, it is difficult to control with a centralized control structure due to the required inherent computational complexity, robustness and reliability problems and communication bandwidth limitations.

For all these reasons, many distributed control structures have been developed and applied over the recent decades.

8.2. The reasons why DMPC is adopted

About MPC. The aim of this section is to review the distributed control approaches adopted, and to provide a wide list of references focusing the attention on the methods based on MPC. This choice is motivated by the ever increasing popularity of MPC in the process industry, see e.g. the survey papers [143, 144] on the industrial applications of linear and nonlinear MPC. Moreover, in recent years many MPC algorithms have been developed to guarantee some fundamental properties, such as the stability of the resulting closed-loop system or its robustness with respect to a wide class of external disturbances and/or model uncertainties, see e.g. the survey paper [2]. Especially, MPC is also a natural control framework to deal with the design of coordinated, distributed control systems because of its ability to handle input and state constraints, and also because it can account for the actions of other actuators in computing the control action of a given set of control actuators in real-time. Therefore, MPC is now recognized as a very powerful approach with well established theoretical foundations and proven capability to handle the problems of large scale systems.

Other control structures

1) *Centralized Control.* MPC is normally implemented in a centralized fashion. One controller is able to acquire the information of the global system, computes all the control inputs for the system, and could obtain a good global performance. In large-scale interconnected systems, such as power systems, water distribution systems, traffic systems, etc., such a centralized control scheme may not suitable or even possible apply to large scale system for some reasons: (1) there are hundreds of inputs and outputs. It requires a large computational efforts in online implementation (2) when the centralized controller fails, the entire system is out of control and the control integrity cannot be guaranteed when a control component fails (3) in some cases, e.g. in multi-intelligent vehicle system, the global information is unavailable to each controller and (4) objections to centralized control are often not computational, however, but organizational. All subsystems rely upon the central agent, making plantwide control difficult to coordinate and maintain. These obstacles deter implementation of centralized control for large-scale plants.

In recent years, there is a trend for the development of decentralized and distributed MPC due to the disadvantages of centralized MPC mentioned above (e.g.,[145, 146]).

2) *Decentralized Control.* Most large-scale and networked control systems are based on a decentralized architecture, that is, the system is divided into several subsystems, each controlled by a different agent that does not share information with the rest. Each of the agents implements an MPC based on a reduced model of the system and on partial state information, which in general results in an optimization problem with a lower computational burden. Figure 5 shows a decentralized control structure, where the system under control is assumed to be composed by two subsystems S1 and S2, with states, control and output variables (x_1, u_1,y_1) and (x_2, u_2,y_2), respectively, and the interaction between the subsystems is due the inputs and the outputs of different pairs are weak. These interactions can either be direct (input coupling) or caused by the mutual effects of the internal states of the subsystems under control, like in Figure 5.

For example, in [147], a MPC algorithm was proposed under the main assumptions that the system is nonlinear, discrete-time and no information is exchanged between local controllers.The decentralized framework has the advantages of being flexible to system structure, error-tolerance, less computational efforts and no global information requirements [148].

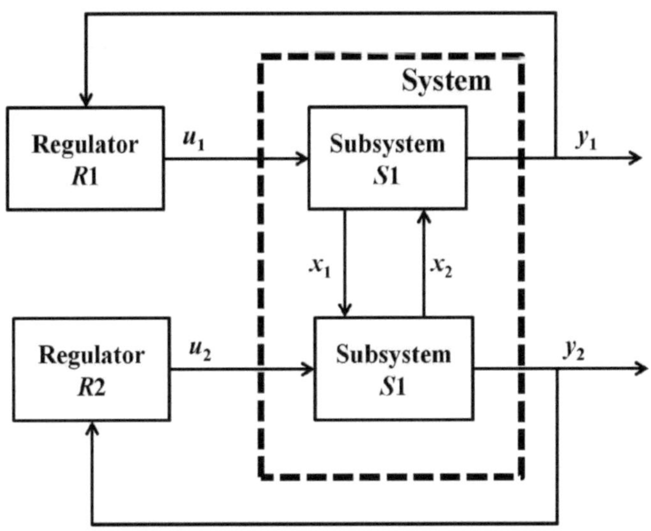

Figure 5. Decentralized control of a two input (u_1,u_2)-two output (y_1,y_2) system.

In plants where the subsystems interact weakly, local feedback action provided by these subsystem (decentralized) controllers may be sufficient to overcome the effect of interactions. For such cases, a decentralized control strategy is expected to work adequately. On the contrary, it is well known that strong interactions can even prevent one from achieving stability and/or performance with decentralized control, see for example [149, 150], where the role played by the so-called fixed modes in the stabilization problem is highlighted.

Distributed MPC. While these paradigms (centralized control and decentralized Control) to process control have been successful, there is an increasing interest in developing distributed model predictive control (DMPC) schemes, where agents share information in order to improve closed-loop performance, robustness and fault-tolerance. As a middle ground between the decentralized and centralized strategies, distributed control preserves the topology and flexibility of decentralized control yet offers a nominal closed-loop stability guarantee.

For each decentralized MPC, a sequence of open-loop controls are determined through the solution of a constrained optimal control problem. A local objective is used. A subsystem model, which ignores the interactions, is used to obtain a prediction of future process behavior along the control horizon. For distributed control, one natural advantage that MPC offers over other controller paradigms is its ability to generate a prediction of future subsystem behavior. If the likely influence of interconnected subsystems is known, each local controller can possibly determine suitable feedback action that accounts for these external influences. Intuitively, one expects this additional information to help improve systemwide control performance. Thus the distributed control framework is usually adopted in large-scale plants [151], in spite of that the dynamic performance of centralized frame work is better than it.

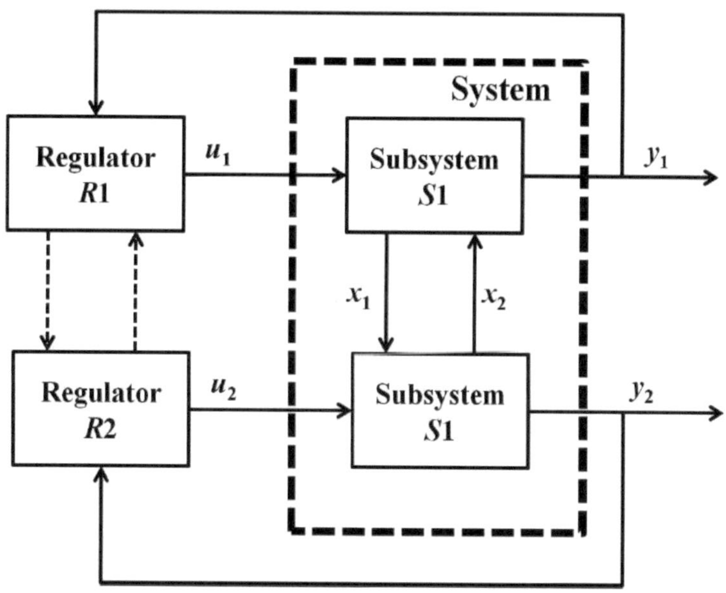

Figure 6. Distributed control of a two input (u_1,u_2)-two output (y_1,y_2) system.

In distributed control structures, like the simple example shown in Figure 6, it is assumed that some information is transmitted among the local regulators ($R_1$and R_2 in Figure 6), so that each one of them has some knowledge on the behavior of the others. When the local regulators are designed with MPC, the information transmitted typically consists of the future predicted control or state variables computed locally, so that any local regulator can predict the interaction effects over the considered prediction horizon. With reference to the simple case of Figure 6, the MPC regulators $R_1$and $R_2$are designed to control the subsystems S_1 andS_2, respectively. If the information was exchange among the local regulators ($R_1$and R_2) concerns the predicted evolution of the system states ($x_1$andx_2), any local regulator needs only to know the dynamics of the subsystem directly controlled (S_1andS_2).

In any case, it is apparent that the performance of the closed-loop system depends on the decisions that all the agents take. Hence, cooperation and communication policies become very important issues.

With respect to available results in this direction, several DMPC methods have been proposed in the literature that deal with the coordination of separate MPCs. These communicate in order to obtain optimal input trajectories in a distributed manner see [145, 146, 152] for reviews of results in this area. Some distributed MPC formulations are available in the literatures [153-157].

8.3. DMPC over network information exchange

However, all of the above results are based on the assumption of continuous sampling of the entire plant state vector and assuming no delays and perfect communication between subsystems. In practice, individual subsystems exchange information over a communication network, especially wireless communication network, where the data is transmitted in discrete packets. These packets may be lost during communication. Moreover, the communication media is a resource that is usually accessed in a mutually exclusive manner by neighborhood agents. This means that the throughput capacity of such networks is limited. Thus, how to improve the global performance of each subsystem with the limited network communication or limited available information is a valuable problem.

Previous work on MPC design for systems subject to asynchronous or delayed measurements has primarily focused on centralized MPC design [158], [159] and little attention has been given to the design of DMPC. In [160], the issue of delays in the communication between distributed controllers was addressed. The authors of [161] consider the design of distributed MPC schemes for nonlinear systems in a more common setting. That is, measurements of the state are not available continuously but asynchronously and with delays.

9. Conclusions

Recently, there has been much interest in model predictive control which allows researchers to address problems like feasibility, stability and performance in a rigorous manner. We first give a review of discrete-time model predictive control of constrained dynamic systems, both linear and nonlinear. The min-max approach for handling uncertainties are illustrated, then the LMIs methods are showed, and the advantages and disadvantages of methods are mentioned. The basic idea of each method and some method applications are stated. Despite the extensive literature that exists on predictive control and robustness to uncertainty, very little attention has been paid to the case of stochastic uncertainty. SMPC is emerging to adopt a stochastic uncertainty description (instead of a set-based description). Some of the recent advances in this area are reviewed. We show that many important practical and theoretical problems can be formulated in the MPC framework, such as DMPC. Some considerable attention has been directed to NCSs. Although the network makes it convenient to control large distributed systems, there also exist many control issues, such as network delay and data dropout, which cannot be addressed using conventional control theory, sampling and transmission methods. Results from our recent research are summarized in Section 7. We have proposed a new networked control scheme, which can overcome the effects caused by the network delay. In the last section we review a number of distributed control architectures based on model predictive control. For the considered architectures, the underlying rationale, the fields of application, the merits and limitations are discussed.

Acknowledgements

The work of Yuanqing Xia was supported by the National Basic Research Program of China (973 Program) (2012CB720000), the National Natural Science Foundation of China (60974011), Program for New Century Excellent Talents in University of China (NCET-08-0047), the Ph.D. Programs Foundation of Ministry of Education of China (20091101110023, 20111101110012), and Program for Changjiang Scholars and Innovative Research Team in University, and Beijing Municipal Natural Science Foundation (4102053,4101001). The work of Magdi S. Mahmoud is supported by the research group project no. RG1105-1 from DSR-KFUPM.

Author details

Li Dai[1], Yuanqing Xia[1*], Mengyin Fu[1] and Magdi S. Mahmoud[2]

*Address all correspondence to: xia_yuanqing@bit.edu.cn

1 School of Automation, Beijing Institute of Technology, China

2 Systems Engineering Department, King Fahd University of Petroleum and Minerals, Saudi Arabia

References

[1] Morari, M., & Lee, J. H. (1999). Model predictive control: past, present and future. *Computers and Chemical Engineering*, 23, 667-682.

[2] Mayne, D. Q., Rawlings, J. B., Rao, C. V., & Scokaert, P. O. M. (2000). Constrained model predictive control: stability and optimality. *Automatica*, 26(6), 789-814.

[3] Bemporad, A. (2006). Model Predictive Control Design: New Trends and Tools. Proceedings of the 45th IEEE Conference on Decision & Control Manchester Grand Hyatt Hotel San Diego, CA, USA, 13-15December 2006.

[4] Garcia, C. E., Prett, D. M., & Morari, M. (1989). Model Predictive Control: Theory and Practice a Survey. *Automatica*, 25(3), 335-348.

[5] Zafiriou, E., & Marchal, A. (1991). Stability of SISO quadratic dynamic matrix control with hard output constraints. *AIChE Journal*, 37, 1550-1560.

[6] Muske, K. R., & Rawlings, J. B. (1993). Model predictive control with linear models. *AIChe J*, 39, 262-287.

[7] Genceli, H., & Nikolaou, M. (1993). Robust stability analysis of constrained l_1-norm model predictive control. *AIChE Journal*, 39, 1954-1965.

[8] Campo, P. J., & Morari, M. (1986). Norm formulation of model predictive control problems. Paper presented at Proc. Am. Control Conf., Seattle, Washington. 339-343.

[9] Polak, E., & Yang, T. H. (1993a). Moving horizon control of linear systems with input saturation and plant uncertainty- Part 1: robustness. *International Journal of Control*, 58(3), 613-638.

[10] Polak, E., & Yang, T. H. (1993b). Moving horizon control of linear systems with input saturation and plant uncertainty- Part 2: disturbance rejection and tracking. *International Journal of Control*, 58(3), 639-663.

[11] Keerthi, S., & Gilbert, E. (1988). Optimal infinite-horizon feedback laws for a general class of constrained discrete-time systems: stability and moving-horizon approximations. *Journal of Optimization Theory and Applications*, 57(2), 265-293.

[12] Bemporad, A., Chisci, L., & Mosca, E. (1994). On the stabilizing property of the zero terminal state receding horizon regulation. *Automatica*, 30(12), 2013-2015.

[13] Nevistić, V., & Primbs, J. A. (1997). Finite receding horizon linear quadratic control: a unifying theory for stability and performance analysis. Paper presented at Technical Report CIT-CDS 97-001California Institute of Technology., Pasadena, CA.

[14] Primbs, J., & Nevistić, V. (1997). Constrained finite receding horizon linear quadratic control. Paper presented at Technical Report CIT-CDS 97-002 California Institute of Technology., Pasadena, CA.

[15] Allgöwer, F., Badgwell, T. A., Qin, J. S., Rawlings, J. B., & Wright, S. J. (1999). Nonlinear predictive control and moving horizon estimation: introductory overview. In: P. M. Frank, editor, *Advances in Control, Highlights of ECC99*, Springer, 391-449.

[16] Nicolao, G. D., Magni, L., & Scattolini, R. (2000). Stability and robustness of nonlinear receding horizon control. In: F. Allgöwer and A. Zheng, editors, *Nonlinear Predictive Control*, Birkhäuser, 3-23.

[17] Keerthi, S. S., & Gilbert, E. G. (1998). Optimal infinite-horizon feedback laws for a general class of constrained discrete time systems: Stability and moving-horizon approximations. *Journal of Optimization Theory and Applications*, 57(2), 265-2938.

[18] Meadows, E. S., & Rawlings, J. B. (1993). Receding horizon control with an infinite horizon. . In Proc. Amer. Contr. Conf., San Francisco , 2926-2930.

[19] Findeisen, R., & Allgöwer, F. (2002). An Introduction to Nonlinear Model Predictive Control. Paper presented at Control, 21st Benelux Meeting on Systems and Control, Veidhoven.

[20] Bellman, R. (1957). Dynamic Programming. Princeton, New Jersey, Princeton University Press.

[21] Xia, Y., Yang, H., Shi, P., & Fu, M. C. (2010). Constrained Infinite-Horizon Model Predictive Control for Fuzzy-Discrete-Time Systems. *IEEE Transactions on Fuzzy Systems*, 18(2), 429-432.

[22] Mayne, D. Q., & Michalska, H. (1990). Receding horizon control of nonlinear systems. *IEEE Transactions Automatic Control*, 35(7), 814-824.

[23] Meadows, E. S., Henson, M. A., Eaton, J. W., & Rawlings, J. B. (1995). Receding horizon control and discontinuous state feedback stabilization. *International Journal of Control*, 62(5), 1217-1229.

[24] Chen, H., & Allgöwer, F. (1998). A quasi-infinite horizon nonlinear model predictive control scheme with guaranteed stability. *Automatica*, 34(10), 1205-1218.

[25] Nicolao, G. D., Magni, L., & Scattolini, R. (1996). Stabilizing nonlinear receding horizon control via a nonquadratic terminal state penalty. In Symposium on Control, Optimization and Supervision, CESA96 IMACS Multi-conference, Lille , 185-187.

[26] Fontes, F. A. (2000). A general framework to design stabilizing nonlinear model predictive controllers. *Systems & Control Letters*, 42(2), 127-143.

[27] Jadbabaie, A., Yu, J., & Hauser, J. (2001). Unconstrained receding horizon control of nonlinear systems. *IEEE Transactions Automatic Control*, 46(5), 776-783.

[28] Mayne, D. Q., & Michalska, H. (1990). Receding horizon control of nonlinear systems. *IEEE Transactions Automatic Control*, 35(7), 814-824.

[29] Michalska, H., & Mayne, D. Q. (1993). Robust receding horizon control of constrained nonlinear systems. *IEEE Transactions Automatic Control*, 38(11), 1623-1633.

[30] Nevistić, V., & Morari, M. (1995). Constrained control of feedback-linearizable systems. In Proc. 3rd European Control Conference ECC95, Rome , 1726-1731.

[31] Primbs, J., Nevistić, V., & Doyle, J. (1999). Nonlinear optimal control: A control Lyapunov function and receding horizon perspective. *Asian Journal of Control J*, 1(1), 14-24.

[32] Chisci, L., Lombardi, A., & Mosca, E. (1996). Dual receding horizon control of constrained discrete-time systems. *European Journal of Control J*, 2, 278-285.

[33] Scokaert, P. O. M., Mayne, D. Q., & Rawlings, J. B. (1999). Suboptimal model predictive control (feasibility implies stability). *IEEE Transactions on Automatic Control J*, 44(3), 648-654.

[34] Bitmead, R. R., Gevers, M., & Wertz, V. (1990). Adaptive optimal control-The thinking man's GPC. Englewood Cliffs, NJ, Prentice-Hall.

[35] Parisini, T., & Zoppoli, R. (1995). A receding horizon regulator for nonlinear systems and a neural approximation. *Automatica*, 31(10), 1443-1451.

[36] Nicolao, D. G., Magni, L., & Scattolini, R. (1996). Stabilizing nonlinear receding horizon control via a nonquadratic penalty. Paper presented at Proceedings of the IMACS Multi-conference CESA, Lille. 1-185.

[37] Michalska, H., & Mayne, D. Q. (1993). Robust receding horizon control of constrained non linear systems. *IEEE Transactions on Automatic Control*, 38(11), 1623-1633.

[38] Michalska, H. (1997). A new formulation of receding horizon control without a terminal constraint on the state. *European Journal of Control*, 3(1), 2-14.

[39] Yang, T. H., & Polak, E. (1993). Moving horizon control of non linear systems with input saturation, disturbances and plant uncertainty. *International Journal of Control*, 58(4), 875-903.

[40] Oliveira, D. S. L., & Morari, M. (2000). Contractive model predictive control for constrained nonlinear systems. *IEEE Transactions on Automatic Control*, 45(6), 1053-1071.

[41] Oliveira, D. S. L., Nevistic, V., & Morari, M. (1995). Control of nonlinear systems subject to input constraints. Paper presented at IFAC symposium on nonlinear control system design,, Tahoe City, CA. 1520.

[42] Kurtz, M. J., & Henson, M. A. (1997). Input-output linearizing control of constrained nonlinear processes. *Journal of Process Control*, 7(1), 3-17.

[43] Keerthi, S. S. (1986). Optimal feedback control of discrete-time systems with state-control constraints and general cost functions. *PhD thesis.*, University of Michigan.

[44] Rossiter, J. A., Kouvaritakis, B., & Rice, M. J. (1998). A numerically robust state-space approach to stable-predictive control strategies. *Automatica*, 34(1), 65-74.

[45] Berber, R. (1995). Methods of Model Based Process Control. NATO ASI series. series E, Applied Sciences Kluwer Academic, Dordrecht, The Netherlands, 293

[46] Zheng, Z. Q., & Morari, M. (1993). Robust stability of constrained model predictive control. Paper presented at Proceedings of the American Control Conference, San Francisco, CA. 1, 379-383.

[47] Zeman, J., & Ilkiv, B. (2003). Robust min-max model predictive control of linear systems with constraints. *IEEE Transactions Automatic Control*, 930-935.

[48] Campo, P. J., & Morari, M. (1987). Robust model predictive control. *Proceedings of the American control conference* , 2, 1021-1026.

[49] Witsenhausen, H. S. (1968). A min-max control problem for sampled linear systems. *IEEE Transactions Automatic Control*, 13(1), 5-21.

[50] Zheng, A., & Morari, M. (1994).)Robust control of linear time varying systems with constraints. Proceedings of the American Control Conference Baltimore, ML , 2416-2420.

[51] Lee, J. H., & Cooley, B. L. (1997). Stable minimax control for state-space systems with bounded input matrix. Paper presented at Proceedings of the American Control Conference,, Alberquerque, NM. 5-2945.

[52] Lee, J. H., & Yu, Z. (1997). Worst-case formulations of model predictive control for systems with bounded parameters. *Automatica*, 33(5), 763-781.

[53] Zheng, Z. Q., & Morari, M. (1995). Control of linear unstable systems with constraints. Paper presented at Proceedings of the American Control Conference, Seattle, WA. 3704-3708.

[54] Zheng, Z. Q., & Morari, M. (1995). Stability of model predictive control with mixed constraints. *IEEE Transactions on Automatic Control*, 40(10), 1818-1823.

[55] Kothare, K. V., Balakrishnan, V., & Morari, M. (1996). Robust constrained model predictive control using linear matrix inequalities. *Automatica*, 32(10), 1361-1379.

[56] Boyd, S., Ghaoui, L. E., Feron, E., & Balakrishnan, V. (1994). Linear Matrix Inequalities in System and Control Theory. SIAM, Philadelphia.

[57] Wan, Z., & Kothare, M. V. (2003). An efficient off-line formulation of robust model predictive control using linear matrix inequalities. *Automatica*, 39, 837-846.

[58] Pluymers, B., Suykens, J. A. K., & Moor, B. D. (2005). Min-max feedback MPC using a time-varying terminal constraint set and comments on efficient robust constrained model predictive control with a time varying terminal constraint set. *Systems & Control Letters*, 54, 1143-1148.

[59] Lee, Y. I., Cannon, M., & Kouvaritakis, B. (2005). Extended invariance and its use in model predictive control. *Automatica*, 41, 2163-2169.

[60] Jeong, S. C., & Park, P. (2005). Constrained MPC algorithm for uncertain time-varying systems with state-delay. *IEEE Transactions on Automatic Control*, 50(2), 257-263.

[61] Sato, T., & Inoue, A. (2006). Improvement of tracking performance in self-tuning PID controller based on generalized predictive control. *International Journal of Innovative Computing, Information and Control*, 2(3), 491-503.

[62] Kemih, K., Tekkouk, O., & Filali, S. (2006). Constrained generalized predictive control with estimation by genetic algorithm for a magnetic levitation system. *International Journal of Innovative Computing, Information and Control*, 2(3), 543-552.

[63] Tuan, H., Apkarian, P., & Nguyen, T. (2001). Robust and reduced-order filtering: new LMI-based characterizations and methods. *IEEE Transactions on Signal Processing*, 19, 2975-2984.

[64] Oliveira, D. M. C., Bernussou, J., & Geromel, J. C. (1999). A new discrete-time robust stability condition. *Systems & Control Letters*, 37, 261-265.

[65] Geromel, J. C., Oliveira, D. M. C., & Bernussou, J. (2002). Robust filtering of discrete-time linear systems with parameter dependent Lyapunov functions. *SIAM Journal on Control and Optimization*, 41, 700-711.

[66] Xia, Y., Liu, G. P., & Shi, P. J. (2008). Robust Constrained Model Predictive Control Based on Parameter-Dependent Lyapunov Functions. *Circuits, Systems and Signal Processing*, 27(4), 429-446.

[67] Calafiore, G. C., Dabbene, F., & Tempo, R. (2000). Randomized algorithms for probabilistic robustness with real and complex structured uncertainty. *IEEE Transactions on Automatic Control*, 45(12), 2218-2235.

[68] Lee, J. H., & Cooley, B. L. (1998). Optimal feedback control strategies for state-space systems with stochastic parameters. *IEEE Transactions on Automatic Control*, 43(10), 1469-1474.

[69] Hessem, V. D. H., & Bosgra, O. H. (2002). A conic reformulation of model predictive control including bounded and stochastic disturbances under state and input constraints. Paper presented at Proceedings of the 41st IEEE International Conference on Decision and Control, Las Vegas, NV,. 4, 4643-4648.

[70] Kouvaritakis, B., Cannon, M., & Tsachouridis, V. (2004). Recent developments in stochastic MPC and sustainable development. *Annual Reviews in Control*, 28(1), 23-35.

[71] Magni, L., Pala, D., & Scattolini, R. (2009). Stochastic model predictive control of constrained linear systems with additive uncertainty. In Proc. European Control Conference. Hungary: Budapest.

[72] Oldewurter, F., Jones, C. N., & Morari, M. (2009). A tractable approximation of chance constrained stochastic MPC based on affine disturbance feedback. In Proc. 48th IEEE Conf. Decision Control. Cancun.

[73] Primbs, J. A. (2007). A soft constraint approach to stochastic receding horizon control. In Proc. 46th IEEE Conf. Decision Control.

[74] Astrom, K. J. (1970). Introduction to stochastic control theory. New York, Academic Press.

[75] Batina, I., & Stoorvogel, Weiland. S. (2002). Optimal control of linear, stochastic systems with state and input constraints. In Proc. 41st IEEE Conf. Decision and Control , 1564-1569.

[76] Munoz, D., Bemporad, A., & Alamo, T. (2005). Stochastic programming applied to model predictive control. In Proc. CDC-ECC'05 , 1361-1366.

[77] Schwarm, A., & Nikolaou, M. (1999). Chance-constrained model predictive control. *AIChE Journal*, 45(8), 1743-1752.

[78] Hessem, V. D. H., & Bosgra, O. H. (2002). A conic reformulation of model predictive control including bounded and stochastic disturbances under state and input constraints. Paper presented at Proc. 41st IEEE Conf. Decision and Control. 4643-4648.

[79] Kouvaritakis, B., Cannon, M., & Couchman, P. (2006). MPC as a tool for sustainable development integrated policy assessment. *IEEE Transactions on Automatic Control*, 51(1), 145-149.

[80] Couchman, P., Cannon, M., & Kouvaritakis, B. (2006). Stochastic MPC with inequality stability constraints. *Automatica*, 42, 2169-2174.

[81] Couchman, P., Kouvaritakis, B., & Cannon, M. (2006). MPC on state space models with stochastic input map. In Proc. 45th IEEE Conf. Decision and Control , 3216-3221.

[82] Cannon, M., Kouvaritakis, B., & Wu, X. J. (2009). Model predictive control for systems with stochastic multiplicative uncertainty and probabilistic constraints. *Automatica*, 45(1), 167-172.

[83] Cannon, M., Kouvaritakis, B., Raković, S. V., & Cheng, Q. (2011). Stochastic tubes in model predictive control with probabilistic constraints. *IEEE Transactions on Automatic Control*, 56(1), 194-200.

[84] Kouvaritakis, B., Cannon, M., Raković, S. V., & Cheng, Q. (2010). Explicit use of probabilistic distributions in linear predictive control. *Automatica*, 46(10), 1719-1724.

[85] Cannon, M., Chenga, Q. F., Kouvaritakis, B., & Raković, S. V. (2012). Stochastic tube MPC with state estimation. *Automatic*, 48(3), 536-541.

[86] Zhivoglyadov, P. V., & Middleton, R. H. (2003). Networked control design for linear systems. *Automatica*, 39, 743-750.

[87] Hespanha, J. P., Naghshtabrizi, P., & Xu, Y. (2007). A survey of recent results in networked control systems. *Proceedings of the IEEE*, 95-138.

[88] Wong, S., & Brockett, R. W. (1999). Systems with finite communication bandwidth constraints II: Stabilization with limited information feedback. *IEEE Transactions on Automatic Control*, 44(5), 1049-1053.

[89] Ye, H., Walsh, G., & Bushnell, L. G. (2001). Real-time mixed-traffic wireless networks. *IEEE Transactions on Industrial Electronics*, 48(5), 883-890.

[90] Zhang, W., & Brannicky, Philips. S. M. (2001). Stability of networked control systems. *IEEE Control Systems Magazine*, 21(1), 84-99.

[91] Walsh, G. C., Beldiman, O., & Bushnell, L. G. (2001). Asymptotic behavior of nonlinear networked control systems. *IEEE Transactions on Automatic Control*, 46(7), 1093-1097.

[92] Yook, J. K., Tilbury, D. M., & Soparkar, N. R. (2001). A design methodology for distributed control systems to optimize performance in the presence of time delays. *International Journal of Control*, 74(1), 58-76.

[93] Park, H. S., Kim, Y. H., Kim, D. S., & Kwon, W. H. (2002). A scheduling method for network based control systems. *IEEE Transactions on Control Systems and Technology*, 10(3), 318-330.

[94] Lin, H., Zhai, G., & Antsaklis, P. J. (2003). Robust stability and disturbance attenuation analysis of a class of networked control systems. in Proc. 42nd IEEE Conf. Control, Maui, HI , 1182-1187.

[95] Lee, K. C., Lee, S., & Lee, M. H. (2003). Remote fuzzy logic control of networked control system via Profibus-dp. *IEEE Transactions on Industrial Electronics* , 50(4), 784-792.

[96] Guerrero, J. M., Matas, J., Vicuna, L. G. D., Castilla, M., & Miret, J. (2006). Wireless-control strategy for parallel operation of distributed-generation inverters. *IEEE Transactions on Industrial Electronics*, 53(5), 1461-1470.

[97] Hespanha, J. P., Naghshtabrizi, P., & Xu, Y. (2007). A survey of recent results in networked control systems. *Proceedings of the IEEE*, 95, 138-162.

[98] Gao, H., Chen, T., & James, L. (2008). A new delay system approach to network-based control. *Automatica*, 44, 39-52.

[99] Gao, H., & Chen, T. (2007). H_1 estimation for uncertain systems with limited communication capacity. *IEEE Transactions on Industrial Electronics*, 52, 2070-2084.

[100] Liu, G. P., Xia, Y., Chen, J., Rees, D., & Hu, W. (2007). Networked predictive control of systems with random networked delays in both forward and feedback channels. *IEEE Transactions on Industrial Electronics*, 54(3), 1282-1297.

[101] Hu, W., Liu, G. P., & Rees, D. (2007). Event-driven networked predictive control. *IEEE Transactions on Industrial Electronics*, 54, 1603-1613.

[102] Yang, S. H., Chen, X., Edwards, D. W., & Alty, J. L. (2003). Design issues and implementation of internet based process control. *Control Engineering Practices*, 11, 709-720.

[103] Christofides, P. D., & El -Farra, N. H. (2005). Control of nonlinear and hybrid process systems: Designs for uncertainty, constraints and time-delays. Berlin, Springer.

[104] Mhaskar, P., Gani, A., Mc Fall, C., Christofides, P. D., & Davis, J. F. (2007). Fault-tolerant control of nonlinear process systems subject to sensor faults. *AIChE Journal*, 53, 654-668.

[105] Nair, G. N., & Evans, R. J. (2007). Stabilization with data-rate-limited feedback: tightest attainable bounds. *Systems & Control Letters*, 41-49.

[106] Tipsuwan, Y., & Chow, M. (2003). Control methodologies in networked control systems. *Control Engineering Practice*, 1, 1099-1111.

[107] Hong, S. H. (1995). Scheduling algorithm of data sampling times in the integrated communication and control-systems. *IEEE Transactions on Control Systems Technology*, 3, 225-230.

[108] Shin, K. G. (1991). Real-time communications in a computer-controlled workcell. *IEEE Transactions on Robotics and Automation*, 7, 105-113.

[109] Nilsson, J. (1998). Real-time control systems with delays. *PhD thesis, Lund Inst. Technol.*

[110] Lian, F. L., & Moyne, J. (2003). Modelling and optimal controller design of networked control systems with multiple delays. *International Journal of Control*, 76(6), 591-606.

[111] Nesic, D., & Teel, A. R. (2004). Input-output stability properties of networked control systems. *IEEE Transactions on Automatic Control*, 49(10), 1650-1667.

[112] Yue, D., Han, Q. L., & Lam, J. (2005). Network-based robust H∞ control of systems with uncertainty. *Automatica*, 41(6), 999-1007.

[113] Brockett, R. W., & Liberzon, D. (2000). Quantized feedback stabilization of linear systems. *IEEE Transactions on Automatic Control*, 45, 1279-1289.

[114] Walsh, G., Ye, H., & Bushnell, L. (2002). Stability analysis of networked control systems. *IEEE Transactions on Control Systems Technology*, 10, 438-446.

[115] Nevsic, V. (2004). Input-output stability properties of networked control systems. *IEEE Transactions on Automatic Control*, 49, 1650-1667.

[116] Ploplys, N. J., Kawka, P. A., & Alleyne, A. G. (2004). Closed-loop control over wireless networks: developing a novel timing scheme for real-time control systems. *IEEE Control Systems Magazine*, 24, 52-71.

[117] Tabbara, M. (2007). Stability of wireless and wireline networked control systems. *IEEE Transactions on Automatic Control*, 52, 1615-1630.

[118] Ye, H., & Walsh, G. (2001). Real-time mixed-traffic wireless networks. *IEEE Transactions on Industrial Electronics*, 48, 883-890.

[119] Ye, H., Walsh, G., & Bushnell, L. (2000). Wireless local area networks in the manufacturing industry. In Proceedings of the American control conference, Chicago, Illinois , 2363-2367.

[120] Hassibi, A., Boyd, S. P., & How, J. P. (1999). Control of asynchronous dynamical systems with rate constraints on events. In Proceedings of IEEE conference on decision and control, Phoenix, Arizona , 1345-1351.

[121] Ritchey, V. S., & Franklin, G. F. (1989). A stability criterion for asynchronous multirate linear systems. *IEEE Transactions on Automatic Control*, 34, 529-535.

[122] Su, Y. F., Bhaya, A., Kaszkurewicz, E., & Kozyakin, V. S. (1997). Further results on stability of asynchronous discrete-time linear systems. In Proceedings of the 36th IEEE conference on decision and control San Diego, California , 915-920.

[123] Nguyen, G. T., Katz, R. H., Noble, B., & Satyanarayananm, M. (1996). A trace based approach for modeling wireless channel behavior. In Proceedings of the winter simulation conference, Coronado, California , 597-604.

[124] Hespanha, J. P. (2005). A model for stochastic hybrid systems with application to communication networks. *Nonlinear Analysis*, 62, 1353-1383.

[125] Mao, X. (1999). Stability of stochastic differential equations with Markovian switching. *Stochastic Processes and Their Applications*, 79, 45-67.

[126] Lin, H., & Antsaklis, P. J. (2005). Stability and persistent disturbance attenuation properties for a class of networked control systems: switched system approach. *International Journal of Control*, 78, 1447-1458.

[127] Imer, O. C., Yüksel, S., & Basar, T. (2006). Optimal control of LTI systems over unreliable communications links. *Automatica*, 42, 1429-1439.

[128] Azimi-Sadjadi, B. (2003). Stability of networked control systems in the presence of packet losses. In Proceedings of the 42nd IEEE conference on decision and control, Maui, Hawaii , 676-681.

[129] Elia, N., & Eisenbeis, J. N. (2004). Limitations of linear remote control over packet drop networks. In Proceedings of IEEE conference on decision and control, Nassau, Bahamas , 5152-5157.

[130] Hadjicostis, C. N., & Touri, R. (2002). Feedback control utilizing packet dropping networks links. In Proceedings of the 41st IEEE conference on decision and control, Las Vegas, Nevada , 1205-1210.

[131] Jeong, S. C., & Park, P. (2005). Constrained MPC algorithm for uncertain time-varying systems with state-delay. *IEEE Transactions on Automatic Control*, 50-257.

[132] Schenato, L. (2009). To zero or to hold control inputs with lossy links?. *IEEE Transactions on Automatic Control*, 50, 1099-1105.

[133] Liu, G. P., Mu, J., Rees, D., & Chai, S. C. (2006). Design and stability of networked control systems with random communication time delay using the modified MPC. *International Journal of Control*, 79, 288-297.

[134] Xia, Y., Fu, M., Liu, B., & Liu, G. P. (2009). Design and performance analysis of networked control systems with random delay. *Journal of Systems Engineering and Electronics*, 20, 807-822.

[135] Liu, G. P., Mu, J., & Rees, D. (2004). Networked predictive control of systems with random communication delays. presented at the UKACC Int. Conf. Control, BathU.K. ; Paper ID-015.

[136] Liu, G. P., Xia, Y., & Rees, D. (2005). Predictive control of networked systems with random delays. Paper presented at IFAC World Congress, Prague.

[137] Liu, G. P., Rees, D., Chai, S. C., & Nie, X. Y. (2005). Design and Practical Implementation of Networked Predictive Control Systems. *Networking, Sensing and Control*, 38, 17-21.

[138] Xia, Y., Liu, G. P., Fu, M., & Rees, D. (2009). Predictive Control of Networked Systems with Random Delay and Data Dropout. *IET Control Theory and Applications*, 3(11), 1476-1486.

[139] Xia, Y., Fu, M., & Liu, G. P. (2011). Analysis and Synthesis of Networked Control Systems. Springer.

[140] Negenborn, R. R, De Schutter, B., & Hellendoorn, H. (2006). Multi-agent model predictive control of transportation networks. Paper presented at Proceedings of the 2006 IEEE International Conference on Networking, Sensing and Control (ICNSC2006),, Ft. Lauderdale, FL,. 296-301.

[141] Yang, T. C. (2006). Networked control systems: a brief survey. *IEE Proceedings Control Theory and Applications*, 152-403.

[142] Neumann, P. (2007). Communication in industrial automation what is going on? *Control Engineering Practice*, 15, 1332-1347.

[143] Qin, S. J., & Badgwell, T. A. (2000). An overview of nonlinear model predictive control applications,. in: F. Allgower, A. Zheng (Eds.), Nonlinear Model Predictive Control, Birkhauser Berlin , 369-392.

[144] Qin, S. J., & Badgwell, T. A. (2003). A survey of industrial model predictive control technology. *Control Engineering Practice*, 11(7), 733-764.

[145] Rawlings, J. B., & Stewart, B. T. (2008). Coordinating multiple optimization-based controllers: New opportunities and challenges. *Journal of Process Control*, 18, 839-845.

[146] Scattolini, R. (2009). Architectures for distributed and hierarchical model predictive control: a review. *Journal of Process Control*, 19, 723-731.

[147] Magni, L., & Scattolini, R. (2006). Stabilizing decentralized model predictive control of nonlinear systems. *Automatica*, 42, 1231-1236.

[148] Vaccarini, M., Longhi, S., & Katebi, M. R. (2009). Unconstrained networked decentralized model predictive control. *Journal of Process Control*, 19(2), 328-339.

[149] Wang, S. H., & Davison, E. (1973). On the stabilization of decentralized control systems. *IEEE Transactions on Automatic Control*, 18, 473-478.

[150] Davison, E. J., & Chang, T. N. (1990). Decentralized stabilization and pole assignment for general proper systems. *IEEE Transactions on Automatic Control*, 35, 652-664.

[151] Du, X., Xi, Y., & Li, S. (2001). Distributed model predictive control for large-scale systems. In: Proceedings of the American control conference , 4, 3142-3143.

[152] Camponogara, E., Jia, D., Krogh, B. H., & Talukdar, S. (2002). Distributed model predictive control. *IEEE Control Systems Magazine*, 22, 44-52.

[153] Dunbar, W. B. (2007). Distributed receding horizon control of dynamically coupled nonlinear systems. *IEEE Transactions on Automatic Control*, 52(7), 1249-1263.

[154] Dunbar, W. B., & Murray, R. M. (2006). Distributed receding horizon control for multi-vehicle formation stabilization. *Automatica*, 42(4), 549-558.

[155] Li, S., Zhang, Y., & Zhu, Q. (2005). Nash-optimization enhanced distributed model predictive control applied to the Shell benchmark problem. *Information Sciences*, 170(2-4), 329-349.

[156] Richards, A., & How, J. P. (2007). Robust distributed model predictive control. *International Journal of Control*, 80(9), 1517-1531.

[157] Venkat, A. N., Rawlings, J. B., & Wright, S. J. (2007). Distributed model predictive control of large-scale systems. In: Proceedings of the assessment and future directions of nonlinear model predictive control. Berlin Heidelberg, Springer, 591-605.

[158] Liu, J., Muñoz la, Peña. D., Christofides, P. D., & Davis, J. F. (2009). Lyapunovbased model predictive control of nonlinear systems subject to time-varying measurement delays. *International Journal of Adaptive Control and Signal Processing*, 23-788.

[159] Muñoz la, Peña. D., & Christofides, P. D. (2008). Lyapunov-based model predictive control of nonlinear systems subject to data losses. *IEEE Transactions on Automatic Control*, 53, 2076-2089.

[160] Franco, E., Magni, L., Parisini, T., Polycarpou, M. M., & Raimondo, D. M. (2008). Cooperative constrained control of distributed agents with nonlinear dynamics and delayed information exchange: a stabilizing receding-horizon approach. *IEEE Transactions on Automatic Control*, 53, 324-338.

[161] Liu, J., de la Peña, D. M., & Christofides, P. D. (2010). Distributed model predictive control of nonlinear systems subject to asynchronous and delayed measurements. *Automatica*, 46, 52-61.

Chapter 5

Stability Analysis of Nonlinear Discrete-Time Adaptive Control Systems with Large Dead-Times - Theory and a Case Study

Mario A. Jordan, Jorge L. Bustamante and
Carlos E. Berger

Additional information is available at the end of the chapter

http://dx.doi.org/10.5772/52224

1. Introduction

Accordingly to modern digital technology in control communications and optic fiber, unmanned underwater vehicles (UUV) are usually controlled digitally. In the case of remotely operated vehicles (ROV), partial control systems are useful, for instance for the roll-pitch stabilization, as long as the main modes of motion are performed basically by teleoperation. In the case of autonomous underwater vehicles (AUV) on the contrary, the control of modes is complete, it means, the advance, the immersion and the roll-pitch stabilization are carried out automatically with a large degree of self-decision both in guidance and control.

In all cases, digital communications between the controller, the guide system and the navigation system are often affected by a pure delay in the control action, which correctively manipulates the vehicle behavior with lateness through their thrusters. Generally speaking, the delay is variable because of the commonly sophisticated nature of protocols involved in the usual communication standards, for instance in the well-widespread protocols RS422/485. In many cases, the delay problem is much more complex and embraces a pure delay for the sensor instruments and other quite different ones for the controller and guidance communications. Moreover, sensors may have different delays each one, due to different hardware and baud rates in data transmission.

Pure delays can influence significantly the stability of UUV's, principally in fast motions like in the modes of pitch and roll, causing, in extreme fall, the capsize of the vehicle. Additionally, the well-known strong interaction among the modes in the dynamics of UUV's may cause large oscillations of the pitch modes that are induced by acelerations in the advance mode. Thus, complex control systems for the whole 6-degrees-of freedom (DOF) dynamics are much more preferable than many single-mode controllers.

Dealing with pure delays in the controller design, a Smith-predictor solution stays in mind at the first place. However, the needs of a precise model to construct the predictor upon the usually uncertain and potentially unstable dynamics of an UUV, makes this alternative quite unfeasible (Leonard and Abba, 2012). On the other way, simple controllers like for instance PID controllers, are viable to be tuned with less dynamics information but generally can not counteract by itself the undesirable effects of relatively large pure delays. Adaptive controllers had proved to work properly in these scenarios with many advantages (Jordán and Bustamante, 2011). Nevertheless, the roll played by pure delays in the stability and performance of control systems for underwater vehicles is much less dealt with in the specialized literature.

In this Chapter we focus the design of a 6-degrees-of-freedom adaptive controller for UUV's directly in the sample-time domain. The controller pertains to the class of speed gradient adaptive control systems. This controller was developed in (Jordán and Bustamante, 2011) and shows clearly advantages in stability over the same digital speed-gradient controller which is first designed in continuous time and finally translated to discrete time. One starts from the fact that the UUV dynamics, together with the control communication link in the feedback, involves a considerable delay. In this work, we depart from a hypothesis that an optimal sampling time for the control stability should have some upper limit for the stability in the presence of pure delays, disturbances in the samples and rapid desired maneuvers. To support our hypothesis, we close the analysis with a classification of certain influence variables on the stability and performance of the proposed digital adaptive control system.

2. UUV dynamics

Let $\eta=[x,y,z,\varphi,\theta,\psi]^T$ be the generalized position vector of the UUV referred to an earth-fixed coordinate system termed O', with displacements x,y,z, and rotation angles φ,θ,ψ about these directions, respectively. The motions associated to the elements of η are referred to as surge, sway, heave, roll, pitch and yaw, respectively.

Additionally let $v=[u,v,w,p,q,r]^T$ be the generalized rate vector referred on a vehicle-fixed coordinate system termed O, oriented according to its main axes with translation rates u,v,w and angular rates p,q,r about these directions, respectively.

The vehicle dynamics with a time delay in the communication system, is described by the ODE (*cf.* Jordán and Bustamante, 2009a; *cf.* Fossen, 1994)

$$\dot{v}=M^{-1}\left(-C[v]v-D[|v|]v-g[\eta]+\tau_c+\tau(t-T_d)\right) \tag{1}$$

$$\dot{\eta}=J[\eta](v+v_c). \tag{2}$$

Here M, C and D are the inertia, the Coriolis-centripetal and the drag matrices, respectively and J is the matrix expressing the transformation from the inertial frame to the vehicle-fixed frame. Moreover, g is the restoration force due to buoyancy and weight, τ is the generalized propulsion force whose action is delayed T_d seconds, τ_c is a generalized perturbation force (for instance due to cable tugs in ROV's) and v_c is a velocity perturbation (for instance the fluid current in ROV's/AUV's), all of them applied to O.

From now on, brackets are employed to indicate functional dependence and parenthesis to denote common factor. Besides vectors are indicated in bold, variables in italics and matrices in capital letters.

Notice from (1) the nonlinear dependence of C, D and $\boldsymbol{g}$ with the states $\boldsymbol{v}$ and $\boldsymbol{\eta}$.

Moreover, we will concentrate henceforth on disturbed measures $\boldsymbol{\eta}_\delta$ and $\boldsymbol{v}_\delta$, and not on exogenous perturbations $\boldsymbol{\tau}_c$ and $\boldsymbol{v}_c$, so we have set $\boldsymbol{\tau}_c=\boldsymbol{v}_c=0$ throughout the Chapter. For more explanations about the influence of $\boldsymbol{\tau}_c$ and $\boldsymbol{v}_c$ on adaptive guidance systems see (Jordán and Bustamante, 2008; Jordán and Bustamante 2007), respectively.

3. Sampled-data behavior

For the continuous-time dynamics there exists an associated exact sampled-data dynamics described by the set of sequences $\{\boldsymbol{\eta}[t_i],\boldsymbol{v}[t_i]\}=\{\boldsymbol{\eta}_{t_i},\boldsymbol{v}_{t_i}\}$ for the states $\boldsymbol{\eta}[t]$ and $\boldsymbol{v}[t]$ at sample times t_i with a sampling rate h. When measures are affected with noise values $\{\delta\boldsymbol{\eta}_{t_n},\delta\boldsymbol{v}_{t_n}\}$, we use $\{\boldsymbol{\eta}_\delta[t_i],\boldsymbol{v}_\delta[t_i]\}=\left\{\boldsymbol{\eta}_{\delta_{t_i}},\boldsymbol{v}_{\delta_{t_i}}\right\}=\{\boldsymbol{\eta}_{t_n}+\delta\boldsymbol{\eta}_{t_n},\boldsymbol{v}_{t_n}+\delta\boldsymbol{v}_{t_n}\}$ instead.

Since the pure delay period is supposed to be originated in the control communication system, we will assume in some particular scenarios that T_d in (1), satisfies

$$T_d = d\,h = d_0\,h + \delta d\,h, \tag{3}$$

which is saying that d is a variable integer, while d_0 is a constant positive integer and δd a sign-undefined integer representing a perturbation that fulfills $d_0 \geq |\delta d| \geq 0$ and d can range between 0 and $2d_0$. Another feature of the communication hardware is that the sample times t_i of the instrument (from Gyro and DVL for instance) are indicated together with the samples, and so, when these are transmitted to the controller, the calculation of d is possible.

Now, let us rewrite the ODE (1)-(2) in a more compact form

$$\dot{\boldsymbol{v}} = M^{-1}\boldsymbol{p}[\boldsymbol{\eta},\boldsymbol{v}]+M^{-1}\boldsymbol{\tau} \tag{4}$$

$$\dot{\boldsymbol{\eta}} = \boldsymbol{q}[\boldsymbol{\eta},\boldsymbol{v}], \tag{5}$$

with $\boldsymbol{p}$ and $\boldsymbol{q}$ being Lipschitz vector functions located at the right-hand memberships of the (1) and (2), respectively. Here no exogenous perturbation was considered as agreed above.

For further analysis, we can state a model-based predictor for one step or more steps ahead. To this end it might employ high order approximators like Adams-Bashforth types, though for perturbed states a simple Euler approximator is more convenient (Jordán and Bustamante, 2009b). So

$$\boldsymbol{v}_{n+1} = \boldsymbol{v}_{t_n}+\delta\boldsymbol{v}_{t_n}+hM^{-1}\left(\boldsymbol{p}_{\delta_{t_n}}+\boldsymbol{\tau}_{n-d}\right) \tag{6}$$

$$\boldsymbol{\eta}_{n+1} = \boldsymbol{\eta}_{t_n}+\delta\boldsymbol{\eta}_{t_n}+h\boldsymbol{q}_{\delta_{t_n}}, \tag{7}$$

where $\boldsymbol{\eta}_{n+1}$ and $\boldsymbol{v}_{n+1}$ are one-step-ahead predictions. Herein it is valid with (1)-(2)

$$p_{\delta_{t_n}} = -\sum_{i=1}^{6} C_i . \times C_{v_{i_n}} v_{\delta_{t_n}} - D_l v_{\delta_{t_n}} - \sum_{i=1}^{6} D_{q_i} |v_{i\delta_{t_n}}| v_{\delta_{t_n}} - B_1\, g_{1_n} - B_2\, g_{2_n} \tag{8}$$

$$q_{\delta_{t_n}} = J_{\delta_{t_n}} v_{\delta_{t_n}} \tag{9}$$

where $C_{v_{i_n}}$ means $C_{v_i}[v_{\delta_{t_n}}]$, g_{1_n} and g_{2_n} mean $g_1[\eta_{\delta_{t_n}}]$ and $g_2[\eta_{\delta_{t_n}}]$ respectively, $J_{\delta_{t_n}}$ means $J[\eta_{\delta_{t_n}}]$ and $v_{i_{t_n}}$ is an element of v_{t_n}. Additionally, the matricial product ".×" in (8) means an element-by-element product between the matrices to both sides. Besides, the control action τ is retained one sampling period h by a sample holder, so it is valid $\tau_n = \tau_{t_n}$. We finally remark that since p, q and r are Lipschitz continuous in the attraction domains in v and η, then the samples, predictions and local errors all yield bounded.

4. Predictions

The accuracy of one-step-ahead predictions (6)-(7) with known perfect model and without perturbation is defined by the local model errors as

$$\varepsilon_{v_{n+1}} = v_{\delta_{t_{n+1}}} - v_{n+1} \tag{10}$$

$$\varepsilon_{\eta_{n+1}} = \eta_{\delta_{t_{n+1}}} - \eta_{n+1}. \tag{11}$$

with $\varepsilon_{\eta_{n+1}}, \varepsilon_{v_{n+1}} \in \mathcal{O}[h]$ and $\mathcal{O}$ being such a function that $f[x] \in \mathcal{O}[x]$ means that there exists a neighborhood of x around null such that $f[x]/x$ is bounded inside the neighborhood.

We have also the goal to predict states counteracting the negative influence of a delay in them. In order to be able to produce a prediction of many steps in advance based upon the last past information known, we can employ (6)-(7) tied in succession in many links of first order.

So we attempt to construct the state predictions η_{n+1} and v_{n+1} taken the sample at t_{n-d} as the unique support to predict at t_n. We start with

$$v_{n-d+1} = v_{\delta_{t_{n-d}}} + h\underline{M}^{-1}\left(r_{\delta_{n-d}} + \tau_{n-d}\right), \tag{12}$$

where $v_{\delta_{t_{n-d}}}$ is the last sample known at the current time, $\underline{M}$ is some known lower matrix of M and

$$r_j = \sum_{i=1}^{6} U_i . \times C_{v_{i_j}} v_j + U_7 v_j + \sum_{i=1}^{6} U_{7+i} |v_{i_j}| v_j + U_{14} g_{1_j} + U_{15}\, g_{2_j}, \tag{13}$$

where the matrices U_i will account for every unknown system matrix in $p_{\delta_{t_n}}$ in (8) with some appropriate value. We will return to these matrices U_i´s later in the controller design.

As there is no information of the sample at t_{n-d+1}, the next prediction is with (12) included

$$v_{n-d+2} = v_{\delta_{t_{n-d}}} + h\underline{M}^{-1}\left(r_{n-d+1} + \tau_{n-d+1}\right) + h\underline{M}^{-1}\left(r_{\delta_{n-d}} + \tau_{n-d}\right). \tag{14}$$

It is noticing the difference between $\boldsymbol{r}_{\delta_{n-d}}$ and $\boldsymbol{r}_{n-d+1}$ from the procedence of their variables, namely $\boldsymbol{r}_{\delta_{n-d}}$ is based upon the samples $\boldsymbol{v}_{\delta_{n-d}}$ and $\boldsymbol{\eta}_{\delta_{n-d}}$, while $\boldsymbol{r}_{n-d+1}$ is based upon the predictions $\boldsymbol{v}_{n-d+1}$ and $\boldsymbol{\eta}_{n-d+1}$.

For control purposes, the prediction for t_{n+1} will be necessary. This is

$$\boldsymbol{v}_{n+1} = \boldsymbol{v}_{\delta_{t_{n-d}}} + h\underline{M}^{-1} \sum_{i=1}^{d} (\boldsymbol{r}_{n+1-i} + \boldsymbol{\tau}_{n+1-i}) + h\underline{M}^{-1} \left(\boldsymbol{r}_{\delta_{n-d}} + \boldsymbol{\tau}_{n-d}\right), \tag{15}$$

$$\boldsymbol{\eta}_{n+1} = \boldsymbol{\eta}_{\delta_{t_{n-d}}} + h \sum_{i=1}^{d} \boldsymbol{q}_{n+1-i} + h\boldsymbol{q}_{\delta_{n-d}}. \tag{16}$$

The same consideration between $\boldsymbol{q}_{\delta_{n-d}}$ and $\boldsymbol{q}_{n-d+i}$ (for $i > 0$) mentioned before can be said as in the comparison made between $\boldsymbol{r}_{\delta_{n-d}}$ and $\boldsymbol{r}_{n-d+i}$ (for $i > 0$) with respect to samples and predictions.

As the so-called local truncation error of the Euler method is bounded, it is for $\boldsymbol{v}$

$$\alpha_0(h, \delta\boldsymbol{\eta}_{t_i}, \delta\boldsymbol{v}_{t_i}) = \max_{t_i > 0} \left| \frac{\boldsymbol{v}_{\delta_{t_i}} - \boldsymbol{v}_{i+1}}{h} - \underline{M}^{-1} \left(\boldsymbol{r}_{\delta_i} + \boldsymbol{\tau}_i\right) \right|, \tag{17}$$

and since the Method is consistent, $\alpha_0(h, \mathbf{0}, \mathbf{0})$ goes to zero as h tends to zero, then global error $\varepsilon_{v_{n+1}}$ has a bound

$$|\varepsilon_{v_{n+1}}| \leq \left(\delta\boldsymbol{v}_{t_{n-d}} - \frac{\alpha_0(h, \delta\boldsymbol{\eta}_{t_i}, \delta\boldsymbol{v}_{t_i})}{\kappa_v} \right) e^{\kappa_v (\frac{T_d}{h} + 1) h}, \tag{18}$$

where κ_v is the Lipshitz constant of $\underline{M}^{-1} (\boldsymbol{p}[\boldsymbol{\eta}, \boldsymbol{v}] + \boldsymbol{\tau})$. The same is said for $\boldsymbol{\eta}$, where there exists a Lipshitz constant κ_η of $\boldsymbol{q}[\boldsymbol{\eta}, \boldsymbol{v}]$ and it is valid

$$|\varepsilon_{\eta_{n+1}}| \leq \left(\delta\boldsymbol{\eta}_{t_{n-d}} - \frac{\beta_0(h, \delta\boldsymbol{\eta}_{t_i}, \delta\boldsymbol{v}_{t_i})}{\kappa_\eta} \right) e^{\kappa_\eta (\frac{T_d}{h} + 1) h}, \tag{19}$$

and

$$\beta_0(h, \delta\boldsymbol{\eta}_{t_i}, \delta\boldsymbol{v}_{t_i}) = \max_{t_i > 0} \left| \frac{\boldsymbol{\eta}_{\delta_{t_i}} - \boldsymbol{\eta}_{i+1}}{h} - \boldsymbol{q}_{\delta_i} \right|. \tag{20}$$

Clearly from (18) and (19), for any $T_d > 0$, the convergence of the predictions is ensured for h tending to zero and with $\delta\boldsymbol{\eta}$, $\delta\boldsymbol{v}$ uniformly null.

5. Design of the controller

Let the control system in Fig. 1 be taken as the basic structure for the next development. The guide system therein generates references in time, denoted by $\eta_r(t)$, of a geometric path in the 6-DOF with some desired kinematic, termed $v_r(\eta_r(t))$, over it. Additionally, it is assumed that the disturbances $\delta\eta_{t_n}$ and δv_{t_n} acting on the samples are uniformly bounded.

We now postulate a functional of the path error energy

$$Q_{t_n} = \breve{\eta}_{t_n}^T \breve{\eta}_{t_n} + \breve{v}_{t_n}^T \breve{v}_{t_n}, \tag{21}$$

with (see Jordán and Bustamante, 2011)

$$\breve{\eta}_{t_n} = \eta_{t_n} - \eta_{r_{t_n}} = \eta_n + \varepsilon_n - \eta_{r_{t_n}} \tag{22}$$

$$\breve{v}_{t_n} = v_{t_n} - J_{t_n}^{-1} \dot{\eta}_{r_{t_n}} + J_{t_n}^{-1} K_p \breve{\eta}_{t_n} = v_{t_n} + \varepsilon_{v_n} - J_{t_n}^{-1} \dot{\eta}_{r_{t_n}} + J_{t_n}^{-1} K_p \breve{\eta}_{t_n}, \tag{23}$$

where $K_p = K_p^T \geq 0$ is a design gain matrix affecting the geometric path errors. Clearly, if $\breve{\eta}_{t_n} \equiv \mathbf{0}$, then by (23) and (2), it yields $v_{t_n} - v_{r_{t_n}} \equiv \mathbf{0}$.

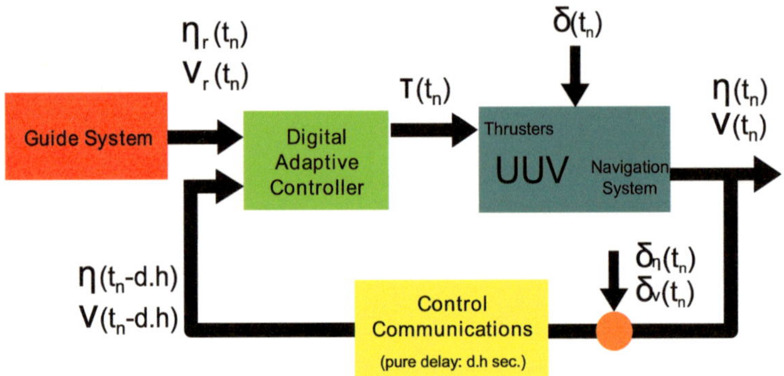

Figure 1. Digital adaptive control system of an UUV with sample disturbances and pure time delay in the control communication link

Then, replacing (6) and (7) in (22) for t_{n+1} one gets

$$\breve{\eta}_{t_{n+1}} = \eta_{n+1} + \varepsilon_{n+1} - \eta_{r_{t_{n+1}}} = \eta_n + h q_n + \varepsilon_n + \varepsilon_{n+1} - \eta_{r_{t_{n+1}}}. \tag{24}$$

Similarly, (6) and (7) in (23) for t_{n+1} one obtains

$$\begin{aligned} \breve{v}_{t_{n+1}} &= v_{t_{n+1}} - J_{t_{n+1}}^{-1} \dot{\eta}_{r_{t_{n+1}}} + J_{t_{n+1}}^{-1} K_p \breve{\eta}_{t_{n+1}} = \\ &= v_n + h \underline{M}^{-1} \left(r_{\delta_{n-d}} + \tau_{n-d} \right) + \varepsilon_{v_n} + \varepsilon_{v_{n+1}} - J_{t_{n+1}}^{-1} \dot{\eta}_{r_{t_{n+1}}} + J_{t_n+1}^{-1} K_p \breve{\eta}_{t_{n+1}}. \end{aligned} \tag{25}$$

http://dx.doi.org/10.5772/52224

The control goal is to construct the force τ_n so as to minimize Q_{t_n} asymptotically, with $\Delta Q_{t_n} := Q_{t_{n+1}} - Q_{t_n} < 0$

$$\Delta Q_{t_n} = \overset{\backsim}{\eta}^T_{t_{n+1}} \overset{\backsim}{\eta}_{t_{n+1}} + \overset{\backsim}{v}^T_{t_{n+1}} \overset{\backsim}{v}_{t_{n+1}} - \overset{\backsim}{\eta}^T_{t_n} \overset{\backsim}{\eta}_{t_n} - \overset{\backsim}{v}^T_{t_n} \overset{\backsim}{v}_{t_n}. \tag{26}$$

Bearing in mind the presence of disturbances and model uncertainties, the practical goal would be at least that $\{\Delta Q_{t_n}\}$ decrease so as to ultimately remain bounded for $t_n \to \infty$. The problem is now to construct the control action τ_n in such a way that this goal be achieved.

With (24), (25) and (21) in (26), one gets

$$\begin{aligned} \Delta Q_{t_n} = & \left(\left(I - hJ_{t_n} J_n^{-1} K_p \right) \eta_n + hJ_{t_n} \overset{\backsim}{v}_{t_n} - hJ_{t_n} \varepsilon_{v_n} - hJ_{t_n} J_n^{-1} \dot{\eta}_{r_{t_n}} - \right. \\ & \left. - hJ_{t_n} J_n^{-1} K_p (\varepsilon_{\eta_n} - \eta_{r_{t_n}}) + \varepsilon_{\eta_n} + \varepsilon_{\eta_{n+1}} - \eta_{r_{t_{n+1}}} \right)^2 - \\ & - \left(\eta_n + \varepsilon_{\eta_n} - \eta_{r_{t_n}} \right)^2 + \\ & + \left(v_n + h\underline{M}^{-1} (r_n + \tau_n) + \varepsilon_{v_n} + \varepsilon_{v_{n+1}} - J_{t_{n+1}}^{-1} \dot{\eta}_{r_{t_{n+1}}} + J_{t_{n+1}}^{-1} K_p \overset{\backsim}{\eta}_{t_{n+1}} \right)^2 - \\ & - \left(v_n + \varepsilon_{v_n} - J_{t_{n+1}}^{-1} \dot{\eta}_{r_{t_n}} + J_{t_n}^{-1} K_p \overset{\backsim}{\eta}_{t_n} \right)^2 . \end{aligned} \tag{27}$$

The desired properties of (27) can be conferred through a suitable selection of τ_n. In (Jordán and Bustamante, 2011) a flexible methodology for constructing τ_n was proposed and could serve to support this control objective. We will briefly review it and add the proper modifications attending the particularities of the pure-delay case.

Analyzing (27) we can conveniently split the control thrust τ_n into two terms as

$$\tau_n = \tau_{1_n} + \tau_{2_n}, \tag{28}$$

We notice that the choice

$$\tau_{1_n} = -K_v v_n - \frac{1}{h} \underline{M} \left(-J_{n+1}^{-1} \dot{\eta}_{r_{t_{n+1}}} + J_{n+1}^{-1} K_p \overset{\backsim}{\eta}_{n+1} \right) \tag{29}$$

is the most convenient to compensate some sign-undefinite terms in (27) and to propitiate a negative definite term in v_n. Herein $K_v = K_v^T \geq 0$ being another design matrix like K_p, but affecting the kinematic errors.

Thus

$$\Delta Q_{t_n} = \left(\left(I - hJ_{t_n}J_n^{-1}K_p\right)\eta_n\right)^2 - \eta_n^2 + \left(\left(I - h\underline{M}^{-1}K_v\right)v_n\right)^2 - v_n^2 -$$
$$- \left(J_{t_n}^{-1}\dot{\eta}_{r_{t_n}} + J_{t_n}^{-1}K_p\breve{\eta}_{t_n}\right)^2 - \eta_{r_{t_n}}^2 + \left(-hJ_{t_n}\varepsilon_{v_n} - hJ_{t_n}J_n^{-1}K_p\varepsilon_{\eta_n} + \varepsilon_{\eta_n} + \varepsilon_{\eta_{n+1}}\right)^2 +$$
$$+2\varepsilon_{\eta_n}^T\eta_{r_{t_n}} - \varepsilon_{\eta_n}^2 + \left(\varepsilon_{v_n} + \varepsilon_{v_{n+1}} - \Delta J_{n+1}^{-1}\dot{\eta}_{r_{t_{n+1}}} + \Delta J_{n+1}^{-1}K_p\breve{\eta}_{t_{n+1}}\right)^2 - \varepsilon_{v_n}^2 +$$
$$+2\left(\left(I - hJ_{t_n}J_n^{-1}K_p\right)\eta_n\right)^T\left(-hJ_{t_n}\varepsilon_{v_n} - hJ_{t_n}J_n^{-1}K_p\varepsilon_{\eta_n} +\right.$$
$$\left. + \varepsilon_{\eta_n} + \varepsilon_{\eta_{n+1}}\right) - 2\eta_n^T\left(\varepsilon_{\eta_n} - \eta_{r_{t_n}}\right) + 2\left(\left(I - h\underline{M}^{-1}K_v\right)v_n\right)^T$$
$$\left(\varepsilon_{v_n} + \varepsilon_{v_{n+1}} - \Delta J_{n+1}^{-1}\dot{\eta}_{r_{t_{n+1}}} + \Delta J_{n+1}^{-1}K_p\breve{\eta}_{t_{n+1}}\right) +$$
$$+ \left(h\underline{M}^{-1}(p_n - r_n)\right)^T\left(\varepsilon_{v_n} + \varepsilon_{v_{n+1}} - \Delta J_{n+1}^{-1}\dot{\eta}_{r_{t_{n+1}}} + \Delta J_{n+1}^{-1}K_p\breve{\eta}_{t_{n+1}}\right) -$$
$$-v_n^T\varepsilon_{v_n} + \left(hJ_{t_n}\breve{v}_{t_n} + hJ_{t_n}J_n^{-1}\dot{\eta}_{r_{t_n}} + hJ_{t_n}J_n^{-1}K_p\eta_{r_{t_n}} - \eta_{r_{t_{n+1}}}\right)^2 +$$
$$+2\left(\left(I - hJ_{t_n}J_n^{-1}K_p\right)\eta_n\right)^T\left(hJ_{t_n}\breve{v}_{t_n} + hJ_{t_n}J_n^{-1}\dot{\eta}_{r_{t_n}} + hJ_{t_n}J_n^{-1}K_p\eta_{r_{t_n}} - \eta_{r_{t_{n+1}}}\right) +$$
$$+ \left(h\underline{M}^{-1}(p_n - r_n)\right)^2 + 2\left(\left(I - h\underline{M}^{-1}K_v\right)v_n\right)^T h\underline{M}^{-1}(p_n - r_n) -$$
$$-2v_n^T\left(-J_{t_n}^{-1}\dot{\eta}_{r_{t_n}} + J_{t_n}^{-1}K_p\breve{\eta}_{t_n}\right) + \left(h\underline{M}^{-1}\tau_{n_2}\right)^2 +$$
$$+2\left(v_n + h\underline{M}^{-1}(p_n - r_n) + \varepsilon_{v_n} + \varepsilon_{v_{n+1}} - \Delta J_{n+1}^{-1}\dot{\eta}_{r_{t_{n+1}}} + \Delta J_{n+1}^{-1}K_p\breve{\eta}_{t_{n+1}}\right)^T h\underline{M}^{-1}\tau_{n_2} \tag{30}$$

where p_n is defined as in $p_{\delta_{t_n}}$ but with predictions v_n and η_n instead of v_{t_n} and η_{t_n}, respectively. Similarly J_n stays for $J[\eta_n]$. Additionally $\Delta J_{n+1}^{-1} = J_{t_{n+1}}^{-1} - J_{n+1}^{-1}$.

Finally, as seen in (30), the unique remaining design variable is τ_{n_2}.

A glance into (30) let us identify sign-undefinite terms which can not be compensated with τ_{n_2}, precisely because they are functions of unknown global prediction errors ε_η, ε_v, and ΔJ. We can group them into the function

$$
\begin{aligned}
f_{\Delta Q_1}[\boldsymbol{\varepsilon}_{\eta_n},\boldsymbol{\varepsilon}_{v_n}] = & \left(-hJ_{t_n}\boldsymbol{\varepsilon}_{v_n} - hJ_{t_n}J_n^{-1}K_p\boldsymbol{\varepsilon}_{\eta_n} + \boldsymbol{\varepsilon}_{\eta_n} + \boldsymbol{\varepsilon}_{\eta_{n+1}}\right)^2 + 2\boldsymbol{\varepsilon}_{\eta_n}^T\boldsymbol{\eta}_{r_{t_n}} - \boldsymbol{\varepsilon}_{\eta_n}^2 + \\
& + \left(\boldsymbol{\varepsilon}_{v_n} + \boldsymbol{\varepsilon}_{v_{n+1}} - \Delta J_{n+1}^{-1}\dot{\boldsymbol{\eta}}_{r_{t_{n+1}}} + \Delta J_{n+1}^{-1}K_p\breve{\boldsymbol{\eta}}_{t_{n+1}}\right)^2 - \boldsymbol{\varepsilon}_{v_n}^2 + \\
& +2\left(\left(I - hJ_{t_n}J_n^{-1}K_p\right)\boldsymbol{\eta}_n\right)^T\left(-hJ_{t_n}\boldsymbol{\varepsilon}_{v_n} - hJ_{t_n}J_n^{-1}K_p\boldsymbol{\varepsilon}_{\eta_n} + \right. \\
& \left. + \boldsymbol{\varepsilon}_{\eta_n} + \boldsymbol{\varepsilon}_{\eta_{n+1}}\right) + 2\left(\left(I - h\underline{M}^{-1}K_v\right)\boldsymbol{v}_n\right)^T \\
& \left(\boldsymbol{\varepsilon}_{v_n} + \boldsymbol{\varepsilon}_{v_{n+1}} - \Delta J_{n+1}^{-1}\dot{\boldsymbol{\eta}}_{r_{t_{n+1}}} + \Delta J_{n+1}^{-1}K_p\breve{\boldsymbol{\eta}}_{t_{n+1}}\right) + \\
& + \left(h\underline{M}^{-1}(\boldsymbol{p}_n - \boldsymbol{r}_n)\right)^T\left(\boldsymbol{\varepsilon}_{v_n} + \boldsymbol{\varepsilon}_{v_{n+1}} - \Delta J_{n+1}^{-1}\dot{\boldsymbol{\eta}}_{r_{t_{n+1}}} + \Delta J_{n+1}^{-1}K_p\breve{\boldsymbol{\eta}}_{t_{n+1}}\right) - \\
& - \boldsymbol{v}_n^T\boldsymbol{\varepsilon}_{v_n} + 2\left(\boldsymbol{\varepsilon}_{v_n} + \boldsymbol{\varepsilon}_{v_{n+1}} - \Delta J_{n+1}^{-1}\dot{\boldsymbol{\eta}}_{r_{t_{n+1}}} + \Delta J_{n+1}^{-1}K_p\breve{\boldsymbol{\eta}}_{t_{n+1}}\right)^T h\underline{M}^{-1}\boldsymbol{\tau}_{n_2}
\end{aligned} \tag{31}
$$

which is consistent with $\boldsymbol{\varepsilon}_{\eta_n}$, $\boldsymbol{\varepsilon}_{v_n}$. So we have

$$
\begin{aligned}
\Delta Q_{t_n} = & \left(\left(I - hJ_{t_n}J_n^{-1}K_p\right)\boldsymbol{\eta}_n\right)^2 - \boldsymbol{\eta}_n^2 + \left(\left(I - h\underline{M}^{-1}K_v\right)\boldsymbol{v}_n\right)^2 - \boldsymbol{v}_n^2 - \left(J_{t_n}^{-1}\dot{\boldsymbol{\eta}}_{r_{t_n}} - J_{t_{n+1}}^{-1}K_p\breve{\boldsymbol{\eta}}_{t_n}\right)^2 - \boldsymbol{\eta}_{r_{t_n}}^2 + \\
& + f_{\Delta Q_1}[\boldsymbol{\varepsilon}_{\eta_n},\boldsymbol{\varepsilon}_{v_n}] + a\left(h\underline{M}^{-1}\boldsymbol{\tau}_{n_2}\right)^2 + \boldsymbol{b}_n^T\left(h\underline{M}^{-1}\boldsymbol{\tau}_{n_2}\right) + c_n,
\end{aligned} \tag{32}
$$

where the last three terms conform a complete quadratic polynomial in $\boldsymbol{\tau}_{n_2}$ with coefficients

$$
\begin{aligned}
a &= h^2 && (33) \\
\boldsymbol{b}_n &= 2h(I - hK_v^*)\boldsymbol{v}_n + 2h\underline{M}^{-1}(\boldsymbol{p}_n - \boldsymbol{r}_n) && (34) \\
c_n &= \left(hJ_{t_n}\breve{\boldsymbol{v}}_{t_n} + hJ_{t_n}J_n^{-1}\dot{\boldsymbol{\eta}}_{r_{t_n}} + hJ_{t_n}J_n^{-1}K_p\boldsymbol{\eta}_{r_{t_n}} - \boldsymbol{\eta}_{r_{t_{n+1}}}\right)^2 + && (35) \\
& +2\left(\left(I - hJ_{t_n}J_n^{-1}K_p\right)\boldsymbol{\eta}_n\right)^T\left(hJ_{t_n}\breve{\boldsymbol{v}}_{t_n} + hJ_{t_n}J_n^{-1}\dot{\boldsymbol{\eta}}_{r_{t_n}} + hJ_{t_n}J_n^{-1}K_p\boldsymbol{\eta}_{r_{t_n}} - \boldsymbol{\eta}_{r_{t_{n+1}}}\right) + \\
& + \left(h\underline{M}^{-1}(\boldsymbol{p}_n - \boldsymbol{r}_n)\right)^2 + 2\left(\left(I - h\underline{M}^{-1}K_v\right)\boldsymbol{v}_n\right)^T h\underline{M}^{-1}(\boldsymbol{p}_n - \boldsymbol{r}_n) - \\
& - 2\boldsymbol{v}_n^T\left(-J_{t_n}^{-1}\dot{\boldsymbol{\eta}}_{r_{t_n}} + J_{t_n}^{-1}K_p\breve{\boldsymbol{\eta}}_{t_n}\right),
\end{aligned}
$$

with K_v^* being an auxiliary matrix equal to $K_v^* = M^{-1}K_v$.

Clearly, for eliminating these terms we need to implement one of the roots of the polynomial, it is

$$
\boldsymbol{\tau}_{2_n} = M\left(\frac{-\boldsymbol{b}_n}{2a} \pm \frac{1}{2a}\sqrt{\frac{\boldsymbol{b}_n^T\boldsymbol{b}_n - 4ac_n}{6}\mathbf{1}}\right), \tag{36}
$$

with $\mathbf{1}$ a vector with all elements equal one. However, there are some variables and parameters in these coefficients that are not known. So we can approximate them to

$$\bar{a} = h^2 \tag{37}$$

$$\bar{\boldsymbol{b}}_n = 2h(I-hK_v^*)\boldsymbol{v}_n \tag{38}$$

$$\begin{aligned}\bar{c}_n = &\left(hJ_n\widetilde{\boldsymbol{v}}_n+h\dot{\boldsymbol{\eta}}_{r_{t_n}}+hK_p\boldsymbol{\eta}_{r_{t_n}}-\boldsymbol{\eta}_{r_{t_{n+1}}}\right)^2+\\ &+2\left((I-hK_p)\,\boldsymbol{\eta}_n\right)^T\left(hJ_n\widetilde{\boldsymbol{v}}_n+h\dot{\boldsymbol{\eta}}_{r_{t_n}}+hK_p\boldsymbol{\eta}_{r_{t_n}}-\boldsymbol{\eta}_{r_{t_{n+1}}}\right)+\\ &-2\boldsymbol{v}_n^T\left(-J_n^{-1}\dot{\boldsymbol{\eta}}_{r_{t_n}}+J_n^{-1}K_p\widetilde{\boldsymbol{\eta}}_n\right).\end{aligned} \tag{39}$$

Finally we get the second component of $\boldsymbol{\tau}_n$ in an implementable way

$$\boldsymbol{\tau}_{2_n}=\underline{M}\left(\frac{-\bar{\boldsymbol{b}}_n}{2\bar{a}}\pm\frac{1}{2\bar{a}}\sqrt{\frac{\bar{\boldsymbol{b}}_n^T\bar{\boldsymbol{b}}_n-4\bar{a}\bar{c}_n}{6}}\mathbf{1}\right). \tag{40}$$

Introducing the expression of $\boldsymbol{\tau}_n$ the functional remains

$$\begin{aligned}\Delta Q_{t_n}=&\left(\left(I-hJ_{t_n}J_n^{-1}K_p\right)\boldsymbol{\eta}_n\right)^2-\boldsymbol{\eta}_n^2+\left(\left(I-h\underline{M}^{-1}K_v\right)\boldsymbol{v}_n\right)^2-\boldsymbol{v}_n^2-\left(J_{t_n}^{-1}\dot{\boldsymbol{\eta}}_{r_{t_n}}-J_{t_{n+1}}^{-1}K_p\widetilde{\boldsymbol{\eta}}_{t_n}\right)^2-\boldsymbol{\eta}_{r_{t_n}}^2+\\ &+f_{\Delta Q_1}[\boldsymbol{\varepsilon}_{\eta_n},\boldsymbol{\varepsilon}_{v_n}]+f_{\Delta Q_2}[\boldsymbol{\varepsilon}_{\eta_n},\boldsymbol{\varepsilon}_{v_n}],\end{aligned} \tag{41}$$

where the new error $f_{\Delta Q_2}$ is

$$\begin{aligned}f_{\Delta Q_2}[\boldsymbol{\varepsilon}_{\eta_n},\boldsymbol{\varepsilon}_{v_n}] &= h\left(\boldsymbol{b}_n-\bar{\boldsymbol{b}}_n\right)^T\left(\frac{-\bar{\boldsymbol{b}}_n}{2\bar{a}}\pm\frac{1}{2\bar{a}}\sqrt{\frac{\bar{\boldsymbol{b}}^T\bar{\boldsymbol{b}}-4\bar{a}\bar{c}}{6}}\mathbf{1}\right)+(c_n-\bar{c}_n)=\\ &=\frac{\underline{M}^{-1}(\boldsymbol{p}_n-\boldsymbol{r}_n)^T\left(2h(I-hK_v^*)\boldsymbol{v}_n+2h\underline{M}^{-1}(\boldsymbol{p}_n-\boldsymbol{r}_n)\right)}{2h}+\\ &+\frac{\underline{M}^{-1}(\boldsymbol{p}_n-\boldsymbol{r}_n)^T}{2h}\sqrt{\frac{\bar{\boldsymbol{b}}^T\bar{\boldsymbol{b}}-4\bar{a}\bar{c}}{6}}\mathbf{1}+(c_n-\bar{c}_n).\end{aligned} \tag{42}$$

The properties of the error functions $f_{\Delta Q_1}$ and $f_{\Delta Q_2}$ and their influence in the stability of the control system is analyzed later. Previous to this task, we will illustrate the way we generate the matrices U_i's so as to calculate the variables $\boldsymbol{r}_i$ in (13).

6. Adaptive laws

The adaptation of the control behaviour to the unknown vehicle dynamics occurs by the permanent actualization of the controller matrices U_i.

Let the following adaptive law be valid for $i = 1, ..., 15$

$$U_{i_{n+1}} \triangleq U_{i_n} - \Gamma_i \frac{\partial \Delta Q_{t_n}}{\partial U_i}, \tag{43}$$

with a gain matrix $\Gamma_i = \Gamma_i^T \geq 0$ and $\frac{\partial \Delta Q_{t_n}}{\partial U_{i_n}}$ being a gradient matrix for U_{i_n}.

First we can define an expression for the gradient matrix upon ΔQ_{t_n} in (30) but considering that M is known. This expression is referred to the ideal gradient matrix

$$\begin{aligned} \frac{\partial \Delta Q_{t_n}}{\partial U_i} &= -2h^2 M^{-T} \left(M^{-1} \boldsymbol{\tau}_{2_n} \right) \left(\frac{\partial \boldsymbol{r}_n}{\partial U_i} \right)^T - \\ &\quad -2h^2 M^{-T} M^{-1} (\boldsymbol{p}_n - \boldsymbol{r}_n) \left(\frac{\partial \boldsymbol{r}_n}{\partial U_i} \right)^T - \\ &\quad -2hM^{-T} (I - hK_v^*) \widetilde{\boldsymbol{v}}_n \left(\frac{\partial \boldsymbol{r}_n}{\partial U_i} \right)^T . \end{aligned} \tag{44}$$

Now, in order to be able to implement adaptive laws like (43) we have to replace the unknown M in (44) by its lower bound $\underline{M}$. In this way, we can generate implementable gradient matrices which will denote by $\frac{\partial \overline{\Delta Q}_{t_n}}{\partial U_i}$ with

$$\begin{aligned} \frac{\partial \overline{\Delta Q}_{t_n}}{\partial U_i} &= -2h^2 \underline{M}^{-T} \left(\underline{M}^{-1} \boldsymbol{\tau}_{2_n} \right) \left(\frac{\partial \boldsymbol{r}_n}{\partial U_i} \right)^T - \\ &\quad -2h^2 \underline{M}^{-T} \underline{M}^{-1} (\boldsymbol{p}_n - \boldsymbol{r}_n) \left(\frac{\partial \boldsymbol{r}_n}{\partial U_i} \right)^T - \\ &\quad -2h\underline{M}^{-T} (I - hK_v^*) \widetilde{\boldsymbol{v}}_n \left(\frac{\partial \boldsymbol{r}_n}{\partial U_i} \right)^T , \end{aligned} \tag{45}$$

and the property

$$\frac{\partial \overline{\Delta Q}_{t_n}}{\partial U_i} = \frac{\partial \Delta Q_{t_n}}{\partial U_i} + \Delta_{U_{i_n}}, \tag{46}$$

where

$$\Delta_{U_{i_n}} = \delta_{M^{-2}} A_{i_n} + \delta_{M^{-1}} B_{i_n}, \tag{47}$$

and $\delta_{M^{-2}} = \left(\underline{M}^{-T}\underline{M}^{-1} - M^{-T}M^{-1}\right) \geq 0$ and $\delta_{M^{-1}} = \left(\underline{M}^{-1} - M^{-1}\right) \geq 0$. Here A_{i_n} and B_{i_n} are sampled state functions obtained from (44) after extracting of the common factors $\delta_{M^{-2}}$ and $\delta_{M^{-1}}$, respectively.

It is worth noticing that ΔQ_{t_n} and $\overline{\Delta Q}_{t_n}$, satisfy convexity properties in the space of elements of the U_i's.

Moreover, with (46) in mind we can conclude for any pair of values of U_i, say U_i' and U_i'', it is valid

$$\Delta Q_{t_n}(U_i') - \Delta Q_{t_n}(U_i'') \leq \frac{\partial \Delta Q_{t_n}(U_i'')}{\partial U_i}\left(U_i' - U_i''\right) \leq \tag{48}$$

$$\leq \frac{\partial \overline{\Delta Q}_{t_n}(U_i'')}{\partial U_i}\left(U_i' - U_i''\right). \tag{49}$$

This feature will be useful in the next analysis.

In summary, the practical laws which conform the digital adaptive controller are

$$U_{i_{n+1}} \triangleq U_{i_n} - \Gamma_i \frac{\partial \overline{\Delta Q}_{t_n}}{\partial U_i}. \tag{50}$$

Finally, it is seen from (45) that also here the noisy measures $\eta_{\delta_{t_n}}$ and $v_{\delta_{t_n}}$ will propagate into the adaptive laws $\frac{\partial \overline{\Delta Q}_{t_n}}{\partial U_i}$.

7. Stability analysis

It is worth noticing that the two first terms in (41) can satisfy $\left(\left(I - hJ_{t_n}J_n^{-1}K_p\right)\eta_n\right)^2 - \eta_n^2 < 0$ by proper selection of K_p and the following two terms can fulfill $\left(\left(I - h\underline{M}^{-1}K_v\right)v_n\right)^2 - v_n^2 < 0$ by proper selection of K_v and so the sign of ΔQ_{t_n} for any trajectories $\widetilde{\eta}_{t_n}$ and $\widetilde{v}_{t_n}$ and initial conditions of them would be depending of error functions $f_{\Delta Q_1}$ and $f_{\Delta Q_2}$ only.

According to (18) and (19), we can argue that $f_{\Delta Q_1}$ in (31) and $f_{\Delta Q_2}$ in (42) are consistent with ε_η and ε_v, it is, in absence of disturbances, they go to zero for h tending to zero. On the other hand, by existing disturbances $\delta\eta_{t_n}$ and δv_{t_n}, and any value of h, the maximal global errors are proportional to the disturbances. Clearly, the more extensive the pure dead time T_d, the larger the magnitude of $f_{\Delta Q_1}$ and $f_{\Delta Q_2}$, and this dependence is exponential.

To focus the stability problem in more detail, let first the controller matrices U_i's to take the values U_i^*'s. So, using these constant system matrices in (1), a fixed controller can be designed.

For this particular controller we consider the resulting $\Delta Q_{t_n}^*$ from (30) accomplishing

http://dx.doi.org/10.5772/52224

$$
\begin{aligned}
\Delta Q^*_{t_n} = &\left(\left(I - hJ_{t_n}J_n^{-1}K_p\right)\boldsymbol{\eta}_n\right)^2 - \boldsymbol{\eta}_n^2 + \left(\left(I - h\underline{M}^{-1}K_v\right)\boldsymbol{v}_n\right)^2 - \boldsymbol{v}_n^2 - \left(J_{t_n}^{-1}\dot{\boldsymbol{\eta}}_{r_{t_n}} - J_{t_{n+1}}^{-1}K_p\breve{\boldsymbol{\eta}}_{t_n}\right)^2 - \boldsymbol{\eta}_{r_{t_n}}^2 + \\
&+ f^*_{\Delta Q}[\varepsilon_{\eta_n}, \varepsilon_{v_n}\delta\boldsymbol{\eta}_{t_n}, \delta\boldsymbol{v}_{t_n}, M^{-1}\underline{M}],
\end{aligned}
\qquad (51)
$$

where $f^*_{\Delta Q_n}$ is the sum of $f_{\Delta Q_1}$ and $f_{\Delta Q_2}$ obtained from (31) and (42), but with the condition $\boldsymbol{p}_n = \boldsymbol{r}_n$

$$
f^*_{\Delta Q_n} = f_{\Delta Q_{1_n}}[\boldsymbol{p}_n = \boldsymbol{r}_n] + f_{\Delta Q_{2_n}}[\boldsymbol{p}_n = \boldsymbol{r}_n]. \qquad (52)
$$

Later, a norm of $f^*_{\Delta Q_n}$ will be indicated.

Since $\varepsilon_{\eta_{n+1}}$, $\varepsilon_{v_{n+1}}$, $\delta\boldsymbol{\eta}$, $\delta\boldsymbol{v} \in l_\infty$. Additionally, $M^{-1}\underline{M}$ is bounded. Thus, one concludes $f^*_{\Delta Q_n} \in l_\infty$ as well.

So, it is noticing that $\Delta Q^*_{t_n} < 0$, at least in an attraction domain equal to

$$
\mathcal{B} = \left\{\breve{\boldsymbol{\eta}}_{t_n}, \breve{\boldsymbol{v}}_{t_n} \in \mathcal{R}^6 \cap \mathcal{B}_0^*\right\}, \qquad (53)
$$

with $\mathcal{B}_0^*$ a residual set around zero

$$
\mathcal{B}_0^* = \left\{\breve{\boldsymbol{\eta}}_{t_n}, \breve{\boldsymbol{v}}_{t_n} \in \mathcal{R}^6 / \Delta Q^*_{t_n} - f^*_{\Delta Q_n} \leq 0\right\} \qquad (54)
$$

and with the design matrices satisfying the conditions

$$
2\frac{J_n J_{t_n}^{-1}}{h} > K_p > 0 \qquad (55)
$$

$$
\frac{2}{h}I > K_v^* \geq 0, \qquad (56)
$$

which is equivalent to

$$
\frac{2}{h}M \geq \frac{2}{h}\underline{M} > K_v \geq 0. \qquad (57)
$$

The residual set $\mathcal{B}_0^*$ depends not only on $\varepsilon_{\eta_{n+1}}$ and $\varepsilon_{v_{n+1}}$ and the measure noises $\delta\boldsymbol{\eta}_{t_n}$ and $\delta\boldsymbol{v}_{t_n}$, but also on $M^{-1}\underline{M}$. In consequence, $\mathcal{B}_0^*$ becomes the null point at the limit when $h \to 0$, $\delta\boldsymbol{\eta}_{t_n}$, $\delta\boldsymbol{v}_{t_n} \to 0$ and $\underline{M} = M$.

7.1. Stability proof

The problem of stability of the adaptive control system is addressed in the sequel. Let a Lyapunov function be

$$V_{t_n} = Q_{t_n} + \frac{1}{2}\sum_{i=1}^{15}\sum_{j=1}^{6}\left(\tilde{\boldsymbol{u}}_j^T\right)_{i_{n+1}} \Gamma_i^{-1}\left(\tilde{\boldsymbol{u}}_j\right)_{i_{n+1}} - \tag{58}$$

$$-\frac{1}{2}\sum_{i=1}^{15}\sum_{j=1}^{6}\left(\tilde{\boldsymbol{u}}_j^T\right)_{i_n} \Gamma_i^{-1}\left(\tilde{\boldsymbol{u}}_j\right)_{i_n},$$

with $\left(\tilde{\boldsymbol{u}}_j\right)_{i_n} = \left(\boldsymbol{u}_j - \boldsymbol{u}_j^*\right)_{i_n}$, where $\boldsymbol{u}_j$ and $\boldsymbol{u}_j^*$ are vectors corresponding to the column j of the adaptive controller matrix U_i and its corresponding one U_i^* in the fixed controller, respectively. Then the differences $\Delta V_{t_n} = V_{t_{n+1}} - V_{t_n}$ can be bounded as follows

$$\Delta V_{t_n} = \Delta Q_{t_n} + \frac{1}{2}\sum_{i=1}^{15}\sum_{j=1}^{6}\left(\Delta\boldsymbol{u}_j^T\right)_{i_n} \Gamma_i^{-1}\left(\left(\tilde{\boldsymbol{u}}_j\right)_{i_{n+1}} + \left(\tilde{\boldsymbol{u}}_j\right)_{i_n}\right) \tag{59}$$

$$= \Delta Q_{t_n} + \sum_{i=1}^{15}\sum_{j=1}^{6}\left(\Delta\boldsymbol{u}_j^T\right)_{i_n} \Gamma_i^{-1}\left(\tilde{\boldsymbol{u}}_j\right)_{i_n} -$$

$$-\frac{1}{2}\sum_{i=1}^{15}\sum_{j=1}^{6}\left(\Delta\boldsymbol{u}_j^T\right)_{i_n} \Gamma_i^{-1}\left(\Delta\boldsymbol{u}_j\right)_{i_n}$$

$$\leq \Delta Q_{t_n} - \sum_{i=1}^{15}\sum_{j=1}^{6}\left(\frac{\partial \Delta Q_{t_n}}{\partial \boldsymbol{u}_j}\right)^T\left(\tilde{\boldsymbol{u}}_j\right)_{i_n}$$

$$\leq \Delta Q_{t_n} - \sum_{i=1}^{15}\sum_{j=1}^{6}\left(\frac{\partial \overline{\Delta Q}_{t_n}}{\partial \boldsymbol{u}_j}\right)^T\left(\tilde{\boldsymbol{u}}_j\right)_{i_n}$$

$$\leq \Delta Q_{t_n}^* < 0 \text{ in } \mathcal{B} \cap \mathcal{B}_0^*,$$

with $\left(\Delta\boldsymbol{u}_j\right)_{i_n}$ a column vector of $\left(U_{i_{n+1}} - U_{i_n}\right)$.

The column vector $\left(\Delta\boldsymbol{u}_j\right)_{i_n}$ at the first inequality was replaced by the column vector $-\Gamma_i\left(\frac{\partial \Delta Q_{t_n}}{\partial \boldsymbol{u}_j}\right)$ and then by $-\Gamma_i\left(\frac{\partial \overline{\Delta Q}_{t_n}}{\partial \boldsymbol{u}_j}\right)$ in the right member according to (46) and (48)-(49). So in the second and third inequality, the convexity property of ΔQ_{t_n} in (48) was applied for any pair $\left(U' = U_{i_n}, U'' = U_i^*\right)$.

This analysis has proved convergence of the error paths when real square root exist from $\sqrt{\overline{\boldsymbol{b}}_n^T\overline{\boldsymbol{b}}_n - 4\bar{a}\bar{c}_n}$ of (40).

If on the contrary $4\bar{a}\bar{c}_n > \bar{\boldsymbol{b}}_n^T\bar{\boldsymbol{b}}_n$ occurs at some time t_n, one chooses the real part of the complex roots in (40). So a suboptimal control action is employed instead equal to

$$\tau_{2_n} = \frac{-1}{2\bar{a}}\underline{M}^{-1}\bar{\boldsymbol{b}}_n = \frac{-\underline{M}^{-1}}{h}(I - hK_v^*)\breve{\boldsymbol{v}}_{t_n}, \tag{60}$$

and yields a new functional $\Delta Q_{t_n}^{**}$ in

$$\Delta V_{t_n} \leq \Delta Q_{t_n}^{**} = \Delta Q_{t_n}^{*} + \bar{c}_n - \frac{1}{4h^2}\bar{\boldsymbol{b}}_n^T\bar{\boldsymbol{b}}_n < 0 \text{ in } \mathcal{B}\cap\mathcal{B}_0^{**}, \tag{61}$$

where $\Delta Q_{t_n}^{*}$ is (51) with a real root of (40) and $\mathcal{B}_0^{**}$ is a new residual set. It is worth noticing that the positive quantity $\left(\bar{c}_n - \frac{1}{4h^2}\bar{\boldsymbol{b}}_n^T\bar{\boldsymbol{b}}_n\right)$ can be reduced by choosing h small. Nevertheless, $\mathcal{B}_0^{**}$ results larger than $\mathcal{B}_0^{*}$ in (59), since its dimension depends not only on $\varepsilon_{\eta_{n+1}}$ and $\varepsilon_{v_{n+1}}$ but also on the magnitude of $\left(\bar{c}_n - \frac{1}{4h^2}\bar{\boldsymbol{b}}_n^T\bar{\boldsymbol{b}}_n\right)$.

This closes the stability and convergence proof.

7.2. Variable boundness

With respect to the boundness of the adaptive matrices U_i´s it is seen from (45) that the gradients are bounded. Also the third term is more dominant than the remainder ones for h small ($h << 1$), and so, the kinematic error $\breve{\boldsymbol{v}}_{t_n}$ influences the intensity and sign of $\partial\overline{\Delta Q}_{t_n}/\partial U_i$ more significantly than the others. From (43) one concludes than the increasing of $|U_i|$ may not be avoided long term, however some robust modification techniques like a projection zone can be employed to achieve boundness. This is not developed here. The author can consult for instance (Ioannou and Sun, 1996).

7.3. Instability for large sampling time and pure delay

Broadly speaking, the influence of the analyzed parameters will play a role in the instability when the chosen h is something large, even smaller than one, because the quadratic terms rise a turn off dominant in the error function $f_{\Delta Q_n}^{*}$.

The study of this phenomenon is rather complex. It involves the function $\Delta Q_{t_n}^{*}$ in (51) and $f_{\Delta Q_n}^{*}$ in (52).

Qualitatively speaking, when

$$f_{\Delta Q_n}^{*} < -\left(\left(I - hJ_{t_n}J_n^{-1}K_p\right)\boldsymbol{\eta}_n\right)^2 + \boldsymbol{\eta}_n^2 - \left(\left(I - h\underline{M}^{-1}K_v\right)\boldsymbol{v}_n\right)^2 + \boldsymbol{v}_n^2 + \left(J_{t_n}^{-1}\dot{\boldsymbol{\eta}}_{r_{t_n}} - J_{t_{n+1}}^{-1}K_p\breve{\boldsymbol{\eta}}_{t_n}\right)^2 + \boldsymbol{\eta}_{r_{t_n}}^2, \tag{62}$$

the path trajectories may not be bounded into a residual set because the domain for the initial conditions in this situation is partially repulsive. So, depending on the particular initial conditions and for $h >> 0$, or similarly for T_d large, the adaptive control system may turn unstable.

In conclusion, when comparing two digital controllers, the sensitivity of the stability to h and indirectly the presence of large pure delays in the dynamics, is fundamental to draw out robust properties and finally to range them.

8. Adaptive control algorithm

The adaptive control algorithm can be summarized as follows.

Preliminaries:

1) Estimate a lower bound $\underline{M}$, for instance $\underline{M} = M_b$ (Jordán & Bustamante, 2011),

2) Select a sampling time h as small as possible,

3) Choose design gain matrices K_p and K_v according to (56)-(57), and simultaneously in order to reduce $f^*_{\Delta Q_n}$ and $\Delta Q^*_{t_n}$ (see related commentary in previous section),

4) Define the adaptive gain matrices Γ_i (usually $\Gamma_i = \alpha_i I$ with $\alpha_i > 0$),

5) Stipulate the desired sampled-data path references for the geometric and kinematic trajectories in 6 DOF´s: $\eta_{r_{t_n}}$ and $v_{r_{t_n}}$, respectively (see related commentary in previous section),

Continuously at each sample point:

6) Calculate the control thrust τ_n with components τ_{1_n}in (29) and τ_{2_n} (40) (or (60)), respectively,

7) Calculate the adaptive controller matrices (44) with the lower bound $\underline{M}$ instead of M,

Long-term tuning:

7) Redefine K_p, K_v and h in order to achieve optimal tracking performance.

Remark

For the present approach, we can summarize the different steps carried out in this Chapter after the control design in order to determine its convergence properties and performance of the control system:

a) Establishment of the adaptive laws for the designed controller using a lower bound of M (Section 6),

b) Stability and convergence analysis of the control system to a residual set dependent of the sign-undefinite terms $f_{\Delta Q_1}$ and $f_{\Delta Q_2}$ in (31) and (42), respectively, which depend on the pure dead-time T_d (Section 7). Moreover, the conjoint incidence of local model errors $\varepsilon_{\eta_{n+1}}$ and $\varepsilon_{v_{n+1}}$, measure noises $\delta\eta_{t_n}$ and δv_{t_n}, and the product $M^{-1}\underline{M}$ in the the convergence of state trajectories to a residual set $\mathcal{B}^*_0$ is illustrated in (Section 7.1).

http://dx.doi.org/10.5772/52224

c) Proof of boundness of the adaptive controller matrices U_i's and the way to ensure this (Section 7.2),

d) Analysis of a stability condition involving both huge sampling times and a large pure delays (Section 7.3).

9. Case study

With the end of illustrating the features of our control system approach, we simulate a path-tracking problem in 6 DOF´s for an underwater vehicle in a planar motion with some sporadic immersions to the floor.

A continuous-time model of a fully-maneuverable underwater vehicle is employed for the numerical simulations and a pure dead time in the control transmission was included. Details of this dynamics are given in (Jordán & Bustamante, 2009a).

We present the simulation of the adaptive control algorithm summarized in the previous section for an immersion in the depth (motion in the heave modus z) with translations aside in the modes surge x and sway y simultaneously.

Fig. 2 illustrates the evolution of the six controlled modes of the UUV in the descending. The initial conditions of the UUV at t_0 were $\boldsymbol{\eta}(0)=[1.1;1.1;1.1;0.1;0.1;0.1]$ and $\boldsymbol{v}(0)=[0.1;0.1;0.1;0.1;0.1;0.1]$. The design matrices were set in $K_p = K_v = I$. The sampling period was selected $h = 0.1$ s.

It is seen that after a short transient, which is not longer than 7 s, the UUV is positioned at the coordinates to the start point. Then it begins to the maneuver of descending. In the meantime the matrices U_i's are adapted and the path tracking result asymptotically convergent with unappreciated stationary errors. The predictors are sufficiently accurate during the evolution of the states.

In the simulation, between 20 s and 30 s, it can be seen a high interaction between the traslational modes which are tracked (namely: x, y, z) and the rotational modes which are regulated about zero only (namely: φ, θ, ψ). In the last ones, it one observes a significant variation of these magnitudes. However, this is reasonable considering the dynamics with large dead-times we are dealing with.

10. Conclusions

Often in complex digital control systems, for instance digital adaptive controllers in conjugation with complex dynamics with high degree of state interaction, the role played by the sampling time h is the algid point in the stability and control performance analysis. This is so because of the potential instability that may occur by improperly selected large h. This phenomenon is commonly magnified when a dead time is present. In any case, the appearance of perturbations and delays together in the dynamics makes the problem difficult to seize and comprehend.

An important example which meets these particularities is found in the control problem represented by the guidance of UUV´s in 6 DOF´s, which was taken here as case study.

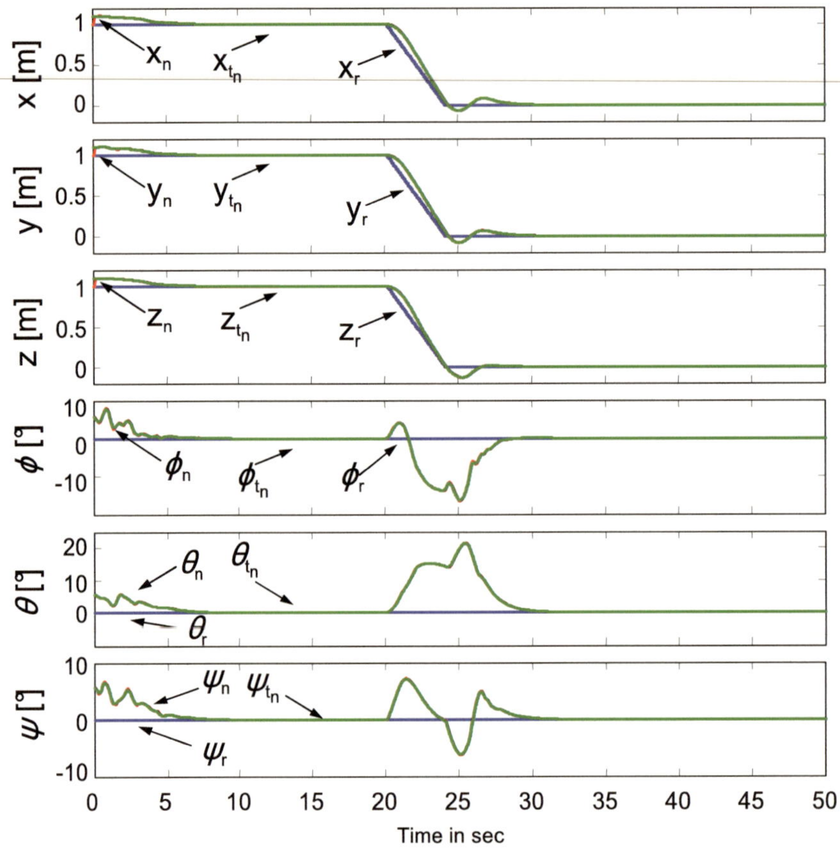

Figure 2. Evolution of the behaviour of a simulated UUV with adaptive control in all its modes.

Taking into consideration the hole of information caused by the presence of a pure delay in the adaptive control, we employs a filter for estimation of the actual state vector based on past measures together with a set of adaptive control matrices available over the delay period. The control end in the design is the minimization of certain incremental functional of the path energies of the geometric and kinematic errors. The control action can be then computed from predictions, as well as from the updating of the adaptive laws which succeeds with a support of filtered data at any discrete time.

We relate the stability and control performance with certain sign non-definite terms that are present in the final incremental functional of energy. From therein it can be concluded about the existence of an attraction domain and a residual set. This last one is influenced in size by the local errors of predictions, the perturbations δ in the measurements and the pure discrete delay d. It was clearly shown, that the presence of d does affect exponentially in magnitude the size of the prediction errors, which may be critical for the control stability if h is not selected sufficiently small.

http://dx.doi.org/10.5772/52224

Author details

Mario A. Jordan[1,2],
Jorge L. Bustamante[1,2] and Carlos E. Berger[1]

1 Instituto Argentino de Oceanografía IADO CCT-CONICET Bahía Blanca, Argentina
2 Universidad Nacional del Sur, Dto. de Ing. Eléctrica y de Computadoras UNS-DIEC, Bahía Blanca, Argentina

References

[1] Fossen, T.I. (1994). *Guidance and control of ocean vehicles*, John Wiley&Sons, New York, USA.

[2] Fradkov, A.L., Miroshnik, I.V. y Nikiforov, V.O. (1999), *Nonlinear and adaptive control of complex systems*, Kluwer Acad. Pub.

[3] Jordán, M.A. and J.L Bustamante (2007). On the presence of nonlinear oscillations in the teleoperation of underwater vehicles under the influence of sea, wave and current. In: *26th American Control Conference (2007 ACC)*. New York City, USA, July 11-13.

[4] Jordán, M.A. and J.L. Bustamante (2008). Guidance of underwater vehicles with cable tug perturbations under fixed and adaptive control modus. *IEEE J. of Oceanic Engineering*, 34(4), 579-598.

[5] Jordán, M.A. and J.L. Bustamante (2009a). *Adaptive Control for Guidance of Underwater Vehicles. In: Underwater Vehicles*, A.V. Inzartev (Editor), Chap. 14, 251-278. In-Tech, Vienna, Austria.

[6] Jordán, M.A. and J.L. Bustamante (2009b). Adams-Bashforth approximations for digital control of complex vehicle dynamics. In: *4th Int. Scientific Conf. on Physics and Control (PHYSCON 2009)*, Catania, Italy, Sep. 1-4.

[7] Jordán, M.A. and J.L. Bustamante (2011). *A General approach to discrete-time adaptive control systems with perturbed measures for complex dynamics. Case Study: unmanned underwater vehicles*. In: *Discrete Time Systems*. M.A. Jordán and J.B. Bustamante (Ed.). Chap. 15, 255-289. In-Tech, Rijeka, Croatia.

[8] Ioannou P. and J. Sun (1996). *Robust Adaptive Control*, Prentice Hall, New Jersey, USA.

[9] Leonard, F. and Abba, G. (2012). Robustness and Safe Sampling of Distributed-Delay Control Laws for Unstable Delayed Systems . *IEEE Transactions on Automatic Control,* 57 (6), 1521-1526.

Chapter 6

Adaptive Step-Size Orthogonal Gradient-Based Per-Tone Equalisation in Discrete Multitone Systems

Suchada Sitjongsataporn

Additional information is available at the end of the chapter

http://dx.doi.org/10.5772/52158

1. Introduction

An all-digital implementation of multicarrier modulation called *discrete multitone (DMT) modulation* has been standardised for asymmetric digital subscriber line (ADSL), ADSL2, ADSL2+ and VDSL [1]- [3]. ADSL modems rely on DMT modulation, which divides a broadband channel into many narrowband subchannels and modulated encoded signals onto the narrowband subchannels [4], [5]. With advanced digital signal processing algorithms, DMT system is to fight the impairments for wired communications such DSL-based technology. The major impairments such as the intersymbol interference (ISI), the intercarrier interference (ICI), the channel distortion, echo, radio-frequency interference (RFI) and crosstalk from DSL systems are induced as a result of large bandwidth utilisation over the telephone line. However, the improvement can be achieved by the equalisation concepts.

ISI and ICI caused by the length of channel impulse response can be eliminated by the use of cyclic prefix (CP) adding a copy of the last ν time-domain samples between DMT-symbols at the part of transmitter. The conventional equalisation in DMT-based systems consists of a (real) time-domain equaliser (TEQ) and the (complex) one-tap frequency-domain equalisers [6]. For a more sophisticated equalisation technique, a frequency-domain equaliser (FEQ) for each tone, called *per-tone equaliser (PTEQ)* has been introduced in order to give the bit rate maximising compared with existing equalisation schemes [7], [8].

The basic structure of the DMT transceiver is shown in Fig.1. The incoming bit stream is likewise reshaped to a complex-valued transmitted symbol for mapping in quadrature amplitude modulation (QAM). Then, the output of QAM bit stream is split into N parallel bit streams that are instantaneously fed to the modulating inverse fast Fourier transform (IFFT). After that, IFFT outputs are transformed into the serial symbols including the cyclic prefix between symbols and then fed to the channel. The transmitted signal sent over the channel with impulse response is generally corrupted by the additive white Gaussian noise and near-end crosstalk. The received signal is also equalised by PTEQs without TEQ concerned. The per-tone equalisation structure is based on transferring the TEQ-operations into the frequency-domain after FFT demodulation, which results in a multitap PTEQ for each tone separately. Then, the parallel of received symbols are eventually converted into serial bits in the frequency-domain.

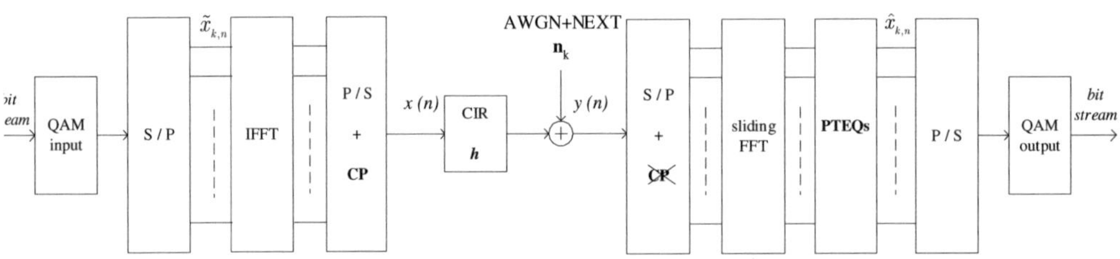

Figure 1. Block Diagram of a Discrete Multitone System.

It is a well known issue that in DMT theory, there is no overlapping between tones due to orthogonality derived from the discrete Fourier transformation among them. In practice, frequency-selective fading channel generally destroys such orthogonal structure leading to information interfering from adjacent tones as commonly known as ICI. In such case, information supposedly belonging to a particular tone generally smear into adjacent tones and leave some residual energy in them. The idea of a mixed-tone PTEQ for DMT-based system has been proposed in [9]. By recovering adaptively the knowledge of residual interfering signal energy from adjacent tones, the mixed-tone exponentially weighted least squares criterion can be shown to offer an improved signal to noise ratio (SNR) of the tone of interest.

In order to improve the convergence properties, the orthogonal gradient adaptive (OGA) has been presented by introducing orthogonal projection to the filtered gradient adaptive (FGA) algorithm. When the forgetting-factor is optimised sample by sample whereas a fixed forgetting-factor is used for FGA algorithm [10]. A normalised version of the OGA (NOGA) algorithm that has been introduced with the mixed-tone cost function and fixed step-size presented in [11]. With the purpose of the good tracking behaviour and recovering to a steady-state, it is necessary to let the step-size automatically track the change of system. Consequently, the concept of low complexity adaptive step-size approach based on the FGA algorithm is introduced for the per-tone equalisation in DMT-based systems in [12].

In this chapter, the focus is therefore to present low complexity orthogonal gradient-based algorithms for PTEQ based on the adaptive step-size approaches related to the mixed-tone criterion. The convergence behaviour and stability analysis of proposed algorithms will be investigated based on the mixed-tone weight-estimated errors. The convergence analysis of mechanisms will be carried out the steady-state and mean-square expressions of adaptive step-size parameter relating to the mean convergence factor.

http://dx.doi.org/10.5772/52158

2. System model and notation

In this section, the basic structure of the DMT transceiver is illustrated in Fig. 1. We describe that the data model and notation based on an FIR model of the DMT transmission channel is presented as [7]

$$\mathbf{y} = \mathbf{H} \cdot \mathbf{X} + \mathbf{n} \ ,$$

$$\underbrace{\begin{bmatrix} y_{k,l+\Delta} \\ \vdots \\ y_{k,N-l+\Delta} \end{bmatrix}}_{\mathbf{y}_{k,l+\Delta:N-1+\Delta}} = \underbrace{\begin{bmatrix} \mathbf{0}_{(1)} & \begin{matrix} [\,\bar{\mathbf{h}}^T\,]\ 0 \cdots \\ \ddots \ \ddots \\ \cdots 0\ [\,\bar{\mathbf{h}}^T\,] \end{matrix} & \mathbf{0}_{(2)} \end{bmatrix} \cdot \begin{bmatrix} \mathcal{P}_\nu & \mathbf{0} & \mathbf{0} \\ \mathbf{0} & \mathcal{P}_\nu & \mathbf{0} \\ \mathbf{0} & \mathbf{0} & \mathcal{P}_\nu \end{bmatrix} \cdot \begin{bmatrix} \mathcal{I}_N & \mathbf{0} & \mathbf{0} \\ \mathbf{0} & \mathcal{I}_N & \mathbf{0} \\ \mathbf{0} & \mathbf{0} & \mathcal{I}_N \end{bmatrix}}_{\mathbf{H}} \cdot \underbrace{\begin{bmatrix} \mathbf{x}_{k-1,N} \\ \mathbf{x}_{k,N} \\ \mathbf{x}_{k+1,N} \end{bmatrix}}_{\mathbf{X}_{k-1:k+1,N}} + \underbrace{\begin{bmatrix} \eta_{k,l+\Delta} \\ \vdots \\ \eta_{k,N-l+\Delta} \end{bmatrix}}_{\eta_{k,l+\Delta:N-1+\Delta}} . \tag{1}$$

where l denotes as the first considered sample of the k-th received DMT-symbol. This depends on the number of tap of equaliser ($\mathbb{T}$) and the synchronisation delay (Δ). The vector $\mathbf{y}_{k,i:j}$ of received samples i to j of k-th DMT-symbol is as $\mathbf{y}_{k,i:j} = [y_{k,i} \ \cdots \ y_{k,j}]^T$. A sequence of the $N \times 1$ $\mathbf{x}_{k,N}$ transmitted symbol vector is as $\mathbf{x}_{k,N} = [x_{k,0} \ \cdots \ x_{k,N-1}]^T$. The size N is of inverse discrete Fourier transform (IDFT) and DFT. The parameter ν denotes as the length of cyclic prefix. The matrices $\mathbf{0}_{(1)}$ and $\mathbf{0}_{(2)}$ are also the zero matrices of size $(N-l) \times (N-L+2\nu+\Delta+l)$ and $(N-l) \times (N+\nu-\Delta)$. The vector $\bar{\mathbf{h}}$ is the $\mathbf{h}$ channel impulse responce (CIR) vector in reverse order. The $(N+\nu) \times N$ matrix $\mathcal{P}_\nu$ is denoted by

$$\mathcal{P}_\nu = \left[\begin{array}{c|c} \mathbf{0}_{\nu \times (N-\nu)} & \mathbf{I}_\nu \\ \hline \multicolumn{2}{c}{\mathbf{I}_N} \end{array}\right] ,$$

which adds the cyclic prefix. The $\mathcal{I}_N$ is $N \times N$ IDFT matrix and modulates the input symbols. The $\eta_{k,l+\Delta:N-1+\Delta}$ is a vector with additive white Gaussian noise (AWGN) and near-end cross-talk (NEXT).

Some notation will be used throughout this chapter as follows: $E\{\cdot\}$ is the expectation operator and diag$(\cdot)$ is a diagonal matrix operator. The operators $(\cdot)^T$, $(\cdot)^H$, $(\cdot)^*$ denote as the transpose, Hermitian and complex conjugate operators, respectively. The parameter k is the DMT symbol index and $\mathbf{I}_a$ is an $a \times a$ identity matrix. A tilde over the variable indicates the frequency-domain. The vectors are in bold lowercase and matrices are in bold uppercase.

3. Per-tone equalisation

In this section, we show the concept of per-tone equaliser (PTEQ). We refer the readers to [7] for more details. The per-tone equalisation structure is based on transferring the

TEQ-operations into the frequency-domain after DFT demodulation, which results in a $\mathbb{T}$-tap PTEQ for each tone separately. For each tone i ($i = 1 \dots n$), the TEQ-operations are shown as follows [7]

$$\tilde{d}_n = \overbrace{\tilde{z}_n}^{\text{1-tap PTEQ}} \cdot \text{row}_n \overbrace{(\mathcal{F}_N) \cdot (\mathbf{Y} \cdot \mathbf{w})}^{\text{1 DFT}}, \tag{2}$$

$$= \text{row}_n \underbrace{(\mathcal{F}_N \cdot \mathbf{Y})}_{\mathbb{T}\text{ DFTs}} \cdot \underbrace{\mathbf{w} \cdot \tilde{z}_n}_{\mathbb{T}-\text{tap PTEQ } \mathbf{v}_n}, \tag{3}$$

where $\tilde{d}_n$ is the output after frequency-domain equalisation for tone n. The $\tilde{z}_n$ is the (complex) one-tap PTEQ for tone n. The parameter $\mathbf{w}$ is of (real) $\mathbb{T}$-tap TEQ and $\mathcal{F}_N$ is an $N \times N$ DFT matrix [7]. Note that $\mathbf{Y}$ is an $N \times \mathbb{T}$ Toeplitz matrix of received signal samples as vector $\mathbf{y}$ in (1). From (3), the $\mathbb{T}$ DFT-operations are cheaply calculated by means of a sliding DFT. It is demonstrated in [7] that every $\mathbb{T}$-tap PTEQ $\mathbf{v}_n$ exists a $\mathbb{T}$-tap PTEQ $\tilde{\mathbf{p}}_n$ which consists of only one DFT and $\mathbb{T} - 1$ real difference terms as its input.

The PTEQ output $\hat{x}_{k,n}$ can be specified as follows

$$\hat{x}_{k,n} = \tilde{\mathbf{p}}_n^H \cdot \underbrace{\left[\begin{array}{c|c|c} \mathbf{I}_{\mathbb{T}-1} & \mathbf{0} & \textbf{-I}_{\mathbb{T}-1} \\ \hline \mathbf{0} & \multicolumn{2}{c}{\mathcal{F}_N(n,:)} \end{array}\right]}_{\mathbf{F}_n} \cdot \mathbf{y}, \tag{4}$$

$$= \tilde{\mathbf{p}}_n^H \cdot \tilde{\mathbf{y}}_{k,n}, \tag{5}$$

where $\tilde{\mathbf{p}}_n$ is the $\mathbb{T}$-tap complex-valued PTEQ vector for tone n. The $\mathbf{F}_n$ is a $(\mathbb{T} - 1) \times (N + \mathbb{T} - 1)$ matrix [7]. The $\mathcal{F}_N(n,:)$ is the nth row of $\mathcal{F}_N$. By using the sliding DFT, the first block row of matrix $\mathbf{F}_n$ in (4) extracts the difference terms, while the last row corresponds to the usual DFT operation as detailed in [7] and [13]. The vector $\mathbf{y}$ is of channel output samples as described in (1). The $\tilde{\mathbf{y}}_{k,n}$ is the sliding DFT output for tone n at each symbol k.

4. A mixed-tone cost function

In this section, we describe a mixed-tone cost function by means of the orthogonal projection matrix. The idea of using orthogonal projection of adjacent equalisers to include the information of interfering tones has been presented firstly in [9]. The illustration of the vector $\hat{\mathbf{p}}_m$ and its orthogonal projection as well as $\tilde{\mathbf{x}}_m$ for 2-dimensional subspace S^2 is shown in Fig. 2. The error vector $\mathbf{e}_m^{\perp}$ associated with the orthogonal projection of vectors $\hat{\mathbf{p}}_m$ and $\Pi_m^{\perp}\hat{\mathbf{p}}_m$, where $\Pi_m^{\perp}$ denotes as the orthogonal projection matrix of $\hat{\mathbf{p}}_m(k)$, will be presented in the update of the vector $\hat{\mathbf{p}}_m(k)$ where $k \neq m$. Therefore, the mixed-tone cost function derived as the sum of weight-estimated errors is optimised in order to achieve the solutions for frequency-domain equalisation. It is designed to work in conjunction with the complex-valued frequency-domain equalisation structure.

http://dx.doi.org/10.5772/52158

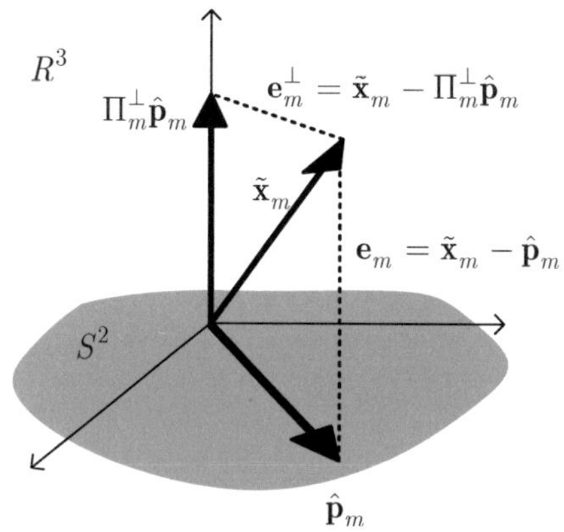

Figure 2. The tap-weight estimated PTEQ vector $\hat{\mathbf{p}}_m$ and its orthogonal projection $\Pi_m^{\perp}\hat{\mathbf{p}}_m$ are illustrated in two dimentional subspace S^2 [9].

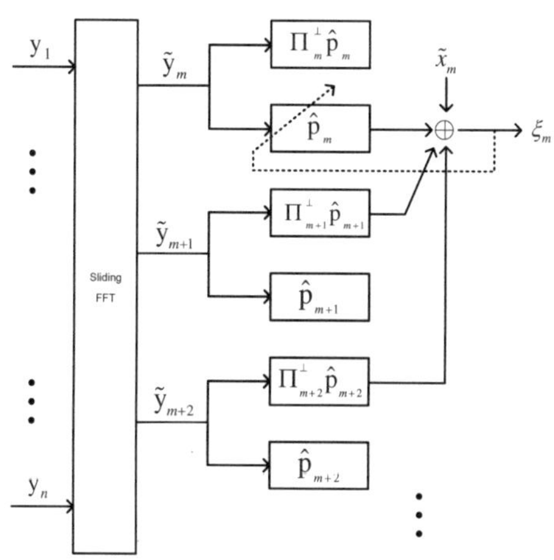

Figure 3. Block structure of the proposed mixed-tone PTEQ $\hat{\mathbf{p}}_m$ for $m \in M$ with the use of combining estimates of M-adjacent tones, where $M = 3$. [11]

A mixed-tone exponentially weighted least squares cost function to be minimised is defined as

$$J(k) = \frac{1}{2} \sum_{m=1}^{M} \sum_{i=1}^{k} \lambda_m^{k-i} \{\xi_m(i)\}^{2}, \tag{6}$$

where λ_m is the forgetting-factor and $\xi_m(k)$ is the mixed-tone weight-estimated error at tone m for $m \in M$. The number of the adjacent tones M is of tone of interest.

$$\begin{aligned}\xi_m(i) = \tilde{x}_m(i) - \hat{\mathbf{p}}_m^H(k)\tilde{\mathbf{y}}_m(i) &- \left(\Pi_l^{\perp}(k)\hat{\mathbf{p}}_l(k)\right)^H\tilde{\mathbf{y}}_l(i)\\ &- \left(\Pi_{l+1}^{\perp}(k)\hat{\mathbf{p}}_{l+1}(k)\right)^H\tilde{\mathbf{y}}_{l+1}(i)\\ &- \ldots - \left(\Pi_L^{\perp}(k)\hat{\mathbf{p}}_L(k)\right)^H\tilde{\mathbf{y}}_L(i)\,,\\ &\qquad \text{for } m \neq l\,,\ L \leq M-1. \end{aligned} \tag{7}$$

where the parameter $\tilde{x}_m(k)$ is the kth transmitted DMT-symbol on tone m. The vector $\hat{\mathbf{p}}_m(k)$ is of complex-valued $\mathbb{T}$-tap PTEQ for tone m. The vector $\tilde{\mathbf{y}}_m(k)$ is the DFT output for tone m at symbol k.

The orthogonal projection matrix $\Pi_l^{\perp}(k)$ which is the matrix difference determined by the tap-weight estimated vector $\hat{\mathbf{p}}_l(k)$ as [14]

$$\begin{aligned}\Pi_l^{\perp}(k) &= \tilde{\mathbf{I}} - \hat{\Pi}_l(k)\\ &= \tilde{\mathbf{I}} - \hat{\mathbf{p}}_l(k)\,[\hat{\mathbf{p}}_l^H(k)\,\hat{\mathbf{p}}_l(k)]^{-1}\,\hat{\mathbf{p}}_l^H(k)\,,\end{aligned} \tag{8}$$

where $\tilde{\mathbf{I}}$ denotes as an identity matrix and $\hat{\Pi}_l(k)$ is the projection matrix onto the space spanned by the tap-weight vector $\hat{\mathbf{p}}_l(k)$. We note that the orthogonal projection matrix $\Pi_l^{\perp}(k)$ is mentioned by the vector $\hat{\mathbf{p}}_l(k)$ for $l \neq m$.

With the definition for this cost function, the mth-term on the right hand side of (9) represents as the estimated mixed-tone error of the symbol k due to the mth-tone of equaliser $\hat{\mathbf{p}}_m(k)$ for $m \in M$ as depicted in Fig. 3.

$$\xi_m(i) = \tilde{x}_m(i) - \hat{\mathbf{p}}_m^H(k)\tilde{\mathbf{y}}_m(i) - \sum_{l=1}^{L}\left(\Pi_l^{\perp}(k)\hat{\mathbf{p}}_l(k)\right)^H\tilde{\mathbf{y}}_l(i)\,, \text{ for } m \neq l\,,\ L \leq M-1. \tag{9}$$

5. Adaptive step-size normalised orthogonal gradient adaptive algorithms

Based on filtered gradient adaptive algorithm, adaptive algorithms employing orthogonal gradient filtering can provide with the development of simple and robust filter across a wide range of input environments. This section is therefore concerned with the development of simple and robust adaptive frequency-domain equalisation by defining normalised orthogonal gradient adaptive algorithm.

In this section, we describe the orthogonal gradient adaptive (OGA) algorithm that is a class of the filtered gradient adaptive (FGA) algorithm using an orthogonal constraint. This employs the mixed-tone criterion described above in Section 4 in order to improve the convergence speed presented in Section 5.1, respectively.

The idea for low complexity adaptive step-size algorithms with the mixed-tone cost function is described in Section 5.2. For a large prediction error, the algorithm will increase the step-size to track the change of system whereas a small error will result in the decreased step-size [15], [16].

5.1. A Mixed-Tone Normalised Orthogonal Gradient Adaptive (MT-NOGA) algorithm

The orthogonal gradient adaptive (OGA) algorithm is formulated from the FGA algorithm [10] by introducing an orthogonal constraint between the present and previous direction vectors [17]. This OGA algorithm employs the optimised forgetting-factor on a sample-by-sample basis, so that the direction vector is orthogonal to the previous direction vector.

We then demonstrate the derivation of the mixed-tone normalised orthogonal gradient adaptive (MT-NOGA) algorithm for PTEQ in DMT-based systems. With this mixed-tone criterion in Section 4, the tap-weight estimate vector $\hat{\mathbf{p}}_m(k)$ at symbol k for $m \in M$ is given adaptively as

$$\hat{\mathbf{p}}_m(k) = \hat{\mathbf{p}}_m(k-1) + \mu_m(k)\,\mathbf{d}_m(k)\;, \tag{10}$$

where $\mu_m(k)$ is the step-size parameter and $\mathbf{d}_m(k)$ is the $\mathbb{T} \times 1$ direction vector.

The direction vector $\mathbf{d}_m(k)$ can be obtained recursively as

$$\begin{aligned}\mathbf{d}_m(k) &= \lambda_m(k)\,\mathbf{d}_m(k-1) + \mathbf{g}_m(k)\\ &= \lambda_m(k)\,\mathbf{d}_m(k-1) - \nabla_{\hat{\mathbf{p}}_m(k)} J(k)\;,\end{aligned} \tag{11}$$

where $\mathbf{g}_m(k)$ is the negative gradient of cost function $J(k)$ in (6) and $\lambda_m(k)$ is the forgetting-factor at symbol k.

By differentiating $J(k)$ in (6) with respect to $\hat{\mathbf{p}}_m(k)$, we then get the gradient vector $\mathbf{g}_m(k)$ as

$$\begin{aligned}\mathbf{g}_m(k) &= -\nabla_{\hat{\mathbf{p}}_m(k)} J(k)\\ &= -\xi_m(k)\,\frac{\partial \xi_m(k)}{\partial \hat{\mathbf{p}}_m(k)} = \tilde{\mathbf{y}}_m(k)\,\xi_m^*(k)\;.\end{aligned} \tag{12}$$

where $\xi_m(k)$ is the *a priori* mixed-tone weight-estimated error at symbol k for $m \in M$ as

$$\xi_m(k) = \tilde{x}_m(k) - \hat{\mathbf{p}}_m^H(k-1)\tilde{\mathbf{y}}_m(k) - \sum_{l=1}^{L} \left(\Pi_l^{\perp}(k)\hat{\mathbf{p}}_l(k)\right)^H \tilde{\mathbf{y}}_l(k)\;,\ \text{for } m \neq l\;,\ L \leq M-1. \tag{13}$$

We introduce the updating gradient vector $\mathbf{g}_m(k)$ by

$$\mathbf{g}_m(k) = \lambda_m(k)\mathbf{g}_m(k-1) + \tilde{\mathbf{y}}_m(k)\xi_m^*(k)\;, \tag{14}$$

where $\xi_m^*(k)$ is the complex conjugate of the mixed-tone estimated error at symbol k for $m \in M$ as given in (13).

A procedure of an orthogonal gradient adaptive (OGA) algorithm to determine $\lambda_m(k)$ has been described in [17] by projecting the gradient vector $\mathbf{g}_m(k)$ onto the previous direction vector $\mathbf{d}_m(k-1)$. This leads us to obtain the direction vector $\mathbf{d}_m(k)$.

By determining the direction vector $\mathbf{d}_m(k)$ through an orthogonal projection of the gradient vector $\mathbf{g}_m(k)$ onto the previous direction vector $\mathbf{d}_m(k-1)$, we arrive

$$\mathbf{d}_m(k) = \mathbf{g}_m(k) - \frac{\mathbf{d}_m(k-1)\,\mathbf{d}_m^H(k-1)}{\mathbf{d}_m^H(k-1)\,\mathbf{d}_m(k-1)}\mathbf{g}_m(k)\,. \tag{15}$$

Thus, $\mathbf{d}_m(k)$ is orthogonal to the previous direction vector $\mathbf{d}_m(k-1)$ weighted by the forgetting-factor $\lambda_m(k)$. We can easily optimise a value of $\lambda_m(k)$ based on a sample-by-sample basis by taking the previous direction vector $\mathbf{d}_m(k-1)$ in (11) and setting to zero as

$$\begin{aligned}\mathbf{d}_m^H(k)\mathbf{d}_m(k-1) &= \lambda_m(k)\mathbf{d}_m^H(k-1)\mathbf{d}_m(k-1) + \mathbf{g}_m^H(k)\mathbf{d}_m(k-1)\\ &= 0\,.\end{aligned} \tag{16}$$

Meanwhile, the gradient vector $\mathbf{g}_m(k)$ becomes the direction vector $\mathbf{d}_m(k)$ when the gradient vector $\mathbf{g}_m(k)$ is orthogonal to previous direction vector $\mathbf{d}_m(k-1)$ by $\mathbf{g}_m^H(k)\mathbf{d}_m(k-1) = 0$. The forgetting-factor parameter $\lambda_m(k)$ can be calculated for each tone m at symbol k as

$$\lambda_m(k) = \left|\frac{\mathbf{g}_m^H(k)\,\mathbf{d}_m(k-1)}{\mathbf{d}_m^H(k-1)\,\mathbf{d}_m(k-1)}\right|\,. \tag{17}$$

According to the results in [10], it is noticed that the results of FGA and OGA algorithms are similar to those obtained by the normalised version of OGA (NOGA) algorithm. The convergence rate of the NOGA algorithm is shown that it is better than that of both FGA and OGA.

Therefore, we introduce the mixed-tone normalised orthogonal gradient adaptive (MT-NOGA) algorithm which can be applied recursively as

$$\tilde{\mathbf{g}}_m(k) = \tilde{\lambda}_m(k)\,\tilde{\mathbf{g}}_m(k-1) + \frac{\tilde{\mathbf{y}}_m(k)\,\xi_m^*(k)}{\|\tilde{\mathbf{y}}_m(k)\|^2}\,, \tag{18}$$

$$\tilde{\lambda}_m(k) = \left|\frac{\tilde{\mathbf{g}}_m^H(k)\,\mathbf{d}_m(k-1)}{\mathbf{d}_m^H(k-1)\,\mathbf{d}_m(k-1)}\right|\,, \tag{19}$$

where $\tilde{\mathbf{g}}_m(k)$ is obtained instead of the gradient vector $\mathbf{g}_m(k)$ in (14) and (17) for this normalised version and $\xi_m^*(k)$ is the complex conjugate of the mixed-tone estimated error at symbol k for $m \in M$ as given in (13).

5.2. Adaptive step-size algorithms

This section describes the proposed low complexity adaptive step-size algorithms with the method of the mixed-tone criterion as described in Section 4 as follows.

5.2.1. *Modified Adaptive Step-size algorithm (MAS)*

Following [18] and [19], the step-size parameter is controlled by squared prediction mixed-tone error. If a large error will be the cause of increased step-size for fast tracking, while a small error will result in a decreased step-size to yield smaller misadjustment. This algorithm can be expressed as

$$\mu_m(k+1) = \gamma\, \mu_m(k) + \beta|\xi_m(k)|^2\,, \tag{20}$$

where $0 \leq \gamma < 1$, $\beta > 0$ and $\xi_m(k)$ is the *a priori* mixed-tone estimated error at symbol k for $m \in M$ as given in (13).

We note that the instantaneous mixed-tone cost function controls the step-size parameter. This idea is that a large prediction error causes the step-size to increase and provides faster tracking, while a small prediction error will result in a decrease in the step-size to yield smaller misadjustment. The step-size parameter $\mu_m(k)$ at symbol k for $m \in M$ is always positive and is controlled by the size of the prediction error and parameters γ and β. The summary of proposed MAS-MTNOGA algorithm is presented in Table 1.

5.2.2. *Adaptive Averaging Step-size algorithm (AAS)*

The objective is to ensure large step-size parameter when the algorithm is far from an optimum point with the step-size parameter decreasing as we approach the optimum [15].

This algorithm achieves the objective using an estimate of the autocorrelation between $\xi_m(k)$ and $\xi_m(k-1)$ to control step-size update $\tilde{\mu}_m(k+1)$. The estimate of an averaging of $\xi_m(k) \cdot \xi_m(k-1)$ is introduced as

$$\tilde{\mu}_m(k+1) = \gamma\, \tilde{\mu}_m(k) + \beta\, |\hat{\zeta}_m(k)|^2\,, \tag{21}$$

$$\hat{\zeta}_m(k) = \alpha\, \hat{\zeta}_m(k-1) + (1-\alpha)|\xi^*_m(k) \cdot \xi_m(k-1)|\,, \tag{22}$$

where $0 \leq \gamma < 1$ and β is an independent variable for scaling the prediction error. The exponentially weighting parameter α should be close to 1. The parameter $\xi^*_m(k)$ is the complex conjugate of the mixed-tone estimated error at symbol k for $m \in M$ as shown in (13). The use of $\hat{\zeta}_m(k)$ responds to two objectives as presented in [15]. First, the error autocorrelation is generally a good measure for the optimum. Second, it rejects the effect of the uncorrelated noise sequence on the update step-size. The summary of proposed AAS-MTNOGA algorithm is presented in Table 2.

6. Computational complexity

In this section, we investigate the additional computational complexity of the proposed low complexity MAS and AAS algorithms. We consider that a multiplication of two complex numbers is counted as 4-real multiplications and 2-real additions. A multiplication of a real number with a complex number is computed by 2-real multiplications.

- Starting with soft-constrained initialisation as : $\hat{\mathbf{p}}_m(0) = \mathbf{0}; \Pi_m^{\perp}(0) = \mathbf{I}; \tilde{\mathbf{d}}_m(0) = \tilde{\mathbf{g}}_m(0) = [1\ 0\ \cdots\ 0]^T$.
- Do for $n \in N_d$ $n = 1, 2, \ldots,$ compute.
  for $m = 1, 2, \ldots, M$.
  for $k = 1, 2, \ldots, K$.

1. To compute $\hat{\mathbf{p}}_m(k)$ as:

$$
\begin{aligned}
\hat{\mathbf{p}}_m(k) &= \hat{\mathbf{p}}_m(k-1) + \mu_m(k)\, \tilde{\mathbf{d}}_m(k)\,, \\
\tilde{\mathbf{d}}_m(k) &= \tilde{\lambda}_m(k)\, \tilde{\mathbf{d}}_m(k-1) + \tilde{\mathbf{g}}_m(k) \\
\tilde{\mathbf{g}}_m(k) &= \tilde{\lambda}_m(k)\, \tilde{\mathbf{g}}_m(k-1) + \frac{\tilde{\mathbf{y}}_m(k)\, \xi_m^*(k)}{\|\tilde{\mathbf{y}}_m(k)\|^2}\,, \\
\text{where} \quad \tilde{\lambda}_m(k) &= \left| \frac{\tilde{\mathbf{g}}_m^H(k)\, \tilde{\mathbf{d}}_m(k-1)}{\tilde{\mathbf{d}}_m^H(k-1)\, \tilde{\mathbf{d}}_m(k-1)} \right| .
\end{aligned}
$$

2. To compute $\mu_m(k)$ as:

$$
\begin{aligned}
\mu_m(k) &= \gamma\, \mu_m(k-1) + \beta\, |\xi_m(k-1)|^2\,, \\
\text{where} \quad \xi_m(k) &= \tilde{x}_m(k) - \hat{\mathbf{p}}_m^H(k-1)\tilde{\mathbf{y}}_m(k) - \sum_{l=1}^{L} \left(\Pi_l^{\perp}(k)\hat{\mathbf{p}}_l(k)\right)^H \tilde{\mathbf{y}}_l(k)\,, \\
& \qquad \text{for } m \neq l\,,\ L \leq M-1. \\
\Pi_m^{\perp}(k) &= \tilde{\mathbf{I}} - \hat{\mathbf{p}}_m(k)\, [\hat{\mathbf{p}}_m^H(k)\, \hat{\mathbf{p}}_m(k)]^{-1}\, \hat{\mathbf{p}}_m^H(k)\,.
\end{aligned}
$$

    end
end
end

Table 1. Summary of the proposed modified adaptive step-size mixed-tone normalised orthogonal gradient adaptive (MAS-MTNOGA) PTEQs.

The proposed AAS mechanism involves two additional updates (21) and (22) as while the proposed MAS approach employs only one update (20) compared with the MT-NOGA algorithm in [11].

Therefore, the computational complexity of the proposed MAS-MTNOGA, AAS-MTNOGA and FS-MTNOGA algorithms are listed in Table 3, where $\mathbb{T}$ is the number of taps of PTEQ. It is shown that the proposed algorithms require a few additional number of operations.

http://dx.doi.org/10.5772/52158

- Starting with soft-constrained initialisation as : $\hat{\mathbf{p}}_m(0) = \mathbf{0}; \Pi_m^{\perp}(0) = \mathbf{I}; \tilde{\mathbf{d}}_m(0) = \tilde{\mathbf{g}}_m(0) = [1\ 0\ \cdots\ 0]^T$.
- Do for $n \in N_d \quad n = 1, 2, \ldots,$ compute.
  for $m = 1, 2, \ldots, M$.
  for $k = 1, 2, \ldots, K$.

1. To compute $\hat{\mathbf{p}}_m(k)$ as:

$$\begin{aligned} \hat{\mathbf{p}}_m(k) &= \hat{\mathbf{p}}_m(k-1) + \tilde{\mu}_m(k)\, \tilde{\mathbf{d}}_m(k)\,, \\ \tilde{\mathbf{d}}_m(k) &= \tilde{\lambda}_m(k)\, \tilde{\mathbf{d}}_m(k-1) + \tilde{\mathbf{g}}_m(k) \\ \tilde{\mathbf{g}}_m(k) &= \tilde{\lambda}_m(k)\, \tilde{\mathbf{g}}_m(k-1) + \frac{\tilde{\mathbf{y}}_m(k)\, \xi_m^*(k)}{\|\tilde{\mathbf{y}}_m(k)\|^2}\,, \\ \text{where} \quad \tilde{\lambda}_m(k) &= \left| \frac{\tilde{\mathbf{g}}_m^H(k)\, \tilde{\mathbf{d}}_m(k-1)}{\tilde{\mathbf{d}}_m^H(k-1)\, \tilde{\mathbf{d}}_m(k-1)} \right|. \end{aligned}$$

2. To compute $\tilde{\mu}_m(k)$ as:

$$\begin{aligned} \tilde{\mu}_m(k) &= \gamma\, \tilde{\mu}_m(k-1) + \beta\, |\hat{\zeta}_m(k-1)|^2\,, \\ \hat{\zeta}_m(k) &= \alpha\, \hat{\zeta}_m(k-1) + (1-\alpha) |\xi_m^*(k) \cdot \xi_m(k-1)|\,, \\ \text{where} \quad \xi_m(k) &= \tilde{x}_m(k) - \hat{\mathbf{p}}_m^H(k-1) \tilde{\mathbf{y}}_m(k) - \sum_{l=1}^{L} \left(\Pi_l^{\perp}(k) \hat{\mathbf{p}}_l(k)\right)^H \tilde{\mathbf{y}}_l(k)\,, \\ & \qquad \text{for } m \neq l\,,\ L \leq M-1. \\ \Pi_m^{\perp}(k) &= \tilde{\mathbf{I}} - \hat{\mathbf{p}}_m(k)\, [\hat{\mathbf{p}}_m^H(k)\, \hat{\mathbf{p}}_m(k)]^{-1}\, \hat{\mathbf{p}}_m^H(k)\,. \end{aligned}$$

    end
  end
end

Table 2. Summary of the proposed adaptive averaging step-size mixed-tone normalised orthogonal gradient adaptive (AAS-MTNOGA) PTEQs.

Algorithm	Number of operations per symbol		
	Multiplications	**Additions**	**Divisions**
MAS-MTNOGA	$8\mathbb{T}+5$	$8\mathbb{T}+5$	1
AAS-MTNOGA	$8\mathbb{T}+8$	$8\mathbb{T}+6$	1
MTNOGA [11]	$8\mathbb{T}+2$	$8\mathbb{T}+4$	1

Table 3. The computational complexity per symbol [21].

7. Performance analysis

The convergence behaviour and stability analysis of the proposed MAS and AAS mechanisms are investigated based on the mixed-tone weight-estimated error. The convergence analysis of both MAS and AAS mechanisms are carried out and the steady-state and mean-square expressions of the step-size parameter relating the mean convergence factor as presented in [21] .

In the following analysis, we study the steady-state performance of the proposed MAS and AAS algorithms. We assume that these algortihms have converged.

7.1. Convergence analysis of the proposed MAS mechanism

Taking expectations on both sides of (20), the steady-state step-size arrives at

$$E\{\mu_m(k+1)\} = \gamma\, E\{\mu_m(k)\} + \beta\, E\{|\varsigma_m(k)|^2\}\,. \tag{23}$$

To facilitate the analysis, the proposed MAS mechanism is under a few assumptions.

Assumption (i). *We consider the steady-state value of $E\{\mu_m(k+1)\}$ by*

$$\begin{aligned}\lim_{k\to\infty} E\{\mu_m(k+1)\} &= \lim_{k\to\infty} E\{\mu_m(k)\} = E\{\mu_m(\infty)\}\,,\\ \lim_{k\to\infty} E\{|\varsigma_m(k)|^2\} &= \varsigma_m^{min} + \varsigma_m^{ex}(\infty)\,,\end{aligned}$$

where ς_m^{min} is the minimum mean square error (MMSE) and $\varsigma_m^{ex}(\infty)$ is the excess of mean square error (EMSE) related with the optimisation criterion in the steady-state condition.

Applying assumption (i) to (23), we obtain

$$\begin{aligned}E\{\mu_m(\infty)\} &= \gamma\, E\{\mu_m(\infty)\} + \beta\,(\varsigma_m^{\min} + \varsigma_m^{\text{ex}}(\infty))\\ (1-\gamma)\, E\{\mu_m(\infty)\} &= \beta\,(\varsigma_m^{\min} + \varsigma_m^{\text{ex}}(\infty))\\ E\{\mu_m(\infty)\} &= \frac{\beta\,(\varsigma_m^{\min} + \varsigma_m^{\text{ex}}(\infty))}{(1-\gamma)}\,.\end{aligned} \tag{24}$$

To simplify these expressions, let us consider another assumptions.

Assumption (ii). *Let us consider that for (24), where*

$$\varsigma_m^{min} + \varsigma_m^{ex}(\infty) \;\approx\; \varsigma_m^{min}\,,$$

and

$$\left(\varsigma_m^{min} + \varsigma_m^{ex}(\infty)\right)^2 \;\approx\; \left(\varsigma_m^{min}\right)^2.$$

We then assume that $\varsigma_m^{ex}(\infty) \ll \varsigma_m^{min}$, when the algorithm is close to optimum.

http://dx.doi.org/10.5772/52158

Employing assumption (ii) to (24), the steady-state step-size for the proposed MAS algorithm becomes

$$E\{\mu_m(\infty)\} \approx \frac{\beta\,(\xi_m^{\min})}{(1-\gamma)}\,. \tag{25}$$

It is noted that the steady-state performance of proposed MAS mechanism has derived in (25) for predicting in the steady-state condition.

7.2. Convergence analysis of the proposed AAS mechanism

Following [20] and [22], the average estimate $\hat{\zeta}_m(k)$ in (22) can be rewritten as

$$\hat{\zeta}_m(k) = (1-\alpha)\sum_{i=0}^{k-1} \alpha^i\,\xi_m^*(k-i)\cdot\xi_m(k-i-1)\,. \tag{26}$$

and

$$|\hat{\zeta}_m(k)|^2 = (1-\alpha)^2\sum_{i=0}^{k-1}\sum_{j=0}^{k-1} \alpha^i\,\alpha^j\,\xi_m^*(k-i)\cdot\xi_m(k-i-1)\cdot\xi_m^*(k-j)\cdot\xi_m(k-j-1)\,. \tag{27}$$

We assume that the proposed algorithm has converged in the steady-state condition. Also, the expectation of (27) can be expressed as

$$E\{|\hat{\zeta}_m(k)|^2\} = (1-\alpha)^2\sum_{i=0}^{k-1} \alpha^{2i}\,E\{|\xi_m(k-i)|^2\}\cdot E\{|\xi_m(k-i-1)|^2\}\,, \tag{28}$$

where α is an exponential weighting parameter.

Using assumption (i) into (28), we have

$$E\{|\hat{\zeta}_m(k)|^2\} = (1-\alpha)^2\,(1+\alpha^2+\alpha^4+\cdots+\alpha^{2k})\cdot(\xi_m^{\min}+\xi_m^{\text{ex}}(\infty))^2\,. \tag{29}$$

For convenience of computation, let

$$E\{|\hat{\zeta}_m(k)|^2\} = (1-\alpha)^2\,\mathcal{A}\,, \tag{30}$$

where

$$\mathcal{A} = (1+\alpha^2+\alpha^4+\cdots+\alpha^{2k})\cdot(\xi_m^{\min}+\xi_m^{\text{ex}}(\infty))^2\,. \tag{31}$$

By multiplying α^2 on both sides of $\mathcal{A}$ in (31), if $k \to \infty$ and $0 < \alpha < 1$, we get

$$\begin{aligned}\alpha^2 \mathcal{A} &= \alpha^2 \cdot (1 + \alpha^2 + \alpha^4 + \ldots + \alpha^{2(k-1)} + \alpha^{2k}) \cdot (\zeta_m^{\min} + \zeta_m^{\text{ex}}(\infty))^2 \\ &= (\alpha^2 + \alpha^4 + \alpha^6 + \ldots + \alpha^{2(k-1)} + \alpha^{2k}) \cdot (\zeta_m^{\min} + \zeta_m^{\text{ex}}(\infty))^2 \\ &= \mathcal{A} - (\zeta_m^{\min} + \zeta_m^{\text{ex}}(\infty))^2 \,. \end{aligned} \tag{32}$$

Rearranging (32) to get $\mathcal{A}$, we arrive at

$$\begin{aligned}(1-\alpha^2) \cdot \mathcal{A} &= (\zeta_m^{\min} + \zeta_m^{\text{ex}}(\infty))^2 \\ \mathcal{A} &= \frac{(\zeta_m^{\min} + \zeta_m^{\text{ex}}(\infty))^2}{(1-\alpha^2)} \,. \end{aligned} \tag{33}$$

Substituting (33) into (30), we get

$$\begin{aligned} E\{|\hat{\zeta}_m(k)|^2\} &= \frac{(1-\alpha)^2 \cdot (\zeta_m^{\min} + \zeta_m^{\text{ex}}(\infty))^2}{(1-\alpha^2)} \\ &= \frac{(1-\alpha) \cdot (1-\alpha) \cdot (\zeta_m^{\min} + \zeta_m^{\text{ex}}(\infty))^2}{(1+\alpha) \cdot (1-\alpha))} \\ &= \frac{(1-\alpha) \cdot (\zeta_m^{\min} + \zeta_m^{\text{ex}}(\infty))^2}{(1+\alpha)} \,. \end{aligned} \tag{34}$$

Taking the expectation on both sides of (21), the mean behaviour of step-size $\tilde{\mu}_m(k)$ is given as

$$E\{\tilde{\mu}_m(k+1)\} = \gamma\, E\{\tilde{\mu}_m(k)\} + \beta\, E\{|\hat{\zeta}_m(k)|^2\} \,. \tag{35}$$

Using assumption (i) and (34) into (35), we get

$$\begin{aligned} E\{\tilde{\mu}_m(\infty)\} &= \gamma\, E\{\tilde{\mu}_m(\infty)\} + \frac{\beta\,(1-\alpha) \cdot (\zeta_m^{\min} + \zeta_m^{\text{ex}}(\infty))^2}{(1+\alpha)} \\ (1-\gamma) \cdot E\{\tilde{\mu}_m(\infty)\} &= \frac{\beta\,(1-\alpha) \cdot (\zeta_m^{\min} + \zeta_m^{\text{ex}}(\infty))^2}{(1+\alpha)} \\ E\{\tilde{\mu}_m(\infty)\} &= \frac{\beta\,(1-\alpha) \cdot (\zeta_m^{\min} + \zeta_m^{\text{ex}}(\infty))^2}{(1-\gamma) \cdot (1+\alpha)} \,. \end{aligned} \tag{36}$$

where $\zeta_m^{\min}$ is the steady-state minimum value and $\zeta_m^{\text{ex}}(\infty)$ is the steady-state excess error of mixed-tone cost function.

By using assumption (ii), the steady-state value of $E\{\tilde{\mu}_m(\infty)\}$ in (36) is approximately as

$$E\{\tilde{\mu}_m(\infty)\} \approx \frac{\beta\,(1-\alpha)\cdot\left(\xi_m^{\min}\right)^2}{(1-\gamma)\cdot(1+\alpha)}\ . \tag{37}$$

We note that (37) has proven for predicting the steady-state performance of proposed AAS algorithm.

7.3. Stability and performance analysis

We introduce the stability and performance analysis of proposed algorithm that is based on the mean-square value of the mixed-tone estimated $\xi_m(k)$.

Let us denote the weight-error vector $\varepsilon_m(k)$ at symbol k for each tone m by following [23] and [24]

$$\varepsilon_m(k) = \mathbf{p}_{opt,m} - \hat{\mathbf{p}}_m(k)\ , \tag{38}$$

where $\mathbf{p}_{\mathrm{opt},m}$ denotes as the optimum Wiener solution for the tap-weight vector.

The estimate tap-weight PTEQ vector $\hat{\mathbf{p}}_m(k)$ can be introduced as

$$\hat{\mathbf{p}}_m(k) = \hat{\mathbf{p}}_m(k-1) + \mu_m(k)\sum_{i=1}^{k}\lambda^{k-i}\frac{\tilde{\mathbf{y}}_m(i)\,\xi_m^*(i)}{\|\tilde{\mathbf{y}}_m^H(i)\,\tilde{\mathbf{y}}_m(i)\|}\ , \tag{39}$$

where $\xi_m(k)$ is the *a priori* mixed-tone estimated error at symbol k for tone m as

$$\xi_m(k) = \tilde{x}_m(k) - \hat{\mathbf{p}}_m^H(k-1)\tilde{\mathbf{y}}_m(k) - \sum_{l=1}^{L}(\Pi_l^{\perp}(k)\hat{\mathbf{p}}_l(k))^H\tilde{\mathbf{y}}_l(k)\ .$$
$$\text{for } m \neq l\ , L \leq M-1 \tag{40}$$

Subtracting $\mathbf{p}_{\mathrm{opt},m}$ from both sides of (39) and using (40) to eliminate $\hat{\mathbf{p}}_m(k)$, we may rewrite as

$$\begin{aligned}\mathbf{p}_{opt,m} - \hat{\mathbf{p}}_m(k) = \mathbf{p}_{opt,m} - \hat{\mathbf{p}}_m(k-1) + \mu_m(k)\sum_{i=1}^{k}\lambda^{k-i}\frac{\tilde{\mathbf{y}}_m(i)}{\|\tilde{\mathbf{y}}_m^H(i)\tilde{\mathbf{y}}_m(i)\|}\Big\{\tilde{x}_m(i) - \hat{\mathbf{p}}_m^H(k-1)\tilde{\mathbf{y}}_m(i)\\ - \sum_{l=1}^{L}(\Pi_l^{\perp}(i)\hat{\mathbf{p}}_l(k))^H\tilde{\mathbf{y}}_l(i)\Big\}^* + \mu_m(k)\sum_{i=1}^{k}\lambda^{k-i}\frac{\tilde{\mathbf{y}}_m(i)}{\|\tilde{\mathbf{y}}_m^H(i)\tilde{\mathbf{y}}_m(i)\|}(\mathbf{p}_{opt,m}^H\tilde{\mathbf{y}}_m(i))^*\\ - \mu_m(k)\sum_{i=1}^{k}\lambda^{k-i}\frac{\tilde{\mathbf{y}}_m(i)}{\|\tilde{\mathbf{y}}_m^H(i)\tilde{\mathbf{y}}_m(i)\|}(\mathbf{p}_{opt,m}^H\tilde{\mathbf{y}}_m(i))^*\ .\end{aligned} \tag{41}$$

Substituting (38) in (41), we get

$$\varepsilon_m(k) = \varepsilon_m(k-1) - \mu_m(k) \sum_{i=1}^{k} \lambda^{k-i} \frac{\tilde{\mathbf{y}}_m(i)\tilde{\mathbf{y}}_m^H(i)\varepsilon_m(k-1)}{\|\tilde{\mathbf{y}}_m^H(i)\tilde{\mathbf{y}}_m(i)\|}$$
$$+ \mu_m(k) \sum_{i=1}^{k} \lambda^{k-i} \frac{\tilde{\mathbf{y}}_m(i)}{\|\tilde{\mathbf{y}}_m^H(i)\tilde{\mathbf{y}}_m(i)\|} \left\{ \tilde{x}_m(i) - \mathbf{p}_{\mathrm{opt},m}^H \tilde{\mathbf{y}}_m(i) - \sum_{l=1}^{L} (\Pi_l^{\perp}(i)\hat{\mathbf{p}}_l(k))^H \tilde{\mathbf{y}}_l(i) \right\}^* . \tag{42}$$

Then, the weight-error vector $\varepsilon_m(k)$ can be expressed as

$$\varepsilon_m(k) = \left[\mathbf{I} - \mu_m(k) \sum_{i=1}^{k} \lambda^{k-i} \frac{\tilde{\mathbf{y}}_m(i)\tilde{\mathbf{y}}_m^H(i)}{\|\tilde{\mathbf{y}}_m^H(i)\tilde{\mathbf{y}}_m(i)\|} \right] \varepsilon_m(k-1) + \mu_m(k) \sum_{i=1}^{k} \lambda^{k-i} \frac{\tilde{\mathbf{y}}_m(i)\, \zeta_{\mathrm{opt},m}^*}{\|\tilde{\mathbf{y}}_m^H(i)\tilde{\mathbf{y}}_m(i)\|} . \tag{43}$$

where $\zeta_{\mathrm{opt},m}^*$ is the complex conjugate of estimation mixed-tone error produced in the optimum Wiener solution as

$$\zeta_{\mathrm{opt},m} = \tilde{x}_m(i) - \mathbf{p}_{\mathrm{opt},m}^H \tilde{\mathbf{y}}_m(i) - \sum_{l=1}^{L} (\Pi_l^{\perp}(i)\hat{\mathbf{p}}_l(k))^H \tilde{\mathbf{y}}_l(i) .$$
$$\text{for } m \neq l\,, L \leq M-1 \tag{44}$$

Assumption (iii). *We consider the condition necessary for the convergence of mean, that is*

$$E\{\ \|\varepsilon_m(k)\|\ \} \rightarrow 0\,,\ \ as\ \ k \rightarrow \infty$$

or equivalently,

$$E\{\,\hat{p}_m(k)\,\} \rightarrow p_{opt,m}\,,\ \ as\ \ k \rightarrow \infty$$

where $\|\varepsilon_m(k)\|$ *is the Euclidean norm of the weight-error vector* $\varepsilon_m(k)$.

We denote the mixed-tone estimated error for tone m at symbol k as

$$\zeta_m(k) = \tilde{x}_m(k) - \hat{\mathbf{p}}_m^H(k)\, \tilde{\mathbf{y}}_m(k) - \sum_{l=1}^{L} (\Pi_l^{\perp}(k)\hat{\mathbf{p}}_l(k))^H \tilde{\mathbf{y}}_l(k) .$$
$$\text{for } m \neq l\,, L \leq M-1 \tag{45}$$

Using (38) into (45), the estimation mixed-tone error $\zeta_m(k)$ at symbol k for each tone m is given as in (46), where $\zeta_{\mathrm{opt},m}$ is the estimation mixed-tone error in the optimum Wiener solution shown in (44).

$$\begin{aligned}
\zeta_m(k) &= \tilde{x}_m(k) - \hat{\mathbf{p}}_m^H(k)\,\tilde{\mathbf{y}}_m(k) - \sum_{l=1}^{L}(\Pi_l^{\perp}(k)\hat{\mathbf{p}}_l(k))^H\tilde{\mathbf{y}}_l(k) \\
&= \tilde{x}_m(k) - (\mathbf{p}_{\text{opt},m} - \varepsilon_m(k))^H\tilde{\mathbf{y}}_m(k) - \sum_{l=1}^{L}(\Pi_l^{\perp}(k)\hat{\mathbf{p}}_l(k))^H\,\tilde{\mathbf{y}}_l(k) \\
&= \tilde{x}_m(k) - \mathbf{p}_{\text{opt},m}^H\,\tilde{\mathbf{y}}_m(k) - \sum_{l=1}^{L}(\Pi_l^{\perp}(k)\hat{\mathbf{p}}_l(k))^H\,\tilde{\mathbf{y}}_l(k) + \varepsilon_m^H(k)\,\tilde{\mathbf{y}}_m(k) \\
&= \;\zeta_{\text{opt},m} + \varepsilon_m^H(k)\,\tilde{\mathbf{y}}_m(k)\,.
\end{aligned} \tag{46}$$

Let $\hat{J}_m(k)$ denotes as the expectation of mean square mixed-tone error at tone m for $m \in M$

$$\begin{aligned}
\hat{J}_m(k) &= E\{\,|\zeta_m(k)|^2\,\} \\
&= E\{(\zeta_{\text{opt},m} + \varepsilon_m^H(k)\tilde{\mathbf{y}}_m(k))^*\,(\zeta_{\text{opt},m} + \varepsilon_m^H(k)\tilde{\mathbf{y}}_m(k))\} \\
&= E\{|\zeta_{\text{opt},m}|^2\} + E\{\tilde{\mathbf{y}}_m^H(k)\varepsilon_m(k)\zeta_{\text{opt},m}\} \\
&\qquad + E\{\varepsilon_m^H(k)\tilde{\mathbf{y}}_m(k)\zeta_{\text{opt},m}^*\} \\
&\qquad + E\{\varepsilon_m^H(k)\varepsilon_m(k)\tilde{\mathbf{y}}_m^H(k)\tilde{\mathbf{y}}_m(k)\}\,.
\end{aligned} \tag{47}$$

By using assumption (iii), we assume that

$$\hat{J}_m(k) = J_m^{min} + J_m^{ex}(k)\,, \tag{48}$$

where J_m^{min} is the minimum mean square mixed-tone error produced by the optimum Wiener filter for tone m as

$$J_m^{min}(k) = E\{|\zeta_{\text{opt},m}|^2\} + E\{\varepsilon_m^H(k)\tilde{\mathbf{y}}_m(k)\zeta_{\text{opt},m}^*\} + E\{\tilde{\mathbf{y}}_m^H(k)\varepsilon_m(k)\zeta_{\text{opt},m}\}\,, \tag{49}$$

and $J_m^{ex}(k)$ is called the excess mean square mixed-tone error (EMSE) at symbol k for tone m as

$$J_m^{ex}(k) = E\{\,\varepsilon_m^H(k)\varepsilon_m(k)\tilde{\mathbf{y}}_m^H(k)\tilde{\mathbf{y}}_m(k)\,\}\,. \tag{50}$$

Since

$$\mathcal{R}_{\tilde{\mathbf{y}}\tilde{\mathbf{y}}} = E\{\tilde{\mathbf{y}}_m(k)\,\tilde{\mathbf{y}}_m^H(k)\}\,, \tag{51}$$

and by the orthogonality principle

$$E\{\zeta_{\text{opt},m}\,\tilde{\mathbf{y}}_m(k)\} \approx 0\,, \tag{52}$$

the excess in mean square mixed-tone error is given by

$$J_m^{ex}(k) = E\{\,\varepsilon_m^H(k)\,\mathcal{R}_{\tilde{\mathbf{y}}\tilde{\mathbf{y}}}\,\varepsilon_m(k)\,\}\,. \quad (53)$$

where $\varepsilon_m(k)$ denotes as the weight-error vector at symbol k for each tone m shown in (38).

8. Simulation results

In this section, we implemented transmission simulations for the ADSL-based downstream including additive white Gaussian noise (AWGN) and near-end crosstalk (NEXT) detailed as follows. The used tones for downstream transmission were starting at active tones 38 to 255 and unused tones including tones 8 to 32 for upstream transmission were set to zero. The samples of reference carrier serving area (CSA) loop were used for the entire test channel, which comprises 512 coefficients of channel impulse response. The ADSL downstream simulations with the CSA loop #4 was the representative of simulations with all 8 CSA loops detailed in [25] as follows. The CSA#4 loop is consisting of 26-gauge bridged tap of length of 400 ft. at 550 ft., of 800 ft. at 6800 ft. and 26-gauge loop of length of 800 ft. at 7600 ft., respectively. Other parameters were as the sampling rate $f_s = 2.208$ MHz and the size of FFT $N = 512$. The length of CP (ν) was identical to 32. The synchronisation delay was of 45. The SNR gap of 9.8dB, the coding gain of 4.2dB, the noise margin of 6 dB, and the input signal power of -40 dBm/Hz were used for all active tones [1]. With the power of AWGN of -140dBm/Hz and NEXT from 24 ADSL disturbers were included in the test channel. The bit allocation calculation requires an estimate of signal to noise ratio (SNR) on tone $n \in N_d$, when the noise energy is estimated after per-tone equalisation.

We compare the proposed MAS-MTNOGA and AAS-MTNOGA PTEQs with variable step-size parameters compared with the fixed step-size MT-NOGA [11] PTEQ. The proposed algorithms were initialised with $\mathbb{T} = 32, \hat{\mathbf{p}}_m(0) = [0\;0\;0\;\ldots\;\;0]^T$, $\tilde{\mathbf{d}}_m(0) = \tilde{\mathbf{g}}_m(0) = [1\;0\;0\;\ldots\;\;0]^T$ and $\Pi_m^{\perp}(0) = \mathbf{I}$, where $\lambda_m(0) = 0.95, \hat{\zeta}_m(0) = \sigma_\eta^2$. The matrix $\mathbf{I}$ is the identity matrix and the parameter σ_η^2 is the variance of AWGN and NEXT. We considered the use of the combining estimated of 3-adjacent tones $(M = 3)$. All the following results were obtained by averaging over 50 Monte Carlo trials.

Fig. 4 and Fig. 5 show the sum of squared mixed-tone errors learning curves of proposed AAS-MTNOGA, MAS-MTNOGA and MT-NOGA PTEQs are illustrated with the different values of fixed step-size parameters for the samples of the active tone at $m = 200$ and 250, respectively. It is observed that the proposed AAS-MTNOGA algorithm can converge more rapidly to steady-state condition than MT-NOGA with the fixed step-size. Learning curves of the excess mean square mixed-tone errors (EMSE) $J_m^{ex}(k)$ of proposed AAS-MTNOGA, MAS-MTNOGA and MT-NOGA PTEQs in Fig. 6 and Fig. 7 are depicted with the different values of fixed step-size parameters for the samples of the active tone at $m = 200$ and 250, respectively. Fig. 8 and Fig. 9 depict the trajectories of step-size parameters $\mu_m(k)$ of proposed MAS-MTNOGA and AAS-MTNOGA algorithms at different initial step-size settings with the sample of the active tone at $m = 250$, respectively. It is shown to converge to its own equilibrium despite large variations of initial step-size parameters.

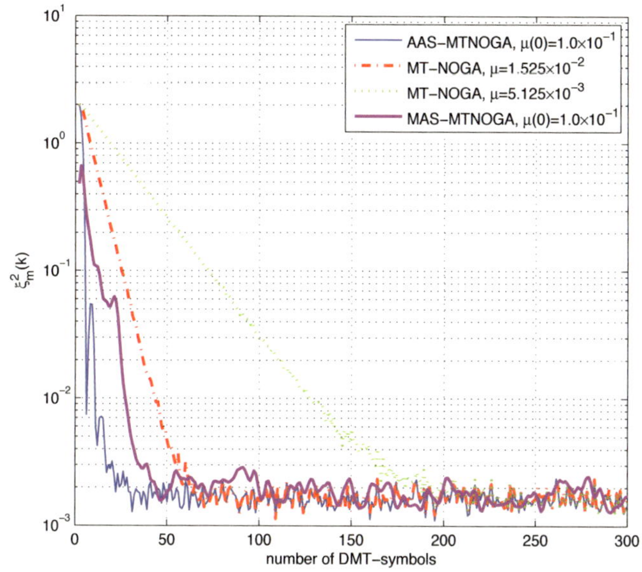

Figure 4. Learning curves of sum of squared mixed-tone errors of the proposed MAS-MTNOGA, AAS-MTNOGA and MTNOGA [11] algorithms with the sample of active tone $m = 200$. The other fixed parameters of the proposed ASS-MTNOGA algorithm are $\gamma = 0.985$, $\beta = 1.25 \times 10^{-2}$, and $\alpha = 0.995$.

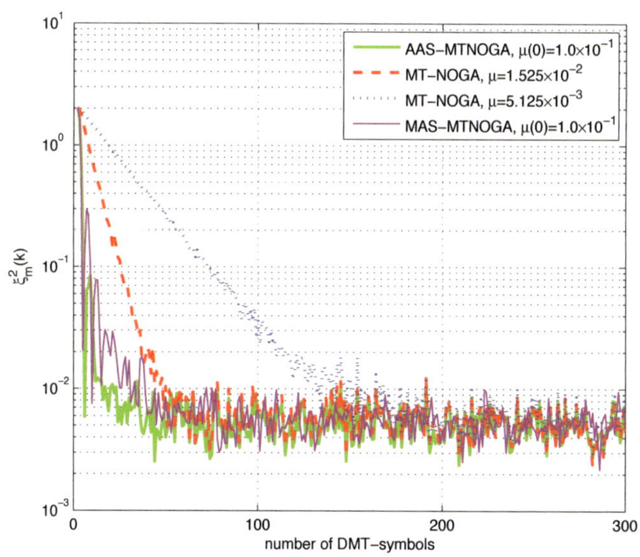

Figure 5. Learning curves of sum of squared mixed-tone errors of the proposed MAS-MTNOGA, AAS-MTNOGA and MTNOGA [11] algorithms with the sample of active tone $m = 250$. The other fixed parameters of the proposed ASS-MTNOGA algorithm are $\gamma = 0.985$, $\beta = 1.25 \times 10^{-2}$, and $\alpha = 0.995$.

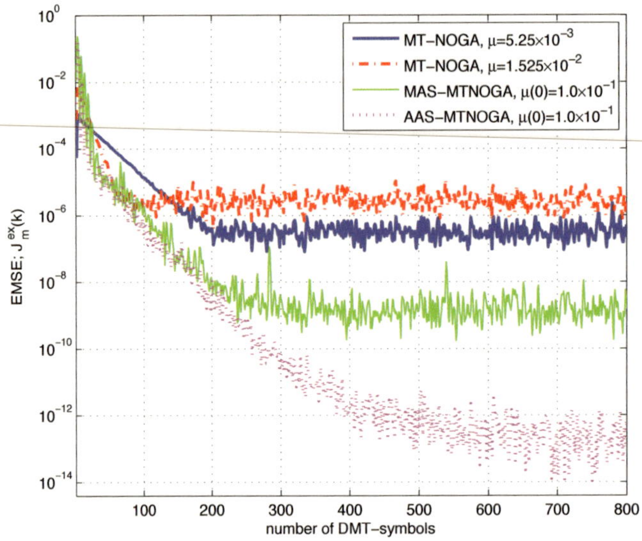

Figure 6. Learning curves of EMSE $J_m^{ex}(k)$ of the proposed MAS-MTNOGA, AAS-MTNOGA and MTNOGA [11] algorithms with the sample of active tone $m = 200$. The other fixed parameters of the proposed ASS-MTNOGA algorithm are $\gamma = 0.985$, $\beta = 1.25 \times 10^{-2}$, and $\alpha = 0.995$.

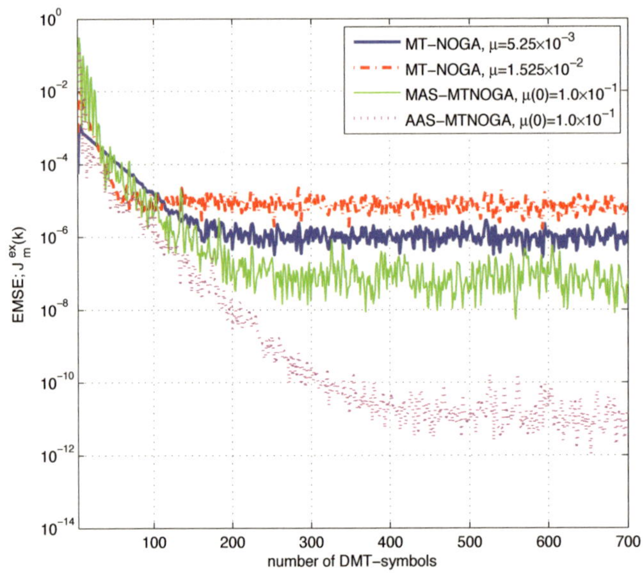

Figure 7. Learning curves of EMSE $J_m^{ex}(k)$ of the proposed MAS-MTNOGA, AAS-MTNOGA and MTNOGA [11] algorithms with the sample of active tone $m = 250$. The other fixed parameters of the proposed ASS-MTNOGA algorithm are $\gamma = 0.985$, $\beta = 1.25 \times 10^{-2}$, and $\alpha = 0.995$.

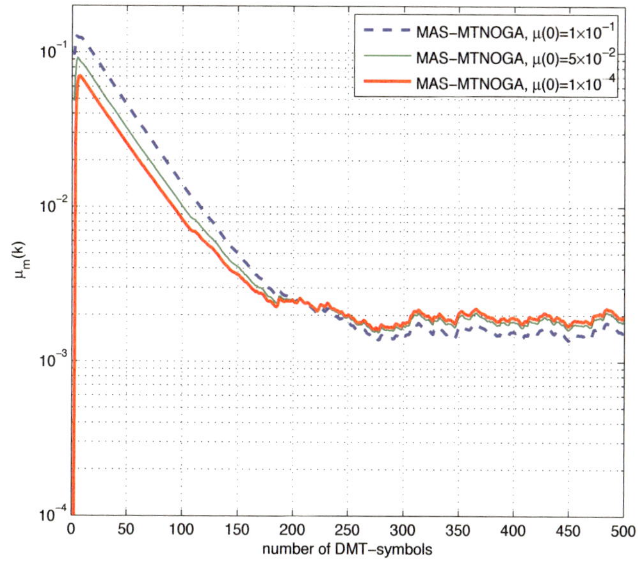

Figure 8. Trajectories of the adaptive step-size $\mu_m(k)$ of the proposed MAS-MTNOGA algorithm using different setting of $\mu(0) = 1 \times 10^{-1}, 5 \times 10^{-2}$ and 1×10^{-4} with the sample of active tone $m = 250$.

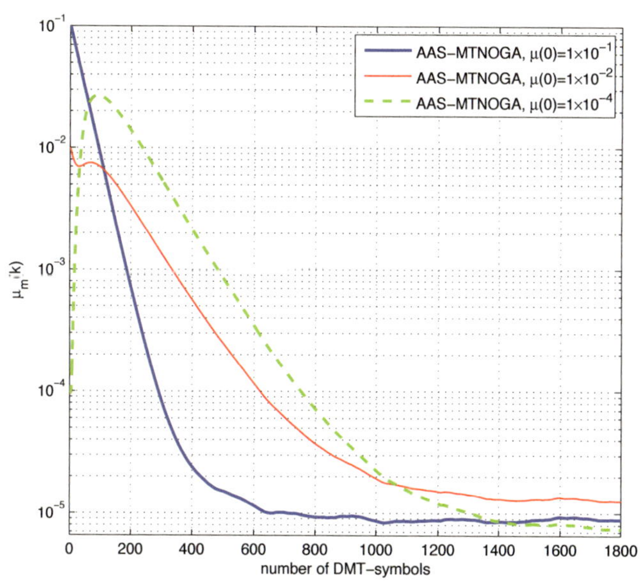

Figure 9. Trajectories of the adaptive step-size $\mu_m(k)$ of the proposed AAS-MTNOGA algorithm using different setting of $\mu(0) = 1 \times 10^{-1}, 1 \times 10^{-2}$ and 1×10^{-4} with the sample of active tone $m = 250$.

9. Conclusion

In this chapter, we present the proposed MAS-MTNOGA and AAS-MTNOGA algorithm for per-tone equalisation in DMT-based systems. We describe the tap-weight estimated PTEQ vector $\hat{\mathbf{p}}_m(k)$ for $m \in M$ of M-combining tones. The mixed-tone cost function is demonstrated as the sum of mixed-tone weight estimated errors of adjacent tones. With the method of adaptive step-size approach and the normalised orthogonal gradient adaptive algorithm, two of low complexity adaptive step-size mechanisms can be achieved for per-tone equalisation based on the mixed-tone criterion. The derivation and analysis of two low complexity adaptive step-size schemes are presented. The adaptation of mean square mixed-tone errors (MSE) and excess mean square mixed-tone errors (EMSE) curves of proposed MAS-MTNOGA and AAS-MTNOGA algorithms are shown to converge rapidly to steady-state condition in the simulated channel. According to simulation results, the proposed algorithms can provide the good performance and are appeared to be robust in AWGN and NEXT channel in comparison with the fixed step-size algorithm of MTNOGA algorithm.

Author details

Suchada Sitjongsataporn

Centre of Electronic Systems Design and Signal Processing (CESdSP),
Mahanakorn University of Technology, Thailand

References

[1] International Telecommunications Union (ITU). Recommendation G.996.1, *Test Procedures for Asymmetric Digital Subscriber Line (ADSL) Transceivers*, February 2001.

[2] International Telecommunications Union (ITU). Recommendation G.992.3, *Asymmetric Digital Subscriber Line (ADSL) Transceivers-2 (ADSL)*, July 2002.

[3] International Telecommunications Union (ITU). Recommendation G.992.5, *Asymmetric Digital Subscriber Line (ADSL) Transceivers-Extened Bandwidth ADSL2 (ADSL2+)*, May 2003.

[4] P.Golden, H.Dedieu, and K.S.Jacobsen, *Fundamentals of DSL Technology*, Auerbach Publications, Taylor&Francis Group, 2006.

[5] P.Golden, H.Dedieu, and K.S.Jacobsen, *Implementation and Applications of DSL Technology*, Auerbach Publications, Taylor&Francis Group, 2008.

[6] S.Sitjongsataporn and P.Yuvapoositanon, "Adaptive Step-size Order Statistic LMS-based Time-domain Equalisation in Discrete Multitone Systems", *Discrete Time Systems*, Mario Alberto Jordán (Ed.), ISBN: 978-953-307-200-5, InTech, April 2011, Available from: http://www.intechopen.com/articles/show/title/adaptive-step-size-order-statistic-lms-based-time-domain-equalisation-in-discrete-multitone-systems

[7] K.V.Acker, G.Leus, M.Moonen, O.van de Wiel and T.Pollet, "Per Tone Equalization for DMT-based Systems", *IEEE Transactions on Communications*, vol. 49, no. 1, pp. 109-119, Jan. 2001.

[8] S.Sitjongsataporn and P.Yuvapoositanon, "Bit Rate Maximising Per-Tone Equalisation with Adaptive Implementation for DMT-based Systems", *EURASIP Journal on Advances in Signal Processing*, vol. 2009, Article ID 380560, 13 pages, 2009. doi:10.1155/2009/380560.

[9] S.Sitjongsataporn and P.Yuvapoositanon, "A Mixed-Tone RLS Algorithm with Orthogonal Projection for Per-Tone DMT Equalisation", in *Proc. IEEE International Midwest Symposium on Circuits and Systems (MWSCAS)*, Knoxville, USA, pp. 942-945, Aug. 2008.

[10] J.A.Apolinário Jr., R.G.Alves, P.S.R.Diniz and M.N.Swamy, "Filtered Gradient Algorithm Applied to a Subband Adaptive Filter Structure", in *Proc. IEEE International Conference Acoustics, Speech, and Signal Processing (ICASSP)*, vol.6, pp. 3705-3708, May 2001.

[11] S.Sitjongsataporn and P.Yuvapoositanon, "Mixed-Tone Normalised Orthogonal Gradient Adaptive Per-Tone DMT Equalisation", in *Proc. IEEE International Conference on Electrical Engineering/Electronics, Computer, Telecommunications and Information Technology (ECTI-CON)*, Pattaya, Thailand, pp. 1151-1154, May 2009.

[12] S.Sitjongsataporn and P.Yuvapoositanon, "Low Complexity Adaptive Step-size Filtered Gradient-based Per-Tone DMT Equalisation", in *Proc. IEEE International Symposium on Circuits and Systems (ISCAS)*, Paris, France, pp. 2526-2529, May 2010.

[13] P.K.Pandey and M.Moonen, "Resource Allocation in ADSL Variable Length Per-Tone Equalizers", *IEEE Transanctions on Signal Processing*, vol. 56, no. 5, May 2008.

[14] G.Strang, *Linear Algebra and Its Applications*, Harcourt Brace Jovanovich, 1988.

[15] L.Wang, Y.Cai and R.C.de Lamare, "Low-Complexity Adaptive Step-Size Constrained Constant Modulus SG-based Algorithms for Blind Adaptive Beamforming", in *Proc. IEEE International Conference Acoustics, Speech, and Signal Processing (ICASSP)*, pp. 2593-2596, 2008.

[16] L.Wang, R.C.de Lamare and Y.Cai, "Low-Complexity Adaptive Step-Size Constrained Constant Modulus SG Algorithms for Adaptive Beamforming", *Signal Processing*, vol.89, pp. 2503-2513, 2009.

[17] J.S.Lim, "New Adaptive Filtering Algorithm Based on an Orthogonal Projection of Gradient Vectors", *IEEE Signal Processing Letters*, vol. 7, no. 11, pp. 314-316, Nov. 2000.

[18] R.C.de Lamare and R.Sampaio-Neto, "Low-Complexity Variable Step-Size Mechanisms for Stochastic Gradient Algorithms in Mimimum Variance CDMA Receivers", *IEEE Transactions on Signal Processing*, vol. 54, pp. 2302-2317, Jun. 2006.

[19] Y.Cai and R.C.de Lamare, "Low-complexity Variable Step-Size Mechanism for Code-Constrained Constant Modulus Stochastic Gradient Algorithms Applied to

CDMA Interference Suppression", *IEEE Transactions on Signal Processing*, vol. 57, no. 1, pp. 313-323, Jan. 2009.

[20] R.H.Kwong and E.W.Johnston, "A Variable Step Size LMS Algorithm", *IEEE Transactions on Signal Processing*, vol.40, no.7, pp. 1633-1642, July 1992.

[21] S.Sitjongsataporn, "Analysis of Low Complexity Adaptive Step-size Orthogonal Gradient-based FEQ for OFDM Systems", *ECTI Transactions on Computer and Information Technology (ECTI-CIT)*, vol. 5, no. 2, pp. 133-144, Nov. 2011.

[22] T.Aboulnasr, and K.Mayyas, "A Robust Variable Step-Size LMS-Type Algorithm: Analysis and Simulations", *IEEE Transactions on Signal Processing*, vol. 45, no. 3, pp. 631-639, Mar. 1997.

[23] P.S.R.Diniz, *Adaptive Filtering: Algorithms and Practical Implementation*, Springer, 2008.

[24] S.Haykin, *Adaptive Filter Theory*, Prentice Hall, 1996.

[25] N.Al-Dhahir and J.M.Cioffi, "Optimum Finite-Length Equalization for Multicarrier Transceivers", *IEEE Transactions on Communications*, vol. 44, pp. 56-64, Jan. 1996.

Section 3

Applications

Chapter 7

An Approach to Hybrid Smoothing for Linear Discrete-Time Systems with Non-Gaussian Noises

Gou Nakura

Additional information is available at the end of the chapter

http://dx.doi.org/10.5772/51385

1. Introduction

It is very important to consider simultaneous estimation of both system states and inaccessible modes for hybrid systems with unknown modes [4,7,24,25]. This estimation is called hybrid estimation. By the hybrid estimation we often want to know both a current mode and system state at each time through information of observation. However there exist cases that we want to know distributions of modes on long run time interval rather than each estimate of the modes themselves at each time to grasp global performance over long time intervals, for example, distributions of active modes in solar systems [5,21], distributions of active agents on formation or consensus via hybrid systems representation and so on.

Much work has been done for smoothing theory for both of continuous- and discrete-time systems ([1,2,3,6,8,9,10,12,13,14,15,18,19,20,22,23] and so on). Various researchers have studied the smoothing problems by various approach, for example, maximum likelihood approach [9,13,19], projection approach [14] and so on. It is well known that smoothers (noncausal estimators) more effectively estimates the states than filters (causal estimators) because of more information of observation.

It is well known that utilization of accumulated information of observation improves estimation performance. Nevertheless, on research of estimation for hybrid systems, little work has been done from the point of view of the noncausal information of observation, i.e., smoothing. In [9] Helmick et al. have presented a fixed-interval smoothing algorithm for discrete-time Markovian jump systems by maximum likelihood (ML) approach. However they have considered only the case with fully accessible modes and their approach is based on approximate approach to probability density functions (PDFs). Therefore they have presented only a nearly optimal smoothing algorithm. While it is significant that optimality is guaranteed for estimation algorithms, in [4] and [7] Costa et al. have presented LMMSE (linear minimum mean square estimate) filters to estimate both system states and inaccessible modes for continuous- and discrete-time Markovian jump systems affected by wide sense white noises, but in these LMMSE filters theory the optimality of estimation isn"t always guaranteed in the meaning that these filters aren"t always MMSE (minimum mean square estimate). To the best of the author"s knowledge the optimal smoothing problems in the cases with inaccessible modes have not yet fully investigated.

In this chapter we study hybrid estimation for linear discrete-time systems with non-Gaussian noises. The concerned systems are general hybrid systems given below which aren"t restricted to Markovian jump systems [4,5,7] and where added noises aren"t restricted to be Gaussian. It is assumed that modes of the systems are not directly accessible throughout this paper. We consider optimal estimation problems to find both estimated states of the systems and an optimal candidate of the distributions of the modes over the finite time interval. We adopt most probable trajectory (MPT) approach to guarantee the optimality of estimation methods. On this approach, given information of observation, we consider optimal control problems where we seek optimal control by which averaged noises energies are minimized for averaged systems throughout the mode distributions. In [24,25] Zhang has presented hybrid filtering algorithm by MPT approach for the continuous- and discrete-time hybrid systems. We consider both filtering and smoothing problems for discrete-time hybrid systems in this chapter. We can expect better estimation performance by taking into consideration noncausal information of observations. The hybrid smoother is realized by two filters approach [2,8,12,20,22,23]. Finally we give numerical examples and verify that we can obtain better estimation performance by smoothing than filtering.

The organization of this chapter is as follows. In section 2 we describe the systems and problem formulation. In section 3 we present the hybrid estimation algorithms by the MPT approach over the finite time interval. In subsection 3.1 we review the hybrid filtering algorithm and in subsection 3.2 we design the backward filters and present the hybrid smoothing algorithm by the two filters approach. In section 4 we consider numerical examples and verify the effectiveness of the estimation algorithms presented in this chapter. In the Appendix we present the principles of hybrid optimality, which give the basis of validity for the hybrid estimation algorithms presented in this chapter

2. Systems and Problems Formulation

Let (Ω, F, P) be a probability space and, on this space, we consider the following system with mode transitions and noises which aren"t restricted to be Gaussian.

$$\begin{aligned} x(k+1) &= A_d(k, \theta(k))x(k) + w_d(k, \theta(k)), \\ x(0) &= x_0, \ \theta(0) = i_0 \\ y(k) &= H_d(k, \theta(k))x(k) + v_d(k, \theta(k)) \end{aligned} \tag{1}$$

where $x \in \mathbf{R}^{\mathbf{n}}$ is the state, $w_d \in \mathbf{R}^{\mathbf{n}}$ is the exogenous random noise, $v_d \in \mathbf{R}^{\mathbf{k}}$ is the measurement noise, and $y \in \mathbf{R}^{\mathbf{k}}$ is the measured output. x_0 is an unknown initial state and it is assumed that a distribution of initial modes i_0 is given. The noises $w_d(\cdot, \cdot)$ and $v_d(\cdot, \cdot)$ aren"t restricted to be Gaussian.

We assume that all these matrices are of compatible dimensions.

Let $\mathsf{M} = \{1, 2, \cdots, m\}$ denote the state space of $\theta(k)$. In this chapter it is assumed that the probability distribution of $\theta(\cdot)$ is unknown or inaccessible. But it is also assumed that a finite number of candidate distributions and the true probability distribution is among the candidate distributions. Let $r \in \mathsf{N}_0 = \{1, 2, \cdots, n_0\}$, and let $\mathsf{P} = \{\phi^{(1)}(\cdot), \cdots, \phi^{(n_0)}(\cdot)\}$ denote the set of such candidate distributions on M, i.e., for $r \in \mathsf{N}_0$ and $k \in [0, N]$, $\phi^{(r)}(k) = (\phi_1^{(r)}(k), \cdots, \phi_m^{(r)}(k))$ with $\phi_i^{(r)}(k) \geq 0$ and $\sum_{i=1}^{m} \phi_i^{(r)}(k) = 1$.

The fixed-interval optimal hybrid estimation problems we address in this chapter for the system (1) are to find the MPT (most probable trajectory) estimate of $x(k)$, $k \in [0, N]$, over the finite horizon $[0,N]$, using the information available on the known part of the observation $y(\cdot)$ for the given distributions of initial mode i_0 and initial state x_0. We define the following performance indices for $r \in \mathsf{N}_0$ and $k \in [0, N]$:

$$\begin{aligned} J_{0k}^{(r)}(x_0, w_d, v_d) := \sum_{l=0}^{k-1} \sum_{i=1}^{m} \phi^{(r)}(l)\big(w_d'(l, i)M_d(l, i)w_d(l, i) + v_d'(l, i)N_d(l, i)v_d(l, i)\big) \\ + (x_0 - \hat{x}_0)' D_0 (x_0 - \hat{x}(0)) \end{aligned} \tag{2}$$

$$\begin{aligned} J_{0N}^{(r)}(x_0, w_d, v_d) := \sum_{l=0}^{N-1} \sum_{i=1}^{m} \phi^{(r)}(l)\big(w_d'(l, i)M_d(l, i)w_d(l, i) + v_d'(l, i)N_d(l, i)v_d(l, i)\big) \\ + (x_0 - \hat{x}_0)' D_0 (x_0 - \hat{x}(0)) \\ + (x(N) - \hat{x}_N)' D_N (x(N) - \hat{x}_N) \end{aligned} \tag{3}$$

where $\hat{x}_0$ is an initial estimate of x_0 and $\hat{x}_{\mathrm{N}}$ is a terminal estimate of $x(N)$. $M_d(l, i) > O$, $N_d(l, i) \geq O$, $D_0 > O$ and $D_N > O$ are symmetric matrices which reflect the uncertainties on the noises $w_d(\cdot, \cdot)$ and $v_d(\cdot, \cdot)$ with the estimates $\hat{x}_0$ and $\hat{x}_{\mathrm{N}}$. Thus these performance indices mean the energies of noises, initial and terminal estimates under some uncertainties averaged by the mode distributions for each $r \in \mathsf{N}_0$. We consider the optimization problems to decide $w_d(\cdot, i)$, $v_d(\cdot, i)$ and $r \in \mathbf{N}_0$ minimizing $J_{0k}^{(r)}$ and $J_{0N}^{(r)}$ utilizing the known parts of the observed information $\mathsf{Y}_N = \{y(l) \mid 0 \le l \le N\}$.

Since the mode $\theta(k)$ at each time is inaccessible, we cannot directly design estimators for the system (1) including the unknown modes. Also, even if the modes are accessible, the computational complexity can exponentially increase with k if we directly design the estimators for the system (1) including $\theta(k)$ explicitly. Hence we introduce the system averaged through the mode distributions for each $r \in \mathbf{N}_0$.

For notational simplicity, we adopt the following notation.

$$\overline{F}^{(r)}(k) = \sum_{i=1}^{m} \phi_i^{(r)}(k) F(k, i)$$

for a matrix function $F(k,i)$ and $r \in \mathbf{N}_0$. Similarly $\overline{F_1 F_2}^{(r)}(k) = \sum_{i=1}^{m} \phi_i^{(r)}(k) F_1(k, i) F_2(k, i)$ for matrix functions $F_1(k,i)$ and $F_2(k,i)$ and so on. Using these notations, we can shift the drift term in the system (1) to $\overline{A_d}^{(r)}(k)$ as follows:

$$x(k+1) = \overline{A_d}^{(r)}(k) x(k) + w_d(k)$$

where

$$w_d(k) = w_d^{(r)}(k) = (A_d(k, \theta(k)) - \overline{A_d}^{(r)}(k)) x(k) + w_d(k, \theta(k)).$$

By replacing the system noise $w_d(k, i)$ by $(\overline{A_d}^{(r)}(k) - A_d(k, i)) x(k) + w_d(k)$ and the observation noise $v_d(k, i)$ by $y(k) - H_d(k, i) x(k)$ in the performance indices (2) and (3), we define

$$\begin{aligned} &L^{(r)}(k, x, w_d, y) \\ &:= \sum_{i=1}^{m} \phi_i^{(r)}(k) ([(\overline{A_d}^{(r)}(k) - A_d(k, i)) x + w_d]' \\ &\qquad \times M_d(k, i) [(\overline{A_d}^{(r)}(k) - A_d(k, i)) x + w_d] \\ &\qquad + (y - H_d(k, i) x)' N_d(k, i) (y - H_d(k, i) x)). \end{aligned}$$

Then we can define the following performance indices:

$$J_f^{(r)}(k, x, w_d(\cdot)) := \sum_{l=0}^{k-1} L^{(r)}(l, x(l), w_d(l), y(l)) + \Phi_0(x(0)) \tag{4}$$

$$J_b^{(r)}(k, x, w_d(\cdot)) := \sum_{l=k}^{N-1} L^{(r)}(l, x(l), w_d(l), y(l)) + \Phi_N(x(N)) \tag{5}$$

$$J_s^{(r)}(k, x, w_d(\cdot)) := J_f^{(r)}(k, x, w_d(\cdot)) + J_b^{(r)}(k, x, w_d(\cdot))$$

where $\Phi_0(x(\cdot)) = (x(\cdot) - \hat{x}_0)' D_0 (x(\cdot) - \hat{x}_0)$ and $\Phi_N(x(\cdot)) = (x(\cdot) - \hat{x}_N)' D_N (x(\cdot) - \hat{x}_N)$.

We consider the optimal control problems to minimize $J_f^{(r)}$ and $J_s^{(r)} = J_f^{(r)} + J_b^{(r)}$ for the given parts of Y_N. Let $V_f^{(r)}(k, x)$ and $V_b^{(r)}(k, x)$ be the value functions of these control problems as follows:

$$
\begin{aligned}
&V_f^{(r)}(k, x) := \inf_{w_d(\cdot)} J_f^{(r)}(k, x, w_d) \\
&V_b^{(r)}(k, x) := \inf_{w_d(\cdot)} J_b^{(r)}(k, x, w_d) \\
&V_s^{(r)}(k, x) := V_f^{(r)}(k, x) + V_b^{(r)}(k, x) \\
&w_{d,f}^{(r)*}(k) := \arg\min\left\{J_f^{(r)}(k, x, w_d(k)) : w \in R^n\right\} \\
&w_{d,b}^{(r)*}(k) := \arg\min\left\{J_b^{(r)}(k, x, w_d(k)) : w \in R^n\right\} \\
&w_{d,s}^{(r)*}(k) := \arg\min\left\{J_s^{(r)}(k, x, w_d(k)) : w \in R^n\right\}
\end{aligned}
$$

Then define

$$
\begin{aligned}
&\hat{x}_f^{(r)}(k) := \arg\min\left\{V_f^{(r)}(k, x) : x \in R^n\right\}, \\
&V_f^{(r)}(k) := V_f^{(r)}\left(k, \hat{x}_f^{(r)}(k)\right)
\end{aligned}
$$

and

$$
\hat{r}_f(k) := \arg\min\left\{V_f^{(r)}(k) : r \in \mathsf{N}_0\right\}.
$$

Then the most probable distribution is $\phi^{(\hat{r}_f(k))}(\cdot)$. Let $\hat{x}_f(k) = \hat{x}_f^{(\hat{r}_f(k))}(k)$ and we have

$$
\begin{aligned}
&V_f^{(\hat{r}_f(k))}\left(k, \hat{x}_f(k)\right) \le V_f^{(r)}\left(k, \hat{x}_f^{(r)}(k)\right) \\
&\le V_f^{(r)}(k, x) = J_f^{(r)}\left(k, x, w_{d,f}^{(r)*}(k)\right) \le J_f^{(r)}\left(k, x, w_d(k)\right).
\end{aligned}
$$

Also define

$$
\begin{aligned}
&\hat{x}_s^{(r)}(k) := \arg\min\left\{V_s^{(r)}(k, x) : x \in \mathbf{R}^n\right\}, \\
&V_s^{(r)}(k) := V_s^{(r)}(k, \hat{x}_s^{(r)}(k))
\end{aligned}
$$

and

$$
\hat{r}_s(k) := \arg\min\left\{V_s^{(r)}(k) : r \in \mathsf{N}_0\right\}.
$$

Then the most probable distribution is $\phi^{(\hat{r}_s(k))}(\cdot)$. Let $\hat{x}_s(k) = \hat{x}_s^{(\hat{r}_s(k))}(k)$ and we have

$$
\begin{aligned}
&V_f^{(\hat{r}_f(k))}\left(k, \hat{x}_f(k)\right) \le V_f^{(r)}\left(k, \hat{x}_f^{(r)}(k)\right) \\
&\le V_f^{(r)}(k, x) = J_f^{(r)}\left(k, x, w_{d,f}^{(r)*}(k)\right) \le J_f^{(r)}\left(k, x, w_d(k)\right).
\end{aligned}
$$

Now we define the following optimal estimators in the sense of most probable trajectory (MPT).

2.1 Definition

Given the matrices M_d, N_d, D_0 and D_N, $(\hat{r}_f(k), \hat{x}_f(k))$, $k \geq 0$, is called an optimal filter (in the MPT sense) if it minimizes $V_f^{(r)}(k, x)$. $(\hat{r}_s(k), \hat{x}_s(k))$, $0 \leq k \leq N$ is called an optimal smoother (in the MPT sense) if it minimizes $V_s^{(r)}(k, x)$.

Then we formulate the following optimal hybrid estimation problems for the performance indices (4) and (5).

The Optimal Hybrid Filtering Problem for Linear Discrete-Time Systems:

Find the pair $(\hat{r}_f(l), \hat{x}_f^{(\hat{r}_f(l))}(l))$, $l \in [0, k]$ minimizing the performance index (4) based on the causal part $\mathsf{Y}_k = \{y(l) \mid 0 \leq l \leq k\}$ of the observed information Y_N.

The Optimal Hybrid Smoothing Problem for Linear Discrete-Time Systems:

Find the pair $(\hat{r}_s(k), \hat{x}_s^{(\hat{r}_s(k))}(k))$, $k \in [0, N]$ minimizing the performance index (4)+(5) based on the whole observed information Y_N.

Remark 2.1. *In general, if we directly adopt dynamic programming (DP) method for mode-dependent systems, it can arise that computational complexity increases exponentially with time k ([5,11]). On the other hand in this chapter we consider the averaged systems and averaged performance indices for them with regard to the candidates of the mode distributions. Note that this introduction of the averaged systems and performance indices prevents the computational complexity from increasing exponentially by applying the dynamical programming (DP) method as seen in the next section.*

3. Hybrid Estimation Algorithms

We assume the following condition:

A1: The matrices $\overline{A_d}^{(r)}(k)$, $k = 0, 1, \cdots$ are invertible.

Remark 3.1. *As described in [24], note that* **A1** *is the reasonable assumption in the discrete-time models. First we consider the following continuous-time model:*

$$\dot{x}_c(t) = A_c(t, \theta_c(t))x_c(t) + w_c(t, \theta_c(t))$$

where $\theta_c(t) \in M$, $t \geq 0$ is the switching mode process. If we discretize this model with stepsize $h \geq 0$, let $x(k) = x_c(kh)$ and the following discretized equation holds:

$$x(k+1) = [I + h\, A_c(kh, \theta_c(kh))]x(k) + w_d(k, \theta(k))$$

where $w_d(k, \theta(k)) = h\, w_c(kh, \theta_c(kh))$. Let

$$A_d(k, i) = I + A_c(kh, i)$$

and then we obtain

$$\overline{A_d}^{(r)}(k)=\sum_{i=1}^{m}\phi_i^{(r)}(k)A_d(k,\ i)$$
$$=\sum_{i=1}^{m}\phi_i^{(r)}(k)[I+h\ A_c(kh\ ,\ i)]$$
$$=I+h\sum_{i=1}^{m}\phi_i^{(r)}(k)A_c(kh\ ,\ i).$$

If we assume that $A_c(t,\ i)$ is uniformly bounded, then $\overline{A_d}^{(r)}(k),\ k=0,\ 1,\ \cdots$ is invertible for h small enough.

3.1 Optimal Hybrid Filtering

The dynamic programming (DP) equations associated with the forward control problem to minimize $J_f^{(r)}$ with regard to $w_d(\cdot)$ are given as follows:

$$V_f^{(r)}(k+1,\ x)=\min_{w_d}\{L^{(r)}(k,\ \overline{A_d}^{(r),-1}(k)(x-w_d),\ w_d,\ y(k))+V_f^{(r)}(k,\ x)\}$$
$$V_f^{(r)}(0,\ x)=\Phi_0(x),\ \ r\in\mathrm{N}_0$$

Let

$$V_f^{(r)}(k,\ x)=x'K_f^{(r)}(k)x+2(p_f^{(r)}(k))'x+q_f^{(r)}(k) \tag{6}$$

for some functions $K_f^{(r)}$ and $q_f^{(r)}$ with appropriate dimensions. Then we obtain the following minimizing $w_d(\cdot)$.

$$w_{d,f}^{(r)*}(k,\ x)=x-\overline{A_d}^{(r)}(k)S_d^{(r)}(k)\big(\overline{A_d'M_d}^{(r)}(k)x+\overline{H_d'N_d}^{(r)}(k)y(k)-p_f^{(r)}(k)\big)$$

where

$$S_d^{(r)}(k)=[\overline{A_d'M_dA_d}^{(r)}(k)+\overline{H_d'N_dH_d}+K_f^{(r)}(k)]^{-1}.$$

Then we obtain the following matrix difference equations, forward vector equations and scalar equations with initial conditions:

$$K_f^{(r)}(k+1)=\overline{M_d}^{(r)}(k)-\overline{M_dA_d}^{(r)}(k)S_d^{(r)}(k)\overline{A_d'M_d}^{(r)}(k),\ K_f^{(r)}(0)=D_0 \tag{7}$$

$$p_f^{(r)}(k+1)=-\overline{M_dA_d}^{(r)}(k)S_d^{(r)}[\overline{H_d'N_d}^{(r)}(k)y(k)-p_f^{(r)}(k)],\ p_f^{(r)}(0)=-D_0\hat{x}_0 \tag{8}$$

$$\begin{aligned}q_f^{(r)}(k+1)=&-[\overline{H_d'N_d}^{(r)}(k)y(k)-p_f^{(r)}(k)]'S_d^{(r)}(k)[\overline{H_d'N_d}^{(r)}(k)y(k)-p_f^{(r)}(k)]\\&+y'(k)\overline{N_d}^{(r)}(k)y(k)+q_f^{(r)}(k),\ q_f^{(r)}(0)=\hat{x}_0D_0\hat{x}_0\end{aligned} \tag{9}$$

For any given k, by letting $\partial V_f^{(r)} / \partial x = 0$, we obtain

$$K_f^{(r)}(k)x + p_f^{(r)}(k) = 0.$$

Since it can be shown that the matrix $K_f^{(r)}(k)$ is positive-definite, we obtain

$$\hat{x}_f^{(r)}(k) = -(K_f^{(r)}(k))^{-1} p_f^{(r)}(k)$$

as the minimizer of $V_f^{(r)}(k,\ x)$. Then we obtain

$$\begin{aligned}
\hat{x}_f^{(r)}(k+1) &= -({}^{K_f^{(r)}k1)}_{(+)} p_f^{(r)}(k+1) \\
&= -[\overline{M_d}^{(r)}(k) - \overline{M_d A_d}^{(r)}(k) S_d^{(r)}(k) \overline{A_d' M_d}^{(r)}(k)]^{-1} \overline{M_d A_d}^{(r)}(k) S_d^{(r)} \\
&\qquad \times [\overline{H_d' N_d}^{(r)}(k) y(k) + K_f^{(r)}(k) \hat{x}_f^{(r)}(k)],\ \hat{x}_f^{(r)}(0) = \hat{x}_0
\end{aligned} \tag{10}$$

and

$$\begin{aligned}
q_f^{(r)}(k+1) &= -[\overline{H_d' N_d}^{(r)}(k) y(k) + K_f^{(r)}(k) \hat{x}_f^{(r)}(k)]' S_d^{(r)}(k) \\
&\qquad \times [\overline{H_d' N_d}^{(r)}(k) y(k) + K_f^{(r)}(k) \hat{x}_f^{(r)}(k)] \\
&\qquad + y'(k) \overline{N_d}^{(r)}(k) y(k) + q_f^{(r)}(k),\ q_f^{(r)}(0) = \hat{x}_0 D_0 \hat{x}_0
\end{aligned} \tag{11}$$

We also obtain

$$V_f^{(r)}(k) = -(\hat{x}_f^{(r)}(k))' K_f^{(r)}(k) \hat{x}_f^{(r)}(k) + q_f^{(r)}(k).$$

Now we have the following filtering algorithm, which gives the solution of **the Optimal Hybrid Filtering Problem for Linear Continuous-Time Systems**.

****Optimal hybrid filtering algorithm****

Step 1) Obtain $K_f^{(r)}(k)$, $\hat{x}_f^{(r)}(k)$ and $q_f^{(r)}(k)$ for $r \in \mathrm{N}_0$ and $k \in [0,\ N]$ by solving (7), (10) and (11) with initial conditions.

Step 2) Choose $\hat{r}_f(k)$ that minimizes

$$V_f^{(r)}(k) = -(\hat{x}_f^{(r)}(k))' K_f^{(r)}(k) \hat{x}_f^{(r)}(k) + q_f^{(r)}(k).$$

Then the most probable distribution is $\phi^{(\hat{r}_f(k))}(k)$ and the optimal filter is given by

$$(\hat{r}_f(k),\ \hat{x}_f(k)) = (\hat{r}_f(k),\ \hat{x}_f^{(\hat{r}(k))}(k)).$$

3.2 Optimal Hybrid Smoothing

The dynamic programming (DP) equations associated with the backward control problem to minimize $J_b^{(r)}$ with regard to $w_d(\cdot)$ are given as follows:

$$V_b^{(r)}(k, x) = \min_{w_d} \{L^{(r)}(k, x, w_d, y(k)) + V_b^{(r)}(k+1, \bar{A}_d^{(r)}(k)x + w_d)\}$$

$$V_b^{(r)}(N, x) = \Phi_N(x), \quad r \in \mathrm{N}_0$$

Let

$$V_b^{(r)}(k, x) = x' K_b^{(r)}(k)x + 2(p_b^{(r)}(k))' x + q_b^{(r)}(k) \tag{12}$$

for some functions $K_b^{(r)}$, $p_b^{(r)}$ and $q_b^{(r)}$ with appropriate dimensions. Then we obtain the following minimizing $w_d(\cdot)$.

$$w_{d,b}^{(r)*}(k, x) = \{-\overline{A_d}^{(r)}(k) + T_d^{(r)}(k)\overline{M_d A_d}(k)\}x(k) - T_d^{(r)}(k)p_f^{(r)}(k+1)$$

where

$$T_d^{(r)}(k) = [\overline{M_d}^{(r)}(k) + K_b^{(r)}(k+1)]^{-1}.$$

Let

$$V_b^{(r)}(k, x) = x' K_b^{(r)}(k)x + 2(p_b^{(r)}(k))' x + q_b^{(r)}(k) \tag{13}$$

for some functions $K_b^{(r)}$, $p_b^{(r)}$ and $q_b^{(r)}$ with appropriate dimensions. Then we obtain the following matrix difference equations, backward vector equations and scalar equations with terminal conditions:

$$\begin{gathered} K_b^{(r)}(k) = \overline{A_d' M_d A_d}^{(r)}(k) - \overline{A_d' M_d}^{(r)}(k) T_d^{(r)}(k) \overline{M_d A_d}^{(r)}(k) + \overline{H_d' N_d H_d}^{(r)}(k), \\ K_b^{(r)}(N) = D_N \end{gathered} \tag{14}$$

$$p_b^{(r)}(k) = \overline{A_d' M_d}(k) T_d^{(r)}(k) p_b^{(r)}(k+1) \text{ - } \overline{H_d N_d}^{(r)}(k) y(k)], \quad p_b^{(r)}(N) = -D_N \hat{x}_N \tag{15}$$

$$\begin{aligned} q_b^{(r)}(k) = & -p_b^{(r)'}(k+1) T_d^{(r)}(k) p_b^{(r)}(k+1) + q_b^{(r)}(k+1) \\ & + y'(k) \overline{N_d}(k+1) y(k), \quad q_b^{(r)}(N) = \hat{x}'_N D_N \hat{x}_N \end{aligned} \tag{16}$$

For any given k, by letting $\partial V_b^{(r)} / \partial x = 0$, we obtain

$$K_b^{(r)}(k)x + p_b^{(r)}(k) = 0.$$

Since it can be also shown that the matrix $K_b^{(r)}(k)$ is positive-definite, we obtain

$$\hat{x}_b^{(r)}(k) = -(K_b^{(r)}(k))^{-1} p_b^{(r)}(k)$$

as the minimizer of $V_b^{(r)}(k, x)$. Then we obtain

$$\hat{x}_b^{(r)}(k) = -(K_b^{(r)}(k))^{-1} p_b^{(r)}(k)$$
$$= [\overline{A_d' M_d A_d}^{(r)}(k) - \overline{A_d' M_d}^{(r)}(k) T_d^{(r)}(k) \overline{M_d A_d}^{(r)}(k) + \overline{H_d' N_d H_d}^{(r)}(k)]^{-1}$$
$$\times [\overline{A_d' M_d}(k) T_d^{(r)}(k) K_b^{(r)}(k+1) \hat{x}_b^{(r)}(k+1) + \overline{H_d' N_d}^{(r)}(k) y(k)], \ \hat{x}_b^{(r)}(N) = \hat{x}_N \tag{17}$$

and

$$q_b^{(r)}(k) = -\hat{x}_b^{(r)'}(k+1) K_b^{(r)}(k+1) T_d^{(r)}(k) K_b^{(r)}(k+1) \hat{x}_b^{(r)}(k+1)$$
$$+ q_b^{(r)}(k+1) + y'(k) \overline{N}_d(k+1) y(k), \ q_b^{(r)}(N) = \hat{x}_N' D_N \hat{x}_N. \tag{18}$$

We also obtain

$$V_b^{(r)}(k) = -(\hat{x}_b^{(r)}(k))' K_b^{(r)}(k) \hat{x}_b^{(r)}(k) + q_b^{(r)}(k).$$

Using (6) and (12), we can express $V_s^{(r)}(k, x)$ as

$$V_s^{(r)}(k, x) = x'[K_f^{(r)}(k) + K_b^{(r)}(k)]x + 2[p_f^{(r)}(k) + p_b^{(r)}(k)]' x + q_f^{(r)}(k) + q_b^{(r)}(k)$$

Let

$$\partial V_s^{(r)} / \partial x = 0$$

and we obtain the following form.

$$\hat{x}_s^{(r)}(k) = -[K_f^{(r)}(k) + K_b^{(r)}(k)]^{-1} (p_f^{(r)}(k) + p_b^{(r)}(k))$$

Since $p_f^{(r)}(k) = -K_f^{(r)}(k) \hat{x}_f^{(r)}(k)$ and $p_b^{(r)}(k) = -K_b^{(r)}(k) \hat{x}_b^{(r)}(k)$, for each candidate r of given distributions, we can obtain the following form of smoothed estimate at time k by the forward and backward filtered estimates.

$$\hat{x}_s^{(r)}(k) = K_s^{(r)}(k)[K_f^{(r)}(k) \hat{x}_f^{(r)}(k) + K_b^{(r)}(k) \hat{x}_b^{(r)}(k)]$$

where $K_s^{(r)}(k) = [K_f^{(r)}(k) + K_b^{(r)}(k)]^{-1}$.

Now we have the following smoothing algorithm, which gives the solution of **the Optimal Hybrid Smoothing Problem for Linear Continuous-Time Systems.**

****Optimal hybrid smoothing algorithm****

Step 1) Obtain $K_b^{(r)}(k)$, $\hat{x}_b^{(r)}(k)$ and $q_b^{(r)}(k)$ for $r \in \mathrm{N}_0$ and $k \in [0, N]$ by solving (14), (17) and (18) with terminal conditions.

Step 2) Choose $\hat{r}_s(k)$ that minimizes

$$V_s^{(r)}(k) = V_f^{(r)}(k) + V_b^{(r)}(k)$$

where

$$V_b^{(r)}(k) = -\hat{x}_b^{(r)'}(k)K_b^{(r)}(k)\hat{x}_b^{(r)}(k) + q_b^{(r)}(k).$$

Then the most probable distribution is $\phi^{(\hat{r}_s(k))}(k)$ and the optimal smoother is given by

$$\begin{aligned}(\hat{r}_s(k), \hat{x}_s(k)) &= (\hat{r}_s(k), \hat{x}_s^{(\hat{r}_s(k))}(k))\\ &= (\hat{r}_s(k), K_s^{(\hat{r}_s(k))}(k)[K_f^{(\hat{r}_s(k))}(k)\hat{x}_f^{(\hat{r}_s(k))}(k) + K_b^{(\hat{r}_s(k))}(k)\hat{x}_b^{(\hat{r}_s(k))}(k)])\end{aligned}$$

where $K_s^{(\hat{r}_s(k))}(k) = [K_f^{(\hat{r}_s(k))}(k) + K_b^{(\hat{r}_s(k))}(k)]^{-1}$.

Remark 3.2. *Note that, if the system (1) is a single mode system, i.e., the system (1) is independent of θ(k), the forms of the filter and smoother presented in this section are reduced to the well-known ones of the Kalman filter and smoother.*

4. Numerical Examples

In this section, we study numerical examples to demonstrate the effectiveness of the presented design algorithms.

We consider the following two mode systems and assume that the system parameters are as follows:

$$\begin{aligned}x(k+1) &= A_d(k, \theta(k))x(k) + w_d(k, \theta(k)),\\ x(0) &= x_0, \ \theta(0) = i_0\\ y(k) &= H_d(k, \theta(k))x(k) + v_d(k, \theta(k))\end{aligned} \tag{19}$$

where

· Mode 1:

$$A_1 = \begin{bmatrix} 0 & 1 \\ -0.8 & 0.6 \end{bmatrix},$$

· Mode 2:

$$A_2 = \begin{bmatrix} 0.5 & 1 \\ -0.4 & 0.6 \end{bmatrix},$$

$$H = [1, 0]$$

and

$$M(t, i) = \begin{bmatrix} 1 & 0 \\ 0 & 1 \end{bmatrix}, \ N(t, i) = 1, \ D_0 = \begin{bmatrix} 1 & 0 \\ 0 & 1 \end{bmatrix}$$

for *i=1,2*. We set $\hat{x}_0 = col(-0.1, 0)$ and the distribution of the initial mode i_0 as (1/ 2, 1/ 2). $w_d(\cdot, \cdot)$ and $v_d(\cdot, \cdot)$ are stochastic noises which aren''t restricted to be Gaussian white. The candidates of mode distributions are given as follows:

$$\phi^{(1)} = \left(\frac{2}{5}, \frac{3}{5}\right), \phi^{(2)} = \left(\frac{1}{2}, \frac{1}{2}\right), \phi^{(3)} = \left(\frac{3}{5}, \frac{2}{5}\right)$$

The paths of $\theta(k)$ are generated randomly, and the performances are compared under the same circumstance, that is, the same set of the paths so that the performances can be easily compared.

We consider the whole system (19) with the true mode distribution $\phi^{(3)}$ over the time interval $k \in [0, 100]$. We verify the effectiveness of the presented hybrid estimation algorithms and compare the estimation performances for the optimal filtering and smoothing algorithms. In order to carry out these algorithms we solve the forward or backward triplet of the difference equations (7)(10)(11) or (14)(17)(18) with the initial or terminal conditions for given observation $y(\cdot)$ and each candidate r=1,2,3 of given distributions, and obtain the pair $(\hat{r}_f(k), \hat{x}_f(k))$ minimizing $V_f^{(r)}(k, x)$ in the filtering case or the pair $(\hat{r}_s(k), \hat{x}_s(k))$ minimizing $V_s^{(r)}(k, x)$ in the smoothing case for $k \in [0, 100]$.

Filtered and smoothed values of the first components of the whole system states are given by Fig. 1 and Fig. 2 respectively. Fig. 3 and Fig. 4 show the square errors between the states and filtered values, and the states and smoothed values respectively. The mean square errors over the time interval *[0, 100]* are 0.0276 in the filtering case, and 0.0151 in the smoothing case respectively. From these figures and calculation results it is shown that the smoother gives better estimation than the filter. Filtered and smoothed values of the second components of the whole system states are given by Fig. 5 and Fig. 6 respectively. Fig. 7 and Fig. 8 show the square errors between the states and filtered values, and the states and smoothed values respectively. The mean square errors over the time interval *[0, 100]* are 0.0151 in the filtering case, and 0.0118 in the smoothing case respectively. From these figures and calculation results it is shown that the smoother gives better estimation than the filter. Filtered and smoothed mode distributions are given by Fig. 9 and Fig. 10. Notice that the vertical axes show the candidates of the mode distributions not the modes themselves. In Fig. 9 the filtered values of the mode distributions rapidly change to be left undecided. To the contrary in Fig. 10 the smoothed values of the mode distributions are firmly decided. Through these ten figures it is shown that the optimal smoother presented in this chapter gives better estimate performance than the optimal filter presented in the previous work [24] from the point of view of both state and modes estimation.

http://dx.doi.org/10.5772/51385

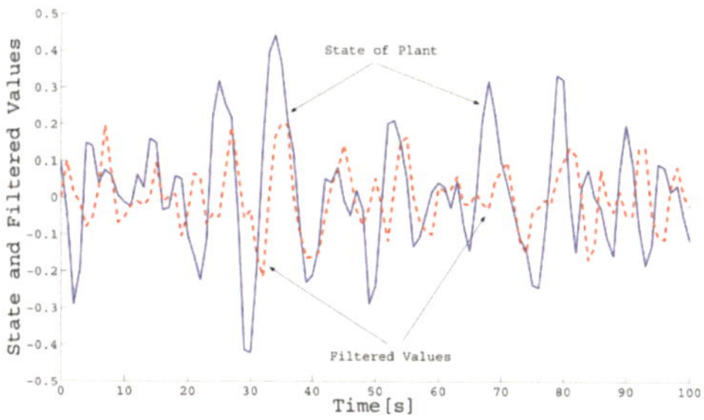

Figure 1. The state of the system and filtered values: 1st components

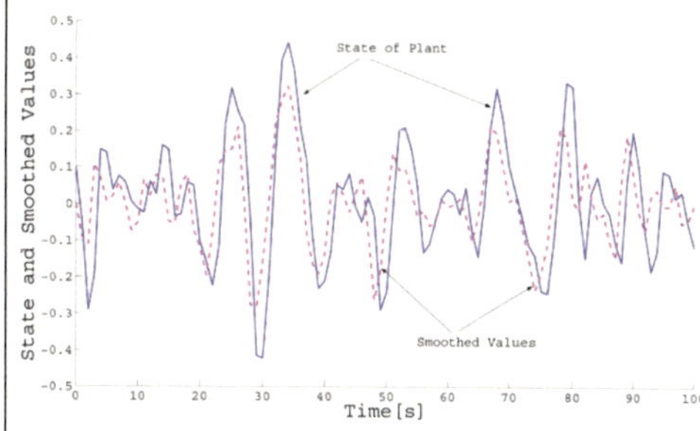

Figure 2. The state of the system and smoothed values: 1st components

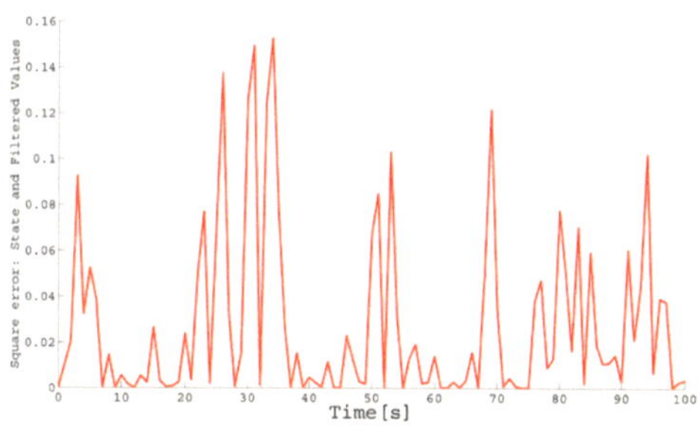

Figure 3. The square errors between the state and filtered values: 1st components

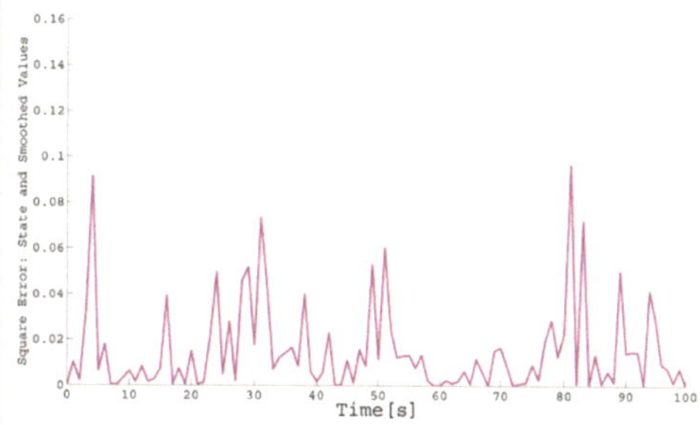

Figure 4. The square errors between the state and smoothed values: 1st components

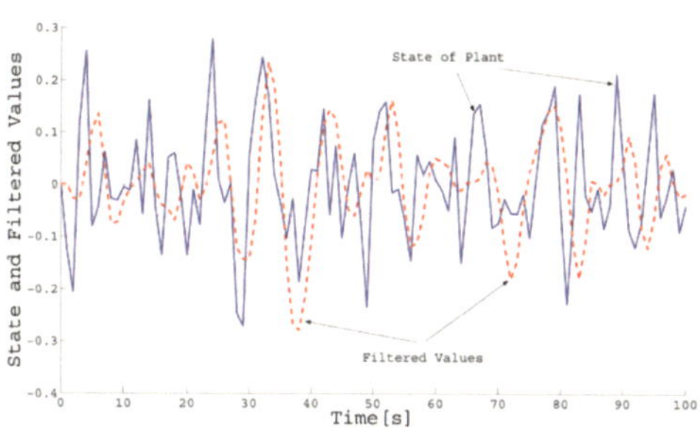

Figure 5. The state of the system and filtered values: 2nd components

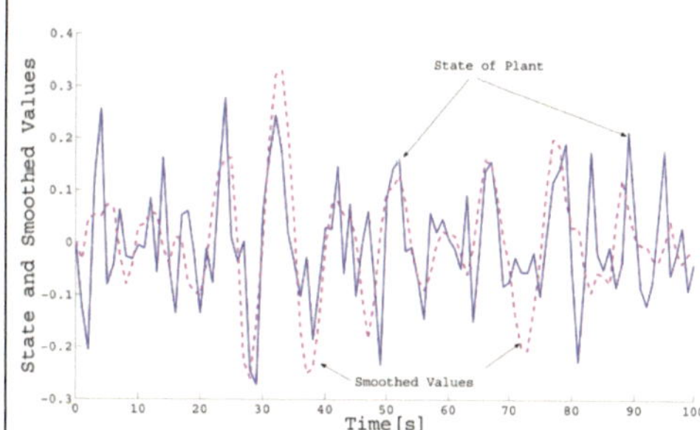

Figure 6. The state of the system and smoothed values: 2nd components

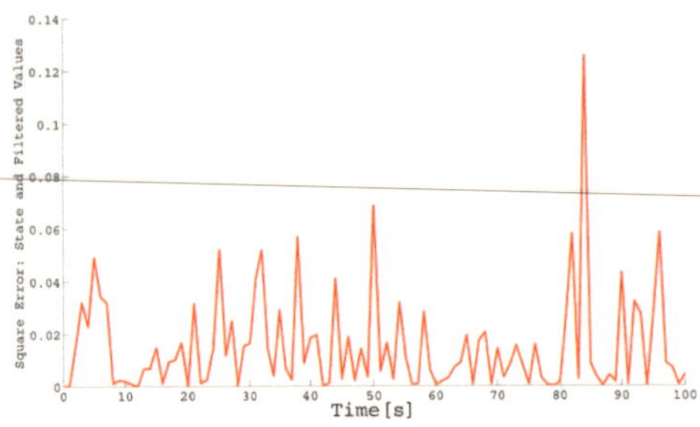

Figure 7. The square errors between the state and filtered values: 2nd components

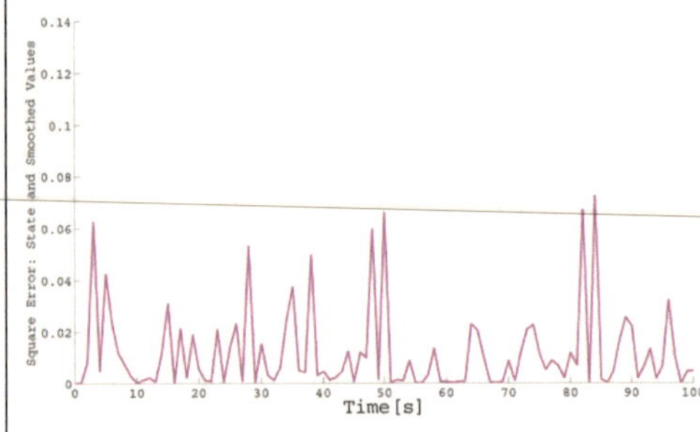

Figure 8. The square errors between the state and smoothed values: 2nd components

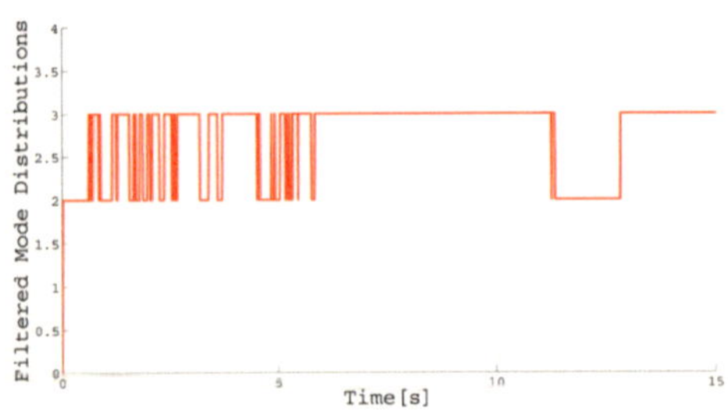

Figure 9. The filtered mode distributions

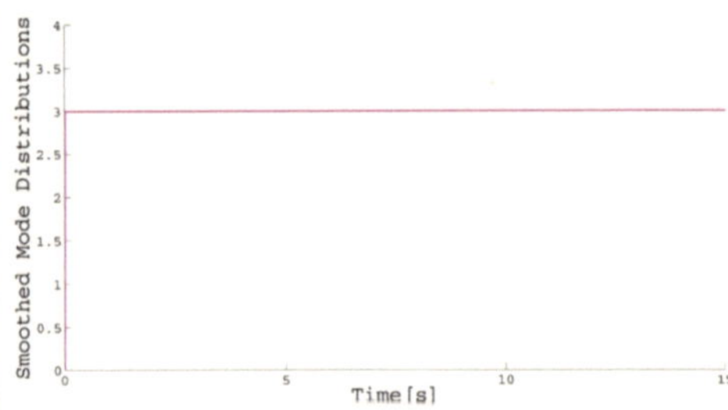

Figure 10. The smoothed mode distributions

5. Concluding Remarks

In this chapter we have studied the state and mode estimation problems for linear discrete-time hybrid systems over the fixed time interval. The systems aren"t restricted to the Markovian jump systems and the added noises aren"t restricted to be Gaussian. With regard to concrete examples of the systems considered in this chapter, refer to [24,25]. Those examples show that the systems and estimation algorithms presented in this chapter cover extreme broad classes of dynamical systems affected by the noises not to be restricted to be Gaussian. We have adopted the MPT approach. The state and mode estimation approach adopted in this paper guarantees the optimality of estimation performance in the meaning of MPT different from the previous work ([4,7]).

In this chapter we have considered the problems that both system state and modes are estimated. However we have considered the problems that the distributions of the modes over the fixed time interval not the modes themselves are estimated to grasp the global behavior of the hybrid systems over the long time intervals. In order to estimate both the system state and distributions of the modes we have introduced the averaged performance indices with respect to the candidates of the mode distributions for the averaged systems. This introduc-

http://dx.doi.org/10.5772/51385

tion of the averaged systems and performance indices prevents the computational complexity from increasing exponentially with time passage. For these performance indices we have formulated the optimal filtering and smoothing problems based on the available observed information. The estimation problems have been reduced to the optimal control problems to find the noises minimizing the introduced performance indices. We have derived the forward and backward matrix difference equations and the forward and backward filter equations with the initial and terminal conditions respectively, which give the necessary conditions for the solvability of the optimal estimation problems. Then we have presented the optimal hybrid smoothing algorithm by the two filters approach. Finally we have studied the numerical examples to compare the estimation performances by filtering and smoothing. We have obtained the better estimation performance by the smoothing algorithm than the filtering algorithm from the point of view of both state and modes estimation.

With regard to continuous-time cases, refer to [16,17,25]. In particular, in [17,25], the cases that concerned systems are assumed to be Markovian jump systems is also considered. In these papers the concept of quasi-stationary distributions is introduced for the Markovian mode processes and near optimality of limiting estimators with the quasi-stationary distributions is shown. It is well known that the concept of quasi-stationary distribution is very important and highly practical to grasp behavior of stochastic processes over long run time. As a further research issue it is very significant that the quasi-stationary distributions of stochastic mode processes and estimator with these distributions are investigated for the discrete-time hybrid systems.

Appendix: Principle of Hybrid Optimality

With regard to the optimal control problems considered in this chapter, it is obvious that principle of optimality does not hold for the optimal trajectory $x^*(\cdot)$ with optimal control input $w_d^{(r)*}(\cdot)$ and each performance index for each mode distribution candidate $r \in \mathrm{N}_0$. However, for the pair $(\hat{r}(\cdot), x(\cdot))$ of the optimal mode distribution candidate and optimal trajectory with the optimal control inputs $w_d^{(r)*}(\cdot)$, the following principles of hybrid optimality hold. These principles give a basis of validity for the hybrid estimation algorithms presented in this chapter.

Consider the following system

$$x(k+1) = \bar{A}_d^{(r)}(k)x(k) + w_d(k) \tag{20}$$

$$y(k) = H_d(k, \theta(k))x(k) + v_d(k, \theta(k))$$

and the performance indices

$$J_f^{(r)}(k,\, x,\, w_d(\cdot))=\sum_{l=0}^{k-1} L^{(r)}(l,\, x(l),\, w_d(l),\, y(l))+\Phi_0(x(0)) \tag{21}$$

$$J_b^{(r)}(k,\, x,\, w_d(\cdot))=\sum_{l=k}^{N-1} L^{(r)}(l,\, x(l),\, w_d(l),\, y(l))+\Phi_N(x(N)) \tag{22}$$

$$J_s^{(r)}(k,\, x,\, w_d(\cdot))=J_f^{(r)}(k,\, x,\, w_d(\cdot))+J_b^{(r)}(k,\, x,\, w_d(\cdot)) \tag{23}$$

where

$$\begin{aligned} &L^{(r)}(k,\, x,\, w_d,\, y) \\ &=\sum_{i=1}^{m} \phi_i^{(r)}(k)([(\overline{A_d}^{(r)}(k)-A_d(k,\, i))x+w_d]' \\ &\qquad \times M_d(k,\, i)[(\overline{A_d}^{(r)}(k)-A_d(k,\, i))x+w_d] \\ &\qquad +(y-H_d(k,\, i)x)' N_d(k,\, i)(y-H_d(k,\, i)x)). \end{aligned}$$

We consider the following three optimal control problems for the system (20) and the performance indices (21)-(23):

Problem (A): Forward Optimal Control Problem

Consider the system (20) with the initial state $x(0)$. Find the pair $(\hat{r}_f(l),\, w_{d,f}^{(\hat{r}_f(l))^*}(l))$, $l\in[0,\, k]$ minimizing the value of the performance index (21) based on the causal part $\mathsf{Y}_k=\{y(l)\mid 0\le l\le k\}$ of the observed information Y_N .

Problem (B): Backward Optimal Control Problem

Consider the system (20) with the initial state $x(k)$. Find the pair $(\hat{r}_b(l),\, w_{d,b}^{(\hat{r}_b(l))^*}(l))$, $l\in[k,\, N]$ minimizing the value of the performance index (22) based on the anti-causal part $\overline{\mathsf{Y}}_k=\{y(l)\mid k\le l\le N\}$ of the observed information Y_N .

Problem (C): Fixed-Interval Optimal Control Problem

Consider the system (20) with the initial state $x(0)$. Find the pair $(\hat{r}_s(k),\, w_{d,s}^{(\hat{r}_s(k))^*}(k))$, $k\in[0,\, N]$ minimizing the value of the performance index (23) based on the whole observed information Y_N .

Proposition A (Principle of Hybrid Optimality (A)) *Consider the optimal control problem (A) on the time interval [0,k]. Also consider the optimal control problem minimizing the performance index*

$$J_f^{(r)}(\tau,\, x,\, w_d(\cdot))=\sum_{l=0}^{\tau-1} L^{(r)}(l,\, x(l),\, w_d(l),\, y(l))+\Phi_0(x(0)),\ 1<\tau<k \tag{24}$$

for the system (20) with the initial state x(0) on the partial time interval [0,τ] and then let the pair of optimal control inputs be $\left(\hat{\hat{r}}_f(l)\, w_{d,f}^{(\hat{r}_f(l))**}(l).\right)$, $l\in[0,\ \tau]$. *Then* $\left(\hat{r}_f(l),\ w_{d,f}^{(\hat{r}_f(l))*}(l)\right)= \left(\hat{\hat{r}}_f(l),\ w_{d,f}^{(\hat{r})**}(l)\right)$, $l\in[0,\ \tau]$ *holds.*

Proposition B (Principle of Hybrid Optimality (B)) *Consider the optimal control problem (B) on the time interval [k,N]. Also consider the optimal control problem minimizing the performance index*

$$J_b^{(r)}(\tau,\ x,\ w_d(\cdot))=\sum_{l=\tau}^{N-1} L^{\ (r)}(l,\ x(l),\ w_d(l),\ y(l))+\Phi_N(x(N)),\ k<\tau<N-1 \tag{25}$$

for the system (20) with the initial state $x(\tau)$ *on the partial time interval* $[\tau,\ N]$ *and then let the pair of optimal control inputs be* $\left(\hat{\hat{r}}_b(l) w_{d,b}^{(\hat{r}_b(l))**}(l)\right)$, $l\in[\tau,\ N]$. *Then* $\left(\hat{r}_b(l),\ w_{d,b}^{(\hat{r}_b(l))*}(l)\right)=\left(\hat{\hat{r}}_b(l) w_{d,b}^{(\hat{r}_b(l))**}(l)\right)$, $l\in[\tau,\ N]$ *holds.*

Theorem C (Principle of Hybrid Optimality (C)) *Consider the optimal control problem (C) on the fixed time interval [0,N]. Split the performance index (23) into the two parts (21) and (22) and also consider the optimal control problems (A) on [0,k] and (B) on [k,N] for the system (20) with initial state x(0) and x(k) respectively. Then at each time k* $\left(\hat{r}_f(l)\, w_{d,f}^{(\hat{r}_f(l))*}(l)\right)$, $l\in[0,\ k]$ *and* $\left(\hat{r}_b(l),\ w_{d,b}^{(\hat{r}_b(l))*}(l)\right)$, $l\in[k,\ N]$ *are optimal input minimizing the values of the (21) and (22) to be used in order to compose the solution of the fixed-interval optimal control problem (C), i.e., any time* $k\in[0,\ N]$ $(\hat{r}_s(l),\ w_{d,s}^{(\hat{r}_f(l))*}(l))=(\hat{r}_f(l),\ w_{d,f}^{(\hat{r}_f(l))*}(l)),\ l\in[0,\ k]$ *and* $(\hat{r}_s(l),\ w_{d,s}^{(\hat{r}_f(l))*}(l))=(\hat{r}_b(l),\ w_{d,f}^{(\hat{r}_b(l))*}(l)),\ \ l\in[k+1,\ N]$ *hold.*

In this appendix we give only a proof of Proposition 7.1. The others can be shown by the similar arguments.

(Proof of Proposition A) We split the pair $\left(\hat{r}_f(l) w_{d,f}^{(\hat{r}_f(l))*}(l)\right)$, $l\in[0,\ k]$ of the optimal control inputs into the following two parts:

$$(\hat{r}_{f,1},\ w_{d,f,1}^{(\hat{r}_{f,1})*})=(\hat{r}_f(l),\ w_{d,f}^{(\hat{r}_f(l))*}(l))\ l\in[0,\ \tau]$$
$$(\hat{r}_{f,2},\ w_{d,f,2}^{(\hat{r}_{f,2})*})=(\hat{r}_f(l),\ w_{d,f}^{(\hat{r}_f(l))*}(l))\ l\in[\tau+1,\ k]$$

Now we assume

$$(\hat{r}_{f,1},\ w_{d,f,1}^{(\hat{r}_{f,1})*})\neq(\hat{\hat{r}}_f,\ w_{d,f}^{(\hat{r}_f)**})\ on\,[0,\ \tau]$$

Then there exists the pair of control inputs $\left(\hat{\hat{r}}_f,\ w_{d,f}^{(\hat{r}_f)**}\right)$ giving less value of the performance index (24) than $\left(\hat{r}_{f,1},\ w_{d,f}^{(\hat{r}_{f,1})*}\right)$ and so the pair of control inputs consisting of $\left(\hat{\hat{r}}_f, w_{d,f}^{(\hat{r}_f)**}\right)$ and $\left(\hat{r}_{f,2},\ w_{d,f,2}^{(\hat{r}_{f,2})*}\right)$ gives less value of the performance index (21) than $\left(\hat{r}_f(l),\ w_{d,f}^{(\hat{r}_f(l))*}(l)\right)$, $l\in[0,\ k]$. This contradicts with the optimality of $\left(\hat{r}_f(l),\ w_{d,f}^{(\hat{r}_f(l))*}(l)\right)$, $l\in[0,\ k]$. Therefore $(\hat{r}_f(l),\ w_{d,f}^{(\hat{r}_f)*})=(\hat{\hat{r}}_f(l),\ w_{d,f}^{(\hat{r}_f(l))**})$, $l\in[0,\ \tau]$ holds. (Q.E.D.).

Author details

Gou Nakura*

Address all correspondence to: gg9925_fiesta@ybb.ne.jp

References

[1] Basar, T. (1991). Optimal Performance Levels for Minimax Filters, Predictors and Smoothers. *Syst. Contr. Lett.*, 16(5), 309-317.

[2] Blanco, E., Neveux, P., & Thomas, G. (2006). The H_∞ Fixed-Interval Smoothing Problem for Continuous Systems. *IEEE Trans. Signal Process.*, 54(11), 4085-4090.

[3] Blom, H. A. P., & Bar-Shalom, Y. (1990). Time-reversion of a hybrid state stochastic difference system with a jump-linear smoothing application. *IEEE Trans. Inform. Theory*, 36(4), 836-847.

[4] Costa, O. L. V. (1994). Linear Minimum Mean Square Error Estimation for Discrete-Time Markovian Jump Linear Systems. *IEEE Trans. Automat. Contr.*, 39(8), 1685-1689.

[5] Costa, O. L. V., Fragoso, M. D., & Marques, R. P. (2005). Discrete-Time Markov Jump Linear Systems. Springer, London.

[6] Cox, H. (1964). Estimation of State Variables via Dynamic Programming. *Proc. 1964 Joint Automatic Control Conf.*, Stanford, California, 376-381.

[7] Fragoso, M. D., Costa, O. L. V., Baczynski, J., & Rocha, N. (2005). Optimal linear mean square filter for continuous-time jump linear systems. *IEEE Trans. Automat. Contr.*, 50(9), 1364-1369.

[8] Fraser, D. C., & Potter, J. E. (1969). The Optimum Linear Smoother as a Combination of Two Optimum Linear Filters. *IEEE Trans. Automat. Contr.*, AC-14(4), 387-390.

[9] Helmick, R. E., Blair, W. D., & Hoffman, S. A. (1995). Fixed-Interval Smoothing for Markovian Switching Systems. *IEEE Trans. Inform. Theory*, 41(6), 1845-1855.

[10] Jazwinski, A. H. (1966). Filtering for Nonlinear Dynamical Systems. *IEEE Trans. Automat. Contr.*, 11, 765-766.

[11] Lincoln, B., & Rantzer, A. (2006). Relaxing Dynamic Programming. *IEEE Trans. Automat. Contr.*, 51(8), 1249-1260.

[12] Ljung, L., & Kailath, T. (1976). Backwards Markovian Models for Second-Order Stochastic Processes. *IEEE Trans. Inform. Theory*, 22(4), 488-491.

[13] Mayne, D. Q. (1966). A Solution of the Smoothing Problem for Linear Dynamic Systems. *Automatica*, 4(2), 73-92.

[14] Meditch, J. S. (1967). Orthogonal Projection and Discrete Optimal Linear Smoothing. *J. SIAM Control*, 5(1), 74-89.

[15] Nakura, G. (2010). H_∞ Estimation for Linear Discrete-Time Markovian Jump Systems by Game Theoretic Approach. *Proceedings of the 42nd ISCIE International Symposium on Stochastic Systems Theory and Its Applications (SSS10)*, Okayama, Japan, 163-169.

[16] Nakura, G. (2011). An Approach to Noncausal Hybrid Estimation for Linear Continuous-Time Systems with Non-Gaussian Noises. *Proceedings of SICE Annual Conference 2011*, Tokyo, Japan, 979-984.

[17] Nakura, G. (2011). An Approach to Hybrid Smoothing for Linear Continuous-Time Systems with Non-Gaussian Noises. *Proceedings of the 43rd ISCIE International Symposium on Stochastic Systems Theory and Its Applications (SSS11)*, Shiga, Japan, 63-72.

[18] Rauch, H. E. (1963). Solutions to the Linear Smoothing Problem. *IEEE Trans., Automat., Contr.*, AC-8, 371-372.

[19] Rauch, H. E., Tung, F., & Striebel, C. T. (1965). Maximum Likelihood Estimates of Linear Dynamic Systems. *AIAA J.*, 3(8), 1445-1450.

[20] Sidhu, G. S., & Desai, U. B. (1976). New Smoothing Algorithms Based on Reversed-Time Lumped Models. *IEEE Trans. Automat. Contr.*, 21, 538-541.

[21] Sworder, D. D., & Rogers, R. O. (1983). An LQG Solution to a Control Problem with Solar Thermal Receiver. *IEEE Trans. Automat. Contr.*, 28, 971-978.

[22] Verghese, G., & Kailath, T. (1979). A Further Note on Backwards Markovian Models. *IEEE Trans. Inf. Theory*, IT-25(1), 121-124.

[23] Wall, J. E., Jr., Willsky, A. S., & Sandell, N. R., Jr. (1981). On the Fixed-Interval Smoothing Problem. *Stochastics*, 5, 1-41.

[24] Zhang, Q. (1999). Optimal Filtering of Discrete-Time Hybrid Systems. *J. Optim. Theory Appl.*, 100(1), 123-144.

[25] Zhang, Q. (2000). Hybrid Filtering for Linear Systems with Non-Gaussian Disturbances. *IEEE Trans. Automat. Contr.*, 45, 50-61.

Chapter 8

Discrete-Time Fractional-Order Systems: Modeling and Stability Issues

Saïd Guermah, Saïd Djennoune and
Maâmar Bettayeb

Additional information is available at the end of the chapter

http://dx.doi.org/10.5772/51983

1. Introduction

The concepts of non-integer derivative and integral are the foundation of the fractional calculus [1–4]. Non-integer derivative has become nowadays a precious tool, currently used in the study of the behavior of real systems in diverse fields of science and engineering.

Starting from the sixties, the research in this domain of interest has progressively put to light important concepts associated with formulations using non-integer order derivative. Indeed, non-integer order derivative revealed to be a more adequate tool for the understanding of interesting properties shown by various types of physical phenomena, that is, fractality, recursivity, diffusion and/or relaxation phenomena. [5–14].

This tool has enabled substantial advances in the accuracy of description and analysis of these phenomena, namely in the domain of electrochemistry, electromagnetism and electrical machines, thermal systems and heat conduction, transmission, acoustics, viscoelastic materials and robotics. At its turn, the community of system identification and automatic control early benefited from this tool. The corresponding system representations are of the types of infinite-dimensional or distributed-parameter systems, enriched by diverse approximating non-integer-order models, indifferently called fractional-order models. There are abundant successful examples in the literature and one can see some for example in [15–30].

An important feature of fractional-order systems (FOS) is that they exhibit hereditarily properties and long memory transients. This aspect is taken into account in modeling, namely with state-space representation, in parameter estimation, identification, and controller design. Besides, these issues can be viewed either in the scope of a continuous time, or a discrete time representation. In this Chapter, we focus on some issues of modeling and stability of LTI FOS in discrete time. The extension of the results obtained with continuous-time representations to the discrete-time case is evidently motivated by the general trend to use digital computer-aided simulations and implementations in control engineering and signal processing. In the particular case of FOS, the discretization methods lead to new models and enlarge the possibilities of representation and simulation of such systems.

More specifically, the familiar state-space representation and its well-established results in the integer-order case receive here an extension to the non-integer case. This extension induces noticeable changes: there appears a neccessity of interpretation of the initial conditions [31] and a neccesity to take into account the history (or memory) of the system from the initial instant, since we have to deal, instead of the classical state, with a so-called "'pseudo state"', that is an expanded state [32, 33]. This infinite-dimensional system, as we expose it in the following sections, has been studied, from the point of view of its structural properties, i.e., controllability, observability [34, 35] and, to some extent, of its stability [36].

2. LTI continuous-time fractional-order modeling

In the beginning, most of the works consecrated to the study of FOS focused on continuous-time representations. The continuous-time state-space FOS representation was introduced in [24, 37–40]. It has been employed in analysis of system performances. The solution of the state-space equation was derived by using the Mittag-Lefller function [41]. Next, the stability of FOS was investigated [42] and a condition based on the argument principle was established to guarantee the asymptotic stability of the fractional-order system. Further, the controllability and the observability properties have been defined and some algebraic criteria of these two properties have been derived in [43]. Another contribution to the analysis of the controllability and the observability with commensurate FOS modeled by fractional state-space equations is brought in [44].

2.1. Definitions of non-integer derivatives

There are different definitions of the non-integer derivatives [1–3, 45]. Let us consider a function $f(t)$ of the real variable t, continuous and integrable on $[a, +\infty[$, where a is the origin of t. Indeed, we usually deal with dynamic systems and $f(t)$ is let to be a causal function of t, with $t \geq a$. Thus $f(t) = 0$ if $t < a$.

Let us introduce the positive integer number m such that $(m-1) < \alpha < m$. We obtain the definition due to A.V. Letnikov

$$ {}_a^L D_t^\alpha f(t) = \frac{1}{\Gamma(m-\alpha+1)} \int_a^t (t-\tau)^{m-\alpha} f^{(m+1)}(\tau) d\tau + \sum_{k=0}^{m} \frac{f^{(k)}(a)(t-a)^{k-\alpha}}{\Gamma(k-\alpha+1)}, \text{ for } t < a. \quad (1) $$

The definition given by (1) assumes that function f is sufficiently differentiable and that $f^{(k)}(a) < \infty$, $k = 0, 1, ..., m$. Γ is the Euler gamma function

$$ \Gamma(\beta) = \int_0^\infty z^{\beta-1} e^{-z} dz \quad (2) $$

in which z is a complex variable. A new version is the Letnikov-Riemann-Liouville definition (LRL) given by

$$ {}_a^L D_t^\alpha f(t) = \frac{d^m}{dt^m}\{\frac{1}{\Gamma(m-\alpha)}\int_a^t \frac{f(\tau)}{(t-\tau)^{\alpha-m+1}}d\tau\} \tag{3} $$

Naturally, as physical systems are modeled by differential equations containing eventually fractional derivatives, it is necessary to give to these equations initial conditions that must be physically interpretable. Unfortunately, the LRL definition leads to initial conditions containing the value of the fractional derivative at the initial conditions. To overcome this difficulty, Caputo proposed another definition given by

$$ {}_a^C D_t^\alpha f(t) = \frac{1}{\Gamma(m-\alpha)}\int_a^t \frac{f^{(m)}(\tau)}{(t-\tau)^{\alpha-m+1}}d\tau \tag{4} $$

Note the remarkable fact that the LRL fractional derivative of a constant function $f(t) = C$ is not zero

$$ {}_a^L D_t^\alpha C = \frac{Ct^{-\alpha}}{\Gamma(1-\alpha)} \tag{5} $$

whereas Caputo's fractional derivative of a constant is identically zero.

2.2. FOS differential equation

Let us now consider a SISO LTI FOS. By means of its dynamic input-output relation and using (4), we can derive its continuous-time models. In all what follows, we use Caputo's definition of a fractional derivative with initial time $t = 0$, *i.e.*, $a = 0$. The derived differential equation is then expressed by [45]

$$ \sum_{i=1}^{n_a} a_i D^{\alpha_i} y(t) = \sum_{j=1}^{n_b} b_j D^{\beta_j} u(t) \tag{6} $$

where $a_i, b_j \in \mathbb{R}$, $\alpha_i, \beta_j \in \mathbb{R}^+$, $u(t) \in \mathbb{R}$ is the input of the system and $y(t) \in \mathbb{R}$ its output. n_a and $n_b \in \mathbb{N}$ are the number of terms of each side of the differential equation. The differential equation is said with commensurate order if all the differentiation orders α_i , β_j are multiple integers of a same base order α. In this case, it can be expressed by

$$ \sum_{i=1}^{n_a} a_i D^{i\alpha} y(t) = \sum_{j=1}^{n_b} b_j D^{j\alpha} u(t) \tag{7} $$

2.3. State-space model derived from a non-integer-order transfer function

By using Laplace transform, assuming null initial conditions, from (6) we derive the following transfer function

$$ G(s) = \frac{Y(s)}{U(s)} = \frac{\sum_{j=0}^{n_b} b_j s^{\beta_j}}{\sum_{i=0}^{n_a} a_i s^{\alpha_i}} \tag{8} $$

To facilitate the development of the so-called construction procedure, (8) is rewritten with coefficients a_i and b_j denoted differently by a'_{2k+1} and a'_{2k} respectively [35]. This gives

$$G(s) = \frac{Y(s)}{U(s)} = \frac{a'_0 + a'_2 s^{\alpha_2} + a'_4 s^{\alpha_4} + \ldots + a'_{2n} s^{\alpha_{2n}}}{1 + a'_1 s^{\alpha_1} + a'_3 s^{\alpha_3} + \ldots + a'_{2n+1} s^{\alpha_{2n+1}}}, \tag{9}$$

in which α_i are the fractional orders that can be either commensurate or non-commensurate, with

$$\alpha_1 \leq \alpha_2 \leq \alpha_3 \leq \ldots \leq \alpha_{2n} \leq \alpha_{2n+1}.$$

The procedure for obtaining a state-space representation from (9) is as follows: firstly, let us introduce an intermediate variable $\mathcal{X}(s)$ such that

$$G(s) = \frac{Y(s)}{\mathcal{X}(s)} \frac{\mathcal{X}(s)}{U(s)}$$

Next, we can write

$$G(s) = \frac{Y(s)}{\mathcal{X}(s)} \frac{\mathcal{X}(s)}{U(s)} = \frac{(a'_0 + a'_2 s^{\alpha_2} + a'_4 s^{\alpha_4} + \ldots + a'_{2n} s^{\alpha_{2n}})\mathcal{X}(s)}{(1 + a'_1 s^{\alpha_1} + a'_3 s^{\alpha_3} + \ldots + a'_{2n+1} s^{\alpha_{2n+1}})\mathcal{X}(s)} \tag{10}$$

Let us put successively

$$\begin{aligned} \mathcal{X}_1(s) &= \mathcal{X}(s) \\ \mathcal{X}_2(s) &= s^{\alpha_1}\mathcal{X}(s) = s^{\alpha_1}\mathcal{X}_1(s) \\ \mathcal{X}_3(s) &= s^{\alpha_2}\mathcal{X}(s) = s^{(\alpha_2-\alpha_1)}\mathcal{X}_2(s) \\ &\vdots \\ \mathcal{X}_{2n+1}(s) &= s^{\alpha_{2n}}\mathcal{X}(s) = s^{(\alpha_{2n}-\alpha_{2n-1})}\mathcal{X}_{2n}(s). \end{aligned} \tag{11}$$

With (10) and relations (11), it is easy to build the following group of equations

$$\begin{aligned} s^{\alpha_1}\mathcal{X}_1(s) &= \mathcal{X}_2(s) \\ s^{(\alpha_2-\alpha_1)}\mathcal{X}_2(s) &= \mathcal{X}_3(s) \\ &\vdots \\ s^{(\alpha_i-\alpha_{i-1})}\mathcal{X}_i(s) &= \mathcal{X}_{i+1}(s) \\ &\vdots \\ s^{(\alpha_{2n+1}-\alpha_{2n})}\mathcal{X}_{2n+1}(s) &= \frac{1}{a'_{2n+1}}[U(s) - \mathcal{X}_1(s) - a'_1\mathcal{X}_2(s) - \ldots - a'_{2n-1}\mathcal{X}_{2n}(s)] \end{aligned} \tag{12}$$

The transposition in the time domain yields a state-space representation of System (9), with $x_i(t)$, $u(t)$ and $y(t)$ the respective inverse Laplace transforms of $\mathcal{X}_i(s)$, $U(s)$ and $Y(s)$

$$\begin{array}{rcl} D^{\alpha_1}x_1(t) & = & x_2 \\ D^{(\alpha_2-\alpha_1)}x_2(t) & = & x_3 \\ \vdots & & \\ D^{(\alpha_i-\alpha_{i-1})}x_i(t) & = & x_{i+1} \\ \vdots & & \\ D^{(\alpha_{2n}-\alpha_{2n-1})}x_{2n}(t) & = & x_{2n+1} \\ D^{(\alpha_{2n+1}-\alpha_{2n})}x_{2n+1}(t) & = & \frac{1}{a'_{2n+1}}[u(t)-x_1(t)-a'_1x_2(t)-\ldots-a'_{2n-1}x_{2n}(t)], \end{array} \tag{13}$$

the expression of the system output being

$$y(t) = a'_0x_1(t) + 0x_2(t) + a'_2x_3(t) + \ldots + 0x_{2n} + a'_{2n}x_{2n+1}(t). \tag{14}$$

The corresponding state-space group of equations is then derived

$$D^{[\gamma]}x(t) = Ax(t) + Bu(t) \qquad x(0) = x_0, \tag{15}$$

where $x(t) = [x_1(t) \quad x_2(t) \ldots \quad x_{2n+1}(t)]^T \in \mathbb{R}^{2n+1}$ is the column state vector and $x(0)$ its initial value. Note that here $x(0)$ can be assumed non null, instead of the assumption of null initial conditions necessary to define the transfer function model. Besides, we have

$$D^{[\gamma]}x(t) = \begin{bmatrix} D^{\gamma_1}x_1(t) \\ \vdots \\ D^{\gamma_{2n+1}}x_{2n+1}(t) \end{bmatrix},$$

in which $\gamma_i \in \mathbb{R}^{\star+}, \gamma_1 = \alpha_1$ for $i = 1$ and $\gamma_i = (\alpha_i - \alpha_{i-1})$ for $i = 2, \ldots, 2n+1$.
The output equation takes the form

$$y(t) = Cx(t) + Du(t), \tag{16}$$

Matrices A, B, C and D are given by

$$A = \begin{bmatrix} 0 & 1 & 0 & 0 & 0 \ldots & 0 \\ 0 & 0 & 1 & 0 & \ldots\ldots & 0 \\ \vdots & \vdots & \vdots & \vdots & \vdots \quad \vdots & \vdots \\ 0 & 0 & 0 & 0 & \ldots\ldots & 1 \\ -\frac{1}{a'_{2n+1}} & \frac{-a'_1}{a'_{2n+1}} & 0 & \frac{-a'_3}{a'_{2n+1}} & 0 \ \ldots & \frac{-a'_{2n-1}}{a'_{2n+1}} \end{bmatrix}, \quad B = \begin{bmatrix} 0 \\ 0 \\ \vdots \\ \frac{1}{a'_{2n+1}} \end{bmatrix},$$

$$C = \left[a'_0 \ 0 \ a'_2 \ 0 \ldots 0 \ a'_{2n} \right].$$

As for direct transmission matrix D, we have

$$D = [\frac{a'_{2n}}{a'_{2n+1}}] \text{ if } \alpha_{2n} = \alpha_{2n+1}, \text{ otherwise } D = [0].$$

The symbol D here should not be confused with the derivation operator $D^{[.]}$.

Remark 1. *The dimension of the model, i.e., its number of state variables $2n+1$ is equal to the total number of non-null terms $a'_l s^{\alpha_l}$ present in the numerator and denominator of $G(s)$. In the following, $2n+1$ is denoted n_d.*

The controllability and observability properties as well as the stability have been well studied when the differentiation fractional-orders γ_i are all equal to a unique value, say α ([43], [42]). In this case, (15) becomes

$$D^{[\alpha]}x(t) = \begin{bmatrix} D^{\alpha}x_1 \\ D^{\alpha}x_2 \\ \vdots \\ D^{\alpha}x_{n_d} \end{bmatrix} = Ax(t) + Bu(t), \qquad x(0) = x_0 \tag{17}$$

Applying the Laplace transform to (17), we have

$$X(s) = [s^{\alpha}\mathbb{I} - A]^{-1}[BU(s) + x(0)],$$

Defining $\Phi(t) = \mathcal{L}^{-1}[s^{\alpha}\mathbb{I} - A]^{-1}$ as the corresponding state transition matrix, we obtain the state response given by

$$x(t) = \Phi(t)x(0) + \int_0^t \Phi(t-\tau)Bu(\tau)d\tau \tag{18}$$

It can be shown that $\Phi(t)$ can be expressed by

$$\Phi(t) = \sum_{k=0}^{\infty} \frac{A^k t^{k\alpha}}{\Gamma(1+k\alpha)} \tag{19}$$

The left side term of this latter equation represents the Mittag-Leffler function [41] :

$$E_{\alpha}(t) \triangleq \sum_{k=0}^{\infty} \frac{A^k t^{k\alpha}}{\Gamma(1+k\alpha)} \tag{20}$$

It has been established in [43] that the controllability and observability conditions of the continuous-time state-space representation of commensurate fractional-order systems are the same as in the integer-order case. Thus, System (17) is controllable if the rank of the controllability matrix

$$\mathcal{C} = [B \quad AB \quad A^2B \quad ...A^{n_d-1}B] \tag{21}$$

is equal to n_d. Besides, this system is observable if the rank of the observability matrix

$$\mathcal{O} = \begin{bmatrix} C \\ CA \\ CA^2 \\ \vdots \\ CA^{n_d-1} \end{bmatrix} \tag{22}$$

is equal to n_d. To our knowledge, no such results have been brought in the literature up to now for FOS with non commensurate fractional-order systems in continuous time. The next section of this chapter constitutes a contribution to the study of structural properties of non-commensurate FOS, using a different approach, that is discrete-time representation [34].

3. LTI discrete-time fractional-order modeling

The development of a discrete-time model is based on the Grünwald-Letnikov's definition of fractional-order operators. This definition is another expression of (1), based on the generalization of the backward difference. The generalization of the integer-order difference to a non-integer-order (or fractional-order) difference is addressed in [33, 47].

3.1. The discrete-time fractional-order difference operator

In what follows, we present a discretized representation of the continuous fractional-order state-space model of Equations (15) and (16), in which the fractional order can be commensurate or non-commensurate.

Let us consider the state-space model with integer-order derivatives

$$D^1 x(t) = Ax(t) + Bu(t) \tag{23}$$

where $x(t) = [x_1(t) \quad x_2(t) \ldots \quad x_{n_d}(t)]^T \in \mathbb{R}^{n_d}$ is the state vector. This latter model can be represented in discrete-time using a forward difference approximation of the derivative of order one of $x(t)$ [32, 33]. For this purpose let us consider a sampling period h. Then for $kh \leq t < (k+1)h$ the integer order first derivative $D^1 x(t)$ can be approximated by

$$D^1 x(t) \approx \Delta^1 x((k+1)h) = \frac{x((k+1)h) - x(kh)}{h}. \tag{24}$$

We can then write

$$\Delta^1 (x(k+1)h) = Ax(kh) + Bu(kh) \tag{25}$$

We start with applying a discretization of (17) with identical fractional orders. The fractional derivatives $D^{[\alpha]} x(t)$ can be approximated by using the definition due to K. Grünwald

$$D^{[\alpha]} x(t) \approx \Delta_h^{[\alpha]} x((k+1)h) = \frac{1}{h^\alpha} \sum_{j=0}^{k+1} (-1)^j \binom{\alpha}{j} x(k+1-j)h) \tag{26}$$

In this equation, $\alpha \in \mathbb{R}^{\star+}$ is the fractional order, t is the current time, $h \in \mathbb{R}^{\star+}$ is the sampling period or time increment. The term $\binom{\alpha}{j}$ is calculated by the relation

$$\binom{\alpha}{j} = \begin{cases} 1 & \text{for } j = 0 \\ \frac{\alpha(\alpha-1)\ldots(\alpha-j+1)}{j!} & \text{for } j > 0 \end{cases} \tag{27}$$

If we drop h (i.e., making $h = 1$), we find the discrete fractional-order difference operator Δ^{α} as defined and used in [32, 33, 46]. Indeed, the choice of the sampling period h is very important when elaborating the discretized model of a given process. h is not necessarily small. It corresponds to an appropriate sampling rate, deduced from the dynamics (or frequency bandwidth) of the process, by using rules of thumbs and criteria, as exposed for example in [48, 49].

3.2. The discrete-time fractional-order state-space model

The previous results conduct to the linear discrete-time fractional-order state-space model

$$\Delta^{[\alpha]}x(k+1) = Ax(k) + Bu(k); \qquad x(0) = x_0 \tag{28}$$

In this model, the differentiation order α is taken the same for all the state variables $x_i(k)$, $i = 1, \ldots, n_d$. Besides, from (27) we have

$$h^{\alpha}\Delta^{[\alpha]}x(k+1) = x(k+1) + \sum_{j=1}^{k+1}(-1)^j\binom{\alpha}{j}x(k-j+1) \tag{29}$$

Substituting (30) into (29) yields

$$x(k+1) = \tilde{A}x(k) - \sum_{j=1}^{k+1}(-1)^j\binom{\alpha}{j}x(k-j+1) + \tilde{B}u(k) \tag{30}$$

with $\tilde{A} = h^{\alpha}A$ and $\tilde{B} = h^{\alpha}B$. By setting $c_j = (-1)^j\binom{\alpha}{j}$, (31) can be rewritten as follows

$$x(k+1) = (\tilde{A} - c_1 I_{n_d})x(k) - \sum_{j=2}^{k+1} c_j x(k-j+1) + \tilde{B}u(k) \tag{31}$$

Let us put now

$$A_0 = (\tilde{A} - c_1 I_{n_d}) \tag{32}$$

and, for all $j > 0$:

$$A_j = -c_{j+1} I_{n_d} \tag{33}$$

This leads to

$$x(k+1) = A_0 x(k) + A_1 x(k-1) + A_2 x(k-2) + ... + A_k x(0) + \tilde{B}u(k) \tag{34}$$

This description can be extended to FOS with different (commensurate or non-commensurate) orders [53]

$$\Delta_h^{[\gamma]} x(k+1) = Ax(k) + Bu(k)$$

$$x(k+1) = \Delta_h^{[\gamma]} x(k+1) + \sum_{j=1}^{k+1} A_j x(k-j+1)$$

where

$$\Delta_h^{[\gamma]} x(k+1) = \begin{bmatrix} h^{\gamma_1} \Delta^{\gamma_1} x_1(k+1) \\ \vdots \\ h^{\gamma_{n_d}} \Delta^{\gamma_{n_d}} x_{n_d}(k+1) \end{bmatrix}$$

in which $\gamma_i \in \mathbb{R}^{\star +}$, $i = 1, 2, \ldots$ denote any fractional orders. Here, we can write

$$A_0 = \tilde{A} + diag\{\binom{\gamma_i}{1}, \ i = 1, \ldots, n_d \ , \tag{35}$$

$$A_j = diag\{-(-1)^{j+1}\binom{\gamma_i}{j+1}, \ i = 1, \ldots, n_d\}, \ j = 1, 2, \ldots \tag{36}$$

Using (35), we obtain the state equation

$$x(k+1) = \sum_{j=0}^{k} A_j x(k-j) + \tilde{B}u(k); \quad x(0) = x_0 \tag{37}$$

In this case, $\tilde{A}$ and $\tilde{B}$ are calculated as follows $\tilde{A}_i = h^{\gamma_i} A_i$; $\tilde{B}_i = h^{\gamma_i} B_i$ where A_i and B_i denote the rows of A and B respectively. The corresponding output equation is

$$y(k) = Cx(k) \tag{38}$$

In this resulting discrete time state-space model, A_j is given by (32) and (33), in the case of a unique fractional-order while it is given by (35) and (36) in the case of different, commensurate or non-commensurate fractional-orders.

Remark 2. *The model defined by (37) and (38) can be viewed as a discrete-time model with time-delay in state. It has a varying number of steps of time-delays, equal to k, i.e., increasing with time. Instead, the models addressed in [50–52] consider a finite constant number of steps of time-delays.*

Define G_k such that

$$G_k = \begin{cases} I_{n_d} & \text{for } k = 0, \\ \sum_{j=0}^{k-1} A_j G_{k-1-j} & \text{for } k \geq 1 \end{cases} \tag{39}$$

Theorem 1. *The solution of (37) is given by*

$$x(k) = G_k x(0) + \sum_{j=0}^{k-1} G_{k-1-j} B u(j) \tag{40}$$

This theorem can be proved by induction [34]. The first part of the solution of (40) represents the free response of the system and the last part takes the role of the convolution sum corresponding to the forced response.
The corresponding transition matrix can be defined as

$$\Phi(k,0) = G_k, \quad \Phi(0,0) = G_0 = I_{n_d} \tag{41}$$

Remark 3. - $\Phi(k,0)$ *exhibits the particularity of being time-varying, in the sense that it is composed of a number of terms* A_j *which grows along with k. This is due to the fractional-order feature of the model which takes into account all the past values of the states.*

By virtue of Equations (37) and (38), the discretization of this state-space realization is

$$x(k+1) = \sum_{j=0}^{k} A_j x(k-j) + Bu(k); \quad x(0) = x_0$$

$$y(k) = Cx(k)$$

Here we have

$$A_0 = A + diag\{\binom{\alpha_i}{1}, \ i = 1, \ldots, n_d\} \tag{42}$$

$$A_j = diag\{-(-1)^{j+1}\binom{\alpha_i}{j+1}, \ i = 1, \ldots, n_d\}, \ j = 1, 2, \ldots \tag{43}$$

The output response for a given input sequence and initial conditions is given by

$$y(k) = CG_k x(0) + \sum_{j=0}^{k-1} CG_{k-1-j} Bu(j) \tag{44}$$

4. Structural properties of LTI discrete-time FOS

4.1. Reachability and controllability

We discuss here a fundamental question for dynamic systems modeled by (37) in the case of a non-commensurate fractional-order. This question is to determine whether it is possible to transfer the state of the system from a given initial state to any other state. We search below to extend two concepts of state reachability (or controllability from the origin) and controllability (or controllability to the origin) to the present case. We are interested in completely state reachable and controllable systems.

Definition 1. *The linear discrete-time fractional-order system modeled by* (37) *is reachable if it is possible to find a control sequence such that an arbitrary state can be reached from the origin in a finite time.*

Definition 2. *The linear discrete-time fractional-order system modeled by* (37) *is controllable if it is possible to find a control sequence such that the origin can be reached from any initial state in a finite time.*

Definition 3. *For the linear discrete-time fractional-order system modeled by* (37) *we define the following*

1. *The controllability matrix*

$$\mathcal{C}_k = \begin{bmatrix} \mathrm{G}_0 B & \mathrm{G}_1 B & \mathrm{G}_2 B & \cdots & \mathrm{G}_{k-1} B \end{bmatrix} \tag{45}$$

2. *The reachability Gramian*

$$\mathrm{W}_r(0,k) = \sum_{j=0}^{k-1} \mathrm{G}_j B B^T \mathrm{G}_j^T, \quad k \geq 1 \tag{46}$$

   It is easy to show that $\mathrm{W}_r(0,k) = \mathcal{C}_k \mathcal{C}_k^T$.

3. *The controllability Gramian, provided that* A_0 *is non-singular*

$$\mathrm{W}_c(0,k) = \mathrm{G}_k^{-1} \mathrm{W}_r(0,k) \mathrm{G}_k^{-T}, \quad k \geq 1 \tag{47}$$

Note that $G_1 = A_0$ and the existence of $W_r(0,1)$ imposes A_0 to be non-singular. However, this is not that restrictive condition because a discrete model is often obtained by sampling a continuous one. Thus, in the remainder of this paper we assume that A_0 is non-singular.

Theorem 2. *The linear discrete-time fractional-order system modeled by* (37) *is reachable if and only if there exists a finite time K such that* $rank(\mathcal{C}_K) = n$ *or, equivalently,* $rank(\mathrm{W}_r(0,K)) = n$. *Furthermore, the input sequence*

$$\mathcal{U}_K = [u^T(K-1) \quad u^T(K-2) \quad \ldots \quad u^T(0)]^T$$

that transfers $x_0 = 0$ *at* $k = 0$ *to* $x_f \neq 0$ *at* $k = K$ *is given by*

$$\mathcal{U}_K = \mathcal{C}_K^T \mathrm{W}_r^{-1}(0,K) x_f. \tag{48}$$

Remark 4. *In the case of an integer order, it is well known that the rank of $\mathcal{C}_k$ cannot increase for any $k \geq n$. This results from the Cayley-Hamilton theorem. On the contrary, in the case of the linear discrete-time non-commensurate fractional-order system (37), the rank of $\mathcal{C}_k$ can increase for values of $k \geq n$. In other words, it is possible to reach the final state x_f in a number of steps greater than n. This is due to the nature of the elements G_k which build up the controllability matrix $\mathcal{C}_k$ and which exhibit the particularity of being time-varying, in the sense that they are composed of a number of terms A_j that grows with k, as already mentioned in Remark 2. The full rank of $(\mathcal{C}_k)$ can be reached in some Step $k = K$ equal to, or greater than n.*

Theorem 3. *The linear discrete-time fractional-order system modeled by (37) is controllable if and only if there exists a finite time K such that $rank(W_c(0, K)) = n$. Furthermore, an input sequence $\mathcal{U}_K = [u^T(K-1) \quad u^T(K-2) \quad \dots \quad u^T(0)]^T$ that transfers $x_0 \neq 0$ at $k = 0$ to $x_f = 0$ at $k = K$ is given by*

$$\mathcal{U}_K = -\mathcal{C}_K^T G_K^{-T} W_c^{-1}(0, K) x_0. \tag{49}$$

4.2. Observability

In this section we aim at extending the concept of observability to the system of Equations (37) and (38), in the case of a non-commensurate fractional-order. We are interested in completely state observable systems.

Definition 4. *The linear discrete-time fractional-order system modeled by Equations (37) and (38) is observable at time $k = 0$ if and only if there exits some $K > 0$ such that the state x_0 at time $k = 0$ can be uniquely determined from the knowledge of u_k, y_k, $k \in [0, K]$.*

Definition 5. *For the linear discrete-time fractional-order system modeled by Equations (37) and (38) we define the following*

1. *The observability matrix*

$$\mathcal{O}_k = \begin{bmatrix} CG_0 \\ CG_1 \\ CG_2 \\ \vdots \\ CG_{k-1}. \end{bmatrix} \tag{50}$$

2. *The observability Gramian*

$$W_o(0, k) = \sum_{j=0}^{k-1} G_j^T C^T C G_j. \tag{51}$$

It is easy to show that $W_o(0, k) = \mathcal{O}_k^T \mathcal{O}_k$.

Theorem 4. *The linear discrete-time fractional-order system modeled by Equations (37) and (38) is observable if and only if there exists a finite time K such that $rank(\mathcal{O}_K) = n$ or, equivalently, $rank(W_o(0, K)) = n$. Furthermore, the initial state x_0 at $k = 0$ is given by*

$$x_0 = W_o^{-1}(0, K) \mathcal{O}_K^T [\tilde{\mathcal{Y}}_K - \mathcal{M}_K \tilde{\mathcal{U}}_K] \tag{52}$$

http://dx.doi.org/10.5772/51983

with

$$\tilde{\mathcal{U}}_K = [u^T(0) \quad u^T(1) \quad \ldots \quad u^T(K-1)]^T,$$

$$\tilde{\mathcal{Y}}_K = [y^T(0) \quad y^T(1) \quad \ldots \quad y^T(K-1)]^T,$$

and

$$\mathcal{M}_K = \begin{bmatrix} 0 & 0 & 0 & \ldots & 0 & 0 \\ CG_0B & 0 & 0 & \ldots & 0 & 0 \\ CG_1B & CG_0B & 0 & \ldots & 0 & 0 \\ CG_2B & CG_1B & CG_0B & \ldots & 0 & 0 \\ \vdots & \vdots & \vdots & \ldots & \vdots & \vdots \\ CG_{K-2}B & CG_{K-3}B & CG_{K-4}B & \ldots & CG_0B & 0 \end{bmatrix}. \tag{53}$$

Remark 5. *From the Cayley-Hamilton theorem, it is well known that for integer-order systems the rank of the observability matrix $\mathcal{O}_k$ cannot increase in Step $k \geq n$. Here too, it is remarkable that this is not true in the case of the discrete-time non-commensurate fractional-order system of (37) and (38). Indeed, rank$(\mathcal{O}_k)$ can increase for values $k \geq n$. We can state that the observability of this type of systems can possibly be obtained in a number of steps greater than n. This is due to the same reasons as those exposed above in Remark 3 for controllability. In [53], the observability condition for the discrete-time fractional-order system as modeled by (37), with non-commensurate order, is that the rank of $\mathcal{O}_k$ should be equal to n at most in Step $k = n$. Our result shows that the full rank of $(\mathcal{O}_k)$ can be reached in some Step $k = K$ greater than n. This can be considered as an extension of the previous result in [53].*

Commensurate fractional-order case In this section we address the particular case of commensurate FOS. The terms A_j are as expressed by $A_j = -c_{j+1}\mathbb{I}_n$, for all $j > 0$. It is clear then that matrices G_k defined by (40) are polynomials in A_0, i.e.,

$$G_k = A_0^k + \beta_{1_k}A_0^{k-1} + \beta_{2_k}A_0^{k-2} + \ldots + \beta_{k_k}\mathbb{I}_n.$$

where the real coefficients β_{j_k} are calculated from the coefficients c_j. In particular, we have

$$G_n = A_0^n + \beta_{1_n}A_0^{n-1} + \beta_{2_n}A_0^{n-2} + \ldots + \beta_{n_n}\mathbb{I}_n.$$

From the Cayley-Hamilton theorem, A_0^n is a linear combination of A_0^{n-1}, A_0^{n-2}, ..., $\mathbb{I}_n$. We deduce that G_{k+n}, for all $k \geq 0$ are linearly dependent on G_{n-1}, G_{n-2}, ..., $\mathbb{I}_n$. This implies the following results

Corollary 1. *The linear discrete-time fractional-order system modeled by Equations (37) and (38) in the commensurate case is reachable if and only if rank$(\mathcal{C}_n) = n$ or, equivalently, rank$(W_r(0,n)) = n$. On the other hand, this system is controllable if and only if rank$(W_c(0,n)) = n$.*

Corollary 2. *The linear discrete-time fractional-order system modeled by (37) and (38) in the commensurate case is observable if and only if rank$(\mathcal{O}_n) = n$ or, equivalently, rank$(W_o(0,n)) = n$.*

Remark 6. *We therefore observe that the controllability and observability criteria for the commensurate fractional-order case are similar to those of the integer-order case, in the sense that if a state cannot be reached in n steps, then it is not reachable at all and that if an initial state cannot be deduced from n steps of input-output data, then it is not observable at all. The result put forward in [53] which states that a necessary and sufficient condition for the discrete-time fractional-order system as modeled in* (37) *and* (38) *to be observable is that the rank of* $\mathcal{O}_k$ *should be equal to n at most in Step* $k = n$ *is true only in the case of commensurate FOS.*

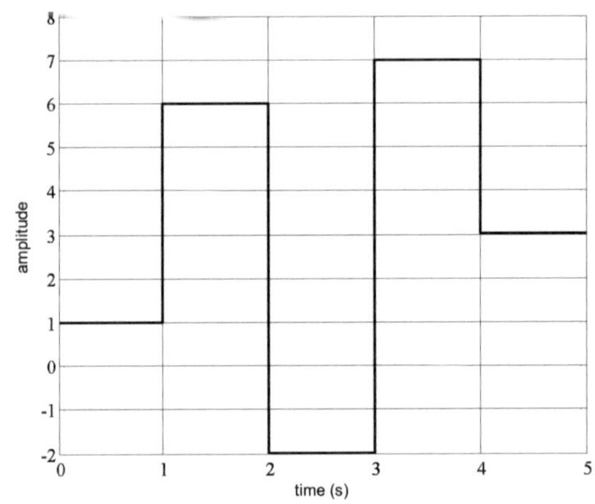

Figure 1. Computed values of the output sequence

4.3. Stability analysis

In this section, we investigate the property of stability of linear discrete-time FOS. We know that the study of the stability of FOS is limited to the result of the "'argument principle"', applicable to the sole category of commensurate-order systems. As far as non-commensurate orders are considered in the new models introduced, other adequate tools are required. In this context, new results concerning asymptotic stability are developed below. Besides, we introduce the concept of practical stability and we establish some mathematical conditions to check this property.

Asymptotic stability Let us consider the state-space model given by (37) and (38)

$$x(k+1) = \sum_{j=0}^{k} A_j x(k-j) + Bu(k), \quad x(0) = x_0,$$

$$y(k) = Cx(k),$$

Its solution, given by (40) is

$$x(k) = G_k x_0 + \sum_{j=0}^{k-1} G_{k-1-j} Bu(j).$$

In order to study the asymptotic stability property of this system, we consider its unforced version, i.e.,

$$x(k+1) = \sum_{j=0}^{k} A_j x(k-j), \quad x(0) = x_0. \tag{54}$$

Definition 6. *System* (54) *is asymptotically stable if for each* $k \geq 1$ *and any initial condition* x_0*, the following equality is verified*

$$\lim_{k \to \infty} \| x(k) \| = 0. \tag{55}$$

We use the 2-norm of the state vector $x(k)$, i.e.,

$$\| x(k) \| = \sqrt{\sum_{i=1}^{n} x_i^2(k)},$$

where $x_i(k)$ are the components of $x(k)$.
The solution to (54) for given initial conditions x_0 is

$$x(k) = G_k x_0, \quad k \geq 1, \; G_0 = \mathbb{I}_n. \tag{56}$$

It follows that System (54) is asymptotically stable if and only if

$$\| G_k \| \leq 1, \quad k \geq 1. \tag{57}$$

The 2-norm of the transition matrix is

$$\| G_k \| = \lambda_{max}^{\frac{1}{2}}(G_k G_k^T) = \sigma_{max}(G_k),$$

where λ_{max} and σ_{max} refer to the maximal eigenvalue and the maximal singular value of G_k respectively.
Let us define the backward shift operator $\mathcal{S}$ as follows ([55], [56]). We consider an infinite sequence of samples of vector x, denoted $\mathbf{x}$, starting from $k = 0$ up to infinity, and with null values for $k < 0$, assuming the system to be causal. Thus, we have

$$\mathbf{x} = \{\ldots, 0, 0, x(0), x(1), x(2), \ldots, x(N), \ldots\}.$$

$\mathcal{S}$ acts on $\mathbf{x}$ as follows

$$\begin{aligned} \mathcal{S}\mathbf{x} &= \mathcal{S}\{\ldots, 0, 0, x(0), x(1), \boxed{x(2)}, \ldots, x(k), x(k+1), \ldots\} \\ &= \{\ldots, 0, 0, 0, 0, x(0), \boxed{x(1)}, x(2), \ldots, x(k-1), \ldots\}. \end{aligned}$$

We then define the column sequence

$$\widetilde{\mathbf{x}} = \begin{bmatrix} \vdots \\ 0 \\ x(0) \\ x(1) \\ \vdots \\ x(k) \\ \vdots \end{bmatrix}$$

Similarly, we can use this representation to rewrite (37) and its output equation

$$y(k) = Cx(k)$$

in the equivalent form

$$\widetilde{\mathbf{x}} = \widetilde{\mathbf{S}}\widetilde{\mathbf{A}}\widetilde{\mathbf{x}} + \widetilde{\mathbf{S}}\widetilde{\mathbf{B}}\widetilde{\mathbf{u}}, \tag{58}$$

$$\widetilde{\mathbf{y}} = \widetilde{\mathbf{C}}\widetilde{\mathbf{x}}. \tag{59}$$

In this representation, the expressions of the different components are

$$\widetilde{\mathbf{u}} = \begin{bmatrix} \vdots \\ 0 \\ u(0) \\ u(1) \\ \vdots \\ u(k) \\ \vdots \end{bmatrix}, \quad \widetilde{\mathbf{y}} = \begin{bmatrix} \vdots \\ 0 \\ y(0) \\ y(1) \\ \vdots \\ y(k) \\ \vdots \end{bmatrix}, \quad \widetilde{\mathbf{S}} = \begin{bmatrix} 0 & 0 & 0 & \ldots\ldots \\ \mathbb{I}_n & 0 & \ldots & \ldots\ldots \\ 0 & \mathbb{I}_n & \ldots & \ldots\ldots \\ 0 & 0 & \mathbb{I}_n & \ldots\ldots \\ \vdots & \vdots & \vdots & \vdots \quad \vdots \end{bmatrix}$$

and

$$\widetilde{\mathbf{A}} = \begin{bmatrix} A_0 & 0 & 0 & 0 \ldots \\ A_1 & A_0 & 0 & 0 \ldots \\ A_2 & A_1 & A_0 & 0 \ldots \\ A_3 & A_2 & A_1 & A_0 \ldots \\ \vdots & \vdots & \vdots & \vdots \quad \vdots \end{bmatrix}, \quad \widetilde{\mathbf{B}} = \begin{bmatrix} B & 0 & 0 & 0 & \ldots \\ 0 & B & 0 & 0 & \ldots \\ 0 & 0 & B & 0 & \ldots \\ 0 & 0 & 0 & B & \ldots \\ \vdots & \vdots & \vdots & \vdots & \vdots \end{bmatrix}$$

and

$$\widetilde{\mathbf{C}} = \begin{bmatrix} C & 0 & 0 & 0 & \dots \\ 0 & C & 0 & 0 & \dots \\ 0 & 0 & C & 0 & \dots \\ 0 & 0 & 0 & C & \dots \\ \vdots & \vdots & \vdots & \vdots & \vdots \end{bmatrix}.$$

Theorem 5. *Putting $\mathcal{A}_s = \widetilde{\mathbf{S}}\widetilde{\mathbf{A}}$, the system*

$$\widetilde{\mathbf{x}} = \widetilde{\mathbf{S}}\widetilde{\mathbf{A}}\widetilde{\mathbf{x}} = \mathcal{A}_s\widetilde{\mathbf{x}} \tag{60}$$

is asymptotically stable if and only if $\rho(\mathcal{A}_s) \leq 1$, where ρ is the spectral radius of operator $\mathcal{A}_s$, defined as

$$\rho(\mathcal{A}_s) = \lim_{i\to\infty} \|\mathcal{A}_s^i\|_*^{\frac{1}{i}}, \tag{61}$$

in which the norm definition is

$$\|\mathcal{A}_s^i\|_* = \sup_{[I,J]} \|\mathcal{A}_{s[I,J]}^i\|,$$

with $\mathcal{A}_{s[I,J]}^i$ denoting the $[I,J]^{th}$ block matrix of $\mathcal{A}_s^i$.

The proof of this theorem is in [36]. In practice, a finite-time observation of the system is desirable. For this purpose, we consider the concept of practical stability ([54], [57]) defined as follows

Definition 7. *System (54) is practically stable in a finite-time horizon $L_h > 0$ if for each $1 \leq k \leq L_h$ and any initial condition x_0 the following inequality is verified*

$$\| x(k) \| \leq M \| x_0 \|, \tag{62}$$

where M is a strictly positive finite given number.

From solution (56), System (54) is practically stable if and only if $\| G_k \| \leq M$ for $1 \leq k \leq L$. Besides, we can write

$$\mathcal{A}_s^L = \begin{bmatrix} G_1 & 0 & 0 & \dots\dots & 0 \\ G_2 & 0 & 0 & \dots\dots & 0 \\ G_3 & 0 & 0 & \dots\dots & 0 \\ \vdots & \vdots & \vdots & \vdots\ \vdots & \vdots \\ G_{L_h} & 0 & 0 & \dots\dots & 0 \\ \times & A_0^{L_h+1} & 0 & \dots\dots & 0 \\ \times & \times & A_0^{L_h+2} & 0\ \dots & 0 \\ \vdots & \vdots & \vdots & \vdots\ \vdots & \vdots \\ \times & \times & \times & \times\ \times & \times \end{bmatrix}$$

Define the block matrix

$$\mathcal{A}_{s\ L_h}^{L_h} = \begin{bmatrix} G_1 & 0 & 0 & \ldots & \ldots & 0 \\ G_2 & 0 & 0 & \ldots & \ldots & 0 \\ G_3 & 0 & 0 & \ldots & \ldots & 0 \\ \vdots & \vdots & \vdots & \vdots & \vdots & \vdots \\ G_{L_h} & 0 & 0 & \ldots & \ldots & 0 \end{bmatrix}.$$

From the above, we can state that System (54) is practically stable if and only if $\| \mathcal{A}_{s\ L_h}^{L_h} \|_* \leq M$. These results are illustrated by a numerical example in [36].

Remark 7. *The state-space representations elaborated in the previous sections for the continuous time and the discrete time were considered for a SISO process. They are easily extended to Multiple Input, Multiple Output (MIMO) systems, with the use of a vector of inputs u instead of a scalar input, and a vector of outputs y instead of a scalar output. MIMO systems are treated with a same procedure. This enables the study of their structural properties and permits to deal with control issues of such systems either in time domain or frequency domain, such as MIMO* H_∞ *problem for example in[58].*

5. Practical example

5.1. Fractional-order modeling of a thermal system

We consider a thermal system consisting in the regulation of the temperature profile of an aluminium rod with constant thermal conductivity κ and diffusivity ξ, as described in [30, 59]. A possible version is shown in Figure 2. Temperature $T(\chi,t)$ is evaluated at abscissa χ

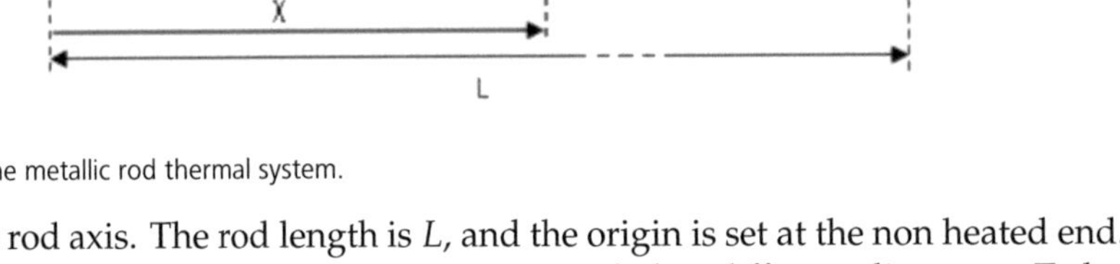

Figure 2. The metallic rod thermal system.

along the rod axis. The rod length is L, and the origin is set at the non heated end. Measuring points of $T(\chi,t)$, by means of probes, are provided at different distances. To build a model of this system, we use an approximation by considering that the temperature diffusion for this type of geometry is governed by the following partial differential equation (PDE)

$$\frac{\partial T(\chi,t)}{\partial t} = \xi \frac{\partial^2 T(\chi,t)}{\partial \chi^2}, \quad \chi \in (0,L), \quad t \geq 0 \tag{63}$$

The Dirichlet boundary condition is stated as follows [59]: we consider the control action that maintains a temperature $u(t)$ fixed at the end point $\chi = L$ and that a temperature measurement can be taken inside the rod, at a fixed abscissa χ_0 (see Figure 2). Therefore, the boundary conditions are

$$T(0,t) = 0. \qquad T(L,t) = u(t). \tag{64}$$

As for the temperature measured at a fixed point χ_0, this represents the observation, that is

$$y(t) = T(\chi_0, t).$$

5.2. Fractional-order state-space model of the aluminium rod

Let us denote the Laplace transforms of $T(\chi,t)$ and $u(t)$ respectively by $\overline{T}(\chi,s)$ and $\overline{u}(s)$. The assumption of null initial conditions is made here, i.e., the rod is left to cool down before experiment. This conducts us to an easier computing process. Indeed non null initial conditions in the fractional case, as exposed for example in [31], conduct to computations that are more complicated to handle. Equation (63) and (64) become

$$\frac{d^2\overline{T}(\chi,s)}{d\chi^2} = \frac{s}{\varsigma}\overline{T}(\chi,s) = 0, \quad \text{with} \tag{65}$$

$$\overline{T}(0,s)) = 0, \qquad \overline{T}(L,s) = \overline{u}(s). \tag{66}$$

The corresponding solution leads to the transfer function

$$H(\chi_0,s) = \frac{\overline{y}(s)}{\overline{u}(s)} = \frac{\overline{T}(\chi_0,s)}{\overline{T}(L,s)} = \frac{sinh\left(\chi_0\sqrt{\frac{s}{\varsigma}}\right)}{sinh\left(L\sqrt{\frac{s}{\varsigma}}\right)}. \tag{67}$$

This expression establishes that the described device exhibits the feature of fractional-order model. It is the case for various other types of diffusion, say chemical diffusion processes, neutron flux, and also for dielectric relaxation, electrode polarization, transmission lines, etc.. The four exp(.) terms composing the last part of (67) are expressed by using a Padé approximation of order 2. Let us recall here that, for instance, for exp(.) with given argument z, a Padé approximation of order P yields

$$\exp(z) \approx \frac{\sum_{k=0}^{P}\frac{(2P-k)!}{k!(P-k)!}(z)^k}{\sum_{k=0}^{P}\frac{(2P-k)!}{k!(P-k)!}(-z)^k}.$$

The determination of $H(\chi_0,s)$ is made for an aluminium rod, with a set of numerical values most of them used in [30]. These are

- rod length $L = 0.4$ m.

- abscissa of the measuring point, set here at $\chi_0 = \frac{2*L}{3}$ m.
- rod thermal conductivity $\kappa = 237$ W/m.K, and diffusivity $\xi = 9975.10^{-8}$ m^2/s.

With this set of practical values, we obtain the following transfer function

$$H(\chi_0, s) = \frac{0.6667 + 22.2501s^{\frac{1}{2}} + 188.1246s - 1982.7s^{\frac{3}{2}} + 5293.9s^2}{1 + 33.3751s^{\frac{1}{2}} + 430.7064s + 1982.7s^{\frac{3}{2}} + 3529.3s^2}. \tag{68}$$

Next we apply to (68) the procedure exposed above from (8) to (17), so as to obtain the corresponding fractional-order state-space model. We find a state-space model with commensurate fractional orders, of the form (17). In our case, it can be reduced to four states, by eliminating redundant states through a variable change. In the resulting model, there exists a direct transmission matrix D, what can be foreseen when considering the monomials of highest degree in s of numerator and denominator of (68).

The computed set of matrices A, B, C, D of the resulting fractional-order state-space model for the rod, in continuous time, is therefore

$$A = \begin{bmatrix} 0 & 1 & 0 & 0 \\ 0 & 0 & 1 & 0 \\ 0 & 0 & 0 & 1 \\ -0.0003 & -0.0095 & -0.1220 & -0.5618 \end{bmatrix}, \quad B = \begin{bmatrix} 0 \\ 0 \\ 0 \\ 0.0002833 \end{bmatrix}, \tag{69}$$

$$C = \begin{bmatrix} -0.8333 & -27.8126 & -457.9350 & -4956.8 \end{bmatrix}, \quad D = [1.5].$$

5.3. Analysis of the discrete-time state-space model of the rod

We convert the continuous-time state space model described by the set of matrices (69) into a discrete-time version. This is done by choosing the sampling period h, making $h = 1$s. The sampling period value taken in [30] for the same aluminium rod is somewhat smaller, that is 0.5s. We set the input variable $u(t) = T(L,t) = 320\ ^oK$. In other words, the temperature at abscissa $\chi = L$ is maintained constant. The observed output $y(t) = T(\chi_0, t)$ is the temperature diffusing at a measuring point at χ_0. The response obtained is shown in Figure 3. It indicates that the output temperature starts increasing from null initial condition set at $T(0,t) = 0\,^oK$, which is an assumption for deriving the model used. In the interval of the experiment over 3000 steps, it diffuses and tends to a value approaching the input fixed value. A detailed plot represented in Figure 4 shows at the beginning an increase of $y(t)$, followed by a brief fall under zero. This type of behaviour at first sight is similar to non-minimum phase system behaviour. However, its interpretation as a physical phenomenon appears to be not realistic, considering the underlying process in study.

Besides, as an example of study of the structural properties of the model proposed, we have led a reachability test, following the theoretical developments of previous Section 4. Starting from a zero initial state $x(0) = [0\ \ 0\ \ 0\ \ 0]'$, we set a final state to be reached as $x_f = [-0.13\quad -0.13\quad -0.13\quad -0.13]'$. The computation achieved yields the result that x_f is exactly reached in four steps, i.e. in a number of steps equal to the rank of the controllability matrix, as depicted in Figure 5. Nevertheless, from the point of view of physical coherence, the result is not satisfactory, since the necessary input sequence yielded is $u(k) = [-278.2396 \quad -99.607 \quad -36.5687 \quad -18.3551]$, that is, with (all) negative elements. Related to this feature, the values of the model output matrix C is found to be made of all negative elements. A further insight should be therefore directed towards the modeling process, initiated with the representation of the diffusive phenomena by PDE equations. Next, a more detailed evaluation of the precision when achieving the Padé approximation would be expectable. It remains that one major improvement to expect is the effective introduction in the modeling of fractional-order systems of non null initial conditions [31]. Taking them into account in the computations is a way to make the representations closer to the reality of the phenomena. The case treated here, which aims to describe the diffusion of a given fixed temperature at one end of the rod, implies to deal with realistic operation conditions. For example, an interesting case to investigate would be to consider the rod set initially at ambient temperature, say currently around 300 ^oK, as a non null initial condition, and to track the diffusion of a given input temperature with a more elaborated model.

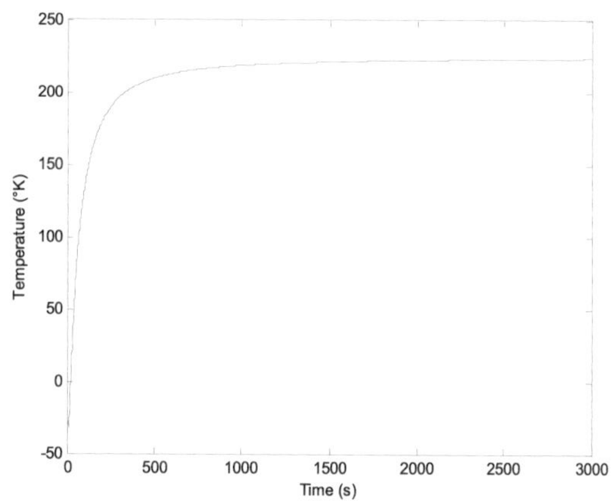

Figure 3. Output temperature evolution over 3000 points (Sampling period: 1s).

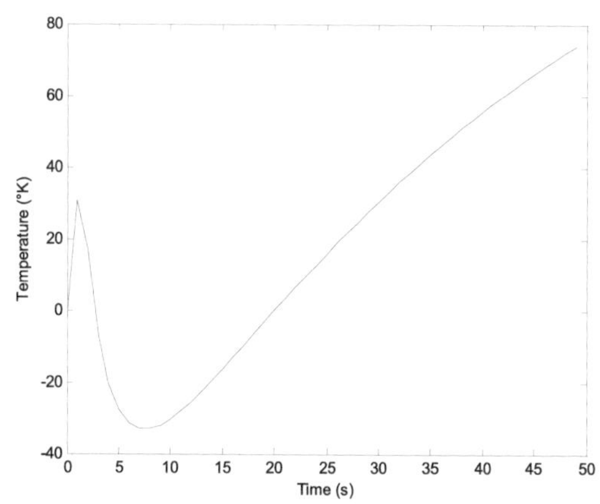

Figure 4. Output temperature evolution, starting from zero initial condition (Detail).

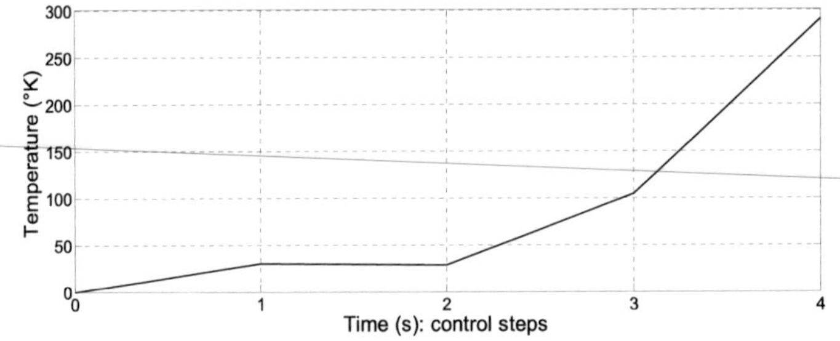

Figure 5. Output temperature evolution during control sequence.

6. Stabilization issue

In this section, we deal with the problem of stabilization. For this purpose, we consider the system given by (37) and (38), which we aim to stabilize, by handling state equation (37)

$$x(k+1) = \sum_{j=0}^{k} A_j x(k-j) + Bu(k), \quad x(0) = x_0.$$

Let us consider the control u as a state-feedback control, in a classical state-feedback control loop, with a null reference input ($r = 0$), as illustrated in Figure 6. We assume that

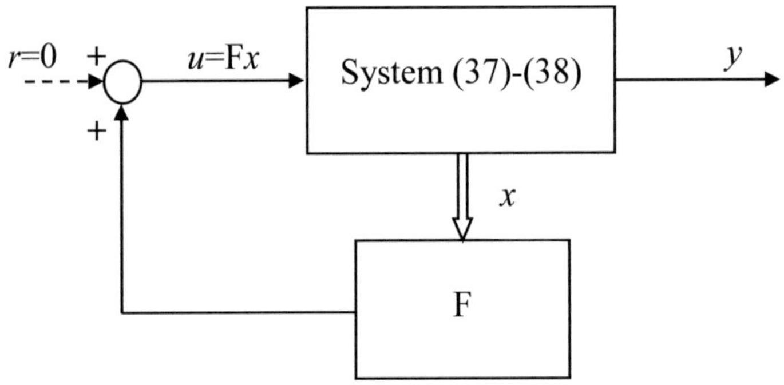

Figure 6. State-feedback control loop.

$$u(k) = \sum_{j=0}^{k} F_j x(k-j), \tag{70}$$

That is

$$u(k) = F_0 x(k) + F_1 x(k-1) + F_2 x(k-2) + \ldots + F_k x(0).$$

In the closed loop, we have

$$x(k+1) = \sum_{j=0}^{k} (A_j + BF_j)x(k-j). \tag{71}$$

Then, putting $A_{Fj} = A_j + BF_j$, we can write

$$x(k+1) = \sum_{j=0}^{k} A_{Fj}x(k-j). \tag{72}$$

Thus, successively, we build the recurrence beginning with

$$x(1) = A_{F0}x(0) = (A_0 + BF_0)x(0),$$

$$x(2) = A_{F0}x(1) + A_{F1}x(0) = (A_0 + BF_0)x(1) + (A_1 + BF_1)x(0),$$

$$x(3) = A_{F0}x(2) + A_{F1}x(1)A_{F2}x(0) = (A_0 + BF_0)x(2) + (A_1 + BF_1)x(1) + (A_2 + BF_2)x(0), \ldots$$

This leads to the following relation between the two column sequences

$$\begin{bmatrix} x(1) \\ x(2) \\ x(3) \\ \vdots \\ x(k+1) \\ \vdots \end{bmatrix} = \begin{bmatrix} (A_0 + BF_0) & 0 & 0 & 0\ldots \\ (A_1 + BF_1) & (A_0 + BF_0) & 0 & 0\ldots \\ (A_2 + BF_2) & (A_1 + BF_1) & (A_0 + BF_0) & 0\ldots \\ \vdots & \vdots & \vdots & \vdots \; \vdots \end{bmatrix} \begin{bmatrix} x(0) \\ x(1) \\ x(2) \\ \vdots \\ x(k) \\ \vdots \end{bmatrix} \tag{73}$$

Similarly to the notations used in (37), i.e., considering an infinite column sequence $\widetilde{\mathbf{x}}$, and using the backward shift $\mathcal{S}$, Equation (58) is rewritten as follows

$$\widetilde{\mathbf{x}} = \widetilde{\mathbf{S}}\widetilde{\mathbf{A_F}}\widetilde{\mathbf{x}}, \tag{74}$$

in which

$$\widetilde{\mathbf{A_F}} = \begin{bmatrix} (A_0 + BF_0) & 0 & 0 & 0\ldots \\ (A_1 + BF_1) & (A_0 + BF_0) & 0 & 0\ldots \\ (A_2 + BF_2) & (A_1 + BF_1) & (A_0 + BF_0) & 0\ldots \\ \vdots & \vdots & \vdots & \vdots \; \vdots \end{bmatrix} \tag{75}$$

Further, we decompose $\widetilde{\mathbf{A_F}}$ as follows

$$\widetilde{\mathbf{A}_{\mathbf{F}}} = \begin{bmatrix} A_0 & 0 & 0 & 0 \dots \\ A_1 & A_0 & 0 & 0 \dots \\ A_2 & A_1 & A_0 & 0 \dots \\ \vdots & \vdots & \vdots & \vdots & \vdots \end{bmatrix} + \begin{bmatrix} B & 0 & 0 & 0 \dots \\ 0 & B & 0 & 0 \dots \\ 0 & 0 & B & 0 \dots \\ \vdots & \vdots & \vdots & \vdots & \vdots \end{bmatrix} + \begin{bmatrix} F_0 & 0 & 0 & 0 \dots \\ F_1 & F_0 & 0 & 0 \dots \\ F_2 & F_1 & F_0 & 0 \dots \\ \vdots & \vdots & \vdots & \vdots & \vdots \end{bmatrix} \tag{76}$$

Equation (58) becomes

$$\widetilde{\mathbf{x}} = \widetilde{\mathbf{S}}\widetilde{\mathbf{A}_{\mathbf{F}}}\widetilde{\mathbf{x}} = \widetilde{\mathbf{S}}\widetilde{\mathbf{A}}\widetilde{\mathbf{x}} + \widetilde{\mathbf{S}}\widetilde{\mathbf{B}}\widetilde{\mathbf{F}}\widetilde{\mathbf{x}}, \tag{77}$$

where

$$\widetilde{\mathbf{F}} = \begin{bmatrix} F_0 & 0 & 0 & 0 \dots \\ F_1 & F_0 & 0 & 0 \dots \\ F_2 & F_1 & F_0 & 0 \dots \\ \vdots & \vdots & \vdots & \vdots & \vdots \end{bmatrix}. \tag{78}$$

The reachability is reformulated here under the operator-theoretic formulation (Equations (58) and (59)) of the discrete-time fractional-order system.

Definition 8. *The pair $(\widetilde{\mathbf{A}}, \widetilde{\mathbf{B}})$ is K-step reachable if the operator reachability Gramian defined by*

$$\widetilde{\mathbf{W}_{\mathbf{r}}^{\mathbf{p}}} = \widetilde{\mathbf{C}}_p^T \widetilde{\mathbf{C}}_p, \tag{79}$$

where

$$\widetilde{\mathbf{C}}_p = [\widetilde{\mathbf{B}} \quad \widetilde{\mathbf{A}}\widetilde{\mathbf{B}} \quad \dots \widetilde{\mathbf{A}}^{p-1}\widetilde{\mathbf{A}}],$$

is invertible.

Similarly to Equation (39), let us now define the transition matrix form G_k such that

$$G_{Fk} = \begin{cases} \mathbb{I}_{n_d} & \text{for } k = 0, \\ \sum_{j=0}^{k-1} A_{Fj} G_{F(k-1-j)} & \text{for } k \geq 1. \end{cases} \tag{80}$$

We now consider the problem of choosing the state feedback operator gain $\widetilde{\mathbf{F}}$ that stabilizes System (77), i.e., which ensures that

$$\| G_{Fk} \| \leq 1 \quad \text{for } k \geq 1.$$

The following statement is derived from Theorem 5 established above, and Lemma 2 in [60].

Corollary 3. *Suppose that $(\widetilde{\mathbf{A}}, \widetilde{\mathbf{B}})$ is K-reachable and let*

$$\widetilde{\mathbf{F}} = -\widetilde{\mathbf{B}}^T \widetilde{\mathbf{A}}^T (\widetilde{\mathbf{W}}_r^p)^{-1} \widetilde{\mathbf{A}}^{p+1},$$

then the closed-loop system (77) is asymptotically stable, that is $\rho(\widetilde{\mathbf{A}}_{Fs}) < 1$, where $\widetilde{\mathbf{A}}_{Fs} = \widetilde{\mathbf{S}}\widetilde{\mathbf{A}}_F$

Remark 8. *The state feedback (70) uses the entire memory of the state variable. In practice, this could be undesirable and computationally unwieldy. It is preferable to design a controller with short-memory [45]. Let be L_h the restricted length of the memory (or horizon). The practical state feedback is formulated as:*

$$u(k) = \sum_{j=0}^{L_h} F_j x(k-j), \qquad for \quad k \geq L_h,$$

and

$$u(k) = \sum_{j=0}^{k} F_j x(k-j), \qquad for \quad k < L_h$$

Stability of the short-memory state feedback controller could be investigated with the same development given in this section.

7. Conclusion

We have reviewed some tools for modeling and analysis of FOS in discrete time, introducing state-space representation for both commensurate and non commensurate fractional orders. These latter new approaches of modeling and analysis of such systems have revealed new properties, not shown in continuous time representations.

Our contribution concerns the analysis of the controllability and the observability of linear discrete-time FOS. We have introduced a new formalism and established testable sufficient conditions for guaranteeing the controllability and the observability. Some aspects of controllability and observability of such systems had not been treated before. Let us recall the remarkable point that, in the case of the linear discrete-time non-commensurate FOS, the rank of the controllability matrix can increase for values greater than the dimension of the system. In other words, it is possible to reach the final state in a number of steps greater than this dimension number. They are expected to give birth to further investigations and applications. With the use of a new formalism, an approach to analysis of asymptotic stability and practical stability of discrete-time FOS has been proposed.

The modeling of a practical system has been treated, which points out theoretical assumptions to match with real conditions.

Finally, the preliminary results presented in this chapter enabled us to make first steps into investigation on stabilization and practical stabilization of linear discrete-time FOS.

Author details

Saïd Guermah[1],
Saïd Djennoune[1] and Maâmar Bettayeb[2]

1 Laboratoire de Conception et Conduite des Systèmes de Production (L2CSP), Faculty of Electrical Engineering and Computer Science, Mouloud Mammeri University of Tizi-Ouzou, Tizi-Ouzou, Algeria

2 Department of Electrical/Electronics & Computer Engineering, University of Sharjah, United Arab Emirates

References

[1] Oldham KB, Spanier J. The fractional calculus. Academic Press. New-York; 1974.

[2] Miller KS, Ross B. An introduction to the fractional calculus and fractional differential equations, Wiley, New-York, 1993.

[3] Samko SG, Kilbas AA, Marichev OI. Fractional integrals and derivatives: theory and applications. Gordon and Breach Science Publisher, Amsterdam, 1993.

[4] Kilbas AA, Srivasta HM, Trujillo JJ. Theory and applications of fractional differential equations, Noth-Holland Mathematics Studies 204, Elsevier, Amsterdam, 2006.

[5] Manabe S. The non-Integer Integral and its Application to Control Systems, ETJ of Japan, 1961; 6 (3/4): 83-87.

[6] Mandelbrot B. The fractal geometry of nature, Freeman, San Fransisco; 1982.

[7] Charef A, Sun HH, Tsao YY, Onaral B. Fractal system as represented by singularity function, IEEE Transactions on Automatic Control, 1992; 37(9): 1465-1470.

[8] Oustaloup A. La dérivation non entière, théorie, synthèse et applications, Hermès Edition, Paris, 1995.

[9] Carpinteri A, Mainardi F. Fractals and Fractional Calculus in Continuum Mechanics, Springer Verlag, Vienna-New York, 1997.

[10] Montseny G. Diffusive representation of pseudo-differential time operator, Proceeding Fractional Differential Equation Systems: Model, Methods and Application, Paris, 1998.

[11] Battaglia JL, Le Lay L, Batsale JC, Oustaloup A, Cois O. Heat flux estimation through inverted non integer identification models, Int J of Thermal Science. 2000; 39 (3): 374-389.

[12] Caputo M. Distributed order differential equations modeling dielectric induction and diffusion, Fractional Calculus Appl. Anal. 2001; 4: 421-442.

[13] Heymans N. Implementation of fractional calculus using hierarchical models: application to the terminal transition of a complex polymer, in the Proc. of DETC 2003/VIB 48396 ASME, Chicago, USA, 2003.

[14] Zhang Yanzhu, Xue Dingyu. Wireless Communications, Networking and Mobile Computing, WiCom 2007.

[15] Ichise M, Nagayanagi Y, Kojima T. An analog simulation of non-integer order transfer functions for analysis of electrode processes, J of Electroanalytical Chemistry; 33: 253-265.

[16] Axtell M, Bise EM. Fractional calculus applications in control systems, in Proceedings of the IEE Nat. Aerospace and Electronics Conf.; 1990 New-York; 536-566.

[17] Bagley RL, Calico RA. Fractional order state equations for the control of viscoelastically damped structures, J of Guidance, Control and Dynamics. 1991; 14: 304-311.

[18] Nakagava N, Sorimachi K. Basic characteristics of fractance device, IEICE Trans. Fund. 1992; E75-A (12):1814-1818.

[19] Matignon D, d'Andréa Novel B, Depalle P, Oustaloup A. Viscothermal losses in wind instrument: a non-integer model, Systems and Networks: mathematical theory and application. Academic Verlag Edition. 1994; 2.

[20] Bidan G. Commande diffusive d'une machine électrique: une introduction, Proceeding Fractional Differential Equation Systems: Model, Methods and Application, Paris; 1998.

[21] Oustaloup A, Sabatier J, Moreau X. From fractional robustness to the CRONE approach, Proceeding Fractional Differential Equation Systems: Model, Methods and Application; 1998; Paris.

[22] Ortigueira MD. Introduction to fractional linear systems, IEE proc. Image signal process; 2000 February; 147 (1).

[23] Cois O, Oustaloup A, Battaglia E, Battaglia JL. Non integer model from modal decomposition for time domain identification; 41 st IEEE CDC'2002 Tutorial Workshop 2; Las Vegas, USA

[24] Vinagre BM , Monje CA, Calderon AJ. Fractional order systems and fractional order actions. Tutorial Workshop 2: Fractional Calculus Applications in Automatic Control and Robotics; 2002; Las Vegas, USA.

[25] Hanyga A. Internal variable models of viscoelasticity with fractional relaxatioon laws. Proc. of DETC 2003/VIB, 48395, ASME, Chicago, USA.

[26] Moreau X, Altet O, Oustaloup A. The CRONE suspension: modeling and stability analysis. DETC, ASME; 2003 Sep 2-6; Chicago, Illinois, USA.

[27] Djouambi A, Charef A, Bouktir T. Fractal Robustness and Parameter Tuning $PI^{\lambda}D^{\mu}$ Controllers. Proc. of the 5th WSEAS Int. Conf. on Signal, Speech and Image Processing; 2005 Aug 17-19:155-162; Corfu, Greece.

[28] Heymans N, Podlubny I. Physical interpretation of initial conditions for fractional differential equations with Riemann-Liouville fractional derivatives, Rheol. Acta. 2006 (45):765-772.

[29] Battaglia JL, Cois O, Puigsegur L, Oustaloup A. Solving an inverse heat conduction problem using a non-integer identified model, Int J of Heat and Mass Transfer 2001; 44(14).

[30] Malti R, Sabatier J, Akçay H. Thermal modeling and identification of an aluminium rod using fractional calculus., 15th IFAC Symposium on System Identification (SYSID); 2009; Saint-Malo, France.

[31] Hartley TT, Lorenzo CF. Dynamics and Control of Initialized Fractional-Order Systems. Nonlinear Dynamics. 2002; 29: 201-233.

[32] Monje CA, Chen YQ, Vinagre BM, Xue D, Feliu V. Fractional-order Systems and Controls: Fundamentals and Applications, ISSN 1430-9491; ISBN 978-1-84996-334-3, e-ISBN 978-1-84996-335-0, DOI 10.1007/978-1-84996-335-0, Springer London Dordrecht Heidelberg New York, 2010.

[33] Dzieliński A, Sierociuk D. Adaptive Feedback Control of Fractional Order Discrete State-Space Systems. Proc of the 2005 International Conference on Computational Intelligence for Modelling, Control and Automation, and International Conference on Intelligent Agents, Web Technologies and Internet Commerce (CIMCA-IAWTIC'05);524-529; 2005; Vienna, Austria.

[34] Guermah S, Djennoune S, Bettayeb M. Controllability and Observability of Linear Discrete-Time Fractional-Order Systems, Int J of Applied Mathematics and Computer Science (AMCS). 2008; 18(2):213-222.

[35] Guermah S, Djennoune S, Bettayeb M. State space analysis of linear fractional order systems. J Européen des Systèmes Automatisés. 2008; 42(6-7-8): 825-838.

[36] Guermah S, Djennoune S, Bettayeb M. A new approach for stability analysis of linear discrete-time fractional-order systems, in New Trends in Nanotechnology and Fractional Calculus Applications, Springer Book, Dimitru Baleanu, Zya Burhanettin, Güvenç JA, Tenreiro Machado Editors; 151-162; ISBN 978-90-481-3292-8, Springer, 2010. DOI 10.1007/978-90-481-3293-5/11

[37] Raynaud HF, Zergainoh A. State-space representation for fractional-order controllers. Automatica. 2000; 36: 1017-1021

[38] Hotzel R, Fliess M. On linear system with a fractional derivation: introductory theory and examples. Mathematics and Computers in Simulation. 1998; 45: 385-395

[39] Dorčák L, Petras I, Kostial I. Modeling and analysis of fractional-order regulated systems in the state-space. Proc. of ICCC'2000: 185-188; 2000; High Tatras, Slovak Republic.

[40] Sabatier J, Cois O, Oustaloup A. Commande de systèmes non entiers par placement de pôles. Deuxième Conférence Internationale Francophone d'Automatique, CIFA. 2002, Nantes, France.

[41] Mittag-Leffler G. Sur la représentation analytique d'une branche uniforme d'une fonction monogène, Acta Mathematica. 1904; 29: 10-181

[42] Matignon D. Stability results on fractional differential equations with application to control processing. In Computational Engineering in Systems Applications. 1996; 963-968

[43] Matignon D, d'Andréa-Novel B. Some results on controllability and observability of finite-dimensional fractional differential systems. In IMACS, IEEE-SMC Proceedings Conference: 952-956; 1996; Lille, France.

[44] Bettayeb M, Djennoune S. A note on the controllability and the observability of fractional dynamical systems, Proceedings of the 2nd IFAC Workshop on Fractional Differentiation and its Applications (FDA'06):506-511; 2006 Jul 19-21; Porto, Portugal.

[45] Podlubny I. Fractional Differential Equations, Academic Press, New York, 1999.

[46] Dzieliński A, Sierociuk D. Reachability, controllability and observability of the fractional order discrete state-space system, IEEE/IFAC International Conference on the Methods and Models in Automation and Robotics, MMAR'2007; 2007 Aug 27-30; Szczecin, Poland.

[47] Lakshmikantham DTV. Theory of Difference Equations: Numerical Methods and Applications, Academic Press, New-York, 1988.

[48] Aström KJ, Wittenmark B. Computer-controlled systems, Theory and design, 2nd edition, Prentice Hall, Englewoods Cliffs, New Jersey, 1990.

[49] Billings SA, Aguirre LA (University of Sheffield, Department of Automatic Control and Systems Engineering, Sheffield, UK). Effects of the Sampling Time on the Dynamics and Identification of Nonlinear Models. Research report 513; Sheffield, 1994.

[50] Peng Y, Guangming X, Long W. Controllability of Linear Discrete-Time Systems With Time-Delay in State, In dean.pku.edu.cn/bksky/1999tzlwj/4.pdf., 2003.

[51] Boukas EK. Discrete-Time Systems with Time-varying Time Delay: Stability and Stabilizability. Hindawi Publishing Corporation, Mathematical Problems in Engineering. 2006; 2006:1-10

[52] Debeljković DL, Aleksendrić M, Yi-Yong N, Zhang QL. Lyapunov and non-Lyapunov Stability of Linear Discrete Time Delay Systems. Facta Universitatis, Series: Mechanical Engineering. 2002: 1(9): 1147-1160

[53] Dzieliński A, Sierociuk D. Observers for discrete fractional order systems, Proceedings of the 2nd IFAC Workshop on Fractional Differentiation and its Applications (FDA'06); 2006 Jul 19-21; Porto, Portugal.

[54] Dzieliński A, Sierociuk D. Stability of discrete fractional-order state-space systems, Proceedings of the 2nd IFAC Workshop on Fractional Differentiation and its Applications (FDA'06): 524-529; 2006 Jul 19-21; Porto, Portugal.

[55] Lall S, Beck C. Error-bounds for balanced model-reduction of linear time-varying systems, IEEE Trans Automat Contr. 2003; 48(6):946-956

[56] Dullerud G, Lall S. A new approach for analysis and synthesis of time-varying systems, IEEE Trans Autom Contr. 1999; 44: 1486-1497

[57] Garcia G, Messaoud H, Maraoui S. Practical stabilization of linear time-varying systems. Sixth International Conference on Sciences and Techniques of Automatic control; 2005 Dec 19-21, Sousse, Tunisia.

[58] Doyle JC. Lectures notes in advances in multivariable control, ONR/Honeywell Workshop, Minneapolis, 1984.

[59] Curtain R, Morris K. Transfer functions of distributed parameter systems: A tutorial. Automatica. 2009; 45: 1101-1116

[60] Iglesias PA (The Johns Hopkins University, Department of Electrical and Computer Engineering, Baltimore, MD 21218). On the stabilization of discrete-time linear time-varying systems. pi@ruth.ece.jhu.edu. Technical report JHU/ECE-94/08; 1994 May 8.

Chapter 9

Investigation of a Methodology for the Quantitative Estimation of Nursing Tasks on the Basis of Time Study Data

Atsue Ishii, Takashi Nakamura, Yuko Ohno and
Satoko Kasahara

Additional information is available at the end of the chapter

http://dx.doi.org/10.5772/51014

1. Background and goals

Estimation of the quantity of nursing care required is regarded as a pressing need from the point of view of the investigation of both patient safety and care provision that meets patient for view of demand. Nursing is a very busy job, and up to now, much attention has been paid to problems arising from the physical and psychological effects of busyness on nurses, and to consequent problems relating to patient safety and quality of care. Because a large part of any estimates of whether a nurse is busy or not depends on subjective judgment, however, it is difficult both to define busyness and to formulate methods of measuring and assessing busyness. It is also true that merely demonstrating busyness will not have a significant effect in solving problems. Consequently, ways of estimating nursing care quantity itself have been sought. If it were possible to make quantitative estimates of necessary nursing care, we could expect to improve patient safety and achieve a better quality of patient care through such elements of nursing care management as appropriate allocation of nursing staff and effective distribution of tasks.

In studies of the measurement of work quantity for the purposes of nursing care management, a typical approach has been to conduct work quantity surveys based on time study (Meyers & Stewart, 2002). Various techniques for calculating work quantity have been used, some of which focus on patient condition (Fagerstom & Rainio, 1999) and others on patient outcomes (Hall et al., 2004), but methods based on time study have the particular advantage that they make it possible to obtain clear quantitative results in the form of work times. Time studies quantitatively examine how much time is spent on what sort of work activities, and yield highly reliable results concerning the amounts of work time expended. They are therefore widely used not only in fields related to nursing but also in clinical locations where doctors and other co-medicals work (Vinson et al., 1996; Langlois et al., 1999; Magnusson et al., 1998). They are carried out in various forms (Thomas et al., 2000; Caughey & Chang, 1998) and in the course of this study also we have used time study to elucidate the actual state of ward nursing care from a variety of perspectives.

In most such studies, however, the analyses of the time study data do not go beyond factual descriptions of the actual state of affairs. So far, almost no methodology has been established for the purpose of linking the data to the calculation of quantities of nursing care required or to nursing care management. The following points may be cited as contributing factors:

1. It is difficult to carry out long-term time studies
2. It is difficult to obtain an overall picture of tasks in hospital wards
3. There is no place for trial and error in the actual execution of the plan devised.

With regard to point 1)→1, for example, researcher-administered time studies (see 2.2.1.1. below) produce what are regarded as the most reliable data, but the outlay in terms of staffing and financial costs, from the pre-survey preparation stage to the results analysis, as well as the high burden on the clinical location concerned, make it difficult to carry out such studies with any great frequency, and the survey periods must also be kept short.

With regard to point 2)→2, where nursing care management matters such as appropriate staff allocation are concerned, inconsistencies in shift conditions will arise (there will be days when shifts have crowded schedules and days when they do not), so it will be necessary to obtain an over-all picture of tasks on the ward based on the evidence of frequent or long-term surveys. For the reason given above, however, time studies are restricted, in almost all cases, to short survey periods. The results obtained therefore provide an interpretation only of the period when the survey was conducted and are confined to the realm of factual description.

With regard to point 3)→3, having obtained an over-all picture of the tasks on the ward, the next step in nursing care management is to formulate a concrete plan that takes into consideration changes in working hours when there is a shortage of nursing staff or when there is an increase in the number of patients admitted. In practice, however, it is difficult to carry out the formulated plan in the actual ward environment because such plans are accompanied by risks and involve many ethical problems. This means that an investigation of a new method of work management is in fact impossible. This has been a major barrier.

Considering the above adverse factors, it would be effective, for the purposes of time-study based management of ward tasks, to establish a methodology of the following kind:

- Estimates of ward task times based on time study data
- Creation of a computer-based virtual ward environment using the estimated values
- Test experiment on a plan for work management using the virtual ward environment

http://dx.doi.org/10.5772/51014

The goal of this study is therefore the formulation of a methodology, based on data from a short-term time study, for estimating ward task times and for creating a virtual ward environment relating to job times.

2. Method

The procedure followed was:

1. Framing a plan for the creation of a virtual environment
2. Computation of basic data required for a virtual environment based on short-term research and long-term cumulative information
3. Construction of a procedure for the creation of a virtual ward environment
4. Trial experiment using the virtual ward environment

2.1. Framing a plan for the creation of a virtual environment

First of all, in order to establish a way of thinking about how to simulate an actual ward environment, we drew up a diagram showing what kinds of factors would have a bearing on the time devoted to nursing tasks (Fig. 1).

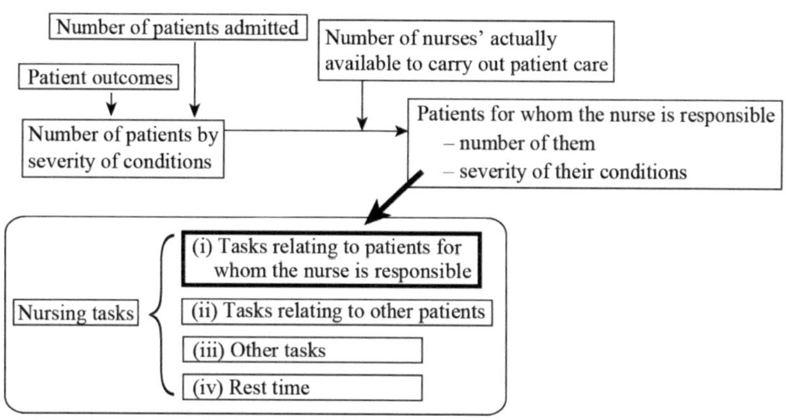

Figure 1. Constituent factors in nursing tasks.

We assumed that the tasks carried out by a given nurse during one shift would comprise (i) tasks relating to patients for whom the nurse is responsible, (ii) tasks relating to other patients, (iii) other tasks, such as those relating to the running of the ward, and (iv) rest time. Task times devoted to these four items would be interdependent and would vary, but we thought that 'task times devoted to patients for whom the nurse is responsible' would have particularly high priority, and would affect 'time devoted to other patients,' 'time devoted to other tasks' and 'rest time.' We also assumed, first, that the number of patients for whom a given nurse is responsible, and the severity of their conditions, would affect 'task times devoted to patients for whom the nurse is responsible'; second, that 'number of patients' in the nurse's charge and 'severity of their conditions' would be affected by 'number of patients by severity of condition' who were on the ward at a given time and 'number of nurses' actually available to carry out patient care; and third, that 'number of patients by intensity of nursing care' would be affected by 'patient outcomes' and 'number of patients admitted.

2.2. Computation of basic data required for a virtual environment based on short-term research and long-term cumulative information

2.2.1. Short-term research

2.2.1.1. Time study

A continuous 24-hour researcher-administered time study was conducted over a total of fifteen days during 1999 and 2000 in a gastrointestinal surgical ward in a university hospital. Of the various forms of time study techniques we adopted the researcher-administered method for the present study because on the basis of the characteristics of the ward studied, we judged that there were limits to the extent to which nurses on duty would themselves be able to keep a record of the content of the tasks in the intervals between the tasks they performed. The survey was conducted in relation to all three work shifts: 'night shift,' 'day shift' and 'evening shift.' The total number of nurses observed was 69 (Table 1).

	Year 1999	Year 2000
Period	Jul. 5th ~ Jul. 14th	Aug 28th ~ Sep. 2nd
Number of days	10 days	5 days
Ward studied	Gastrointestinal surgical ward in a university hospital	
Number of nurses	13 (total 46)	6 (total 23)

Table 1. Time study period and subjects.

The ward studied was a fifty-bed ward with a staff of 23 nurses, including the head nurse. The average number of staff actually on duty on weekdays was 8.6. The ward's nursing system combined a three-module organization, under which ward nursing staff were divided into three groups, A, B and C, and a 'primary nursing' model, under which the same nurse was responsible for a given patient throughout, from admission to discharge (Fig. 2). When the primary nurse was not on duty, a nurse from the same group took responsibility for the patient. Information was gathered during the period of the survey on both the nurses being surveyed and the patients for whom they were responsible.

After completion of the time study, the task content recorded was coded in accordance with a specially created system of task classification and entered into a database. The nursing task classification was based on the Public Health Nurse, Midwife and Nurse Law [1948]. The four principal categories were 'clinical nursing,' 'consulting support nursing,' 'other nursing,' and 'non-nursing tasks.' At the most detailed level, there were 92 headings altogether. The overall number of individual task action-units recorded was 46,775.

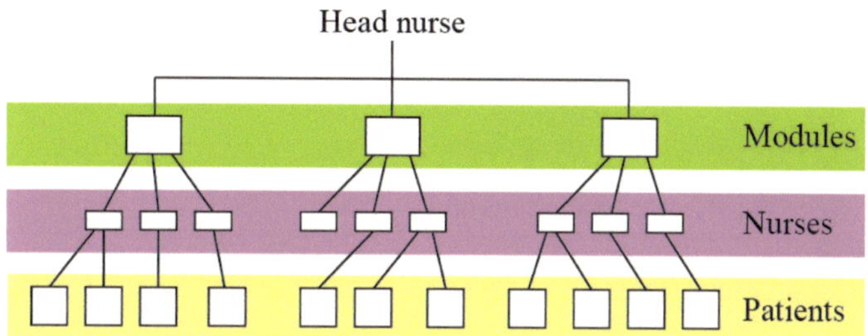

Figure 2. Module system and primary nursing model.

2.2.1.2. Patient condition information

Patient condition information for each patient on the ward was collected and recorded daily throughout the fifteen days of the time study period. 'Patient condition information' means information that indicates a hospital patient's condition, such as how many times in the course of the day vital signs are checked, whether an artificial respirator is in use, or whether there is any fever or bleeding. About 70 items are covered. Information collected during the day shift, at about 10 a.m., served as the base, and was incrementally updated for any patient who underwent an operation or other invasive procedure during the day shift and whose nursing intensity changed. The information recorded was entered into a database. Ultimately, the overall number of patient-shift units recorded was 2,015.

Nursing intensity, assessed daily by an experienced nurse, was included in patient condition information. Nursing intensity is a method of classifying patient severity from two points of view – 'level of observation' and 'freedom of life' – that was proposed in 1984 in a report by the Study Group on Nursing Systems set up by the Ministry of Health, Labor and Welfare (formerly the Ministry of Health and Welfare) (Table 2). In the process of the present study, it was suggested that patient severity observations collected on the ward being studied could be regarded as 'level of observation' for the purpose of assessing nursing intensity and these were used in carrying out our analysis.

By integrating the time study database and the patient condition information database on the basis of 'day of survey,' 'shift,' 'nurse ID' and 'patient ID,' we created a data set that made it possible to tell which nurse had spent how much time performing what tasks for patients in what condition. We assumed that among the task actions, subject patients would be available for nursing task classifications from 10101 to 301T1.

The names of nurses and patients included in the survey records, as well as any other items of information from which it would be possible to identify individuals, were all coded and only if this used for analysis after the information had been made secure.

Level of observation	A	Need continuous observation
	B	Need observation at regular (one to two hour) intervals
	C	Do not need regular observation
Freedom of life	I	Lie in bed at all times
	II	Be able to sit up in bed
	III	Be able to walk around the ward
	IV	No inconvenience in daily life

Table 2. Nursing intensity.

2.2.2. Long-term cumulative information

2.2.2.1. Information concerning patient outcomes

In order to understand over-all patterns of change in nursing intensity for the patients on the ward being studied, we obtained information from the HIS (Hospital Information System) under the headings 'date of admission,' 'date of discharge,' 'date of update ofnursing intensity,' and 'nursing intensity' covering the period from January 1, 2000, to December 31, 2000. This information was obtained in addition to the patient condition information gathered during the time study period.

'Pattern of change in nursing intensity' shows the outcome for a given patient. We defined it in terms of the number of days for which the patient was hospitalized and any changes in nursing intensity during that period. Pattern of change in nursing intensity varies according to individual factors, such as the disease from which the patient is suffering, surgical procedures undergone, and medical treatment. For example, patient J is in hospital for 3 days. On the first day nursing intensity is B, on the second day C, and again on the third day C. The pattern of change in nursing intensity for this patient is 'BCC.' Patient S is in hospital for four days. On the first two days nursing intensity is A, and on the remaining two days B. The pattern of change of nursing intensity for this patient is 'AABB.' It is no exaggeration to say that, except in the cases of patients where there is no clinical pathway variance, each individual patient exhibits a unique pattern of change in nursing intensity during the period of hospitalization.

2.3. Basic data

Basic data required for the creation of a virtual environment was calculated from a short-term survey and a long-term cumulative information survey.

2.3.1. Ward environment

On the basis of time study data and patient condition information, we found recorded statistical values relating to the number of patients admitted to the ward studied. The results were as follows. Average daily number of patients on the ward was 44.2, and the standard deviation (SD) was 2.3. The greatest number of patients on the ward at one time was 49, the smallest 42. The average number of patients for whom one nurse was responsible was 4.9. The largest number was 7, the smallest 3. A total of 281 patterns of change in nursing intensity was abstracted from the HIS information in relation to admissions to the ward in question in the year 2000.

2.3.2. *Task times by purpose*

From the data set obtained by integrating time study data and patient condition information, we calculated, for individual nurses on the day shift, time spent on 'patients for whom the nurse is responsible,' time spent on 'other patients,' time spent on 'other duties' and 'rest time.' Results showed that the greatest amount of task time was spent on 'patients for whom the nurse is responsible.' Next came 'other patients' and 'other duties,' almost the same amount of time being spent on each. Average rest time was less than the 60-minute rest period stipulated by law (Table 3).

	Patients for whom the nurse is responsible	Other patients	Other tasks	Rest time
Average time (minute)	323.0	92.5	104.6	49.0
SD (minute)	73.4	40.2	33.3	11.6
Max (minute)	440.8	162.6	197.2	64.2
Min (minute)	158.1	25.8	58.9	17.9

Table 3. Recorded statistical quantities for task times by purpose.

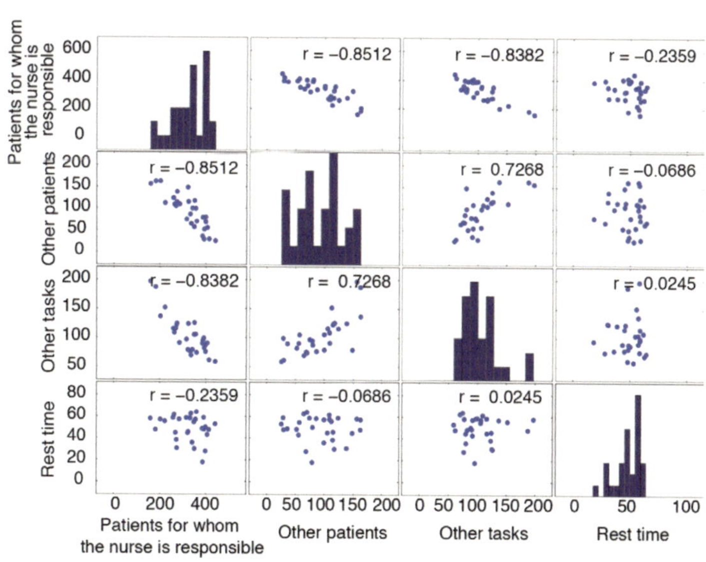

Figure 3. Correlations between task times by purpose.

Fig. 3 shows that there was a strong negative correlation between time spent on 'tasks relating to patients for whom the nurse is responsible' and time spent on 'tasks relating to other patients' and 'other tasks,' and that the correlation of 'rest time' with other task items was low. It appears at first glance that the correlation coefficient between 'tasks relating to other patients' and 'other tasks' is high at 0.727, but the partial correlation coefficient of the two is 0.019 and almost no direct correlation was observed. We were therefore able to judge that this was a spurious correlation influenced by 'tasks relating to patients for whom the nurse is responsible.' In other words, what this shows is that the relationship between the two is not such that when one increases the other decreases, but such that when time spent on 'patients for whom the nurse is responsible' increases, the two decrease together.

2.4. Construction of a virtual ward environment

In accordance with the plan formulated under 2.1, a virtual ward environment was created according to the following procedure:

1. Construction of a model for estimation of task time devoted to patients for whom the nurse is responsible.

   Construct a model to estimate the kinds of factors that influence care time devoted to a given patient.

2. Calculation of number of patients for whom one nurse is responsible and of care time

   Determine which patients a given nurse is responsible for and find the total task time spent by that nurse on patients for whom she is responsible.

3. Estimation of task time by purpose

   On the basis of the total task time devoted to 'patients for whom the nurse is responsible' calculated under 2., estimate time spent on 'patients for whom the nurse is not responsible,' 'other tasks,' and 'rest time,' all of which are correlated.

2.5. Test experiments in virtual ward environment

In the virtual environment we had created, we carried out the following test experiments and investigated the difference from actual data.

1. Estimation of number of patients on the ward by nursing intensity
2. Estimation of task times by purpose
3. Effect of increase or decrease in number of nurses on each task time

3. Results

3.1. Construction of a model for estimation of task time devoted to patients for whom nurse is responsible

Our 'model for estimation of task time devoted to patients for whom nurse is responsible' is a regression analysis model using 'care time devoted to a given patient for whom a given nurse is responsible' as the dependent variable. When formulating a plan for the creation of a virtual environment, we entered the factor 'nursing intensity' as an independent variable on the assumption that task time devoted to patients for whom a nurse is responsible would be affected by patient severity. Bearing in mind that changes in shift time and in the number of nurses actually on duty on a shift would also have a great effect on care time devoted to patients, we included the factor 'shift' as well.

The subject of analysis consisted of records, extracted from the data set created by integrating time study data and patient condition information, which revealed responsibility relationships between nurses and patients. The data extracted related to a total of 425 patients (a total of 57 nurses on 57 shifts).

3.1.1. Multilevel analysis

A multiple regression analysis model is generally formulated as

$$y = \beta_0 + \beta_1 x_1 + \cdots + \beta_p x_p + \varepsilon \tag{1}$$

where y is a dependent variable, there are p independent variables $\{x_k\}$ that have fixed effects and ε is margin of error. As opposed to this, Multilevel Analysis (Jones, 1991; Goldstein, 2003) is a method of estimating parameters (coefficients) in which, by assuming random effects resulting from a given phenomenon j, it is possible to take into account internal correlations between data with the same value for j in relation to the correlation $\{\beta_k\}$ between an intercept β_0 in (1) and independent variables.

Because the time study survey periods were continuous, the same patients were included in different shifts in the data set relating to 425 patients subject to analysis. This means that there were elements that affected the care time, which is a variable dependent on patient identity (i.e., there were internal correlations in the data), although it was difficult to treat these elements as regular fixed effects, as in the case of the patient's bodily strength or personality.

In order to estimate parameters having variable effects that explained these internal correlations, we constructed, for the purposes of this study, a model for the estimation of task time devoted to patients for whom the nurse was responsible using Multilevel Analysis, introducing randomness for each 'patient' with respect to the intercept.

3.1.2. Optimal model

Rather than a model in which the actual care times are regressed in their original dimensions, we judged that the optimal model was one in which logistic conversion was performed with regard to the dependent variable.

Our reasons were as follows.

Because it is a mathematical model for explaining task times, when the estimated expected value y is negative, there is a marked lack of conformance of the times. For this reason, it is necessary to perform logarithmic conversion such that the time value that is the dependent variable does not appear as a negative value.

In the later creation of the virtual ward environment, we used this model for estimation of task time devoted to 'patients for whom the nurse is responsible,' which used normal random numbers (see 3.2.4. below). Because the distribution of the raw data values (here, the distribution of the raw care times) was reproduced using normal random numbers, it was necessary at the point where random number values were generated to convert the raw data so that it showed a data distribution close to a normal distribution (see 3.3.1. for details) (Fig. 4).

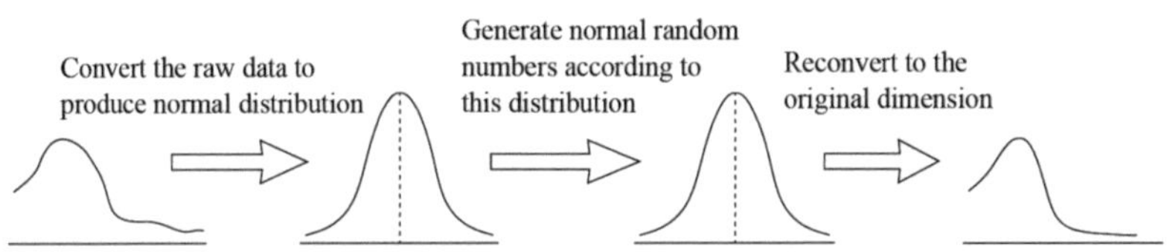

Figure 4. Conversions for the purpose of recreating actuality using normal random numbers.

We found parameters for a logistic conversion that would give real upper and lower limits by minimizing AIC (Akaike's Information Criterion) after performing logistic conversion. The data set used for this analysis included some extremely small time values, so we fixed the lower limit at zero. AIC for the case where the upper limit was a was calculated as follows:

$$AIC = n\log\hat{\sigma}^2 - 2n\log a + 2\sum_{i=1}^{n}\log\left\{y_i(a-y_i)\right\} + 2(p+1) \tag{2}$$

Here, $\hat{\sigma}^2$ is a maximum likelihood estimator, y_i are individual time values, n is a sample number, and p is an estimated parameter number.

This means that the smaller the AIC value the closer to a normal distribution; we used MLwiN ver. 1.1 for model analysis.

The constant a that ultimately produced the smallest AIC was 300, and we used the conversion method

$$\log[y/(300-y)] \tag{3}$$

The result was that a data conversion close to normal distribution became possible, as seen in Fig. 5.

$$\begin{aligned}\log[y_{ij}/(300-y_{ij})] = \beta_{0ij} + \beta_{NA}N_{ij}^{A} + \beta_{NB}N_{ij}^{B} + \\ \beta_{NC}N_{ij}^{C} + \beta_{DA}D_{ij}^{A} + \beta_{DB}D_{ij}^{B} + \beta_{DC}D_{ij}^{C} + \beta_{EA}E_{ij}^{A} + \beta_{EB}E_{ij}^{B}\end{aligned} \tag{4}$$

http://dx.doi.org/10.5772/51014

	β_0	β_{NA}	β_{NB}	β_{NC}	β_{DA}	β_{DB}	β_{DC}	β_{BA}	β_{BB}
coefficient	-3.834	1.653	0.704	-0.312	2.695	1.945	1.207	1.814	1.044
SE	0.245	0.296	0.260	0.256	0.289	0.253	0.245	0.301	0.266

$u_j \sim N(0,\ 0.674) \qquad \beta_{0ij} = \beta_0 + u_j + e_{ij}$

$e_{ij} \sim N(0,\ 0.794)$

With regard to the method of entering independent variables, we found as a result of repeated investigation that a model using 3x3 items in which 'shift' and 'nursing intensity' were confounded, as in 'night shift, nursing intensity A,' was optimal (equation 0.4→4). This numerical formula is a model for the estimation of nursing time devoted to one patient by the nurse responsible. Here, y_{ij} are i th care times on nursing occasions for the j th patient, N, D, and E are respectively 'night shift,' 'day shift' and 'evening shift,' and superscript A, B, and C show nursing intensity. In this model, the value taken by a given independent variable is dichotomous, either (1) or (0), as, for example, in 'night shift nursing intensity is A (1)' or 'is not A (0),' so that when they are looked at as a whole, they form a categorical variable group in which if 'is (1)' appears with respect to an independent variable in a particular place, any other independent variables are necessarily 'is not (0).' For this reason, the independent variable 'evening shift, nursing intensity C' becomes the intercept itself, and in the case of 'day shift is nursing intensity A (1),' the parameter 'day shift, nursing intensity A' added to the intercept becomes the care time prescribed for 'day shift, nursing intensity A'. β_{0ij} is the intercept (evening shift, nursing intensity C), u is variability depending on the patient, and e_{ij} is margin of error (chance variability).

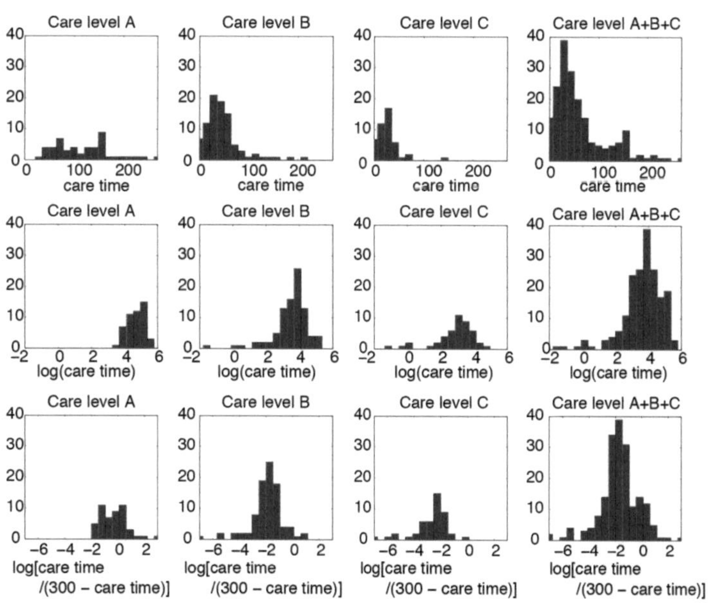

Figure 5. Data distributions after conversions.

According to the results of estimation using this model, given a patient with 'day shift, nursing intensity A,' adding the parameter value 2.695 of 'day shift, nursing intensity A' to the intercept -3.834, then adding variability due to the individual patient and margin of error, gives the care time for this patient. Returning to the time dimension by using the reverse logistic conversion shows it to be about 72.8 minutes. In the same way, in the case of 'day shift, nursing intensity B' the time is about 39.4 minutes, and in the case of 'day shift, nursing intensity C' about 20 minutes.

3.2. Estimation of number of patients for whom one nurse is responsible, and care times

Next, we determined the number of patients for whom one nurse was responsible and estimated the total time spent on those patients. At this point we embarked on the construction of an algorithm using a Monte Carlo Simulation.

A Monte Carlo Simulation is a method of obtaining approximate solutions to problems when simulating the processes of chance phenomena by carrying out numerical value calculations using random numbers. In this study, we used normal random numbers and created algorithms for them using MATLABR2012a. This simulation was conducted with respect to the day shift.

3.2.1. Bed matrix

We went through the process of recreating the actual bed occupancy status, which changes daily as a result of the admission and discharge of patients.

Since the ward studied was a 50-bed ward, we created a matrix for use in the simulation (hereafter 'bed matrix') consisting of vertical columns of 50 cells representing the beds, and on the horizontal time axis (representing days elapsed) we used rows containing enough cells to cover a long time period (for reasons explained later, we used rows of 1,000 cells in this study). Each cell in the bed matrix represents one bed-day.

3.2.2. Determination of number of patients on ward

By randomly determining the daily number of patients on the ward from the average number of patients on the ward already calculated and its standard deviation, we recreated the changes in the actual number of patients on the ward. In the case of Fig. 6, for example, the number of patients on the ward over a seven-day period is randomly divided up and shaded cells show patients on the ward.

3.2.3. Determination of patients on ward

Having determined the number of patients on the ward each day, we simulated the state of affairs relating to patients on the ward whose condition underwent change by inserting the patterns of change in nursing intensity by number of patients on the ward. For this purpose we apportioned patterns randomly chosen from among the total of 281 patterns of change in nursing intensity found under 2.3.1. At this time, the patients on the ward were present for the number of days shown by the patterns of change. The patterns were inserted in column direction.

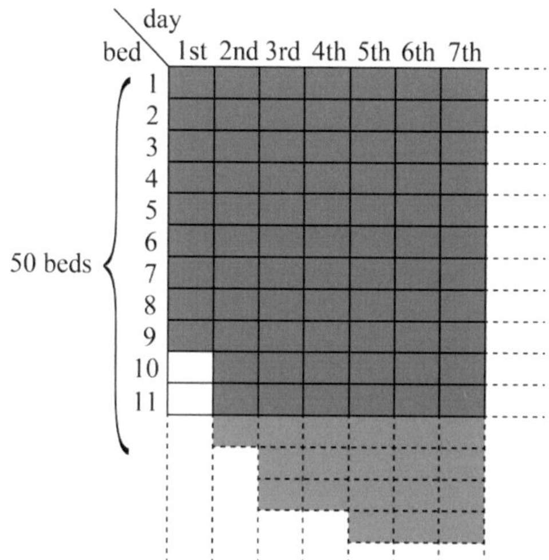

Figure 6. Determination of number of patients on ward.

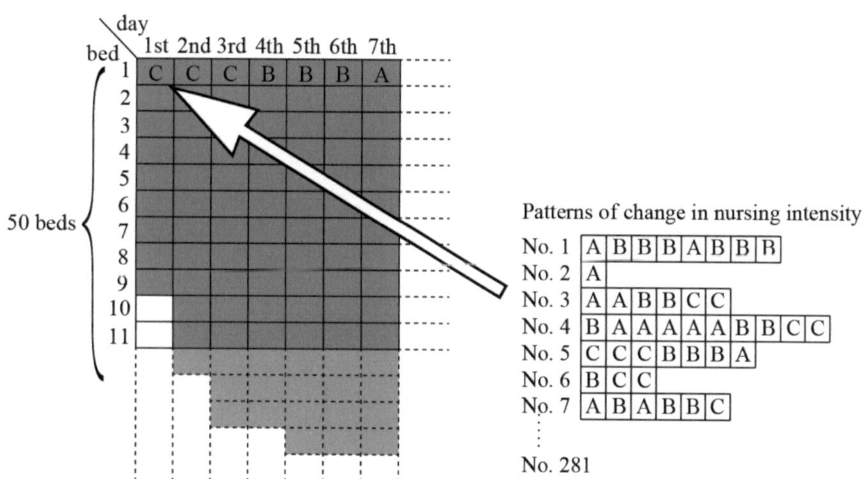

Figure 7. Layout of patterns of change in nursing intensity.

For example, in Fig. 7, pattern No. 5 was chosen and 'CCCBBBA' was inserted horizontally, one letter per cell, starting in bed number 1 on day number 1. At the beginning of the simulation there were no patients at all, and patterns of nursing intensity were allocated for the number of allocated patients on the ward. The pattern of nursing intensity differed depending on the number of days for which a patient was on the ward, so as days elapsed, patients began to be discharged. In cases where the total number of patients given by change in patterns of nursing intensity for a given day fell below the specified minimum number of patients for the ward, we apportioned new patients randomly from the patterns of change in nursing intensity. At this point, we had reached the stage where the set number of days per patient and patients on the ward were shown by nursing intensity in the bed matrix.

3.2.4. Calculation of care time for each patient

On the basis of this nursing intensity, we calculated the care time believed necessary using the previously constructed model for estimating task time devoted to patients for whom the nurse is responsible. From equation (4) we saw that care time is not simply a function of nursing intensity but is the sum of (i) a quantity depending on nursing intensity, (ii) variability depending on the individual patient, and (iii) other chance variability. The average of each of the latter two items was 0, and they were the parts that varied according to a normal distribution with certain variances. For the calculation of care time, first we took as the basis an estimated value for care time corresponding to nursing intensity, then generated a normal random number with a certain estimated variance and an average of 0 as the common value for all the days the patient spent in hospital and added that number. We then added a normal random number with another estimated variance and an average of 0 as chance variability.

In Fig. 8, the right-hand side is an example of the bed matrix when there are patients on the ward. The figure shows the method of calculating care time for a given patient *j*, represented by the lightly shaded cells. This patient is on the ward for three days. On the first day, nursing intensity for this patient is B. On the second day it is C and on the third day also C, at which point the patient is discharged. Care time on the first day has the coefficient for day shift, nursing intensity B, of '–3.834+1.945.' Next, we take the value 0.21, randomly generated from the normal distribution average 0, variance 0.674, as the individual variability for patient *j*. The care necessary for this day has a total of –1.23, including the randomly generated value 0.45, generated from the normal distribution with average 0 and variance 0.794. We now perform reverse conversion of the logistic conversion previously performed and express the result in the time dimension: 68.1 minutes. Next, the care time for the second day has a total of –1.81, including the coefficient for day shift nursing intensity C, '–3.834+1.207,' the variable effect depending on patient *j* 0.21, and the randomly determined value 0.6. The care time ultimately obtained is calculated as 42.1 minutes. The variable effect depending on patient *j* has the same value from when patient *j* is admitted up to the time the patient is discharged. For another patient, *k*, a value for *k* is allotted which is also the same from admission to discharge. Further, the required care time on a given day changes at random daily with regard to every patient, and is allotted randomly each day. Consequently, on the third day, in spite of the fact that nursing intensity for the same patient *j* is the same, care time ultimately differs from that on the second day. By means of the above operations, a bed matrix of the kind shown in Fig. 9 is created, showing care time devoted to each patient for whom a given nurse is responsible.

http://dx.doi.org/10.5772/51014

3.2.5. Assignment of patients to nurses and total task times devoted by nurses to patients for whom they are responsible

On the basis of the statistical values already found for numbers of patients for whom nurses are responsible, we simulated the allocation of responsibility for these ward patients to individual nurses. The following two points suggested themselves as factors in determining the patients for whom nurses are responsible in the actual ward environment:

1. Number of patients for whom the nurse is responsible
2. Severity of the conditions of those patients

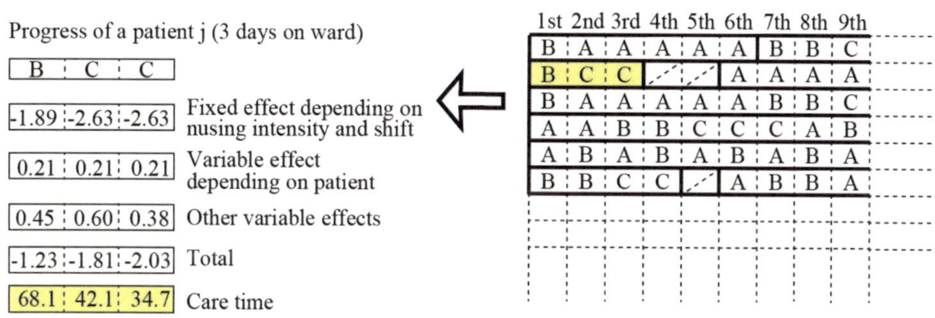

Figure 8. Method of calculating care time for each patient.

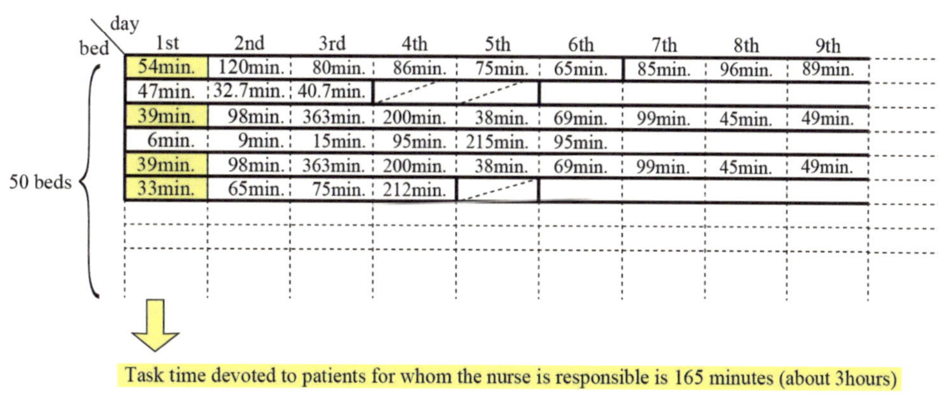

Figure 9. Task times devoted to patients for whom nurse is responsible.

When the number of patients for whom a given nurse is responsible is large, or when they include patients whose condition is very severe, no further patients can be assigned to that nurse, and the quantity of tasks is distributed so that, for example, new patients are apportioned among other nurses with a relatively small number of patients in their charge or nurses whose patients have relatively mild conditions. Consequently, in the virtual environment, first, at the point where patients were randomly admitted to the ward, we totaled the number of patients for whom each nurse was responsible and specified that if the number was 0, priority would be given to the assignment of patients to that nurse. We also controlled assignment of patients so that, as far as possible, each nurse was responsible for no fewer than 4 and no more than 7 patients. In addition, we carried out weighting such that extra patient responsibility was first given to nurses who were devoting a relatively small amount of task time to the patients for whom they had already been assigned responsibility.

In this way, we determined which patients a given nurse was responsible for. The shaded cells in the example shown in Fig. 9 show the task times devoted by one nurse to the patients in her charge. The total, 165 minutes, is the 'task time devoted to patients' by that nurse. At this stage, we have created a virtual simulation of the approximate amount of time a nurse devotes in reality to all the patients for whom she is responsible.

3.3. Estimation of task time by purpose

Next, on the basis of 'care time devoted to all patients for whom the nurse is responsible' by a single nurse found in 3.2.5, we randomly generated 'task time devoted to other patients,' 'time devoted to other tasks' and 'rest time' for the day shift and proceeded to simulate actual task times by purpose. As mentioned in 3.1.2, it is necessary to bear the following points in mind when carrying out these simulations.

1. It is a prerequisite that the random numbers generated should follow a normal distribution

In this study we have employed a Monte Carlo simulation using normal random numbers, and it is a prerequisite that the distribution for the generation of random numbers should be a normal distribution.

2. Negative values are to be avoided among randomly generated values

Since the units in the results obtained are times, task times that have negative values are not realistic and will prevent the simulation results from conforming to reality.

3. Covariance among the four task times by purpose is to be maintained

The generation of random values in which covariance among the variates is not taken into consideration makes it impossible to recreate the characteristic feature that they vary in relation to one another.

Bearing these points in mind, we carried out the following operations.

3.3.1. Logistic conversion

As Fig. 3 shows, a certain amount of skew with regard to all four of the items 'tasks performed for patients for whom the nurse is responsible,' 'tasks performed for other patients,' 'other tasks,' and 'rest time' and a degree of unevenness (probably attributable to sampling limitations) were observed. It is not possible to recreate the distribution exhibited by these original data even if one generates normal random numbers using only the average values and variance of the original data. In order to recreate the distribution of the original data using normal random numbers, it is necessary to think of a conversion in which a distribution based on the conversion of the original is as close as possible to a normal distribution and, after having generated random numbers that have the post-conversion average and variance, it is then necessary to perform reverse conversion to obtain a value. At the same time, it is necessary to ensure that the randomly created values do not have a negative value. For these reasons, we decided in this study to perform the following logistic conversion with respect to task times by purpose y in order to solve problems 1), 2)→ 1 ,2 above.

$$\log[(y-b)/(a-y)] \tag{5}$$

We used AIC (Akaike's Information Criteria) to evaluate whether distribution of the post-conversion values was close to a normal distribution. We looked for an upper limit value a and a lower limit value b that would minimize AIC values. AIC were calculated by means of the following expression.

$$\mathrm{AIC}=n\log\hat{\sigma}^2-2n\log(a-b)+2\sum_{i=1}^{n}\log\{(y_i-b)(a-y_i)\}+2(p+2) \tag{6}$$

As in formula (2), $\hat{\sigma}^2$ is a maximum likelihood estimator, y_i are individual time values, n is a sample number and p is an estimated parameter number.

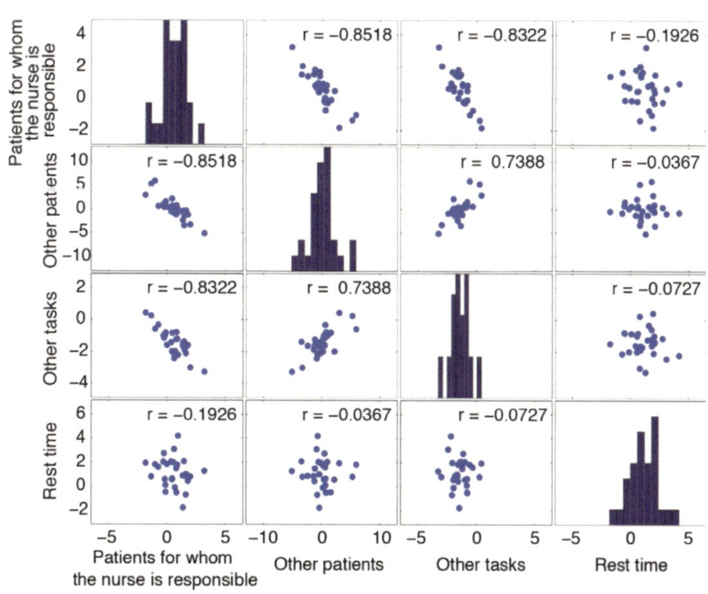

Figure 10. Conversion data plots.

The upper limit *a* and lower limit *b* for each task time by purpose that minimized AIC are as shown in Table 4.

It will be seen from scrutiny of the post-conversion data plots (Fig. 10) that in each of the variables, data distribution is closer to a normal distribution than before conversion (Fig. 3).

	a	b
Tasks relating to patients for whom the nurse is responsible	454	111
Tasks relating to other patients	163	25
Other tasks	295	50
Rest time	65	10

Table 4. Upper and lower limits of conversion functions.

3.3.2. Simulation of task times by purpose using covariance

Using the above conversion data, we generated random numbers that maintained covariance among the 4 variables (the third point to be borne in mind). Here, *X* is 'tasks performed for patients for whom the nurse is responsible,' *Y* is 'tasks performed for other patients,' *Z* is 'other tasks,' and *W* is 'rest.' In this study, we constructed the simulation algorithms on the basis of the hypothesis that 'tasks performed for patients for whom the nurse is responsible' would exert an influence on the allocation of task times to other tasks, and therefore designed the model so that *X* would exert an influence on *Y*, *Z*, and *W*.

If the equation

$$\begin{aligned} Y &= \alpha + \beta X + \varepsilon \\ \varepsilon &\sim N(0, \sigma^2) \end{aligned} \tag{7}$$

is used when generating *Y* with a given covariance, expected value E(*Y*), variance Var(*Y*) and covariance Cov(*X*, *Y*) become

$$\begin{aligned} \mathrm{E}(Y) &= \alpha + \beta E(X) \\ \mathrm{Var}(Y) &= \beta^2 \mathrm{Var}(X) + \sigma^2 \\ \mathrm{Cov}(X, Y) &= \beta \mathrm{Var}(X) \end{aligned} \tag{8}$$

and the unknown quantities α, β, σ^2 are found by means of

$$\begin{aligned} \beta &= \mathrm{Cov}(X, Y) / \mathrm{Var}(X) \\ \alpha &= E(Y) - \beta E(X) \\ \sigma^2 &= \mathrm{Var}(Y) - \beta^2 \mathrm{Var}(X) \end{aligned} \tag{9}$$

If coefficient values with regard to X are calculated in the same way for Z and W, with a given covariance, the result is

$$\begin{aligned} Y &= \alpha_1 + \beta_1 X + \varepsilon_1 \\ Z &= \alpha_2 + \beta_2 X + \varepsilon_2 \\ W &= \alpha_3 + \beta_3 X + \varepsilon_3 \end{aligned} \tag{10}$$

In this way, it is possible to maintain covariance between (X, Y), (X, Z), and (X, W). That is to say, it is possible to recreate changes in Y, Z, and W that occur when X changes, but because $\varepsilon_1, \varepsilon_2, \varepsilon_3$ are independent normal random numbers, covariance between (X, Y), (X, Z), (X, W) is 0, and it is not possible to recreate changes based on the residual in 'other tasks' and 'rest' that occur when 'tasks performed for other patients' changes. So in order to maintain covariance between$\varepsilon_1, \varepsilon_2, \varepsilon_3$ we decided to find the covariance structure of $(\varepsilon_1, \varepsilon_2, \varepsilon_3)$ by means of the equations

$$\begin{aligned} \varepsilon_1 &= Y - (\alpha_1 + \beta_1 X) \\ \varepsilon_2 &= Z - (\alpha_2 + \beta_2 X) \\ \varepsilon_3 &= W - (\alpha_3 + \beta_3 X) \end{aligned} \tag{11}$$

and generate 3-dimensional normal random numbers with this covariance.

Substituting the various coefficients calculated as a result of the above into formula (10) gives the result

$$\begin{aligned} Y &= 1.04 - 1.77X + \varepsilon_1 \\ Z &= -1.04 - 0.64X + \varepsilon_2 \\ W &= 1.26 - 0.22X + \varepsilon_3 \end{aligned} \tag{12}$$

Covariance structure of $(\varepsilon_1, \varepsilon_2, \varepsilon_3)$ is shown in Table 5.

	ε_1	ε_2	ε_3
ε_1	1.40	0.06	-0.56
ε_2	0.06	0.21	-0.24
ε_3	-0.56	-0.24	1.49

Table 5. Covariance structure of residuals.

Using residuals with these regression coefficients and covariances, we generated random numbers. Fig. 11 shows on the same plots the values obtained after logistic conversion of the original data (red dots) and the random numbers generated (blue dots). It can be seen that they have almost identical distributions. This shows that it is possible to generate random numbers that maintain the correlation structure between the variates (covariance).

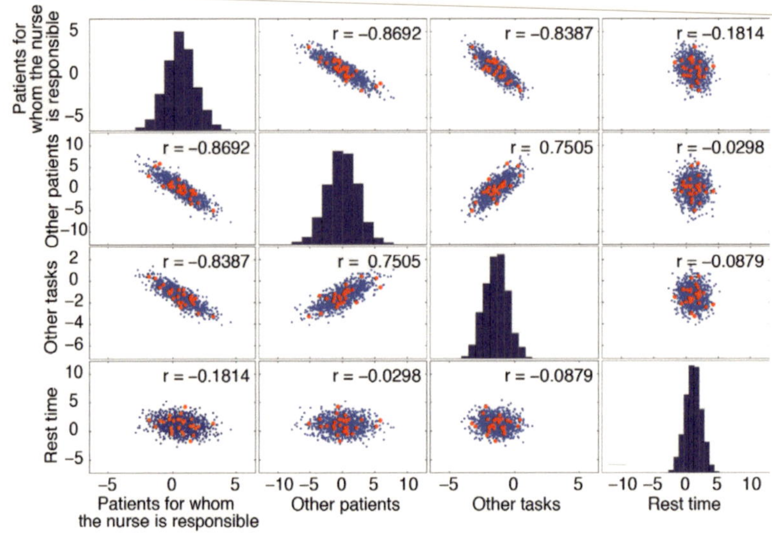

Figure 11. Random number values and logistic conversion values.

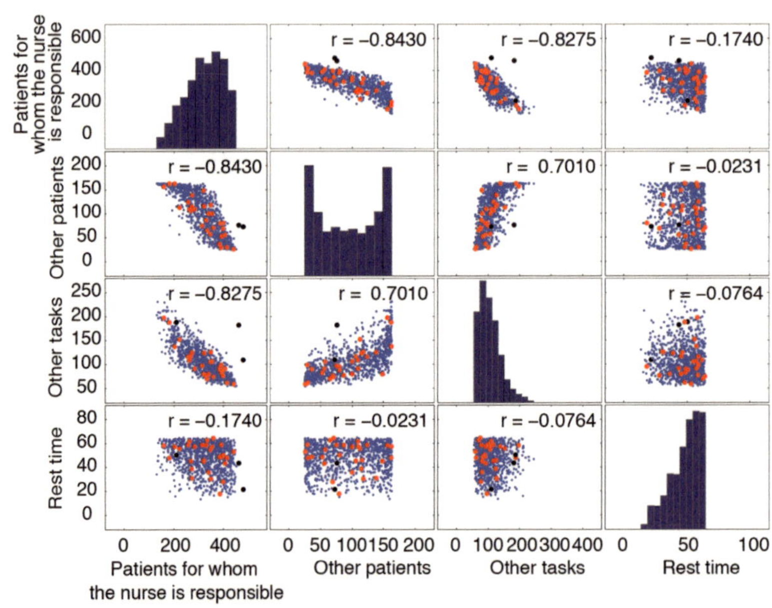

Figure 12. Time dimensions and random number values.

http://dx.doi.org/10.5772/51014

Fig. 12 shows together the original data (red dots) and the values obtained after performing reverse conversion on the logistic conversions of the random numbers generated (blue dots). It can be seen that the distribution of the original data relating to time dimensions has been almost exactly recreated. The black dots represent what we judged to be anomalies in the original data. These data relate to anomalous tasks, such as receiving training or attending meetings, that were performed in the afternoons, with only the mornings being spent on ward duties. We therefore decided to exclude them from the analysis.

Following the above procedure, we randomly generated individual task times while maintaining associations between 'tasks performed for patients for whom the nurse is responsible,' 'tasks performed for other patients,' 'other tasks,' and 'rest.' At this point, we had completed construction of a virtual ward environment for the purpose of simulating actual 'time devoted to tasks performed for patients for whom the nurse is responsible,' 'time devoted to tasks performed for other patients,' 'time devoted to other tasks,' and 'rest time' for one nurse, and for conducting test experiments.

3.4. Test experiments in the virtual ward environment

Using the virtual ward environment we had constructed, we simulated long-term ward task times. On the first day of simulation the situation was that all patients were admitted to the ward at once, so none would be discharged for some time. As days passed in the simulation, gradually some patients began to be discharged. We disregarded simulation results obtained up to the point where it seemed that a stable situation had eventually been reached, with a balance between admissions and discharges. From that point, we specified 1,000 days of simulation. For the purposes of the simulation, we also specified that from the point of view of the work system, every day was a weekday.

3.4.1. Changes in patient numbers by nursing intensity

The result of the simulation was as follows: the total number of patients was 44,846; totals by nursing intensity were: A=11,193 (25.0%), B=26,469 (59.0%), and C=7,184 (16.0%). The largest cohort of patients comprised those subject to nursing intensity B, the next largest those subject to nursing intensity A, and the smallest those subject to nursing intensity C. Unsurprisingly, this trend reflected almost exactly the trend in the 281 nursing intensity patterns we had established, where the frequency of nursing intensity A was 3,287 (24.2%), that of B 8,010 (59.1%), and that of C 2,265 (16.7%).

Fig. 13 is a graph showing changes in number of patients by nursing intensity. The vertical axis shows number of patients and the horizontal axis days elapsed. The upper panel is a graph showing nursing intensity. The daily number of patients at nursing intensity C, the lowest level of severity, is smallest, and the number at B, the intermediate level, is highest. The lower panel shows cumulative totals by nursing intensity. It will be seen, first, that almost all patients on the ward are accounted for by nursing intensity A and B, and, second, that once the number of patients has risen, it remains for some time at the higher level.

3.4.2. Task times devoted to patients for whom the nurse is responsible from the point of view of nursing intensity

The quantity of care time per patient necessary when patients for whom the nurse was responsible were at nursing intensity A was on average 93.5 minutes. For patients on nursing intensity B the average time was 57.1 minutes, and for those on nursing intensity C the average time was 31.6 minutes.

3.4.3. Changes in task times by purpose for the whole ward

The upper panel in Fig. 14 shows changes in task times by purpose for the ward as a whole. The horizontal axis shows number of days elapsed and the vertical axis shows times. 'Task times devoted to patients for whom the nurse is responsible' show large fluctuations, while 'rest times' display nowhere near as large a range of variation. Further, it can be seen that when 'task times devoted to patients for whom the nurse is responsible' decrease, 'task times devoted to other patients' and 'times devoted to other tasks' increase; and when 'task times devoted to patients for whom the nurse is responsible' increase, 'task times devoted to

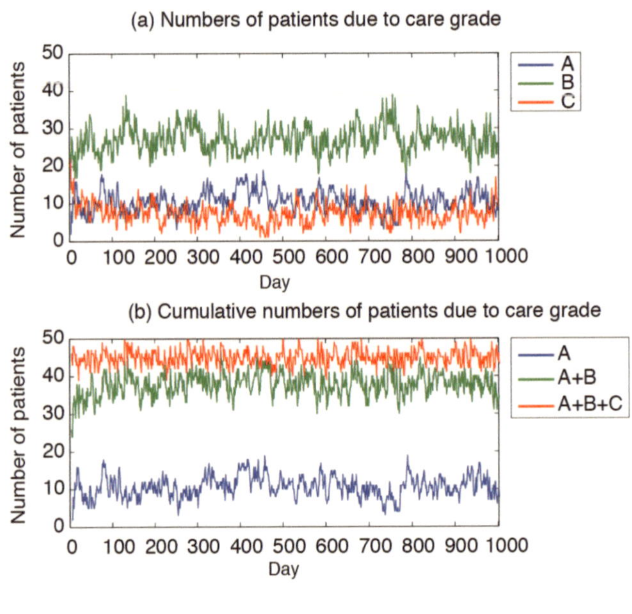

Figure 13. Changes in patient numbers by nursing intensity.

other patients' and 'times devoted to other tasks' decrease.

The lower panel in Fig. 14 shows cumulative totals of task times by purpose. In spite of the fact that 'task times devoted to patients for whom the nurse is responsible' and 'task times devoted to other patients' fluctuate widely, total task times as a whole are kept to an almost uniform level.

http://dx.doi.org/10.5772/51014

3.4.4. Changes in task times by purpose

We simulated changes in task times by purpose for an individual nurse when the number of nurses on a single day shift was increased gradually from 8 to 15. Assuming that the number of nurses actually on duty on a single day shift is 8, a 1,000 day simulation is equivalent to 8,000 nurse-shifts; assuming that the number is 9, a 1,000 day simulation is equivalent to 9,000 nurse-shifts, and so on. Figures 15-18 show the distribution of the number of patients for whom nurses are responsible when the total task times for the entire ward are shared by 8 to 15 nurses, and the frequency distribution of task times per nurse in each of those cases (Horizontal axis: minutes. Vertical axis: number of persons).

Let us look first at the situation where the number of nurses specified is lowest. Almost every nurse is responsible for between 5 and 7 patients. The largest number of nurses has overall task times of between 560 minutes (9.3 hours) and 570 minutes (9.5 hours). The average time for the whole group is 530 minutes. It can be seen that there are some nurses whose overall task time exceeds 10 hours (over 600 minutes). Next, with regard to 'patients

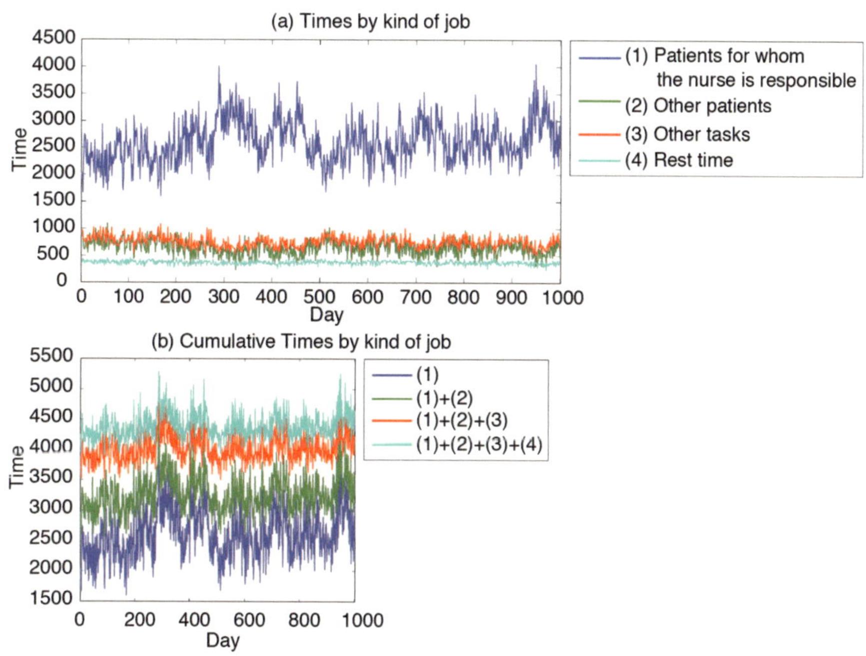

Figure 14. Changes in task times by purpose.

for whom the nurse is responsible,' the largest number of nurses have times corresponding to the median of 312 minutes, or about 5 hours. Time spent on 'tasks performed for other patients' is about 30 minutes, and the number of nurses who spend about 60 minutes on 'other tasks' stands out. With regard to 'rest time,' it will be seen that almost no nurses were able to take the 60 minutes of rest prescribed by law.

As the number of nurses on duty progressively increases, the number of patients for whom each nurse is responsible gradually decreases, until a situation is reached in which some nurses are responsible for 0 patients, and where the ward's nurse requirement can be said to be satisfied.

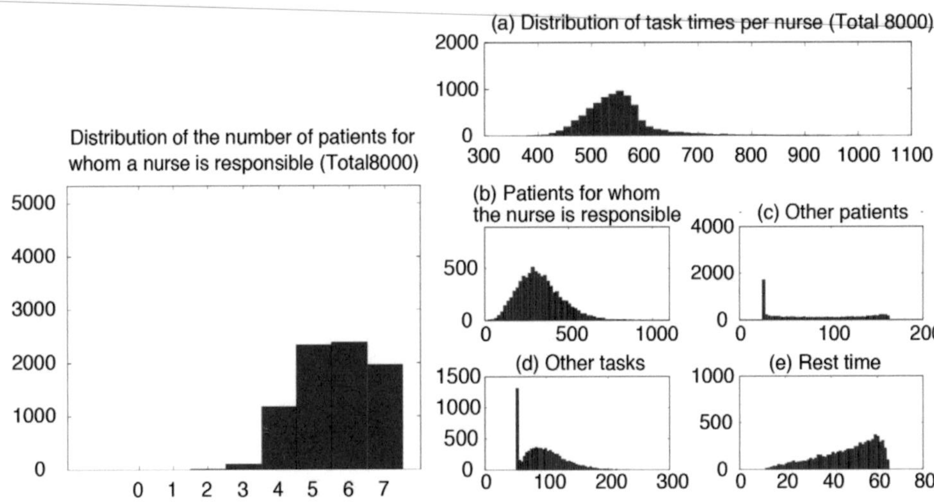

Figure 15. Tasks times when number of nurses is 8.

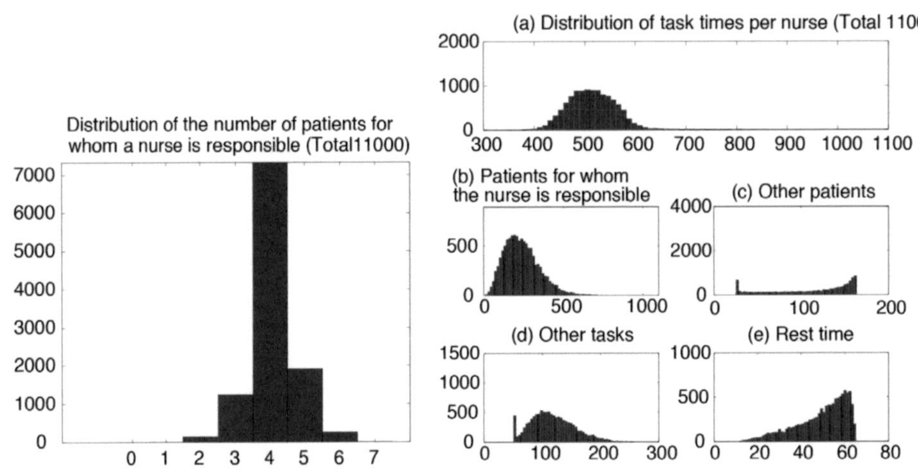

Figure 16. Tasks times when number of nurses is 11.

In addition, while time spent on 'tasks performed for patients for whom the nurse is responsible' decreases along with this variation in the number of patients for whom a nurse is responsible, more nurses are able to increase the time they spend on 'task times devoted to other patients' and 'time spent on other tasks,' while the number able to take a rest period approaching 60 minutes will be seen to have increased.

http://dx.doi.org/10.5772/51014

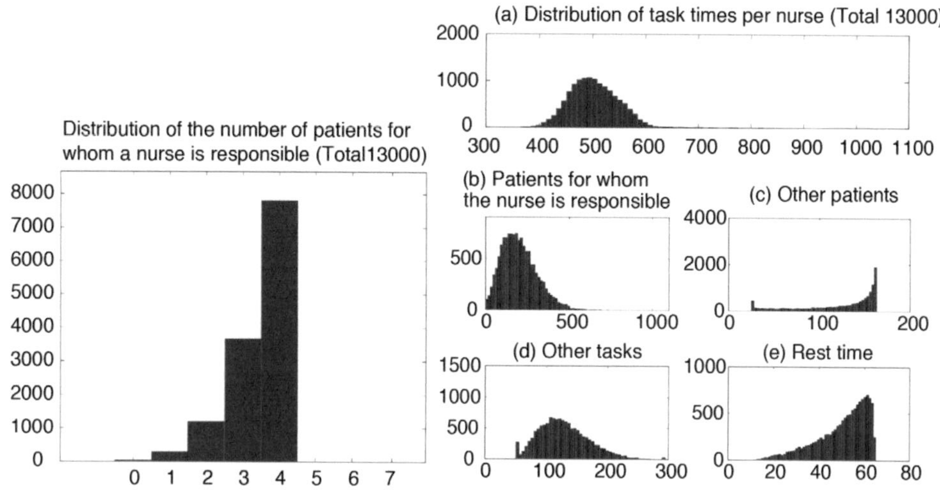

Figure 17. Tasks times when number of nurses is 13.

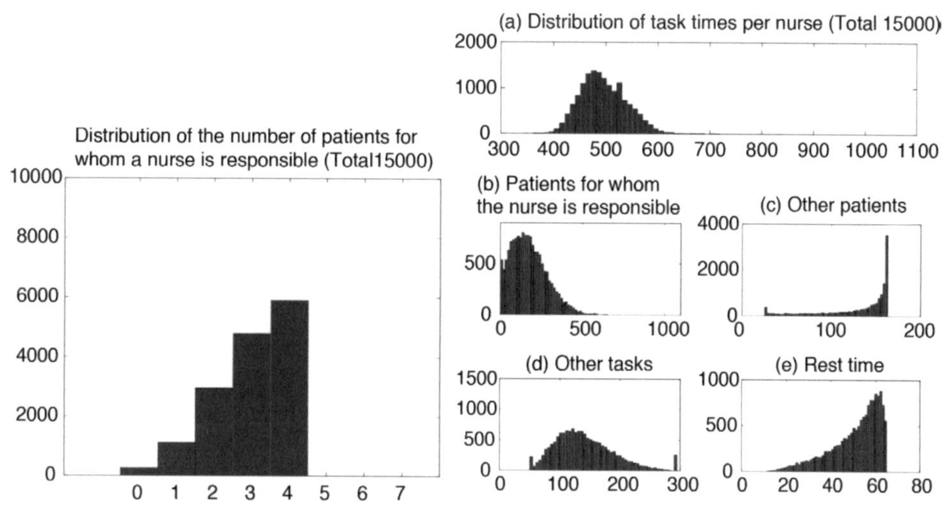

Figure 18. Tasks times when number of nurses is 15.

4. Observations

We carried out an evaluation of whether the simulation algorithms we constructed might be incompatible with reality.

4.1. Changes in numbers of patients by nursing intensity

We were able to judge whether the cohort of patients on the ward reflected the real-world situation, in which patients still requiring assistance are in a majority. The reasons are as follows.

The ward studied was a surgical ward, so for almost all patients the period immediately following surgery or related tests was when their condition was at its severest. After a few days they would emerge from the acute stage (when nursing intensity was A) and enter a period during which they received intravenous drugs or other active treatments as their wounds followed the healing process (the period of nursing intensity B). This follow-up period was the longest. As soon as the outlook was such that the patient could be sent home or return to work (the period of nursing intensity C), discharge followed within 1 to 2 days. In our simulation results also, almost all the patients on the ward were at nursing intensity A or B.

In addition, it seemed that not only nurses but also all medical professionals agreed that they had a sense that on occasion, after the number of patients in a severe condition increased, that state of affairs would continue for some time, and then the patients would all recover at once.

4.2. Task times devoted to patients for whom the nurse is responsible, by nursing intensity

It is, of course, entirely natural that care time required increases with severity of nursing intensity. The results we obtained conformed to this observation and thus seemed to reflect reality.

4.3. Changes in task time by purpose for the whole ward

There are some tasks that need to be performed when spare time becomes available, but, because there is a fixed limit on task time, tasks are in fact omitted. Our simulation appeared to reflect this reality. The reasons are as follows.

An increase in the amount of care time devoted to the patients for whom a nurse is responsible means that the quantity of care, in the form of treatment and observation of the patient, is greater. But on closer examination it appears that the number of drugs prescribed increases, many tests have to be carried out, extra treatments and prescriptions are added, tasks such as changing dressings increase in number, or the procedures involved become more complicated. This affects the usage quantities of documents, medicines, and other materials managed by the ward. The result is that management task time also expands. In theory, therefore, it seems that if 'task time devoted to patients for whom the nurse is responsible' increases, 'time devoted to other tasks' that have no direct connection with patients should also increase, and as a consequence overall task time (shift time) ought to increase. The results of our simulation show, however, that when 'task time devoted to patients for whom the nurse is responsible' increases 'task time devoted to other tasks' is reduced and overall task time does not increase very much. No extension of time devoted to 'other tasks' or of overall task time was observed.

4.4. Work time per nurse

The 9-hour work shift prescribed by law comprises 8 hours of working time and 1 hour of rest time. There was no marked deviation from this time in our simulation results.

4.5. Changes in task time by purpose

When task time available for completion of 'tasks performed for patients for whom the nurse is responsible' is insufficient, the nurse is unable to carry out 'tasks for other patients' and 'other tasks.' But when the number of nurses increases and adequate care time can be devoted to patients for whom a nurse is responsible, time can be found to spend on aspects of nursing care such as tasks performed for 'other patients' and 'other tasks' that have had to be neglected before the increase in nursing staff. Our simulation appeared to reflect this reality. This is also a reflection of the fact that, as noted under 4.3, there are tasks that are omitted because working time is limited. Specific examples are given below. There are occasions when a nurse is so busy providing care to patients for whom she is responsible that she is unable to respond to a call from another patient, even one she is responsible for. On occasion, under these conditions, if a nurse passing along a corridor discovers a patient whose intravenous drip is leaking, if that patient is not one for whom she is responsible the series of tasks involved in dealing with a leaking intravenous drip assume a low priority for her and she must call the nurse who is responsible for the patient in question. If the nurses continue to be fully occupied with patient care, they are unable to tidy up the ward or put things in order. As a result, the ward declines into a state where in an emergency staff must look for a wheelchair that is not in its proper place, or they trip over or bump into things that are in places that should be empty, or they find that when they need to fix a drip in place quickly the tape they need has run out, or that there are not enough specimen containers when specimens are needed for urgent tests, or when pressure of work slackens a little and they set out to update their records they find that the necessary forms have run out. However, when the patients on the ward are in a relatively settled state and care time requirements are met, if a nurse discovers a patient with a leaking intravenous drip in a corridor she will undertake the series of measures necessary to replace it, even if the patient is not one for whom she is responsible, and will fully carry out administrative and management tasks such as tidying the ward and putting things in order.

We observed in our simulation results also that when the number of nurses on a shift was increased, there was a decrease in the number of nurses who spent a very large amount of time on 'tasks performed for patients for whom the nurse is responsible' (unbalanced workloads were resolved) and at the same time there was an increase in the number of nurses who spent a large amount of time on 'tasks performed for other patients' and 'other tasks.'

We concluded from the above that the simulation algorithms constructed in this study conformed to reality.

5. Conclusions

We created a formula for the nursing times provided on the basis of time study data obtained through a short-term survey and patient condition information, and quantified factors governing tasks.

2) We constructed simulation algorithms combining the results under 1) with information accumulated over an extended period on the length of hospitalization and patient condition (nursing intensity).

6. Topics for further research

We believe that there is scope for further investigation of the points below to enable the algorithms constructed for this study to reflect reality more accurately.

6.1. On nursing intensity

Given that it is based on subjective observation, the concept of nursing intensity is lacking in objectivity. Evaluation of patient nursing intensity was carried out on the ward studied by highly experienced nurses. Fixed evaluation standards exist on certain wards and confidence is high with respect to the replicability of judgments on those wards, but it is clear that these standards differ from one ward to the next. In order to make clear what factors enter into evaluations relating to nursing intensity, it is necessary to secure methods of evaluation of patient condition that use phenomena observable by anyone, with objective indicators such as 'how many drains have been inserted.' We believe it is necessary to investigate objective indicators to replace nursing intensity, or to attempt to effectively quantify nursing intensity.

6.2. On the collection of patient condition information

Since there is a time-lag between actual patient condition and the collection of patient condition information, there may be some margin of error in estimated care times. The patient condition information used in this study was based on information gathered at about 10:00 a.m. during the day shift. Information on patients who underwent surgery or other invasive procedures during the day shift and whose nursing intensity changed was incrementally updated and adjusted appropriately. The reason for carrying out the evaluation at 10:00 a.m. was simply that this was a convenient time from the point of view of the running of the ward, and in spite of the fact that patients' conditions were actually changing hour by hour, care time was only estimated for one shift at a time. In the present study, we regarded this as a limitation about which nothing could be done, but we believe that it will be necessary to carry out further investigations in the future, as developments in IT systems within institutions make it possible to accumulate information concerning changes in patient condition in real time.

6.3. On the statistical values for numbers of patients on the ward

There is a need to calculate averages and variances for changes in number of patients on the ward over a relatively long period. For this study, averages and standard deviations for numbers of patients on the ward were calculated using data from a short-term time study

http://dx.doi.org/10.5772/51014

and cannot be used as population means with any confidence. But when long-term changes in numbers of patients on the ward are used, it has to be borne in mind that numbers of patients on the ward fluctuate markedly during holiday periods such as New Year and the summer O-bon Festival, on weekends, and at times when conferences attended by large numbers of doctors are held.

6.4. Handling skewed values

As mentioned in 3.3.2, data relating to anomalous tasks deviated from normal distribution and was therefore excluded from the present analysis. However, it is a fact that nurses may carry out duties on the ward in the morning and undertake anomalous tasks such as attending meetings in the afternoon. Such anomalous tasks occur in a certain proportion throughout the year and a special distribution, different from those of ordinary tasks, must be assumed for them. We believe that we need to improve the accuracy of our simulation by actively seeking to include data concerning unusual phenomena as variables.

6.5. Seasonality

In this study, as we explained under 'Method,' only simulations of day-shifts on weekdays were carried out and we were unable to accommodate the special systems in force on weekends and at the holiday times mentioned above. Under these special systems, the numbers of nurses on duty and of patients on the ward fluctuate considerably. Because this greatly affects task times, we believe that there is room here for future investigation.

6.6. On the roles and level of experience of nurses

We have not incorporated into our simulation the difference in function of nurses such as team leaders, who head and support a team rather than taking responsibility for patients, or nurses that have responsibility for a small number of patients and carry out management tasks alongside these duties, as is very often the case with ward supervisors. We assumed for the purpose of the present simulation that all nurses were nurses whose actual work involved being responsible for patients, but in fact there are nurses who perform their roles in different ways. In addition, each year there are new recruits who need constant guidance from experienced nurses. They may, after some months, be able to cope with basic tasks, but they still have limitations, such as not being able to take responsibility for patients whose condition is severe. Further investigation of a methodology that will reflect this state of affairs is needed.

6.7. Comparison with the real world

It is not possible at this stage, but an evaluation that compared simulation results with reality would be the most reliable form of evaluation. In recent years, computer systems such as ordering systems, distribution systems, and electronic patient charts have been actively adopted as hospital information systems, and even more widespread use of IT→it can be expected in the future. We believe that if it becomes possible to collect task time data without committing large amounts of effort and funding, as required for time studies at present, this is an approach that must be investigated.

7. Outlook for the future

7.1. Standardization of methodology

We believe that it would be useful to standardize the methodology for carrying out the series of operations that was constructed for this study. Some reasons are suggested below.

Because each institution and each ward has different attitudes towards individual patient characteristics and tasks, and different methods of executing tasks, it is difficult to calculate universal quantities for essential nursing tasks that can be applied in any institution. In addition, there are cases in which it would be dangerous, or lead to the loss of desirable qualities, if a fixed value were applied to all institutions. It is desirable to go through the following series of operations. Having considered the task management appropriate to the ward, while preserving the ward's characteristics, a time study of the ward should first be carried out, then a virtual environment simulating the actual ward should be created, making use of existing cumulative information, and test experiments should be conducted using that virtual environment.

7.2. Combination with other information

7.2.1. Relationship to incidents and accidents

We believe that it is possible, on the basis of information derived from incident and accident reports, to explore the relationship between medical errors and task times from a number of viewpoints. As medical malpractice suits have increased in recent years, consciousness of medical errors by nurses has increased and the number of nursing departments that make it a requirement to write near-miss incident reports has grown. Protection of patient safety requires maintenance of minimum standards in all medical jobs, including nursing, and is of the utmost importance. Fujita et.al. have pointed out that there are errors that are related to busyness and errors that are not related to busyness. It is possible to extract from the analysis results the answers to such questions as: 'What kinds of incidents and accidents increase with an increase in task time?' 'What amount of task time elapses before the number of cases reported begins to increase?' and 'After how many hours of overtime work over how many days in a row does the number of cases reported begin to increase?' These analysis results will also provide important material for the investigation of task allocation and assignment of nursing staff with a view to minimizing medical errors.

7.2.2. Patient satisfaction

It is possible to explore the relationship between nurse's task time, particularly 'time devoted to patients for whom the nurse is responsible,' and patient satisfaction. We believe that this has great significance for the improvement of nursing care. We are entering an era when patients are expected to draw sharp distinctions among hospitals. As a result, more and more hospitals are increasing the number of their private rooms, where patients can spend their hospital stay in privacy, and are giving thought to the appearance of the hospital's interior and the richness of its amenities. But we believe that what is more important to patients than the physical elements of the institution is that they should be able to receive care that they are satisfied with in an atmosphere based on a relationship of trust with the medical personnel. Sickness is a special condition, and patients need warm-hearted support at all times. The nurses, who spend more time in contact with the patient than any other medical personnel, have a particularly large role to play, and are at the forefront of ensuring customer satisfaction.

7.2.3. Level of fatigue

In the present study we analyzed only the day shift, but we believe that by constructing a virtual ward environment that takes other shifts into account and carrying out simulations, it would be possible to show the relationship between task time and nurses' fatigue. It has been pointed out that symptoms of fatigue among nurses are greatest after the evening shift and that where the night shift is concerned there is considerable fatigue before the shift begins. There is concern that the physical and mental fatigue of nurses on the night shift has a negative effect on their work. Attempts have long been made to reduce the burden on nurses and to establish an efficient nursing system. One notable example was the introduction of the two-shift system, but no reference has been made to investigation of specific aspects of this working system, such as how its merits and demerits are related to the characteristics of the ward. It is important to re-investigate nurses' work systems, including conditions such as these.

7.2.4. Link between patterns of change in nursing intensity and clinical path

In this study we chose pattern of nursing intensity as the clinical path and, having fixed patient severity as a definite condition, it was possible to make a preliminary calculation of actual nursing task times. In recent years, much has been made of efficiency of treatment, and an increasing number of institutions have introduced the clinical path as a specific methodology. Among city hospitals and privately run general hospitals, there are institutions and wards that have almost completely adopted clinical paths, and that have been successful in the management of planned admission with almost no variance. We believe that in hospital institutions like this, it will be possible to effectively apply patterns of change in nursing intensity to items such as preliminary calculations of nursing personnel costs, which have a great influence on hospital management.

We feel that a combination of the experimental results derived from virtual environments as described in this study and other information will be helpful in the management of nursing tasks suited to various goals.

Acknowledgements

This study was supported in part by research grants of 22792142 Grant-in-Aid for Young Scientists (B) from the Ministry of Education, Culture, Sports, Science and Technology of Japan and in part by the Osaka University Program for the Support of Networking among Present and Future Researchers.

Author details

Atsue Ishii[1*], Takashi Nakamura[2], Yuko Ohno[1] and Satoko Kasahara[3]

*Address all correspondence to: atsue@sahs.med.osaka-u.ac.jp

1 Osaka University, Japan

2 The Institute of Statistical Mathematics, Japan

3 Graduate School of Health Care Sciences, Jikei Institute, Japan

References

[1] Burke, T. A., Mc Kee, J. R., Wilson, H. C., et al. (2000). A Comparison of Time-and-Motion and Self-Reporting Methods of Work Measurement. JONA, , 30(3), 118-125.

[2] Caughey, M. R., & Chang, B. L. (1998). Computer Use and Nursing Research Computerized Data Collection:Example of a Time-Motion Study. *Western Journal of Nursing Research*, 20(2), 251-256.

[3] Fagerstom, L., Rainio, A., & , K. (1999). Professional Assessment of Optimal Nursing Care Intensity Level: A New Method of Assessing Personnel Resources for Nursing Care. *Journal of Clinical Nursing*, 8, 369-379.

[4] Goldstein, H. (2003). *Multilevel Statistical Models* (Third Edition), Oxford University Press Inc., New York.

[5] Hall, L. M., Doran, D., Pink, G. H., et al. (2004). Nurse Staffing Models, Nursing Hours, and Patient Safety Outcomes. *JONA*, 34(1), 41-45.

[6] Jones, K. (1991). Specifying and Estimating Multi-Level Models for Geographical Research. *Trans. Inst. Br Geogr. N. S.*, 16, 148-160.

[7] Langlois, S. L., Vytialingam, R. C., & Aziz, N. A. (1999). A Time-Motion Study of Digital Radiography at Implementation,. *Australasian Radiology*, 43, 201-205.

[8] Magnusson, A. R., Hedges, J. R., Ashley, P., et al. *Resident Educational Time Study: A Tale of Three Specialties, Academic Emergency Medicine*, 5(7), 718-725.

[9] Meyers, F. E., & Stewart, J. R. (2002). *Motion and Time Study for Lean Manufacturing* (3rd ed.), New Jersey, Prentice Hall.

[10] Vinson, D. C., Paden, C., & Amelia-Sales, Devera. (1996). Impact of Medical Student Teaching on Family Physicians' Use of Time. *The Journal of Family practice*, 42(3), 243-249.